# CLASH
## OF THE
# TITANS

How the Unbridled Ambition of Ted Turner and Rupert Murdoch Has
Created Global Empires That Control What We Read and Watch

# Richard Hack

New Millennium Press

Library of Congress Cataloging-in-Publication Data Available

ISBN 1-893224-60-0


Printed in the United States of America

New Millennium Press
301 North Canon Drive
Suite 214
Beverly Hills, CA 90210

www.newmillenniumpress.com
*Please visit our website for a complete list of all book
and periodical sources for this title.*

Book design by Carolyn Wendt

10 9 8 7 6 5 4 3 2 1

For Robert Elias Deaton

a Southern gentleman

and faithful friend

**Also by Richard Hack**

*Madness in the Morning*

*When Money Is King*

*Jackson Family Values*

*Memories of Madison County*

*Next to Hughes*

*Richard Hack's Complete Home Video Companion for Parents*

*Hughes*

*And those fathers of America
thought also that they had but to leave the Press free
and everyone would live in the light.
They did not realize that a free press could develop
a sort of constitutional venality
due to its relations with advertisers,
and that large newspaper proprietors
could become buccaneers of opinion
and insensate wreckers of good beginnings.*

H. G. Wells, *The Outline of History*

# CONTENTS

# CLASH
## OF THE
# TITANS

# Hatfield and McCoy, Meet Turner and Murdoch

*It's true that I am a low, mean snake.*
*But you, sir, could walk beneath me*
*wearing a top hat.*

> Rupert Murdoch describing Ted Turner
> by quoting British statesman and
> author Benjamin Disraeli
> Washington, D.C.
> February 26, 1996

Ted Turner and Rupert Murdoch are two storm fronts colliding. And like weather patterns, no amount of scientific analysis can accurately predict the outcome when these two astonishing individuals interact, cross paths, play God. For these are not ordinary men. They are manipulators of world opinion—nothing less.

Turner—the high front that swings erratic, pushing his way into the spotlight through his outrageous statements, flirtatious escapades, nautical adventures, and environmental causes while maintaining a grip on our everyday lives through his status as vice chairman of AOL Time Warner. His Cable News Network gives people around the world instant access to one another's events, attitudes, moods, and problems, all distorted through a liberal glass, molded in an aspic of responsibility and truth.

Murdoch—the low front that appears at rest, then moves with amazing speed, absorbing all in his path. Controlling, influencing, interfering, irritating, obscuring, Murdoch is the billionaire head of News Corporation, owner of the Fox News Channel and a ragtag collection of newspapers, home to the conservative Right, to strident dictates and bullying tactics delivered as fact and reality.

From their perches high atop their media empires, these two executives control information: the news we read, the news we watch, the news we hear, the news we believe. The same news that presidents, prime ministers, kings, dictators, and terrorists read, watch, and hear as well. Turner and Murdoch, Murdoch and Turner, possessors of the ultimate power. Two men with incalculable riches and influence, destined by their careers and success to be bitter enemies. In another time, they might have dueled on a grassy plain with muskets, or faced each other at high noon at opposite ends of a dusty street, holsters slung low on their hips. When, in fact, their differences of opinion and position finally clashed head-on, the fight filled headlines and television screens, spilling out onto the streets of Manhattan. Naturally, it was September and it was raining. That's what happens when storm fronts collide.

The rainstorm had been predicted for several days and was a welcome relief from an arid New York summer that had left parched dust bowls in place of the pansied window boxes clutching the sills of East Side brownstones. Yet the fierceness of this particular storm, pounding the ground in a staccato rhythm that managed to drown out even the loudest of city sounds, brought out the warrior in those who chose to emerge on the saturated streets. As the combatants jockeyed for position under umbrellas and canopies, accompanied by the shrill whistles of doormen attempting in vain to summon infrequent cabs splashing waves of muddy water from well-worn tires, they were innocents in the real battle around them. Turner and Murdoch were about to duel.

The man who facilitated their fight and gave it volatility in the guise of business as usual was as unlikely a midwife as one might imagine: Gerald M. Levin. As chief executive officer of Time Warner Inc., Levin was head of the media giant that published *Time, People, Fortune,* and *Sports Illustrated* magazines, as well as the man who ran the company that owned Warner Bros. Studios and the second largest cable television system in the United States. He was known for his literate, cerebral, nearly stoic approach to administrating authority—more anti-mogul than intense autocrat.

On September 16, 1996, however, he stepped into the rain less the head of a giant conglomerate than a peacemaker, one who found himself in the middle of a power play, admittedly one of his own making. He was, after all, the man who for months courted Turner in order to gain control of the billionaire playboy's Atlanta-based Turner Broadcasting System (TBS).

Ironically, Murdoch, too, wanted TBS, or at least parts of it, but when bargaining stopped and contracts delivered, it was Levin who convinced Turner to sell his company to Time Warner in a stock swap worth $6.5 billion plus change. Of course, along with Turner came something else: his mouth, his opinions, and his enemies.

It pleased Turner to enter the world's largest media conglomerate at the top, turning his gap-toothed smile into a dimpled grin as his sparkling eyes saw more than mere dollar signs. Folding Turner's Cable News Network, with its 67 million viewers, into the Time Warner empire seemed a perfect fit. And Turner's other holdings—Turner Classic Movies, Turner Network Television, and Cartoon Network—added gold to an already gem-laden treasure chest.

It was not until weeks later that the consequences of his decision became obvious. To his dismay, Turner discovered that despite tripling his wealth through the deal and receiving the fancy title of vice chairman of Time Warner Inc., he had absolutely no responsibilities at the conglomerate. A million-dollar salary, a spectacular office, and no job for the first time in his adult life.

At 57, Turner had not spent the past 35 years working long hours in a scramble for achievement and recognition only to be showcased on a corporate pedestal. No stranger to speaking his mind, Turner lamented his displeasure to all who would listen—chief among them Jerry Levin. In an effort to placate the man who was about to become Time Warner's largest shareholder, Levin flew to Turner's 105,000-acre bison ranch outside Bozeman, Montana, on Labor Day weekend in 1996. There, inside Turner's rustic log cabin, under the stuffed heads of game appropriated from the property, Levin cajoled. He listened. Then he acquiesced. In a move obvious in its logic, Levin agreed to Turner's request to head all of Time Warner's cable operations—that is to say HBO and Cinemax, plus the about-to-be-acquired elements of Turner Broadcasting.

When Levin eventually escaped the muddy roads of Turner's Flying D Ranch, he had every reason to believe he had made a wise decision. Now, as he stepped into the rainstorm two weeks later, he was not so certain. He had neglected to factor into the scenario the impact of Rupert Murdoch, the *other* self-made media mogul—this one not on the Time Warner payroll.

At 65, the Australian-born Murdoch was chairman of a media conglomerate that owned some 85 newspapers, with a plenary thirst for scandal and naked women (whose pictures often appeared on page 3). Through the years Murdoch had jockeyed with Turner for a leadership position in many of the same markets. It therefore came as no surprise when, in early 1996, Murdoch announced his intention to launch his own 24-hour news network in direct competition with CNN. Turner himself had welcomed the challenge, claiming during a speech at a cable convention that he was "looking forward to squishing Rupert like a bug."

All of this would have been of little more than passing interest to Jerry Levin if he had not had a conversation with Murdoch at the annual powerfest held over the Fourth of July weekend that year at the Sun Valley, Idaho, estate of investment banker Herbert A. Allen. In addition to the golf and tennis tournaments, skeet shoots, massage therapy, white-water rafting, fly-fishing expeditions, and rollerblading, Levin and Murdoch shared some private time. The result of their conversation found Levin agreeing to carry Murdoch's new Fox News Channel on Time Warner's Manhattan cable service, a system that served 1.1 million subscribers, including most of Madison Avenue's all-important advertising community. Murdoch, in turn, promised Levin that he would pay Time Warner $25 per subscriber, an amount *far* in excess of the industry standard. A handshake confirmed the $125 million deal, and both men returned to their power bases pleased with the arrangement.

In Washington, D.C., the Federal Trade Commission (FTC) was busy evaluating the Time Warner/Turner Broadcasting merger. Despite seeming conflicts in the merger, the FTC was willing to give the fusion its blessing. Its only stipulation was that Time Warner add another news channel to its cable system to compete against Turner's CNN. Murdoch's Fox News Channel would qualify, of course. So too would yet another start-up news service, this one the result of a joint effort between NBC and Microsoft and saddled with the awkward moniker MSNBC.

MSNBC was launched on July 15, 1996, and spent the following months attempting to gain access to Time Warner's Manhattan system. With the merger, MSNBC saw an open door and began to campaign for the opportunity. Time Warner's cable chief, Joe Collins, suggested carrying *both* networks. That way Levin could keep his promise to Murdoch, MSNBC would be pleased, Time Warner would make an enormous profit, and the FTC would get three news channels instead of one. Everyone agreed—everyone, that is, except Ted Turner, the man who had just been nominated to head all of Time Warner's cable operations.

Insiders insist that Turner's objection to carrying both news networks was based on his desire to conserve Time Warner's channels for offerings from Turner Broadcasting. Of course, he also wanted to limit direct competition with his beloved CNN. Logic apparently forced Levin to agree with Turner's reasoning. For reasons unknown at the time, Levin made his selection.

By September 17, Levin telephoned NBC with the good news that MSNBC had a home on Time Warner, and then slipped into his rain gear to take the short walk from the Time Warner building in Rockefeller Center to Fox News, several blocks away, to advise Murdoch of his decision.

As Levin entered the Time Warner lobby, three young secretaries braced themselves for the downpour by leaning into one another like exhausted geraniums. Levin hardly heard their squeals of excitement (or was it desperation?) as they moved in a huddle into the weather. He had more important things to consider: keeping the peace with Rupert Murdoch without losing the good graces of his new vice chairman. The rain had managed to soak through Levin's overcoat by the time he arrived at Murdoch's efficient Fox News office. Perhaps it was the extraordinary effort that Levin had made to deliver his bad news in person, or perhaps Murdoch was being particularly cautious in his interaction with Levin. In any case, when Levin informed Murdoch that Fox News would not have the promised channel on Time Warner's Manhattan cable system, Murdoch's reaction was muted. His unmade-bed-of-a-face remained solemn, his lined brow unfurrowed. Levin was as surprised as he was relieved, encouraged by the professionalism of the meeting.

It was no longer raining when Levin left the Fox News building. The street-corner skirmishes aimed at hailing cabs had given way to concern over disheveled hairdos in the gusting autumn wind. As Murdoch and Levin parted, they had clasped hands, two executives in seeming agreement, and Levin's sigh of relief as he walked back to his own office reflected his mood of accomplishment. According to Time Warner president Richard Parsons, when Levin returned he said, "Rupert took it very well."[1] As it turned out, Levin had only hours to savor his victory.

By the next morning, the war that had taken place on the sidewalks of New York moved decidedly into its boardrooms. Murdoch was outraged at Time Warner's blatant disregard for its commitment, saying, "We have a contract and we expect Time Warner to live up to it. Two weeks ago, they were within a half-hour of signing a contract with us, which Mr. Levin assured me was totally on track. Mr. Levin and I had a friendly understanding that we would make our channels of distribution open to each other. We're just going to have to see whether they are going to live up to that."[2]

Chase Carey, chief executive officer of Fox Television, got drawn into the fight: "We were dealt with in a duplicitous manner and essentially lied to."[3] Carey placed a heated call to Fred Dressler, Time Warner's vice president. "He went crazy," said Dressler. "He called me a lot of nasty names. Said we were out to screw him. That we were disingenuous."[4]

What Carey dished out to Dressler, Murdoch himself leveled at Levin. "What the hell happened?" Levin later asked Dressler. "I came back and everything was fine. Then Rupert called and he went crazy on me."[5]

As the war of words spat from the telephone onto the streets and into the headlines of New York's newspapers, the spectacle of an outraged Murdoch and an innocent-acting Levin left many of Time Warner's customers amused by what they saw as rich men's games. Somehow lost in the threats and excuses was the reality that Murdoch was not simply attempting to launch another news network unto cable television for mere monetary gain. Murdoch was seriously trying to present an alternative to what he saw as the liberal news bias offered by Turner's CNN and other national media outlets. "They reflect the almost mono-lithic attitude of the press coming out of the *New York Times,* the *Boston Globe,* the *Washington Post,* and the three networks follow it exactly," Murdoch claimed.[6] Fox News was to be different. While many suspected that it would be a mouthpiece for Murdoch's conservative views, Fox News president Roger Ailes was quick to label the news network as "devoid of bias or conservative/liberal viewpoints."[7] Label it "fair"; label it "accurate." Ailes bantered both words as synonyms.

It was only a matter of hours before Murdoch ordered that the Time Warner deal be dusted for the fingerprints of his nemesis Turner. He did not have any direct proof of his involvement, but then, he did not need it. "When you smell a skunk, you don't have to see it,"[8] he said, according to a source close to Murdoch. With this implication of impropriety, Turner joined the fight, not merely leaping into the fray, but becoming central to the most tumultuous media turf war in recent memory.

As Levin and Turner began to cross the country in an effort to sell the still-tenuous Time Warner/Turner Broadcasting merger to its divergent stockholders, Turner used the stage to criticize the Murdoch-owned newspaper the *New York Post* for its "yellow journalists." "Our [CNN] journalists, unlike Murdoch's journalists, are not told what to say. We play by the rules. Murdoch is like the late Führer,"[9] Turner said, suggesting that Murdoch used his media properties to mold public opinion.

The following day, Murdoch's *Post* made certain that no one missed the slur by headlining the news: TURNER COMPARES MURDOCH TO ADOLF HITLER. News Corporation attorney Arthur Siskind called the statement "one more expression of [Turner's] personal animosity toward Mr. Murdoch. [It] must be viewed as deeply offensive not only to Mr. Murdoch and his associates at News Corporation, but to all people of good will."[10]

If the executives of Time Warner took any umbrage to Turner's remarks, they gave no indication of it during a press luncheon at which Levin labeled Turner his "new best friend" and gave a champagne toast to the Time Warner vice chairman. Even as they touched glasses, Murdoch was beginning to circle the warriors around the conglomerate's wagons by calling in some political favors. His first stop: New York's Gracie Mansion.

Mayor Rudolph Giuliani had been running Manhattan and the four boroughs that surround it for only 33 months in September 1996, but had succeeded in pulling the city out of a nervous breakdown that had witnessed 2,000 murders, vagrants with bags of street trash for beds, and a Times Square that was closer to Sodom and Gomorrah than the Great White Way. Under his watch, police patrols were increased, shelters were opened, drug dealers were arrested, and Broadway returned as the entertainment heart of the city.

As a leader, Giuliani rushed impulsively toward the sound of gunfire, eager to be on the front line. At the first rumble of the Time Warner/Fox News debate, Giuliani became involved. It did not hurt that Fox News president Roger Ailes had once been a Republican media consultant for several presidents, and had worked with Giuliani when he ran unsuccessfully for mayor of New York in 1988. Ailes telephoned Giuliani, explained the situation, and then sat back and watched as Giuliani moved with dispatch to help his old friend. For Giuliani, born into a third generation of working-class Italian immigrants from Brooklyn, it became a personal challenge, and as the wheels of politics churned in their own fashion, they dug into soil that managed to dirty every side.

None of that was particularly obvious when, under an enormous white tent outside Fox News' 48th street headquarters, Giuliani joined New York governor George Pataki to welcome Fox News and applaud Murdoch's decision to base the channel in New York City—the only national news service with such a distinction.* He also proudly announced that Cablevision, the sixth largest cable carrier in the United States, would carry Fox News, including 1.6 million subscribers in Brooklyn, the Bronx, and Long Island, plus sections of Connecticut and New Jersey. Although it wasn't Time Warner, it was *something*, and Murdoch savored the moment.

---

*CNN is based in Atlanta and Washington, D.C.; MSNBC is based in Fort Lee, New Jersey.

Time Warner executives, who were not invited to the party, made their own voices heard two days later, responding to a formal request from the city for a legal waiver that would allow the use of the *city-run* channels to broadcast Fox News on the Time Warner system. In a word, *no*. "However innocent in its intent," a Time Warner attorney wrote in response, "any waiver would be in violation of Time Warner Corporation's franchise rights with the city, the Federal Cable Act and other law."[11]

It was with no small amount of irony that on Monday, October 7, 1996, the very day that Fox News debuted in 17 million homes across America, Time Warner was summoned by the Giuliani administration to appear before the city's Franchise and Concession Review Committee to examine its cable franchise in Manhattan. And while Time Warner's franchise agreement may have been the subject, the object of the inquiry quickly turned to the ongoing Turner-Murdoch fracas. "Ted Turner made clear that his personal vendetta and financial interest would be exalted over the interest of New York City and its cable subscribers," Roger Ailes testified before the committee, the loose skin of his double chin quivering as he steeled his jaw in anger. "New York City now has a cable-system czar who can control access and tell New Yorkers what they can and cannot see. Unfortunately, the New York City cable czar lives in Atlanta. His name is Ted Turner."[12]

The following day, Time Warner president Richard Parsons joined the dispute by broadly denouncing the city's effort to dictate Time Warner policy. In a letter released at the hearing, Parsons stated: "The city's effort to influence programming violates Federal law, the First Amendment, and is inappropriate. Even if it were not your intention, the nature and timing of your request creates the clear impression that the city is seeking to use its regulatory leverage to influence our programming decision-making."

Giuliani seized on Parsons' response to lambaste the media company for further suggesting that Murdoch was influence peddling in his move to involve the mayor's office. "That has nothing to do with it," Giuliani said, appearing on the local news that evening. "We go very, very far to try to help preserve jobs for the City of New York; 1,400 jobs are at stake here and a headquarters is at stake here that has been located in the City of New York."[13] Giuliani made no mention of the 10,000 people then employed by Time Warner.

New Yorkers awakened to the sound of bundles of the *New York Daily News* hitting the sidewalk on October 10 with the headline RUDY VOWS HE'LL SET FOX ON FOE. The unflappable mayor of America's largest city had decided to raise the stakes a few notches on his push-and-shove match with Time Warner. He instructed David Klasfeld, chief of staff to his deputy mayor, to inform the cable franchise holder of the city's intention to begin televising both Fox News and the competitive Bloomberg Television News on two of its community service Crosswalks channels. "We're going to put them on the air whenever we can, as soon as we can, whatever it takes," Klasfeld said. He kept his word.

Even as Ted Turner and Jerry Levin were celebrating the news that shareholders of both Time Warner and Turner Broadcasting had approved the merger of the two companies, Bloomberg Television News began airing over the city's Channel 71. It lasted all of one day. The following morning, viewers looking for Bloomberg or any other news service on the city's channels had to turn to a local station to learn that U.S. District Court Judge Denise Cote granted Time Warner a temporary court order overnight, blocking the two all-news stations from airing on city channels. In the kind of petty bickering better suited to dodge-ball courts and playground brawls, Murdoch screamed politics while Turner likened Murdoch's success with the mayor to a payoff. "He tried to pay off Newt Gingrich.** He must have paid off somebody."[14]

---

**The Murdoch-owned publishing house HarperCollins paid a $4.5 million advance to Gingrich for his book *To Renew America* in 1994. Gingrich, then Speaker of the House, later returned the money.

With each passing day, the controversy continued to escalate, rolling snowball turned avalanche, pushed along by media hype controlled by the two opposing sides. For several weeks, no newscast or newspaper missed an opportunity to update the conflict that found ever-increasing volume through the court system. News Corporation's $2 billion lawsuit against Time Warner for breach of contract and antitrust violations filed in U.S. District Court was countered by a Time Warner suit against News Corporation for interfering with its First Amendment right to determine programming.

Murdoch began running a series of advertisements with the headline TED TURNER AND TIME WARNER DON'T WANT YOU TO SEE THIS CHANNEL over the image of a television set featuring the Fox News Channel logo. Each featured a tag line aimed at pricking the thick skin of Turner, including one that read: "They should know that **censorship** and **monopoly** control are never a pretty picture."[15]

Having flown into Manhattan for the official merger of Time Warner and TBS, Turner had only to open the local newspaper to be taunted by Murdoch's insidious baiting. His silence amazed members of the press, who wondered why the man, nicknamed "the Mouth of the South" by his detractors, had not countered Murdoch's punch. On October 18, they received their answer when Turner was summoned into the Eighth Avenue offices of Time Warner's law firm, Cravath Swaine and Moore. He was to be deposed by Murdoch's attorneys in response to an order by U.S. District Court Judge Denise Cote. In his three-hour deposition, Turner again accused Murdoch of influence peddling. "I was just appalled that he *bought* the government of New York City. Murdoch is a pretty slimy character. I can understand him doing it in England, maybe Australia or China. But here, having it happen in New York, it really surprises me," Turner stated.[16]

Denying any suggestion by Murdoch's attorneys that he played a part in the Time Warner decision to ban Fox News from a place in Manhattan's cable channel lineup, Turner said he was in favor of splitting the decision, airing Fox News on some of Time Warner's franchises and MSNBC on others. It was an idea overruled by Levin, he said. "Basically, my suggestions weren't followed at all. But I didn't have any direct authority to do anything. I just made an unsolicited suggestion or two."[17]

When pressed by Murdoch's lawyers, Turner insisted he did not prefer MSNBC over Fox News. "I don't really favor one over the other. . . . It would be like, would you rather be defeated by the Nazis or Japanese in World War II? Neither one of them is going to give you much of a break. You die in one concentration camp as fast as another."[18]

The attorneys quickly segued from World War II to Hitler and to Turner's earlier portrayal of Murdoch. If Turner had been coached to sidestep any controversy by the Time Warner attorneys, the company's new vice chairman ignored the advice and renewed his flagrant attack on the News Corporation head: "The late Führer, first thing he did, like all dictators, was take over the press and use it to further his agenda. Basically, that is what Rupert Murdoch does with his media," Turner swore. "His journalistic credentials are a joke. He is a disgrace to journalism."[19]

At the end of his deposition, in which Turner labeled Murdoch "a scumbag," he eschewed the side-door exit from the lawyer's office and headed directly out the front door into the arms of the waiting press. As questions were shouted in unison, Turner eyes flashed. He absorbed the spotlight like a sun lamp, holding up a finger to silence the crowd. "I can tell you one thing and only one thing," he teased, pausing as the cameras flashed in his direction. "We'll see the Yankees at Yankee Stadium tonight."[20] Murdoch's Fox Network was televising the first game of the World Series between the New York Yankees and the Time Warner–owned Atlanta Braves; just another opportunity for fans to take sides and for Turner to joust with Murdoch.

While the press was wondering if boxing gloves would be handed out at Yankee Stadium, Murdoch was several continents away, having concluded the annual meeting of his News Corporation Ltd. in Australia. In his absence, his *New York Post* took up the fight by bannering: TIME WARNER MOGUL'S BIZARRE OUTBURST: IS TED TURNER NUTS? YOU DECIDE. Under the headline THE CONFESSIONS OF TED TURNER, *Post* political cartoonist David Smith had drawn a caricature of Turner in a straitjacket with the caption "Does He Need a Straitjacket? Ted Turner sees Hitler and Hirohito hiding under the bed in his battle with rivals Fox and General Electric." The cartoon further accused him of being off his manic-depression pills and "veering dangerously toward insanity."[21]

As the Yankees beat the Braves 12–1 in the World Series opener, Ted Turner and his wife, Jane Fonda, were in the stadium, but not on the air, an apparent victim of a Murdoch decree to keep the Turners' faces off the screen. The press called the stands a "no Ted zone,"[22] and it wasn't until game four that he showed up on camera, standing right behind a banner hung with the words FOX NEWS.

By that time, Fonda had also entered the imbroglio by giving an exclusive interview to the *New York Daily News* that was headlined I'M NOT FONDA RUDY. In the piece, Fonda claimed that Giuliani's actual motive for favoring Murdoch in the ongoing cable war was to curry favors for his wife, Donna Hanover, who worked for the Murdoch-owned television station WNYW. "It's hard to think otherwise when his wife works for Rupert Murdoch and he's gotten such considerable contributions from Rupert Murdoch. It's the Margaret Thatcher syndrome all over again," Fonda said, referring to Thatcher's $5 million book deal with a Murdoch-owned publisher that happened to coincide with Murdoch's merger of two British cable stations.[23]

Labeling the attack "jerky," Giuliani called Fonda's charges "probably one of the cheapest attacks ever made, at least on me."[24]

By the time Murdoch returned to Manhattan in time for the final game of the World Series, testimony in Judge Cote's courtroom had concluded, but the jury was still out in Middle America.

Proof positive flew over Yankee Stadium midway through the championship game. A small plane hired by the Fox Network made several passes across the playing field as it flashed the message "Hey Ted. Be Brave. Don't Censor the Fox News Channel." Cheers from the stands indicated amusement if not agreement.

The bickering would continue in public and in private for another month, with no definite movement in any direction, especially in the courts. The stagnation allowed the melodrama of name-calling and political maneuvering to climb the ladder of assumed respectability, peaking with an appearance by Turner at the United Nations for a meeting of television executives from five continents. While the subject of the conference was officially the global impact of television, the course skewed downward when Turner ascended the podium.

"[Time Warner] is very benign," he said. "There is a new group coming, however, led by that no-good SOB Rupert Murdoch. They want to control the world. We have got to do everything we can to stop them. Murdoch wants to control Indian television in India; he wants to control Chinese television in China. Bullshit! This is a battle between good and evil," he railed before suddenly stopping and adding, "I don't want to talk about that no-good bastard anymore."[25]

The legitimacy of Turner's argument is questioned only to the extent that he paints his own involvement as being non-threatening and harmless. Turner is equally as ruthless as Murdoch; these are two enormously successful media moguls who have moved from personal dislike and loud pontificating to gerrymandering. Borders had been crossed and boundaries had been stretched in the search for personal gain. Through the manipulation of the various media outlets under their control, Murdoch and Turner are the brave new world's ultimate power brokers; Attila the Hun gone high-tech.

These men of seemingly limitless ambition have discovered what all of us know on a far more local level. All of us, across the globe, accept as true what we read in newspapers and watch on television, regardless of the slant and despite the spin. Murdoch and Turner cloak this power in the fabric of responsibility, firmly believing that as protectors of the media they must assist viewers and readers in understanding the reality of our predicament as humans of the earth, 2003. Turner rails against the horrors of population growth and environmental pollution. Murdoch launches media campaigns in support of political candidates he deems worthy. Each molds popular opinion in his image to better mankind.

This is not to say that the results of their efforts are not positive, for quite often they are. The problem is that they determine the problems and influence the outcomes with the kind of far-reaching impact and control unprecedented in history.

"There have been press barons for decades," commented media analyst Andrew Tyndall. "Men of huge egos like William Randolph Hearst. They are the kind of characters Orson Welles made movies about. But they must have this drive to succeed, and the drive is to have their product in everyone's house."[26]

Turner and Murdoch (along with Disney/ABC, General Electric/NBC, and Westinghouse/CBS) now determine what reaches American families and a growing number of homes around the world. While the networks have always been run as pseudomonopolies, they are ruled by committee and are not likely to reflect the opinions of single individuals. Murdoch and Turner, however, have both the power and the inclination to determine policy and content, and operate largely outside the walls that have served to contain media barons of old. Through their combined ownership or control of news channels, publishers, newspapers, magazines, satellites, and Internet delivery services, these men possess extremely loud bullhorns that are nearly impossible to escape or ignore.

Gone are the days when governments operated behind castle moats and guarded chambers. Since Franklin Roosevelt sold his

New Deal—and with it himself—on the radio, politics and broadcasting had been joined at the hip. Yet it had always been the politicians running the ship, allowing access as was deemed beneficial. Now, with the advances in technology allowing channels such as CNN and Fox News to broadcast news continually from around the globe as it happens, world leaders are *themselves* turning to these sources to keep abreast of breaking events.

The relevance of that subtlety was not wasted on Turner when he launched CNN on a shoestring budget and a bag of hope. Nor did Murdoch miss the point when he attempted first to buy CNN away from Turner and then to create his own news network when he failed. To have the men now insulting each other with exposed talons and raised blood pressures meant far more than the amusing *affaire d'honneur* being played out in the daily headlines in New York City. This was a joust for the right to hold the key to the executive washroom of world leaders and public opinion.

Just how Mr. Turner and Mr. Murdoch came to this place of backstabbing and name-calling is a tale of adventure traveling on serpentine routes that eventually intersect on a rainy day in Manhattan in 1996. This is a road littered with the stuff of melodrama: courage, deceit, betrayal, obsession, and tragedy—a clash of titans who are at once brave and bizarre, captivating and dangerous, as any men born before or since.

# ONE

# Keith Rupert Murdoch

*He was a rather ordinary child.*

Dame Elisabeth Murdoch of her only son
Cruden Farm, Langwarrin
Summer 1991

Melbourne was a gentle place then. The Yarra River flowed thick as maple syrup, stained brown from suspended particles of dirt, as its north bank edged the city that sat poised around Port Phillip Bay. Icemen carried enormous chunks of frozen water wrapped in burlap and slung across thick backs to waiting chests that protected meat and vegetables from the Australian heat. Despite having just given birth to her first son, whom she named Rupert, 22-year-old Elisabeth Joy Murdoch appeared cool; the smooth, pale skin of her face brushed the red cheek of the baby bundled beside her in the bed at Avonhurst Private Hospital. It was March 11, 1931, and outside the walls of the maternity, the Great Depression had hit Australia with the force of a wave that sucks life from everything in its path.

At 45, Elisabeth's husband, Keith, was 23 years her senior and Australia's most noted newspaperman. As he stood next to his wife's bed, he swelled with pride as he dreamed of a time when his son would inherit his publishing empire, which included several of Australia's most respected newspapers as well as multiple magazines. Tall, husky, and energetic, Keith Murdoch seemed bred to be among the ink and presses of Melbourne's Flinders Street. Few realized that this man, who carried influence and wealth with unassuming ease, had come from parochial roots and a troubled childhood.

Keith Arthur Murdoch was born in West Melbourne in 1885, the son of a Presbyterian minister and his wife, who emigrated from Scotland the year before. One of six children, including four brothers, Keith developed a psychologically debilitating stammer, and routinely dissolved into a private world of fantasy rather than face the cruel taunts of his classmates at Camberwell Grammar School. As the shy youth moved from school to school, he grew into a tall teenager with a thick mane and engaging eyes. Keith found his adventure in reading, following the exploits of politicians and executives whose stories unfolded in the leading local newspaper, the *Age*.

Eager for the perceived excitement of a reporter's life, Keith languished through his final year before graduating from Camberwell. There was to be no ministry in his future, or a college education for that matter. Keith Murdoch knew his calling and leaped at the opportunity to meet David Syme, owner of the *Age* and a friend of Keith's father. A fellow Scot, the humorless Syme hired young Murdoch on a temporary basis, offering to pay him a halfpenny a line for every news item he placed in the paper. Murdoch's beat was the Malvern area of Melbourne, a middle-class inner suburb where the competing paper, the *Argus,* was firmly entrenched.

The enthusiasm that Keith displayed in his effort to gather news was boundless. For the first time in his life, his stammer actually contributed to his success as an assortment of politicians, police officers, and athletes came to his aid during interviews, not only completing his sentences but in the process also offering more information than they had ever intended. By 1907, Keith had saved up enough halfpennies to accumulate $500—by his calculation, enough to grubstake a year in Great

Britain, where the excitement of London's greatest newspapers beckoned.

There is a certain exuberance that comes with youth, and for the next year and a half that was all that sustained the naive Australian. It was a world gaudy with possibilities, yet empty of inspiration. His letters from London to his father revealed a Spartan existence. Home was a room in a boardinghouse "over a singing school, and under a drunkard's home . . . the bath is next door, and there are fleas in the bed."[1]

Despite the wealth of learning experiences, Keith found little in the way of paying jobs, and as his money ran short, so did his hope. "London does not agree with me," he wrote his father in 1909. "I keep cheery when there is the least excuse for it, but I have insomnia here and indigestion. 'Tis the lack of exercise and the lack of good air, and of good solid work and of any mental and spiritual comfort whatever."[2]

Keith was unaware that as he wrote his letter and sent it to Australia, a daughter was being born to a pipe-smoking gambler named Rupert Greene and his ethereal wife, Bairnie, not far from where the elder Murdochs made their home. Pemberley, as the Greenes' house was known, was located in the luxurious Toorak suburb of Melbourne, home to the colonial estates of rich gold barons and bankers. The Greenes named their baby Elisabeth, and she soon joined her two sisters on the lush lawns of Pemberley under the watchful eyes of their governess. Despite her father's trouble holding on to money, the household still found the cash needed to pay for maids and nannies for the girls, even if it meant subletting their home and moving in with relatives for several months at a stretch. Elisabeth's mother was wise in the way of thrift and always managed to save enough to keep her daughters in crinoline and herself in tonic from her physician, Dr. Morrison.

It was a lesson that Keith Murdoch never quite mastered. Having run out of funds and hope in London, he wired his father for capital to make the return trip to Australia. Plans called for Keith to sail aboard the Cunard line's *Mauretania* in steerage. Once the ship arrived at Ellis Island in New York harbor and Murdoch first set foot in America, he wrote his father in outrage:

> [It's] a small place in the harbour where all immigrants are taken. Yes, that day was the roughest I have spent. We were treated like cattle; big-mouthed filthy officials and heartless bullying doctors bullied us for five hours after which we were chucked ashore at New York, starving, weak and, oh, so angry! I could have escaped of course, but wished to experience the emotions of a new arrival without money, without friends, without strength. My tender soul was stirred to its depths, and passions and sensations I knew not made my blood boil and my senses reel.[3]

Tender soul aside, Keith made it safely back to Melbourne, where he once again found employment with *Age* owner David Syme, who hired the 24-year-old as a reporter for a salary of four pounds a week, with a two-pound raise several months later. Thus established, Murdoch began what was a rather meteoric rise in journalism, first by accepting a position with the Sydney *Sun* as its Melbourne correspondent, then by returning triumphantly to London in 1915 as manager of United Cable Service.

On the way to his London assignment, Keith chanced to stop in Gallipoli, where General Sir Ian Hamilton was commanding the British forces against Turkey during World War I. While there, Murdoch discovered the horrors of war, witnessing what he saw as "deplorable" conditions. More important, he talked with Australian soldiers. For days he listened to their souls, saw their fears laid bare in front of a man their own age, and wept alongside them with untethered compassion. After leaving Gallipoli, he wrote an 8,000-word letter to his friend, Australian prime minister Andrew Fisher, in which he denounced Hamilton's command and revealed the Commonwealth's casualties, the courage of its soldiers, and the futility of the assault. He also broke the law, having neglected to clear the letter with Hamilton's censors.

Keith had been in London less than 48 hours when word of his letter reached British cabinet ministers, who persuaded the newsman to repeat his information directly to British prime minister Herbert Henry Asquith. The British government classified the content of the Gallipoli letter until the mid-sixties, when Keith Murdoch's charges were made public. While some of his allegations and statistics were faulty, the thrust of his assertions was nonetheless true. His candor and patriotism served him well, for Murdoch not only became a trusted friend of the British prime minister and his cabinet, but he also began a rather opportune association with Lord Northcliffe. Northcliffe, born Alfred Harmsworth, was a charismatic and noble man who had turned newspaper publishing on its head with innovations such as the banner headline, tabloid-size paper, the extensive use of photographs, exclusive interviews, serialized stories, and highly publicized promotional campaigns. The pair gradually developed a father-son relationship that influenced the reporter for the rest of his life.

As Keith Murdoch rose in stature in London, young Elisabeth Greene was maturing into a slim, teenage tomboy whose reckless exploits pleased her father and caused her mother to flex her muscles as a disciplinarian before doubling up on her tonic in distress. At age 13, Elisabeth went to live at Clyde, a fashionable girls' school surrounded by the woods of Mount Macedon some 60 miles north of Melbourne. It was a place that Elisabeth described in 1985 as "rugged during the long, cold winters, but I believe we were the healthier for those Spartan conditions which today would be considered unbearable—as indeed would be the isolation."[4]

Elisabeth left Clyde after five years and returned home to Pemberley. She volunteered in Lady Northcote's kindergarten class and prepared to make her debut in society, as all proper young ladies of Toorak did. Her fresh-faced beauty contrasted with the heavily made-up look of the day and set Elisabeth apart from the other girls who went to dances squired by the elegantly uniformed naval officers currently in port. It was only miles, but really a world away, from where Keith Murdoch had grown in fame.

After five years in London, Keith accepted the editorship of the *Herald,* Melbourne's evening newspaper, and for the next five years reworked it into the image of Lord Northcliffe's finest efforts. The paper took on larger headlines, gossip stories, and action photographs, which sent subscriptions soaring right along with Murdoch's wealth and prestige.

Elisabeth was not a *Herald* reader, and Keith had no time for debutante balls, making their meeting at Eilyer, the Toorak home of socialite Albert Austin, that much more amazing. Credit belongs to the tenacity of society matron Rosamund Spowers, whose husband, Allan, was part owner of Melbourne's popular *Argus* newspaper. It was Mrs. Spowers who pressured Murdoch to attend a fund-raising dinner-dance to benefit the Australian Red Cross—an invitation he initially refused.

Returning to his work, Keith happened upon the photograph of a rather fetching debutante in one of his own publications, a woman's magazine called *Table Talk*. The picture was of 18-year-old Elisabeth Joy Greene. For a confirmed bachelor seemingly set in his ways, Murdoch wasted little time in lifting the telephone receiver and reconnecting with Mrs. Spowers. As he gazed at the portrait of the lovely teenager with large eyes and a Mona Lisa smile, he announced to the surprised dowager that he had changed his mind and could indeed find time to attend the fund-raiser if, and only if, a certain debutante would be present and Mrs. Spowers could guarantee him an introduction. He was breathless as a schoolboy when he received the news that Miss

Greene did indeed plan to attend, and immediately cleared his calendar for the evening.

When Elisabeth Greene walked into the foyer of Eilyer House, her entrance lacked only musical fanfare. She carried herself with a grace that transcended her years as she moved toward her table, accepting with a glance the homage paid by the more socially ambitious of the young men present. She danced long into the night, though never once with Keith Murdoch. Too shy to make his intentions known, Keith waited until Elisabeth was sipping punch and then skillfully allowed Mrs. Spowers to make his introduction to the young woman.

It was only the following day, when he telephoned Elisabeth at her parents' home, that she realized his interest was more than casual. He asked her to accompany him on a day trip to Sorrento, a tranquil seaside town two hours' drive from Melbourne. Elisabeth answered with an excited yes. "He turned up outside Pemberley in his big Itala sports car and immediately there were terrific ructions in the family, but I said I was going and there would be no stopping me," she said in her memoirs.[5]

Elisabeth proceeded to conquer the enraptured newsman, who, despite his middle age and celebrity, had a dearth of romantic experience. Their whirlwind courtship had the support of her sister Marie, who labeled Keith "such a charming, kindly, nice, gentle and interesting man."[6] Family friends were not so gracious. "That poor mother of ours," Elisabeth's sister Sylvia told the biographer John Monks. "She had a lot to put up with over Elisabeth's engagement. You see, some people looked upon it as if she was selling her daughter. Mother really had an awful time."[7]

The wedding of Elisabeth Joy Greene and Keith Arthur Murdoch took place on June 6, 1928, at the Scots Church in Melbourne, with Keith's father, the Reverend Patrick Murdoch, performing the ceremony. A champagne reception followed at Pemberley, and the couple honeymooned at Cruden Farm, the 90-acre property that Keith gave to his new wife as a wedding gift. Cruden Farm received its name from the Scottish parish in which Keith's grandfather, George Brown, was minister of the Free Church. The property included a small weatherboard cottage surrounded by ti trees, honeysuckle, and roses that grew wildly over the veranda, their thorns piercing the lattice. Their only neighbors were the possums that had nested in the farmhouse roof, and the cook, valet, and maid who had arrived in advance of the newlyweds.

The Murdochs' more traditional residence was a large home on Walsh Street in the Melbourne suburb of South Yarra. With Elisabeth as official hostess, the home became a salon of some note, catering to prime ministers, artists, writers, and military officers. She assumed her role with an ease that belied the fact that she was still a teenager, moving in elite circles as an accomplished member of privileged society. Not even the birth of their first child, a daughter named Helen, in April 1929 slowed their social schedule. It was an event timed to coincide with Keith's promotion to managing director of the *Herald* and the *Weekly Times*. As he rose in professional stature, so did the demands of the workplace. A mere four months after Helen's birth, the Murdochs left their baby in the care of a nanny, Sarah Russell, and began a round-the-world tour of newspapers in Europe and America. "I had to go," Elisabeth said. "I knew I was leaving Helen in the hands of this superb nanny who was to stay with us almost forever and who was really the most wonderful surrogate mother."[8]

As the Murdochs toured, remodeling work began on the house at Cruden Farm, turning the cottage into a colonial mansion with tall porch columns more associated with an antebellum plantation than with a farmhouse. The scope of the change shocked the unpretentious Elisabeth, who had worked passionately to preserve the farm as a family sanctuary free from the growing pressures of the Murdoch business. It was a media empire that now included papers in Brisbane, Perth, and Adelaide, as well as a radio station, 3DB, which was received across Australia and as far away as New Zealand.

Few realized that Keith did not own the newspapers he managed to record profits, and he did nothing to discourage the impression that he was the largest media baron on the Australian continent. It was into that world of illusion that his son was born in 1931. Keith Rupert Murdoch was heir to a heritage of hard work but few physical assets at a time when the Depression was causing staggering losses around the globe.

Undaunted by what others saw as impending disaster, Keith moved his growing family into Heathfield, the largest home in all of Melbourne. A massive brick structure with towering chimneys and leaf-covered walls, the house was on five acres of manicured lawns and gardens designed for William Lawrence Baillieu, an Australian entrepreneur who made and lost millions before his death in 1936. While Keith ran his businesses, Elisabeth managed Heathfield, where she supervised a staff that included six upstairs maids, a downstairs valet, a butler and his wife, and a full-time laundress. "You had to be a juggler," Elisabeth remembered in her memoirs, "when you were entertaining, as we were, with past, present and future prime ministers, businessmen, musicians and artists visiting us for dinners or musical evenings."[9]

As the children were capably cared for by Sarah Russell (now known as Nanny Murdoch), Keith continued expanding his media presence to include publications in every state of Australia. He was knighted for his efforts in journalism and thereafter was to be called Sir Keith. Elisabeth was now Lady Elisabeth, and she joined the management committee of the Royal Children's Hospital at the University of Melbourne. Ironically, her friendships with its staff of doctors proved beneficial when her husband suffered a heart attack while playing tennis on their grass court at Heathfield in 1933.*

---

*Keith Murdoch had been playing tennis with pastoralist Neville Fraser, whose son Malcolm was prime minister of Australia from 1975 to 1983.

For the next year, Keith removed himself from work at Elisabeth's insistence, spending an increasing amount of time in the company of his children at Cruden Farm, where picnics and play created a strong sense of family. More than any other time in his life, Murdoch became aware of his own mortality and struggled to bridle his instinct to return to the *Herald*. When his heart had healed sufficiently, however, he immediately thrust himself back into work, spearheading a move to harvest the rain forests of Tasmania for newsprint. To survey the trees, he recruited several staff members and took Elisabeth on horseback through the muddy forest. Dressed in their finest riding gear from Saville Row in London, the pair looked more prepared for dressage than the rugged Tasmanian trek through tall eucalyptus forests and dunes of buttongrass. Ultimately, Keith was successful in utilizing the ancient trees as raw material for his first pulp mill, long before nature conservancies succeeded in restricting the practice.

After the birth of a second daughter, Anne, in 1936, the Murdochs cruised aboard the 1,700-passenger Orient Navigation liner *Otranto* from Melbourne to London. In addition to the three children, they reserved staterooms for Nanny Murdoch as well as a sewing maid named Edith. Inlaid mahogany walls and crystal chandeliers from Austria gave the ship a palatial mood, at least from across the first-class decks that the Murdochs walked.

Five-year-old Rupert, taking his first vacation by sea, claimed that his mother tossed him into the deep end of the pool to teach him how to swim. "I clearly recall my mother throwing me in the ship's pool, and not letting anyone rescue me. I had to dog paddle to the side and I was screaming," he said, though his mother refutes the story.[10]

They agree that when the family arrived in Gibraltar, Keith and Elisabeth disembarked and the children continued on to Southampton with their nanny. When Rupert's parents finally arrived in England nearly a month later, having traveled to Spain and France, the family settled in Queen Anne's Mansions, a West

End apartment in the tallest building in London. Outfitted in custom-made riding breeches, helmets, and boots, Rupert and Helen took private equestrian lessons despite Rupert's protests at the absurd formality of the sport and the discomfort of the uniforms. The children also enrolled at the nearby Holland School, while Keith traveled to Germany to attend Hitler's Olympic Games in Berlin. When he returned, he was full of foreboding about Hitler's intentions for war and made plans to return his family to the safety of Australia. Intent on continuing the children's schooling, Elisabeth hired a British governess named Joan Kimpton, affectionately called Kimpo by the household. Upon their return to Heathfield, a classroom was set up in the mansion where the six-foot-tall, angular, and often strict Kimpo began to formalize the children's education.

On New Year's Day 1939, Elisabeth Janet Murdoch was born. The family called her Janet, and she bubbled happiness into a household already full of joy. The laughter was silenced and the rooms of Heathfield were suddenly hushed, however, when Anne fell ill with osteomyelitis, an infection of the bone or bone marrow, and endured several life-threatening surgeries. Her long and agonizing recovery deeply affected the family, who rallied behind their invalid sibling during months of painful therapy.

In September, as Hitler was invading Poland at the start of World War II, Rupert entered the private Advalton boys' school in Malvern, outfitted in a uniform of double-breasted blazer and knee-high socks. His classes with Kimpo still continued at Heathfield, and Rupert complained bitterly about his double dose of education, naively unaware that the war would soon dramatically alter his life. When the Japanese attacked Pearl Harbor in 1941 and the inclemency of the war heightened because of it, the Murdochs offered their city estate to the United States as a command post for American troops in Australia. The offer was both fortuitous and appreciated. Keith was having difficulty handling the financial responsibilities of

Heathfield and its staff, and moved out with no small degree of relief.

Soon after the family retreated to Cruden Farm, Rupert was sent to board at Geelong Grammar School, an all-boys academy associated with the Anglican Church. Victoria's second largest city, Geelong fronts the spectacular Corio Bay and the nearby Barwon River. The school is one of Australia's oldest private campuses and rates high on the scale of academia. For the 11-year-old Rupert, Geelong Grammar was a joyless place, a winter that lasted throughout the year and those that followed. Rupert later referred to his tenure at the school as the least happy of his life, his first time away from his family and his first exposure to life without the protective shield of his father.

"He did of course adore being with his father," Elisabeth recalled in an Australian Broadcasting Corporation documentary on her son. "I think perhaps there was a slight feeling of resentment that he'd been sent away to boarding school. Perhaps his Scottish blood was dominant in this respect. My grandparents were shocked that I was so keen on boarding school. And I'm not certain really that my husband was so very keen about it [either]. I was very young, rather determined, and perhaps I wasn't always very wise. But I think Rupert perhaps wasn't a conventional schoolboy, insofar as he didn't excel or wish to excel at sport."[11]

Unfortunately, her only son did not excel in the classroom either, ranking near the bottom scholastically, a standing that prompted his mother to say that he was "not academically brilliant."[12] Yet, Rupert's extracurricular activities more than complemented his education. By the time he turned 16, he was an editor of the school newspaper, the *Corio Courier*, and formed an early appreciation for left-wing politics.

The following year, Rupert helped form a debate society called the Areopagus,** and after its first meeting was mentioned

---

**Areopagus* means "Hill of Ares" in Greek, and was the name of the council that was the central governing body of Athens in ancient Greece.

in the school's magazine, the *Corian,* for his outspoken attack on a debater. "Mr. R. K. Murdoch found fault with the Hon. Proposer who in turn found fault with Mr. Murdoch for misrepresentation," the magazine reported.[13] In subsequent meetings, members of the Areopagus listened to Rupert's disputatious theories on nationalism and socialism and his open ridicule of America for its rampant capitalism, racist behavior, and unmanageable political system.[14] The shyness of youth found its voice in the rantings of one longing to carve his own place among contemporaries who had already found theirs.

On weekends, while other students were taking hikes in the hills or rowing in Corio Bay, Rupert journeyed alone to a nearby garage. There, among the oil cans and greasy tools, he secretly kept a motorbike gassed and ready to deliver him to the provincial racetrack at Geelong. Rupert Greene had taught his grandson well. During school breaks, young Murdoch returned home to Cruden Farm, where his mother had workers construct "Rupert's hut" in the garden. This wooden shed was Rupert's summer room, the place where he slept until he was 16. Despite the hut's lack of electricity, water, heat, fans, or glassed-in windows, Rupert considered it a rather fun place to camp out, never realizing that his mother had conceived of the room as a form of toughening for her pampered son.

During the day, the teenager turned manipulator, coaxing his two older sisters out to catch rabbits and river rats and to collect manure from the horse paddocks and nearby Davies Bay. The girls' enterprising brother then sold the animals' skins and the bagged manure to local families, keeping the cash for himself in an early example of commercial savvy. "I always said that Rupert got his start in life from rabbits and manure," his sister Helen said. "I never saw any of the money. Rupert did. He spent it on gambling at school."[15]

As Rupert continued to do battle at Geelong Grammar, his family remained ensconced for the most part at Cruden Farm, while his father leased a small apartment in the city. After the war, Keith loaned Heathfield Mansion to the Salvation Army, and then to the Royal Children's Hospital before eventually selling it in 1947 to the Colonial Mutual Life Insurance Society. Since Keith's growing empire still required an in-town base for entertaining, he used the money from the sale to purchase a large colonial home at 39 Albany Road, Toorak. Though substantially smaller than Heathfield, with its dining room that seated 24, Albany Road continued to be the scene of dinner parties and musicales that rivaled any in Melbourne for their opulence.

Rupert graduated in 1948 from Geelong with a diploma in English Expression but with little direction in life. Elisabeth, knowing of his uncertainty, which she credited to his age, mandated that Rupert return for an additional year at Geelong, much to his distress. She would later question her motive by admitting, "I think that I myself sometimes did put Keith before the children."[16] Taking advantage of his lightened scholastic load, Rupert launched his first magazine, a sequel to the school's defunct literary journal *If*. He called his new magazine *If Revived* and populated its pages with the finest in student writing—for all of its two issues.

When at last he bid Geelong Grammar good-bye, Rupert joined the staff of his father's *Herald* newspaper as a reporter on the crime beat. His father knew of Rupert's penchant for gambling; he also knew of his love for newspapers. Together the pair spent evenings at Keith's enormous desk in the Albany Street house, scanning the various pages of the *Herald*, critiquing layout and editing. "I think every father of an only son sees this son as a successor. Keith always hoped for that, but he was very anxious Rupert should be worthy of it," Elisabeth said.[17]

By April 1950, a certain contentment had spread its salve over the family. Keith had survived a bout with colon cancer and the surgery that followed, and he excitedly enrolled his son at Oxford University's Worcester College to gain the advanced education he himself never achieved. First, however, with the younger children left in the watchful care of Nanny Murdoch, Keith and Elisabeth flew with their son to Rome for an audience with the pope. "Rupert was unimpressed," his mother said, "particularly with the little silver medals the Pope gave him."[18]

The family was met in Rome by the *Herald*'s London correspondent, Rohan Rivett, and his wife, whom Keith had requested drive them across the continent to England and arrange for economy hotel lodging along the way. From there they continued to Canada, where Murdoch led the Australian delegation at the Empire Press Union.[†] Keith met with Pat Gibson, director of Westminster Press, a company that published more than 80 newspapers in Great Britain, including the *Birmingham Gazette*. As a personal favor, Keith asked Gibson to give his son a summer job as a reporter with the *Gazette*. On-the-job training, one newsman to another. However, neither man had counted on the young Murdoch's forthright spirit as he threw himself into his work, toiling overtime to perfect his skill. At the end of several months at the *Gazette*, Rupert wrote to Gibson recommending that *Gazette* editor Charles Fenby be fired, charging that his style with the staff was too remote and insufficiently hands-on. Gibson wisely ignored the advice.

By October, the Murdochs had returned to Australia, and son Rupert was again on his own. He was hardly without support, however. As an Oxford freshman, he not only had an automobile garaged nearby, but he also was housed in one of its largest dormitory quarters—the de Quincey room, a rather dark and formally paneled place named after British essayist Thomas de Quincey, who attended Oxford and began his lifelong addiction to opium there.

It is said that those who stand very still can hear the wisdom of Oxford's long-dead scholars: Quaker reformer and founder of

---

[†] The union was founded by Sir Harry Brittain as a means of promoting freedom of the press among members of the Commonwealth, and as a lobbying force to oppose any measures that limit such freedom.

Pennsylvania William Penn, British prime minister Harold
Macmillan, authors J. R. R. Tolkien, Evelyn Waugh, Iris Murdoch, and T. S. Eliot, and financier Cecil Rhodes. Their heritage
resides within the cherished academic halls—at least it does to
many. Rupert Murdoch apparently escaped their clairvoyant wisdom, contenting himself with posturing on the merits of socialism, a performance made even more convincing with the
installation of a bust of Vladimir Lenin on the mantle in his
room. He joined the Oxford Labour Club and thoroughly reveled
in his antiestablishment reputation despite the growing resentment of his classmates, who never could justify the incongruence
of Rupert's wealth and his political stance.

   With few friends, Rupert came to depend on Rohan Rivett
and his wife and children. Rivett, whom Keith Murdoch had
asked to keep watch over young Rupert, regularly corresponded
with his employer in Melbourne, updating him on his son's
progress. "I am inclined to prophesy that [Rupert] will make his
first million with fantastic ease," Rivett wrote in late 1950.[19] After
Rupert completed his first year at Oxford, one highlighted by
dismal grades and sporadic study, Rivett informed Keith that he
felt the young man had the innate ability to "work things out
and get things done."[20] Not surprisingly, the senior Murdoch
remained unconvinced. His son's lack of recognizable skill, coupled with poor grades, weighed heavily on the newspaperman as
his health began to fade.

   It was with Keith's remaining strength that he made one last
trip to the United States and had a brief audience with President
Harry S. Truman. On his way back to Australia, Murdoch
stopped in London and offered Rivett the editorship of the *Adelaide News*. More than a mere thank-you for the shepherding of
his son, Murdoch had full confidence in Rivett's ability to handle the position and expand the newpaper's readership.

   Rupert reveled in the news, but not for the obvious reasons.
With Rivett and his family transferred to Australia, Rupert was

freed of all constraints. He indulged himself in the year that followed by purposefully misbehaving much in the way children do to draw attention to themselves. But Rupert was no longer a child. Rather, he was a pampered, privileged son whose academic future looked less than promising. He outraged college advisers when he ran for secretary of the Labour Club using methods that mocked the school's rules. In his zest for campaigning, Rupert flagrantly solicited votes through a mailed advertisement that bannered *Rooting for Rupert* on the envelope. The school paper, *Cherwell*, noted the gaffe with: "Rupert Murdoch, cataclysmic chauffeur from the outback, prototype of Hollywood's peripatetic publicists, has plastered the town and papered the noticeboards."[21] When his methods were revealed, an outraged faculty banned him from holding *any* office in the club, effectively ending his political career. He did not, however, stop vocalizing his politics or cease attending meetings, nor did he stop gambling, a habit at odds with his socialist doctrine.

The two factors came together during his summer break in 1952, a time that Rupert used to tour Europe and frequent the casinos in Monte Carlo and Deauville, France, before heading to Blackpool, England's largest seaside resort and the site of the national Labour Party Conference, plus various prerequisite gambling halls. He gained entrance to the meeting at Blackpool's Convention Center by sporting press credentials from the *Adelaide News,* and later wrote to his father with what Elisabeth Murdoch said was "an objective and penetrating account" of the conference. The letter arrived in Melbourne on October 2, 1952, and when Keith Murdoch read what his son had written, his normally tense face melted into a smile. "I think the boy's got it!" he exclaimed to his wife in what was the first real acknowledgment of his son's talent. Three days later, on October 5, Keith Murdoch died in his sleep of a massive coronary.

As he lay in bed the night before he died, Sir Keith began a letter to his daughter Anne, then attending boarding school at

Clyde. "My beautiful and good Anne," it began. "We have had a splendid letter from Rupert and he is forgiven some of his misdemeanours."[22]

Rupert learned of his father's death via a cable sent to his favorite professor at Oxford, the noted British historian Asa Briggs. It had been more than a year since Rupert last saw his father. After Keith's visit to London, he and his son had taken a drive through Switzerland, Italy, Austria, Yugoslavia, and Greece, where they stayed at the Hotel Grande Bretagne. There, amid the stained-glass ceilings and mirrored salons, the two men watched the sun set on the Acropolis, never dreaming it would be their last moments together.

It took Rupert three full days of flying to reach Melbourne, only to discover that his father had been buried the day before. He swallowed his anger, but his disappointment shattered what remained of his confidence. The sole male heir to the Murdoch throne was neither consulted nor considered when the arrangements were made.

He heard from his sisters that several hundred attended the private service held at Toorak Presbyterian Church. Pallbearers included members of government, business, and publishing, and flowers and wreaths spilled across the front lawn of the sanctuary. The Reverend A. C. Watson called Sir Keith Murdoch "an outstanding leader in the business and private life of this nation, a great Australian and a beloved husband and father."

It was the first of many tributes that continued for days following the funeral. "For all the spread of his interests, every one of which was his by his own efforts, he was regarded as a model and human employer," Australian prime minister Robert Menzies said. "As a nation, Sir Keith Murdoch left us in his debt."

In America, the *New York Times* published an editorial claiming that Sir Keith's most outstanding quality "was not ambition for personal success. It was friendliness . . . friendships both personal and national. No one ever questioned his courage or his integrity. He belonged to the pure of heart."[23]

The *Adelaide News* said Murdoch was "one of the very few great Australians of his age . . . a romantic success story beyond the dreams of fiction."

The reading of Keith Murdoch's will, written in 1948, removed any shred of doubt that he expected his son to follow his lead:

> WHEREAS I desire that Queensland Newspapers Pty Ltd of Queen Street Brisbane and another Newspaper Company approved by my trustees should continue to express my ideals of newspaper and broadcasting activities in the service of others and these ideals should be pursued with deep interest AND WHEREAS I desire that my said son Keith Rupert Murdoch should have the great opportunity of spending a useful altruistic and full life in newspaper and broadcasting activities and of ultimately occupying a position of high responsibility in that field with the support of my trustees if they consider him worthy of that support.

Rupert felt ready to accept his leadership role but was dissuaded by his mother from entering the publishing world until after graduating from Oxford. Nevertheless, when he reluctantly returned to England, he launched an intense letter-writing campaign to Rohan Rivett, querying the *Adelaide News* editor about salaries, costs, expenses, and profits. Where Sir Keith was concerned about the editorial slant, young Rupert worried about the bottom line—and with good reason.

With his father's extensive art collection, the home on Albany Road, and newspaper shares sold to pay estate taxes, Rupert Murdoch's only inheritance was the *News,* the struggling evening paper in Australia's third largest city. It was the most mundane of his father's possessions, and now it was his. After graduating from Oxford with a degree in philosophy in 1953, Rupert did not rush to claim his birthright. Instead, with his university diploma shoved in his back pocket, he went to work learning his trade at the feet of Lord Beaverbrook, owner of the London *Daily Express,* the voice of intellectual populism at the time. Its glaring head-lines and concise copy set the standard for which Rupert's empire would eventually become known. But for the moment, that was all in the future.

When Rupert finally arrived back in Australia in September 1953 at the age of 22, the boy whom classmates had called Rupert the Red leaped blindly onto a road he would eventually pave into a highway leading directly to the Information Age—a journey that could change the entire world forever.

# Robert Edward Turner III

*Ninety percent of the arguments I had with [my husband]
were over his beating Ted too hard.*

Florence Turner
Cincinnati
Spring 1977

938. Winter came early to Cincinnati that year, blowing an overcast sky into the amphitheater of hills above the Ohio River. Not the kind of winter that was common in the Northeast; no snow or even freezing temperatures. The locals called it a lazy sky, for it crept up on the town with damp, cold air that chilled right to the bone. Florence Turner felt it more than most. Nearly 10 months pregnant and overdue, she lowered herself into the large claw-foot tub of her bathroom in the apartment on Dana Avenue and melted into a puddle of relaxed muscles and soothed nerves.

Her husband, Ed, had been drinking again, and when Ed drank, Florence knew it was best to avoid the man who loved to fight when he got drunk. This night, her husband had had only a few beers, at least as far as she could tell, but she did not want to risk confrontation and the shouting matches that always followed. She was too sore, too tired for that now. All she wanted to do was relax in the tub and go quietly to bed.

Florence had lived in Cincinnati all her life, mostly at her grandmother's elegant residential hotel. The lobby was grand,

41

with large Oriental carpets on the hardwood floors. As a young woman, Florence reclined every evening on a deep-violet chaise in a corner of that grand room and watched the parade of guests pass by. It was there that she met her future husband, Robert Edward Turner Jr. Ed was born in Sumner, Mississippi, which explained his charming Southern accent, and after a brief stint at the University of Mississippi had traveled around in search of a career. He tried carpentry and plumbing before moving to Memphis, Tennessee, where he found a job counting the cars that passed by billboards owned by the General Outdoor Advertising Company.

The promise of a sales job at Queen City Chevrolet brought him to Cincinnati, where he sold Florence's brother, George, a maroon two-door Trunkback Town Sedan for $721 cash and the promise of an introduction to his sister. Florence fell for the suave Southerner's glib tongue and affectionate ways, and found nothing rushed in his marriage proposal six months later.

The storm clouds that threatened to ruin their wedding day on August 17, 1937, were a harbinger of things to come. At the time, however, Florence failed to see the warnings in her husband's addiction to liquor or his propensity toward violence. She was simply in love with the star car salesman from Queen City Chevrolet, and the Reverend Monsignor Henry Schengber gave the couple his blessing.

Florence recalled that day on the steps of St. Frances de Sales Church, its towering gray limestone edifice a monument to eternity. Then, as she slid lower into the tub, she tried to remember happiness. It was an emotion in scarce supply in the Turner apartment, replaced by the unpredictability of alcohol and the temper it released. It was only as she left the bath that she felt her first contraction, and realized her life was about to change with or without her consent. She told herself she was ready for a child. *But is my husband?* she wondered to herself in the silence of the night.

When the contractions began to increase in frequency during the predawn hours of November 19, 1938, Florence woke Ed out of a liquor-induced sleep and hurried to get dressed. Their home was surrounded by medical facilities, giving the area of North Avondale its nickname, Pill Hill. That night, Ed drove Florence to nearby Christ Hospital, where Dr. James Pierce attended the birth of Robert Edward Turner III at 8:50 in the morning.

Florence called the baby Teddy and placed blue ribbons in his fine blond hair as Ed looked on in anticipation of a future partnership with his firstborn. For the next few years, Ed became enamored with the idea of a family business. Turner and Son, he said he would call it: business billboards located along Cincinnati's burgeoning highway system. To gain needed experience, he left Queen City Chevrolet and joined the Central Outdoor Advertising Company, developing corporate contacts with some of the city's largest businesses—Procter & Gamble, General Motors, Cincinnati Gas & Electric.

He even gave up drinking for a while, took up smoking in its place, and then ended up smoking and drinking to excess. While Florence stayed at home with Ted, Ed flirted with indiscretion, romancing women he met in Cincinnati bars—girls from Idlewild, Norwood, Walnut Hill, each younger and more available than the last. Florence knew about his cheating. Keeping a secret in their Avondale neighborhood was about as easy as getting lost in a two-seater. There were moments when Florence thought of leaving, of course. Nearly every day, she said. Yet her Catholic faith told her to be patient.

Ed was not a Catholic and had little time for the theatrics that the religion involved. He was raised a Methodist but compromised on his Episcopalian faith after his son was born. And when Florence became pregnant with their second child, he put his hand on a Bible and swore he would reform.

Mary Jane Turner was born dark-haired and healthy on September 18, 1941, and for a while Ed stayed at home and played the part of proud papa. Seeing his father's attention devoted to the baby, little Ted became quickly bored, then jealous, then outraged, and showed his frustration through rebellious fits of anger. Ed reacted with a rage of his own, grabbing, shaking, and beating the child into submission. "Ted was a little on the mischievous side," his mother admitted, "but he was never really bad. His daddy just ruled with an iron hand."[1]

Moreover, as Ted matured, Ed failed to stop at just his hand. He turned to belts and then to wire hangers, yet nothing broke his determined son's spirit. It was for that reason, Ed said, that when he enlisted in the Navy in 1944, he decided to take along his wife and daughter to a succession of naval installations, leaving Ted behind in Cincinnati with his maternal grandmother, Florence Rooney. Mrs. Rooney fared no better in disciplining the child, and sent Ted, at the age of six, to live in a boarding school on the other side of town.

Completely alone for the first time in his young life, Ted turned inward for solace, refusing to express his despair and loneliness. Uncertain, unwanted, unpopular. The blond-haired boy with the cleft chin thought his world could not possibly get any bleaker. He was wrong.

When Ed brought his entire family back home after the war, he opened his own business: Turner Advertising, across the Ohio River from Cincinnati in the town of Covington, Kentucky. The city was located a few miles from a new airport created when the War Department gave up control of the Air Force landing field constructed during World War II. With his Southern accent and conversational ways, Ed began to sell his billboards along the road to the single brick terminal. It didn't matter that only one American Airlines flight flew back and forth to Cleveland each day. Ed had gotten there first, and his business prospered.

Eager for new markets, Turner next looked farther south to Savannah and felt the untapped Georgia cotton belt was ripe with possibilities. He admired the tall moss-veiled oaks and expansive parks, and thought the quiet charm of Savannah was the perfect place to raise a family—all his family, that is, except Ted. Once again, as bags were packed and the family Chevrolet loaded with household goods, Ed Turner told his only son he was not invited. This time, however, his fate was not a mere boarding school. This time Ed had different plans. Ted needed discipline, and his father knew the place.

Georgia Military Academy,* located 20 minutes south of Atlanta, was designed around regimen. Founded in 1900 by Colonel John Charles Woodward, the academy centered itself on strong Christian ethics and military conditioning. Each day began with a 7:30 A.M. chapel service, where the school's president, Colonel William Brewster, son-in-law of the founder, gave a daily sermon on responsibility, manners, and volition. Classes in math, history, and English were followed by military drills and exercise on the parade field.

When nine-year-old Ted Turner entered the academy through its memorial gate in the fall of 1947, it was six weeks into the fall term. Ed had been too busy traveling to Savannah on business to arrange for his son's transportation to the academy. When Ted finally did arrive, not only was he thrust into a strange environment, but his classmates also ostracized him, singling him out as the Yankee among them. The young Turner did little to ingratiate himself with his peers, preferring to challenge their friendships and traditions. "I was from Ohio," Turner said in 1973. "I was a northerner. I don't know what it was. Yes, I do know what it was. The other kids thought I was a show-off and a smart ass."[2] And for good reason. He was.

For the next two years, Ted remained at the military academy, growing increasingly fond of its structure and predictability. He spent the summers in Sumner, Mississippi with his paternal grandfather, the first Robert Edward Turner. There, among the

---

*The academy stopped accepting boarding students in 1964, when it became a coeducational private school and changed its name to Woodward Academy.

moss-covered cypress trees of the murky Cassidy Bayou, Ted felt at peace. It was exceedingly flat land, a place where the water tower provided the only true vista, so people tended not to look far down the road or into the future, content to be coping with today. Ted spent his days watching his grandpa's coondogs, trolling for catfish, playing with toads. Lonely, but not lonesome.

The blues of the Mississippi floated across the flat land from the juke joints scattered along the stream, accompanied by screams of excitement as old friends sang and played, got drunk, fell down on calloused hands, and then stayed put because it was the easiest thing to do. No one bothered to tell Ted of the racial atrocities that took place there in the name of progress, or of the poverty that was as pervasive as it was accepted.

Ted learned about poverty by experiencing the lack of it when he finally joined the family in Savannah in the summer of 1949. His father was flush with success and had taken to wearing custom-made Irish linen suits and Panama hats. He drove a big Lincoln Continental, boasted about the size of his bank account, and spread the news around to make certain no one missed the point. Ed lived with Florence and Mary Jane in a five-bedroom home at 3204 Abercorn Street, in a tree-lined historic section of the city that allowed him easy access to his affluent neighbors and nearby banks. Ted had his own room down the hall from that of his sister and of Jimmy Brown, a 17-year-old Geechee black from Hope, Georgia, whom Ed had retained as the family factotum.

As Ed's success grew, so too did his expectations of his son, whose own abilities fell far short of his father's dream. In a sense, Turner planned it that way, purposefully pushing his goals for Ted higher just before the boy reached any plateau. Yet, the frustration of continuous failure was still ahead for Ted that summer—a period during which he was introduced to the sport that was to determine his course for the next 30 years.

When Ed first joined the Savannah Yacht Club, it was more for social contacts than for the pleasure he found in sailing. He purchased a 45-foot ketch-rigged yawl with a distinctive high-broad foredeck that he named the *Merry Jane,* and with the aid of Jimmy Brown began entertaining on the yacht. Florence did not join him often at these parties, preferring to stay with the children out of "tattling range."[3] She knew about the women her husband had on board for his own enjoyment, but preferred to ignore his indiscretions in favor of a stable home life.

Ted received his own boat that summer, a classic Phil Rhodes–designed dinghy that cost his father $300.[4] It was Brown who first taught Ted to sail. A reluctant pupil, the young Turner took a few months to warm to the subtleties of the sport. When the boy first sailed the 13-foot boat, he earned the nickname the Capsize Kid for his frequent tipping of the wooden craft. In his rush to sail, he pushed past the basics and took years to master the art of keeping his craft in correct position. "But I just kept working and working and working," he said, until finally he figured it out himself.[5]

By then, of course, his father had moved on to another challenge kept just slightly out of his son's eager reach. He put Ted to work in his company pulling weeds around billboard signs. It was backbreaking work and caused additional friction between husband and wife. "Oh, I used to fuss a lot when Ed would send Ted out at the age of ten to cut weeds around the signs that were in swampy places full of snakes. But he would jolly me along. He really was witty. With that thick Southern accent of his, he could be hilarious at times. He called me 'the avenging angel,' and 'his little nubbin.' I thought that was cute until I found out a nubbin is a deformed ear of corn."[6]

For all the disappointment he saw in his son, Ed managed to allow the child to stay in Savannah through an entire school year. Ted began attending sixth grade at the nearby Charles Ellis Academy. The two-story redbrick school in Ardsley Park produced well-adjusted, self-confident students and managed to have a small impact on Ted's education. At the Ellis school the 11-year-old acquired neighborhood friends but not a quest for knowledge, his teachers at the time reporting that he was working far below his potential.

"I don't think Ted was any great student," his mother agreed. "He loved the outdoors, but he was not really too interested in schoolwork. It didn't move fast enough for him."[7]

For his father, unrealized potential was akin to failure, and failure he would not tolerate. Ed rationalized that if the local school could not stimulate Ted, perhaps another dose of military school would. On the recommendation of the president of Savannah's Southern Bank & Trust Company, Turner enrolled his son at McCallie Military School in Chattanooga, Tennessee.

The road to McCallie was an ominous one, shrouded in a reputation of enforced discipline, mandatory athletics, and Christian ethics. The more Ted studied the catalog his father brought home and left in plain view, the more certain he was that his life was over. It didn't help that he refused to go. It only made his father more determined to see that it happened. Throughout the summer, it was the only topic of discussion between father and son; the cause of beatings that left both battered. In the end, of course, the bruises healed, and Ted became the youngest boarder at McCallie Military—in fact, he was the only boarding student in the entire seventh grade.

His dormitory was a place called Douglas Hall, not far from the very spot where the Union army overran the Confederates led by General Braxton Bragg, who lost the Battle of Chattanooga. Ted had no thoughts of Bragg or the Confederate troops for that matter. What little knowledge he did have he wore heavily. He dressed in blue, wore a cap, marched in line, and wished he was anywhere but McCallie Military. He missed his boat; he missed Jimmy Brown; he even missed the ladies of Savannah, with their perfumed hair, plucked eyebrows, and scarlet lips. But he did not miss his father, the man he blamed for being sent packing to Tennessee.

According to the school catalog at the time, "Honor may be the most valuable lesson McCallie teaches. McCallie is the school for the boy who wants to work—and be known by his work."[8] Young Ted wanted none of it.

"I did everything I could to rebel against the system," he said. "I was always having animals in my room . . . and getting into trouble one way or another, and then having to take my punishment like a man. I had more demerits than anyone in the history of the school. They used to give demerits for dirty shoes and things like that. Well, there was only so much time you could walk [off your demerits] on any weekend and anything left over was carried over."[9]

In the first year Ted spent at McCallie, he walked a lot. So much so, in fact, that his mother later said, "I had to buy him new shoes every time he came home."[10]

It wasn't an easy reunion, that first summer back in Savannah. Jimmy Brown came to fetch his 12-year-old charge and needed to wait several days for Ted to finish walking off his demerits. When the pair finally were ready to leave McCallie, Brown pulled out of the driveway so slowly that a single moth, up past its bedtime, flew in and out of the car window. Jimmy was dreading the news he had to deliver. Ted's sister, Mary Jane, was hospitalized in a coma. She was suffering from systemic lupus erythematosus,** a normally fatal disease at the time, had contracted encephalitis, and had been rushed to Johns Hopkins Hospital in Baltimore. When she finally emerged from her coma three months later, her condition only worsened.

"Her brain [was] totally destroyed," Ted remembered years later. "It was a horror show of major proportions. A padded room. Screaming day and night. It was something right out of

---

**An autoimmune disorder that can affect many parts of the body, including the joints, skin, kidneys, heart, lungs, blood vessels, and brain.

*Dark Shadows*."[11] As the young boy watched his sister writhe in agony, he matured in ways that defied his youth. No longer the carefree irritant, he became subdued and turned inward.

At home his mother spent every available moment caring for his sister, while his father buried himself in his business, leaving Ted on his own yet again despite the fact that he was just down the hall. Mary Jane's illness became a constant source of argument for his parents, who disagreed on her care. Ed wanted his daughter in a hospital; Florence wanted her at home, refusing to leave her bedside.

Ed put his son back to work in the business, painting billboards in the field with other day laborers. The pay was a modest $50 a week, from which Ed deducted $25 for room and board. Unable to understand his father's frugality, particularly in light of the hard work he contributed, the youngster complained, only to be told to check around town. "If you can find a better deal, take it," Ed told him. And his son knew he meant every word.

When Ted returned to McCallie that fall, the school played a different role in his life. Defiance was replaced with determination; argumentativeness with purpose. If he did not manage to reduce his demerits, at least now they were for things that mattered to the boy—caring for sick animals in his dorm room and cutting class to sail on Lake Chattanooga. He organized a sailing club and began teaching other cadets how to judge the winds and work the rigging. Ted also discovered a passion for reading, especially classics about the sea. "I read C. S. Forester's books, and [Charles] Nordhoff and [James Norman] Hall about ten times—*Mutiny on the Bounty, Men against the Sea,* and *Pitcairn's Island*. I read about the War of 1812, and about the *Constitution*— you know, the ship."[12]

His fondness for sailing returned with him to Savannah each summer. Reading too. It was a pastime encouraged by his father, who mandated that his son read at least one book every two days. "I never considered not doing it, because I was instructed with wire coat hangers when I didn't get them read. I learned quickly not to question the word of the big chief."[13] Ted stole moments during his lunch break to disappear into the world of buccaneers and buried treasure, of survival against insurmountable odds. At night he escaped the muffled screams of his sister by retreating into the adventure of a bygone age.

Ed had rented out the family's colonial home on Alden Road, and moved the household to larger quarters in an expansive Tudor house, wedged on a triangular piece of property several blocks away at 302 East 46th Street. It was a massive structure, with high ceilings and ornate fireplaces, and represented Ed's success in advertising for all Savannah to see. The opulence hid a tragic secret behind the home's thick walls and closed windows, however.

Unable to bear the continuing horror of his daughter's illness, Ed moved the child to her own room above the garage, as if separation could mend the pain. A dazed, broken man, he would stare across the kitchen table, the extinguished cigarette in his hand a smudge pot of unreachable dreams. Despite her own selfless efforts to save Mary Jane, Florence thought herself responsible for her child's pain, and internalized her grief through long periods of stricken silence.

The couple began to consider divorce, a subject that had surfaced before, but never with the certainty following Mary Jane's illness. Ted refused to believe that his parents might actually separate, let alone divorce, preferring to delude himself with the impression that his own performance would have an effect on their marriage. Returning to McCallie, he redoubled his efforts to become the perfect cadet, was awarded a blue ribbon for tidiness, and upon graduation in 1956, received the Holton Harris Oratorical Medal for excellence on the school's debate team. "I just wanted to be the best," Ted said. "And I saw that it could be done if you worked at it."[14]

Regardless of their son's efforts to please them, however, the Turners were silent strangers sharing a home as if stranded in a world of disagreement. As their indifference began crossing the line to hate, Ted made every effort to shift their attention. He wanted to go to the U.S. Naval Academy in Annapolis, he said. "Honor, Courage, Commitment"—the academy's motto was one even his father could appreciate, yet not enough to give his blessing. Ed Turner wanted his son at Harvard University, "the finest school in the nation," he said.

Unfortunately, Harvard wasn't as impressed with Ted as his father was with Harvard. When the school turned down his son's application for admission, Ed decided to try another Ivy League school—Brown University in Providence, Rhode Island. Nearly as old and equally as prestigious as Princeton, Brown overlooked Ted's average grades and saw potential in his skills at debate, noting on his application, "outspoken advocate of eccentricities."[15]

Ted was unfamiliar with Brown and its Baptist heritage. Founded just prior to the American Revolution, the school's first building, now known as University Hall, was denounced by the *Boston Gazette* as being "near as large as Babel; sufficient to contain ten times the number of students" that the school could ever anticipate matriculating. By the time Ted Turner arrived in September 1956, there were just under 6,000 students enrolled on Brown's 140-acre campus, resplendent with its century-old trees and historic buildings.

Into this refined conclave of academia stormed a very loud, very determined, and very handsome Robert Edward Turner III. He arrived at Brown after a summer spent pushing the envelope of misconduct as if every last ounce of human civility had to be challenged. Like his daddy before him, Ted regularly drove to Charleston in search of girls, routinely breaking the speed limit and daring the local police to risk entering the race. He also inherited Ed's familiarity with liquor, preferring bourbon to beer. Ted explored his sexuality with the available women of Savannah, Charleston, and eventually Providence, the notches of conquest tabulated in his nearly photographic memory. The cocky, over-confident loudmouth joined roommates Carl Wattenberg of Missouri and Doug Woodring of Pennsylvania in room 310, Maxcy Hall.[16] The dormitory was ill prepared for a boy like Ted.

Drawing on his love of literature, he regularly spouted poetry, usually at full volume and always to make an impression on one person or another. A Southern boy in a Northern bastion of culture and respectability, Ted defended the Confederate army and the War of Northern Aggression without ever mentioning Cincinnati or his birth on the wrong side of the Mason-Dixon Line. For all his classmates knew, he was a gregarious prankster from the South who had an annoying habit of firing his rifle out his dormitory window in search of unlucky squirrels. He stayed up late playing poker and drinking booze, slept through classes, and established his only credibility when he wandered into the Marston boathouse on the Seekonk River. On the water, his expertise at sailing replaced his need to compensate with loud pontification. With the wind catching his sail, Ted was suddenly in control, a man at peace. And if not at peace, at least with less to prove.

Though he made it through his first year without any casualties (unless you count Wattenberg and Woodring, who moved out of room 310 in desperation at the end of the second semester), Ted did not find Brown a particular easy place to exist. Without the structure of McCallie, he was ill equipped to handle his freedom. Too much time, too little discipline, and an abundance of bourbon found the 18-year-old drifting without purpose.

After winning nine dinghy regattas during his freshman year, Ted asked his father to allow him to spend the summer working in Connecticut at the Noroton Yacht Club on Darien Harbor, just west of Long Neck Point. He held no illusion that Ed would give his blessing readily, and he was not disappointed. Though his father's exact reply has been lost to history, Ted was nevertheless summoned back to Georgia, where the Turner home was a combat zone.

Early June in Savannah spins moist heat around lazy breezes, and Ted felt its welcome as he drove back into town. He needed family, or at least the Turner version of it. What he received was isolation. Ed and Florence had failed to reconcile their bitterness over the illness of their only daughter, and the chasm that split husband and wife was not a place that welcomed their son home from college. Now standing six-feet-two and several inches taller than his father, Ted no longer had to fear wire hangers. Now his fear was something far more terrifying: avoidance.

On the advice of his attorney, Ed Turner left Savannah soon after Ted's arrival to establish a legal residence in Reno, Nevada, and file for divorce from Florence. He made the action official on August 22, 1957, in the Second Judicial District Court of the State of Nevada. For Florence, the news brought relief but no joy. Ted accepted the fact with halting disbelief.

Ed agreed to pay Florence $15,000 a year for 15 years, barring remarriage, and awarded her title to the East 46th Street residence. The settlement also gave Florence sole responsibility for the care and medical expenses of Mary Jane. Ted remained in Ed's custody by his father's own insistence. According to court documents, Ed was awarded "the sole and absolute care, custody and control of Robert Edward Turner III during his minority, and . . . the right to make all decisions relating to his health, education and welfare."[17]

The arrangement left Ted, his father, and Jimmy Brown on Abercorn Street, and his mother and sister around the corner. In between creosoting poles for billboards, Ted read books and began spontaneous oration of poetry. "Therefore, 'tis with full happiness that I will trace the story of Endymion. The very music of the name has gone into my being and each pleasant scene is growing fresh before me as the green of our own valleys," he recited at full pitch in the kitchen, arms akimbo.

"What the hell's he talking about, Sport?" Ed shouted down the hallway to Jimmy.

"Don't know, Mr. T. But it sure was purdy," came the diplomatic response.

Listening in unenthused amazement as his son quoted John Keats should have been Ed's first clue that the nine months Ted had spent at Brown had radically altered his thinking. Over dinner, while Ed remarked about Charleston whores, Ted recited tales of Alexander the Great in the battle at Gaugamela. It didn't matter that he called it Guacamole. Ted had *learned*.

The issue became more than just idle table talk when the teenager returned to Brown for his sophomore year. He enrolled in classes with noted professor John Rowe Workman and actually began to study. Not study seriously, of course, but at least he began to read bits of classic literature and history.

The majority of Ted's schedule, however, revolved around Kappa Sigma, the fraternity he had pledged in his freshman year, and in whose house he now resided. He drank despite his father's pledge of $5,000 if he did not, though liquor was hardly the worst of his offenses. According to William Kennedy, Brown class of 1960, "Ted was a bigot as maybe all of us were in a sense at that time. Often he would go out in a group, after a lot of drinking, and sing Nazi songs outside the Jewish fraternity, or he would put signs reading WARNINGS FROM THE KU KLUX KLAN on the doors of the few blacks at Brown. He wasn't vicious. He was just trying to be one of the boys."[18]

His room was on the first floor of the large redbrick structure, making for easy access when he wanted to ignore house rules and bring home girls from nearby Pembroke College and Wheaton College. And he wanted to ignore the rules frequently—if not at Brown, then at Pembroke and Wheaton.

During one of his off-campus excursions, Ted's luck at escaping the notice of campus police ran out. It didn't help that he had been drinking, was loudly serenading his current girlfriend, and had stolen the sign-in register from her dormitory to lace it with obscenities. Legend has it that he was midway through "Wake Up

Little Susie" when the local gendarmes arrived and placed him under arrest. When word got back to Brown, Ted's sophomore year was over. The university suspended him for a semester and sent him back to Savannah and his unsuspecting father.

Though Ed had been divorced for less than four months, he had quickly found a replacement for Florence in the tall, attractive daughter of a business associate, William Dillard. Dillard was president of the Central of Georgia Railway Company, which, like so many railroads of the time, was suffering from loss of business. His losses, however, did not stop Dillard from gambling every Friday night in a regular game of poker, a game to which Ed Turner was invited. Jane Dillard found Ed to be a charming, funny whale of a man—his weight having increased to more than 200 pounds from his unabashed intake of liquor. He got along well with the woman and her teenage son, Marshall, and asked her to become his second wife.

Ted discovered the news only upon arriving back in Savannah, and found his father drinking less and smiling more, the joy of romance echoed in a tempered disposition. His father's mood collapsed into an adrenaline rage, however, when Ted delivered the news of his suspension. Ed made the decision right there and then that more military discipline was needed, and he pushed his son into the Coast Guard—a decision that pleased Ted, given his love of the sea.

After his father's wedding, Ted traveled to the Coast Guard Recruit Receiving Station at Sewell Point in Cape May, New Jersey, where he endured basic training with his usual exuberance. When he completed his first six-month tour, he had hardly sailed the seven seas but did manage to achieve the rank of fireman's apprentice.

As Ted returned to Brown in the fall of 1958, his father and stepmother moved to Cotton Hall, a 956-acre plantation in Yemassee, South Carolina, an hour's drive from Savannah. The large white wooden structure, originally constructed in the thirties for New York businessman Harry Payne Bingham and his wife, sat neglected on an expansive lawn of flowering trees that transported the Turners back to a gentler age. Its impressive vistas and expansive size suited Ed's self-image of a Southern gentleman of obvious wealth.

While the father settled down, however, the son was only beginning to play. Back in Kappa Sigma, Ted returned to familiar habits with reckless devotion, learning nothing from his past transgressions. He continued to sail, continued to drink, and continued to seduce nameless local girls with uncorrupted zeal, the concept of study a distant priority. The single exception was his ongoing fascination with literature—the betrayals, sacrifices, vows, and passions of life on the sea in the eighteenth century a particular obsession. He found an eager mentor in Professor Workman, a man known for his dramatic presentation, clarity of voice, and reputation as a saint of lost causes. Coached by Workman, Ted devoured the classics, often at the expense of his other courses. Yet, thanks to a mind that memorized facts with seeming ease, and to compassionate professors willing to accept his inventive excuses, Ted's second attempt at finishing his sophomore year was successful.

Living on luck and outrageous behavior had its limits, however, as he discovered in his junior year. The 1958–59 year began predictably enough, with Ted living at Kappa Sigma. With a glass of bourbon and a stogie to accessorize his look, the 20-year-old aggressively pursued his passion for sailing and women, reading literature as time allowed. As soon as he had returned to his classes with Workman, he sent his father a note informing him of his decision to major in classical literature. He was stunned at the response. Ed wrote a letter back that illustrates their relationship better than any memory could. The missive might have been lost forever if Ted had not been so hurt and outraged by its message. He gave it to the editor of the student tabloid, the *Brown Daily Herald,* to run anonymously on its editorial page.

My dear son,

I am appalled, even horrified, that you have adopted Classics as a Major. As a matter of fact, I almost puked on the way home today. I suppose that I am old-fashioned enough to believe that the purpose of education is to enable one to develop a community of interest with his fellow man, to learn to know them, and to learn how to get along with them. In order to do this, of course, he must learn what motivates them, and how to impel them to be pleased with his objectives and desires.

I am a practical man, and for the life of me I cannot possibly understand why you should wish to speak Greek. With whom will you communicate in Greek? I have read, in recent years, the deliberations of Plato and Aristotle, and was interested to learn that the old bastards had minds which worked very similarly to the way our minds work today. I was amazed that they had so much time for deliberating and thinking and was interested in the kind of civilization that would permit such useless deliberation. Then I got to thinking that it wasn't so amazing after all. They thought like we did, because my Hereford cows today are very similar to those ten or twenty generations ago. I am amazed that you would adopt Plato and Aristotle as a vocation for several months when it might make pleasant and enjoyable reading to you in your leisure time as relaxation at a later date. For the life of me, I cannot understand why you should be vitally interested in informing yourself about the influence of the Classics on English Literature. It is not necessary for you to know how to make a gun in order to know how to use it. It would seem to me that it would be enough to learn English literature without going into the influence this or that ancient

mythology might have had upon it. As for Greek literature, the history of Roman and Greek churches and the
art of those eras, it would seem to me that you would be
much better off by learning something about contemporary literature and writings and things that may have
some meaning to you with the people with whom you
are to associate.

These subjects might give you a community of
interest with an isolated few impractical dreamers and
a select group of college professors. God forbid!

It would seem to me that what you wish to do is to
establish a community of interest with as many people
as you possibly can. With people who are moving, who
are doing things and who have an interesting, not a
decadent outlook.

I suppose everybody has to be a snob of some sort,
and I suppose you will feel that you are distinguishing
yourself from the herd by becoming a Classical snob. I
can see you drifting into a bar, belting down a few, turning around to the guy on the stool next to you—a contemporary billboard baron from Podunk, Iowa, and
saying, "Well, what did you think of old Leonidas?"[†] He
will turn to you and say, "Leonidas who?" You will turn
to him and say, "Why, Leonidas, the prominent Greek of
the twelfth century. He will, in turn, say to you, "Well,
who in the hell was he?" You will say, "Oh, you don't
know anything about Leonidas?" and dismiss him. And
not discuss anything else with him for the rest of the
evening. He will feel that you are a stupid snob and a flop
and you will feel that he is a clodhopper from Podunk,
Iowa. I suppose this will make you both happy and as a
result of it, you will wind up buying his billboard plant.

---

†King of Sparta, killed in 480 B.C. by the Persians at Thermopylae.

There is no question but this type of useless information will distinguish you, set you apart from the doers of the world. If I leave you enough money, you can retire to an ivory tower and contemplate for the rest of your days the influence that the hieroglyphics of prehistoric man had upon the writings of William Faulkner. We speak the same language—whores, sluts, strong words, and strong deeds.

It isn't really important what I think. It's important what you wish to do with your life. I just wish I could see that the influence of those oddball professors and the ivory towers were developing you into the kind of man we can both be proud of. I am quite sure that we both will be pleased and delighted when I introduce you to some friend of mine and say, "This is my son. He speaks Greek."

I had dinner during the Christmas holidays with an efficiency expert, an economic adviser to the nation of India, on the Board of Directors of Regents at Harvard University, who owns some 80,000 acres of valuable timber land down here, among his other assets. His son and his family were visiting him. He introduced me to his son, then apologetically said, "He is a theoretical mathematician. I don't even know what he is talking about. He lives in a different world." After a little while I got to talking to his son, and the only thing he would talk to me about was his work. I didn't know what he was talking about either, so I left early.

If you are going to stay on at Brown, and be a professor of Classics, the course you have adapted will suit you for a lifetime association with Gale Noyes.§ Perhaps he will even teach you to make jelly. In my opinion, it won't do much to help you learn to get along with the

---

§The noted Brown professor of restoration drama and eighteenth-century English fiction.

real people in this world. I think you are rapidly becoming a jackass and the sooner you get out of that filthy atmosphere, the better it will suit me.

Oh, I know everybody says that a college education is a must. Well, I console myself by saying that everybody said the world was square, except Columbus. You go ahead and go with the world, and I'll go it alone.

I hope I am right. You are in the hands of Philistines, and dammit, I sent you there. I am sorry.

Devotedly,
DAD

Ted's pain at reading the letter manifested itself in several ways. First, he got drunk. Next, he mailed a copy of the published letter in the *Brown Daily Herald* to his father. Then he changed his major to economics without communicating the news back to Yemassee.

Frustrated, incensed, and apparently helpless in light of his father's rejection, Ted blazed a trail of revenge through Brown that screamed for attention. Among his more memorable acts was burning down his fraternity's homecoming display, a 25-foot statue of Paul Bunyan crafted from papier-mâché.[19] The fraternity responded by tossing their brother out of the house and telling him he was no longer welcome.

Moving his rifle, duffel bag, and assorted books to a nearby Brown dormitory, Goddard House, the disenfranchised Turner soothed his emotions the only way he knew—through liquor and sailing. Of the former, his poison of choice was Jack Daniel's. Of the latter, he was co-captain of the Brown Sailing Club (with Bud Webster) the year it went on to win the Professor Schell Trophy Regatta on the Charles River at the Massachusetts Institute of Technology in Cambridge. The trophy awards the best sailing team from among 18 East Coast colleges. Among them was the Coast Guard Academy, which finished eighth.

The following year, with Webster graduated, Ted was com-modore and sole captain of the team. While there was not to be a repeat of the Schell victory, he won something far more impor-tant when he traveled with the club to Chicago just before Thanksgiving in 1959 to compete in the Timme Angsten Trophy Regatta on icy Lake Michigan. He met the skipper of the team from Northwestern University, Judy Gale Nye.

Judy was the daughter of Harry Nye, a two-time winner of sailing's International Star Championship and a sail maker of world renown. In the proverbial luck of the draw, Judy and Ted raced against each other in the regatta. Ted won the race; Judy won his attention. So much so that he remembered her name *and* phone number, and used both to invite her to visit Brown. It was fortunate she arrived when she did just before Christmas, for not long into 1960, Ted was discovered with yet another girl in his room. This time, however, suspension was not even discussed. He was expelled. Ted Turner's college days were over.

For lack of anything better to do, he drove to Miami with visions of sailing across the Atlantic to live a bohemian life in Europe. He recruited another malingerer from Brown, Peter Dames, and together they hit the open highway. After a brief pit stop at the Turner family plantation in Yemassee, the pair con-tinued down Route 1 and found a $10-a-night room above the White Horse Bar in Miami's Little Cuba. As Ted Turner would later tell the story, the adventure lasted all of a month, by which time the pair had spent their money and were reduced to using pages torn from the phone book as toilet paper and eating peanut butter sandwiches on week-old bread. "We were miser-able, to tell the truth," Turner said.[20]

Peter Dames made the decision to travel back to Charleston and beg a job from Ted's father. It was a choice worse than death for Ed's defeated son. Rather than admit to his father that he failed even at being a bum, he reenlisted in the Coast Guard to complete his active duty. In later years, Turner would glamorize

the tour, claiming to have cruised to the Mexican Riviera, enjoy-
ing the local señoritas and a heavy dose of margaritas. In truth,
his ship, the *Travis,* only did laps up and down the Florida coast
the few times it ever left port at all.

Tanned, toned, and rested, Ted left active duty to return to
Georgia, where he officially became a full-time employee of Turner
Advertising. His father put him to work in the Savannah office,
selling billboard space to new clients. His salary: $75 a week. Based
on a guaranteed income, he renewed his correspondence with Judy
Nye and proposed marriage via letter in mid-April 1960. She was
still attending Northwestern, and while eager to become Mrs. Ted
Turner, was not about to forsake her college degree.

The hurried event nevertheless took place two months later at
a formal ceremony on June 22, 1960, at St. Chrysostom's Episco-
pal Church on Chicago's North Dearborn Parkway.[21] Ed Turner
and his second wife attended, as did Florence Turner, who was living in Cincinnati and still caring for her gravely ill daughter. The
reception at the prestigious Saddle and Cycle Club on Chicago's
North Side was elegant and refined, and spoke more of the Nyes'
wealth than the Turners' love of parties.

Immediately after the ceremony, the newlyweds returned to
Georgia and set up housekeeping in a rather unglamorous one-
bedroom apartment. Ted expressed his chauvinistic attitudes by
issuing ultimatums of "me breadwinner, you homemaker," and
he played his role by working increasingly long hours plying his
trade. He thought of Turner Advertising as his legacy and billboards as his future.

Any spare moments Ted spent sailing, occasionally with Judy,
more often not. The Savannah River was his playground, and the
hours he spent there the most relaxing of his life. Yet, as enjoyable as sailing was for the newlywed, his biggest thrill came with
the closing of a new billboard rental or the installation of a new
location. It made his subsequent move up to the Turner Advertising office in Macon a promotion of sorts—if not in cash, at

least in personal prestige. Now out from under his father, he moved his boat, his sails, and his wife into a basement apartment in the city that boasted itself as "the Soul of the South," with more buildings listed on the National Register of Historic Places than any other city in Georgia.

It was here that he learned of the death of his sister, Mary Jane, on December 15, 1960, as well as the news that his wife was pregnant with their first child. The 22-year-old took both revelations in stride—his sister having long been a distant memory, and his wife performing with expected fertility. When Judy gave birth to Laura Lee Turner the following July, Ted was not at the hospital but busy sailing on the Atlantic. He returned to see Judy and the baby the following day, accepting his new daughter's arrival with blasé enthusiasm.

Ed kept Ted's independence in check through twice-monthly meetings in Savannah that typically including outings to familiar clubs and alliances with unfamiliar women. As word of his womanizing reached Judy, she responded with petulant scenes that increased in violence until she removed herself and their baby from the war zone, divorcing her husband in the fall of 1962. Only then, after moving to Fort Lauderdale, Florida, did reality set in. Ted was alone and miserable, and Judy was pregnant with their second child.

When Ted learned of his ex-wife's condition, he invited her to move back to Macon, but not as his wife. Despite Judy's wish that their child not be born out of wedlock, her former husband refused to consider remarrying her, at least until after the birth of the baby. "You're big and pregnant," Ted said, not even trying to be subtle. "I'm not taking a pregnant lady to City Hall to get married all over again."[22]

As his son and former daughter-in-law battled, Ed and Jane moved to another plantation. Like Cotton Hall, this home was large and surrounded by mature oaks, but Binden Hall (as the new place was known) had an added feature. It was a former hunting lodge, with a charming creek casually in motion outside the front door and wandering through the 800 acres that comprised the plantation. Jane had reworked the lodge into a comfortably elegant home, the nicest in all of Beaufort County, South Carolina.

From this imposing base, Ed enlarged his scope of what Turner Advertising could be. He wanted to be more than a big fish in a small pond and sought to expand and explore his options on a national level. He saw himself as the billboard king, and got the opportunity to prove himself with the purchase of a portion of his old employer, the General Outdoor Advertising Company. For $4 million, he bought billboard factories in Richmond and Roanoke, Virginia, as well as the biggest billboard plant in all of Atlanta. Bob Naegele, a friend from Minneapolis, took the remainder of GOA, and both men were pleased with the final arrangement. Naegele bought his portion outright. To fund the $750,000 down payment, Ed sold off his Savannah business and mortgaged his other properties.

Initially Ed was buoyed by his purchase, opening a large headquarters office in Atlanta and renting an apartment in the tony Buckhead section of the city. Plagued by pain from a stomach ulcer and intent on weaning himself off booze and nicotine, Ed gave his son free rein over the sales division of Turner Advertising by making him assistant general manager. Ed then checked himself into Silver Hill Hospital, a psychiatric and addiction center in New Canaan, Connecticut. Silver Hill sat on 60 acres of rolling countryside intersected by the Silvermine River, and featured elegant suites, gourmet meals, and an assortment of amenities geared toward its affluent clientele. Almost as soon as Ed Turner arrived in December 1962, however, he began to worry about his business and have doubts about his ability to handle his large debt load. Though each of the offices of Turner Advertising was making money and his payment schedule was well in hand, the effects of his detox program, coupled with his medication, ripped Ed's courage from his body and hid it from his confused mind.

He called Naegele from his bed in Silver Hill and openly panicked over his perceived vulnerability. He wanted to sell out and sell out quickly. "He was terribly upset," Naegele remembered. "Not making any sense at all. He told me he was having second thoughts about the properties he had just acquired. I'll never forget what he said: 'It's a long way from the master bedroom to the cellar.'"[23]

After leaving Silver Hill in February, Ed returned to Binden Hall and continued to pursue his effort to jettison his debt. Naegele attempted to reassure his colleague that his position was sound and his business far from being at risk. But a terrorized Turner would listen to no one. He sank into a dangerous depression, eating little while continuously pacing the wide-plank floors of Binden Hall. When Naegele's representatives visited Turner at his home, he insisted that they immediately write a check for $50,000 to indicate their fair intent. Reluctantly they did, still concerned about a deal that was being rushed to fruition.

Upon hearing of his father's plans, Ted raged into a fury. He drove to Binden Hall intent on changing his father's mind and was determined not to leave until he did. He laid out his argument in persuasive terms, calmly explaining to his father that all of their company's offices were producing well in excess of their own projections, and they had a full five years to service the $4 million in debt.

Ed listened, or if not listened, at least patiently didn't speak until Ted was done. His son returned to Macon, convinced that he had changed his father's mind. He was unaware that Ed thought him too young to be able to handle the business. He did not realize the extent of his father's depression or the depth of his resolve.

When Ed next spoke to Ted, he was unnaturally calm, as if in a trance. He spoke of his need to sleep and his resolve to sell at least the Atlanta plant to Naegele. The words spoke to Ted's own insecurity, and he became outraged at his father's weakness. He ridiculed him, labeling him a "quitter, a loser."[24]

Instead of fighting back, Ed remained stoic, hardened to the words and unmoved by emotion. "We can do this," Ted implored over the phone. "You and me. We can do this together." And as he hung up, Ted thought his father actually believed him.

On the morning of March 5, 1963, Ed Turner awoke late, showered and dressed, and walked downstairs to join Jane for breakfast. The weather outside was warm for a South Carolina winter, but then it had been that way for weeks. As usual, Jimmy Brown was serving a succulent meal, and both servant and wife were happy to see a renewed sparkle in Ed's eyes as he crossed the dining room and took his seat. Watching him enjoy his meal and hearing him speak, Jane dared to think that perhaps he was returning to his old self and regaining his strength and his determination.

His smile was sincere as he pushed away from the table, touched Jane's shoulder, and walked back upstairs. When he reached the second floor, instead of returning to his bedroom, he walked toward the guest room down the hall. There, in the bathroom, he removed a .38-caliber pistol from his pocket, felt the cold barrel enter his mouth, and calmly pulled the trigger.

# THREE

# From Boys to Men

*Just because I haven't managed to get the right
working relationship with every single editor I've appointed
doesn't for a minute suggest that I'm ruthless.
In fact, if you'd known the precise reasoning at the time . . .
and the sort of settlement these people got,
I think one would consider me—a lot of people did consider me—
rather ridiculously soft . . . I'm far too easygoing as a rule.*

Rupert Murdoch
London
September 1970

When Jimmy Brown heard the sound of a gunshot, he was washing dishes in the kitchen at the back of the house. He dropped the damp cloth and didn't stop to remove the suds from his hands as he raced through the dining room and up the stairs. Jane found herself unable to move. Only her eyes dared follow.

Ed Turner lay bleeding from a gaping wound in his head, torn open by a bullet that had removed half his skull. His body twitched in a convulsion from the shock to his brain as Brown stared in horror, screaming "Mr. T! Mr. T!" He raced downstairs, yelling for Jane to telephone for help. "Mr. T had a terrible accident! Call the doctor!"

The doctor Jane called was Irving Victor. A urologist, Dr. Victor was also a family friend. He was like a brother to Ed, who had given him the Turner home on Abercorn Street as a gift. By the time Victor arrived at Binden Hall, Ed had died from his self-inflicted wound. Ted was away on business and could not be reached immediately. It was Jimmy Brown who finally tracked him down, and it fell to the black man who had raised Ted Turner to tell him that his father was dead.

The funeral was held in the grand Greek Revival mansion of Sipple's Mortuary a mile down the street from Irving Victor's home. Young Charles Sipple received the body from the coroner and was shocked by the sight of the body. R. E. TURNER DIES OF GUNSHOT WOUND read the headline in the *Savannah News* the morning of the funeral, with many of the city's business and political leaders among the mourners that day.[1]

For Ted, time stood still in the sense that clouds are still, yet moving so slowly as to be unapparent. Gone was the verbosity of his youth, replaced by a silence that found its foundation in grief. He remained quiet at the graveside at Savannah's Green-wich Cemetery and for the next several days to follow. Only then, after the reading of Ed's will, did Ted turn back to business. Moreover, his first act shocked everyone who knew the situation well. He not only intended to run his father's business as his own, but he also planned to sue Bob Naegele to halt the sale of the Atlanta billboard plant. He was determined to stop the deal that would have put a million dollars in his pocket, and left no doubt who was now firmly in charge.

Halfway around the world, Rupert Murdoch was just getting off a plane in Perth, Australia, in what was the fourteenth hour of a 16-hour workday. Now known throughout the continent as the Boy Publisher, Murdoch had spent the decade expanding his fledgling empire one newspaper at a time.

When he arrived in Adelaide to take charge of the *Adelaide News* in 1953, the paper was struggling as an also-ran in the mar-ketplace. Advertising was down, readership was a distant third, and the paper's editor, Rohan Rivett, was as mercurial as he was pedantic. Into this rather dismal place Murdoch enmeshed him-self, determined to pull the *News* into profitability and success. For several years he was content to concentrate on advertising, distribution, and the labor unions. Bubbling over with youthful enthusiasm and baby fat, Murdoch appeared to be bursting out of the three-piece suits mandated by the publishing world, yet cinched by its trademark respectability. By 1956, however, all that was about to change.

Though he was loath to dance and preferred racetracks to nightclubs, Murdoch managed to meet and propose to a girl named Pat Booker, who worked at Myers, Australia's largest department store. She was slim, blond, attractive, and nothing at all like Rupert Murdoch. While her family questioned the relationship and Lady Elisabeth Murdoch saw the match as perplexing, the two nevertheless were married on March 1, 1956, with news of the event carried in the *Adelaide Advertiser,* but not in Murdoch's own paper.

Several months later, Murdoch agreed to purchase the *Sunday Times,* a struggling paper in Perth. With that purchase, he was emancipated as if previously bound by some ancient rite of solemnity. He took a personal interest in the *Sunday Times,* and stunned local readers who were used to its rather ordinary reporting and predictable style. Perhaps *amazed* is a better word, for he revitalized the readership by plunging the newspaper into what would ultimately be known as "Murdoch journalism," and they loved it.

Murdoch flooded the pages with hyperbole. He sensationalized the stalest stories. He used "eye-shattering, usually ungrammatical, irrelevant and gratuitously blood-curdling headlines (LEPER RAPES VIRGIN, GIVES BIRTH TO MONSTER BABY read a typical early front page), all wrapped in cheap, smudgy tabloid form and promoted with the apocalyptic fervor and energy of Bible Belt evangelism."[2] Rupert Murdoch had arrived.

While the *Adelaide News* began to produce a steady profit, albeit without the tawdry spectacle being unleashed in Perth, Murdoch found his most profitable discovery outside the newspaper arena entirely. In 1957, Australia was just beginning to enter the television age, and Murdoch intended to be a principal player. Competing against the long-established publishing magnates—Sir Frank Packer (who owned the *Daily Telegraph* and Channel 9 in Sydney) and John Fairfax (who published the Sydney *Morning Herald* and *Sun,* and controlled that city's Channel 7)—Murdoch was determined to run the first station in Adelaide. Although he had no experience in television, Murdoch was saved by the fact that *no one* had television experience in Australia. He leaped onto the wagon of technology without a shred of knowledge and bluffed his way into acquiring the license to run Adelaide's Channel 9.

To compensate for his ignorance, Murdoch embraced America, the fountainhead of all that was television. With naïve exuberance, he accidentally uncovered what became a fount of programming for the new television outlet when he was introduced to Leonard Goldenson, chairman of ABC Inc. Perhaps it was his enthusiasm, perhaps it was the fact that both men saw themselves as underdogs. For whatever reason, Goldenson liked Murdoch from his first introduction. "I was very impressed with him from the start," Goldenson later wrote.[3] Impressed enough that he bought 6 percent of Murdoch's News Corporation and established a friendship that lasted until Goldenson's death in 1999.

Friendships were not easy for Murdoch to sustain, as he demonstrated in 1959 with *News* editor Rohan Rivett. Rivett became obsessed with the story of Rupert Max Stuart, a carnival roustabout who was on trial for the murder in Thevenard of a nine-year-old girl named Mary Olive Hattam. Stuart, an illiterate and barely articulate Aborigine, was eventually convicted of the crime based on footprints identified by Aboriginal trackers as belonging to the defendant. The police also had a confession delivered in perfect English, a fact Rivett found incredible, since the man could barely communicate in pidgin.

With the full support of Murdoch, Rivett used the columns of the *News* to urge that Stuart be given a reprieve from his death sentence. Furthermore, he recommended that the entire trial be investigated on the grounds of racist corruption. To calm public outcry, Prime Minister Sir Thomas Playford appointed three special commissioners to investigate the allegations.

As it happened, one of the commissioners was Justice Reed, the original trial judge, and another, Sir Mellis Napier, the judge who denied Stuart his appeal. Rivett took this as further indication of collusion and began leading each day's edition with blaring headlines and plastering posters on newsstands advertising the issue at hand: THESE COMMISSIONERS CANNOT DO THE JOB (a quote attributed to J. W. Shand, Stuart's chief counsel), SHAND QUITS: "YOU WON'T GIVE STUART FAIR GO" and COMMISSION BREAK UP—SHAND BLASTS NAPIER.[4]

The newspapers made their way to Parliament, and on September 2, Playford labeled Murdoch's papers as containing the "gravest libel ever made against any judge in this state." At issue was the use of quotation marks when Shand had never uttered the words. In an effort to control the damage done by the rather obvious breach of journalistic standards, Murdoch composed an editorial that ran on the front page of the next day's *News*. In it he admitted that the headline should not have run as it did, but remained adamantly in support of Rivett's right to ferret out the truth.

The state's prosecutor charged the *News* with nine counts of libel. During the trial that followed, Rivett revealed that Murdoch had seen, composed, or authorized all the headlines and posters. Ultimately the jury dismissed all but one of the libel charges, and the last charge eventually was dropped by the court. Just over a month later, Murdoch fired Rivett, his friend since college. He sent him a letter, which Rivett found on his desk, instructing him to be gone by the end of the day. It was the first example of a habit that Murdoch continues to exercise to this day: the abandonment of those who cease to be useful. It makes no difference if they are old friends, old employees, or influential. To be no longer useful is to be no longer around.

At home Pat Murdoch made herself useful by getting pregnant, giving birth in 1959 to the couple's first child, a daughter they named Prudence. A robust child with large eyes and a disarming smile, Prudence was at her best when demanding to be fed, and she demanded quite regularly—and loudly.

Murdoch was now living in Sydney, having moved his family there in anticipation of bursting onto the scene of the largest newspaper market in Australia. It was the big time, the ultimate in Murdoch's world of the moment, and required more than money, of which he had precious little, to be successful. Fortunately, the Packers were flourishing with their *Daily Telegraph*, and the Fairfaxes had the market cornered with the *Morning Herald* and their popular evening paper, the *Sun*. Thus preoccupied, the Fairfax family fought casually among themselves but with little sincerity before deciding to sell Murdoch the "other" Sydney evening newspaper, the little-read *Daily Mirror*, along with its Sunday counterpart. The entire operation cost Murdoch $2 million ($600,000 down) and provided the foundation for every corporate move he has made since.

For Murdoch, the key to attracting readers was to deliver something different from the competition. In Sydney, the *Sun* was offering its customers intelligent, rather stodgy news coverage. At first Murdoch attempted to refine the market and produced a product that was upscale and sophisticated. When that failed to invigorate the *Mirror*, there was always gutter sensationalism, and in that Murdoch triumphed.

He was not above rewriting stories, inventing quotes, or creating entire scenarios for that matter. Reporter Brian Hogben learned that lesson when he went to New Guinea in 1961 to cover the clan wars. When he disappeared into the rain forest and sent no copy back to Sydney, Murdoch and crew, fearing intense coverage from the competition, wrote a rather inventive piece of journalism and published it under Hogben's name. It was the stuff of jungle lore, including man-eating cannibals and shrunken heads.

When Hogben eventually resurfaced in New Guinea and read "his" report on the country, he fired off a telegram to Murdoch: "Nearest shrunken heads to Dutch New Guinea are in Sydney."[5]

With the purchase of the *Mirror* and the unceremonious dumping of Rivett, Murdoch was clearly marching to his own drummer. No longer hidden in the shadow of his late father, the Boy Publisher became a whirling icon, moving from paper to paper, irritating, cajoling, inspiring. With baby fat providing the fuel for his seemingly boundless energy, Murdoch was not yet Citizen Kane, but well on his way to national recognition. Certainly, within his own mini-empire, his employees assimilated the Murdoch code and incorporated it as their own. Sensationalism, of course, was in, but only in the headlines. In the city room itself, a certain decorum was mandated. Women were not to wear slacks, and men were not to wear brightly colored shirts. No dirty jokes, no crude remarks. And never, *never* suede shoes, which, according to Murdoch, were worn only by "homos," a group that was invisible, if it existed at all.[6]

Though newspapers formed the core of his business, Murdoch still saw television as an arena of unlimited expansion potential. As his baby station in Adelaide kept pumping money into his coffers, he yearned for an outlet in Sydney, and carefully structured his bid for a license when the government introduced a third station into the market.

Camouflaging his interest through a series of consortiums that included a multitude of proper and long-established Sydney businesses, Murdoch nevertheless lost his campaign for Sydney's Channel 10 to United Telecasters Sydney Ltd. Undaunted by what to anyone else would have been a major setback, Murdoch sniffed around the neighborhood and discovered the town of Wollongong, 90 minutes south of Sydney. Wollongong, Australia's eighth largest city, was known for its farming and its coal and steel plants, plus a stretch of pristine beaches. It also had a television station, WIN 4, whose signal reached Sydney if one's antenna was turned just right. For Murdoch, the challenge was clear: invest in the nearly bankrupt station and then attract attention.

To get viewers watching the distant Channel 4, he needed programming—American programming, preferably, since it was then, as now, the most popular. At the time, Australia's TV programmers had a gentlemen's agreement among themselves that limited license fees for shows to $5,000 an episode. In international terms, it was pocket change. Armed with cash from a loan provided by the new Commonwealth Bank in Sydney, Murdoch flew to New York and arranged a meeting with pal Leonard Goldenson, and like an eagle dropping from the clouds above, grasped all of ABC's programming in his talons. The cost: $3 million.

The move got the attention not only of viewers of WIN 4 in Wollongong, but also of Sir Frank Packer, who offered to sell Murdoch a one-fourth share in each of his stations (Channel 9 in Sydney and Channel 9 in Melbourne) in exchange for the right to broadcast ABC shows. "It didn't give me control or much say in anything," Murdoch said in a 1967 television interview. Looking back, he thought, "I might really have overstepped myself in taking the gamble in Wollongong. I think they were probably right."[7]

Now traveling between Sydney, Perth, and Adelaide, with side trips to London and America, Murdoch had precious little time for family. The toll on his marriage was predictable, and Murdoch spent little effort in attempting to change the outcome. "There were all sorts of sad domestic complications which nobody could ever be judgmental about now, least of all Rupert," his mother said. "His way of life was impossible for her and her handling of life was impossible for him."[8]

With a string of suburban papers and magazines purchased as the Cumberland Newspapers Group, the *Mirror* in Sydney, the *Sunday Times* in Perth, and the *Adelaide News* and *Sunday Mail*, its Channel 9 television station, and the stations in Sydney, Melbourne, and Wollongong, Murdoch had bought himself a mini-empire, and a wife played little part in that. Prudence, now nearing grade-school age, was another story. Pat Booker Murdoch was expendable; Murdoch's only child was not. While Murdoch and his wife shared custody of the child, Prudence initially went to live with her mother. It was an arrangement that ultimately proved ineffective, with Prudence eventually rejoining her father who welcomed the opportunity to raise the child.

That subject never entered Ted Turner's mind when his former wife, Judy, stormed out of his life a second time at virtually the same moment that Pat walked out of Murdoch's. Whereas Murdoch was busy loving his businesses, Turner was loving every available woman he chose. From Macon to Atlanta, Turner's eye for long legs and big breasts was the stuff of legend. His reputation as a cad was certainly not hurt when his ex-wife, eight months pregnant with his second child, walked into his Atlanta office and discovered him having sex with a complete stranger.[9] She demanded no explanation and he never thought of giving one; such was the nature of their relationship.

Robert Edward Turner IV, called Teddy, was born in May 1963, and by the following March, Judy and the children moved quietly out of the house in Macon. Judy's mother arrived to bring her daughter back to Chicago. Ted remained in Atlanta, his thoughts not on reconciliation or custody, but rather on his growing business.

Having salvaged the Atlanta billboard plant from Bob Naegele, who agreed to disregard his contract of sale in exchange for a profit of $125,000, Turner had used his personality and couth to ink billboard leases up and down the state of Georgia. "I was sad, pissed, and determined," he said. "I was only a kid, but I had learned how to hustle. I went out and convinced the employees to buy stock in the company. I sold off all the real estate that I possibly could to raise cash. I sold my father's plantation. I borrowed against our accounts receivable. I squeezed the juice out of everything."[10] Turner Advertising, for all its debt, was an extremely successful business, one that Ed Turner certainly would have been able to develop. In the hands of his unflappable son, sales soared—and quickly.

After Judy's departure, Turner shattered the quiet Southern ambience of Macon by racing his newly purchased red Ferrari through the streets of town, along Georgia Avenue to College, past the post office and the Federated Garden Club Center, housed in an English Tudor mansion designed in 1910 by architect J. Neel Reid. He closed up his home there and relocated to Atlanta without so much as a single glance back.

Judy had not even found a permanent home before Turner was romancing her replacement, a Delta Airlines flight attendant named Jane Smith. She was born in Birmingham, Alabama, had a y'all sweetness to her smile, and was introduced to Turner by mutual friends at a meeting of Young Republicans. Jane found Turner rude, insistent, and very disarming, which may explain why, two months later, on June 2, 1964, they were married. Turner was drinking, Jane was pregnant, and Jimmy Brown, as usual, was there to take care of the details.[11] Those details included moving the Turners and himself into a large colonial home on Atlanta's Carriage Drive, where babies began to arrive in assembly-line fashion. Rhett was first in 1965, named for Margaret Mitchell's Rhett Butler, whom Turner became to emulate in look (by growing a mustache) and action ("Frankly, Jane, I don't give a damn"). Another son, Beauregard, arrived in 1967, with daughter Jennie following a year after that.

"I cried a lot when I found out [about the last pregnancy]," Jane said. "My friends thought it was vulgar. I love babies but I nearly died. I thought my back was broken. I stayed home for five years. It would have made anyone crazy."[12]

The neighbors in their Cobb County suburb just shook their heads in wonder when two *more* Turners showed up on the doorstep. Teddy and Laura came for Christmas in 1965 and never returned to their mother. Judy had married a brute of a weightlifter who took his steroid-fueled aggression out on

Teddy, and the sight of his battered son convinced Turner to keep the children in Atlanta.

Not that *he* was looking after them. "He's almost never here," Jane said, though it should have come as little surprise.[13] Early on in their relationship, Ted made no secret of his priorities: first came sailing, then came business. Jane and their children came last.

Soon after marrying Jane, Turner's wild debauchery had evaporated into an intoxication of all things nautical. Although his interest in sailing had never wavered since those days on the Savannah River with Jimmy Brown, after his father's death sailing became a daily obsession. The competitive spirit he demonstrated as a salesman only intensified on the water. Turner the captain charged through the churning waves of lakes, rivers, and the Atlantic, pushed by the air and exhilarated by the sea. He was in command as he was everywhere, but on the water it was different. There he could conquer without fear of being called a pig or callous or—worse still—a sexist.

Turner's first season of competing in the Southern Ocean Racing Conference was 1965. He lost nearly every race he entered, and he entered them all. With typical Turner logic, he laid the blame for his poor performance on his boat, and soon thereafter ordered a custom-made 40-foot racer he christened the *Vamp X*. The Cal 40 was a hard-chined, fin-keeled, spade-ruddered Bill Lapworth design that revolutionized the sailing world in the mid-sixties. At the helm of the *Vamp X*, Turner won the 1966 SORC by the largest margin in the history of the sport.

"You can't win races without working harder than the other guys," Turner told a *New York Times* reporter in his first quote in the newspaper.[14] Turner did work harder, and longer, and more aggressively, often leaving home for weeks at a time, chasing the circuit like surfers chase waves.

Now spending more than $100,000 a year on ocean racing, Turner was burning through money as fast as his billboard company could generate it. More than mere cash, however, Turner needed another challenge. Selling billboards was tough only when the company was down on its luck. Now Turner was Jack, and the beanstalk was his. Where his father paced in desperation, Turner paced in confinement. The caged tiger was eager to explore new arenas, and unlike his father, he did not mind the risks.

Radio—that was the ticket, or at least Turner thought so at this moment in 1968, feeling his way blindly on instinct toward the shadowy promise of adventure. Through sheer nonstop verbal assault, he convinced another billboard man, Jim Roddey, to leave behind his own company, Rollins Outdoor Advertising, and join him in a radio buy: WAPO Chattanooga, Turner's favorite when he attended McCallie. With Roddey as Turner's new president and point man with the banks, Turner Advertising acquired the station, changed the call letters to WGOW, and became Turner Communications overnight.

Once stung by the excitement of instant access to customers via WAPO, Turner envisioned an entire network of radio stations linked via ownership and capable of sending an advertising message across the country. It was hardly a new concept—just new to him—and in quick succession, stations in Charleston and Jacksonville were added to the Turner collection.

Rupert Murdoch wanted to reach a national audience as well, though his vehicle of choice was what he knew best—newspapers, specifically the *Australian,* a brand-new paper created from whole cloth. For Murdoch, it was an adventure as rich as any Turner had taken on the high seas. From its inception to its first issue, the publication took Murdoch only four months of harassing, begging, commandeering, and demanding to launch. In the end, he produced a poorly read, widely praised newspaper that lost money. Lots of money.

Whenever Murdoch thought about losing money, his eyes blinked and narrowed, their lashes enlarged behind the thick magnification of his glasses, forming wispy smears on the lenses to soften the weariness they echoed. He hated losing money. But fortunately for the *Australian,* he hated defeat even more. So the *Australian* remained, draining precious funds needed for expansion throughout his corporation, yet providing him with a national foundation of power. To Rupert Murdoch, that was priceless.

In another, rather prophetic coincidence, Murdoch also had a love of the sea. He purchased a sailing yacht named the *Ilina,* and after running it aground on a reef off the Queensland coast, actually managed to become a rather dependable sailor. Good enough, in fact, to compete in several Sydney to Hobart Yacht Races, Australia's most difficult open-ocean challenge. However, he did not devote himself to the sport with the enthusiasm that Turner did. Murdoch reserved that kind of passion for acquisitions and a young blonde named Anna Maria Torv.

Anna had moved to Australia from her native Glasgow, Scotland, at the age of nine, when her parents sold their dry-cleaning business and sailed halfway around the world to immigrate Down Under in search of riches and a renewed happiness. Borrowing money to buy land, Anna's father, Jakub, started a picnic-and-sports park along remote Easter Creek. "My mother worked even harder at it than my father," Anna remembered, "but eventually the place was repossessed by the bank. My mother developed tuberculosis and had a complete breakdown."[15]

The Torv family moved to Blacktown, a tired city west of Sydney that would later gain fame as the home of softball during the 2002 Summer Olympics. But in the late fifties, the Blacktown landscape was that of cheap high-rises and inexpensive houses in need of repair. The Torvs lived on the eighth floor in an apartment complex where a cacophony of music drifted out windows and dissipated against the soot-covered walls. Through open doors, men in stained T-shirts played cards and drank beer, and bags full of garbage told pungent tales of leftover food from corner restaurants.

Anna was left in charge of her younger brothers and sister while her father worked in a chemical plant. In her diary, she wrote about her dream of being a famous actress one day. Instead, she discovered her true talent was writing, and at the age of 18 was hired by the *Daily Mirror*.

When she walked into her boss's office that day, a year and a half after starting her job, she was poised, confident, and strikingly beautiful. Rupert Murdoch found it difficult to stop gazing at her pale blue eyes as she spoke. She had been assigned to write a piece about his life, and she had had a difficult time scheduling an interview with him. Now he wouldn't let her leave. One look and the incredibly busy, incredibly preoccupied Murdoch cleared his desk *and* his calendar.

At the time, Anna was still an entry-level cadet reporter, having only caught glimpses of her publisher during his frequent sweeps through the newsroom to intimidate his editors with dictatorial suggestions. "A lowly cadet sees very little," Anna said. "You're lucky if you see the editor. You're usually being sent out by the finance editor to buy iced buns with extra butter on the side."[16] Her interview with the chief was therefore something of a coup; her subsequent marriage to him in 1967 an outright *coup de foudre*.

She was Cinderella marrying a rather out-of-shape Napoleonic Prince Charming 13 years her senior, and together they swept into Jamaica on their honeymoon, followed by a business trip to Manhattan. It was a time of change in New York as throughout the rest of America—of war protests and civil rights movements, and Manhattan was awash with the excitement of revolution. Murdoch, of course, was more concerned about reinforcing his friendship with Leonard Goldenson than about protests in Central Park, leaving Anna to explore the city and fall in love with its energy and assortment of players.

When Murdoch returned to Australia with his new bride, they moved into Cavan, an enormous estate outside Canberra, on the

Murrumbidgee River. The river ends in the Burrinjuck Dam, a summer playground for waterskiers, campers, and hikers, which turned Cavan into a home typically filled with houseguests eager to enjoy the countryside. Murdoch lavished attention on his guests, and they in turn fed his need for appreciation. After years of being overlooked both in school and in business, Rupert Murdoch was ignored no more. If his rise to prominence had not been exactly rapid, it was nevertheless steady and consistent.

Yet, for Murdoch as well as Turner, the year ahead would catapult them both into a predominance neither anticipated nor initially cultivated. Once achieved, however, each in his own way relished the attention and maneuvered the spotlight to his advantage. In doing so, they not only changed the way the world received its news, but also altered its perception of its safety and security.

# F O U R

## The Competitive Spirit

*I just love it when people say I can't do something.*
*There's nothing that makes me feel better,*
*because all my life people have said*
*I wasn't going to make it.*

Ted Turner
Atlanta
Summer 1971

**D**owntown Atlanta, 1970. It was a day like any other really. Impossible to tell that the world as we knew it was about to change. True, it was miserable outside. Arctic air from Canada had blown across the Atlantic states, reaching as far as Buford, Georgia, and bringing a messy weather pattern to the rest of the South punctuated by high winds and sleet. The rain froze before it hit the ground, and cars danced like hippos on the slick roads that circled the city of Atlanta.

Over at WJRJ, Atlanta's Channel 17 on the UHF dial, station engineer Gene Wright took a hard hat off the wall next to the back-door exit and secured it firmly on his head. He was leaving for the night after another long day of trying to keep the low-rated TV outlet on the air, and he needed sleep. Still, the worst part of his day lay ahead: the mad dash to his car, parked in the employee lot situated next to the station's 1,093-foot-high transmission tower. This time of year, the tower was covered with ice and, with each gust of wind, swayed perilously in the night air, sending shards of icicles raining down with deadly force.[1]

Any similarity between WJRJ and Atlanta's other three stations was purely accidental. Housed in a concrete-block building with all the eye appeal of a bunker, the station had been losing money, most likely because more than half the people in Atlanta could not even get the signal on television sets that stopped at Channel 13. And those who could rarely watched its assortment of old black-and-white movies and ancient TV series. It was little wonder that Jack Rice, owner of the station and the publicly traded Rice Broadcasting, wanted to dump it. The real problem, of course, was finding a buyer dumb enough to want the business.

Ted Turner was not dumb, but then again, he never watched television. Didn't have the time, between sailing in regattas and driving his Ferrari a hundred miles an hour up Peachtree Street. When his stockbroker, Lee McClurkin, mentioned that a UHF television station was for sale, Turner only heard the word *television* and immediately paid attention. "I had no idea what UHF stood for," Turner said. "But the owner had taken a billboard, and I read it on the board."[2]

The more he heard, the more the challenge appealed to his instincts. "I could *feel* it was right," he later said. "Television!"[3]

Whatever he was feeling, those around him were not. "We tried everything we could do to keep Ted from buying that station," his financial adviser, Irwin Mazo, said. "We didn't have any money to lose in a television station."[4] If Turner heard Mazo, he paid no attention.

"God almighty, the station was within thirty days of going off the air," continued Mazo. "I had been through one big crisis when he took back the billboard company from Bob Naegele, and I said I just couldn't take it another time. [Turner's point man] Jim Roddey was with me. He said, 'Why are we doing this?' It was just an atrocious business proposition."[5]

Yet, the more Turner heard about the risk, the more he became convinced WJRJ held the future. Though it was an unusual maneuver at the time, McClurkin constructed a reverse merger between Rice Broadcasting and Turner Communications, in which Rice absorbed Turner through the issue of $2.5 million in Turner stock. As soon as the deal was completed, Turner changed the name from Rice Broadcasting to Turner Broadcasting System and made it a publicly traded company. The name change became official on September 9, 1970, the day Robert Edward Turner III became a television tycoon—albeit one with a business losing more than half a million dollars a year.

With typical verve and energy, Turner plunged passionately into television. No longer stopping by the billboard plant, he made his way every morning across town to Channel 17, now renamed with the call letters WTCG (Turner Communications Group). He learned to read ratings demographics, only to discover that virtually no one was watching his station regardless of sex or age. Undaunted, he energized his sales team with his mantra: "Programming, personnel, promotion, penetration, and profits. The five P's," he called them.[6]

He flew to California and made the rounds of the Hollywood studios looking for cheap product—MCA-Universal, Paramount, United Artists, Viacom, Warner Bros., MGM. "And they helped me whenever they could," he said.[7] They helped in the sense that they supplied him with programming no one else in the continental United States was interested in buying. Turner ended up with a grab bag of shows that included *Star Trek, The Beverly Hillbillies, Petticoat Junction, Gomer Pyle, Gilligan's Island,* and *The Andy Griffith Show,* and enough black-and-white horror films and Westerns to populate Transylvania and assorted suburbs of Boot Hill.

Because the Federal Communications Commission required that all stations carry a news broadcast, Turner acquiesced by putting his newscast on during the dark hours of 3 A.M. He had inherited a weatherman named Bill Tush from WJRJ and handed him the assignment. The young, erudite, and mustached Tush rose to the occasion by reading the news hidden behind a mask that looked suspiciously like Walter Cronkite. On other occasions,

Turner sat a German shepherd dressed in a coat and tie in the co-anchor chair to keep Tush company at the ungodly hour. All in the name of spontaneity—or at least Ted Turner's version of it.

This taste of show business became nectar to the gods. Turner began to envision himself having a network of television stations, all programmed according to his taste and all running 24 hours a day. It was an unheard-of practice at the time, but then most things Turner were unheard of at the time—his type of television included.

To accomplish his goal, he attempted to buy a second station—Channel 36, Charlotte, North Carolina. Turner Broadcasting System's board of directors absolutely refused to go along with the plan, certain it would put the company permanently out of business. Refusing to doubt his instincts, Turner mortgaged his house and used his own money to purchase the station, changing the call letters to WRET, by no small coincidence his initials, though he claimed he named it in honor of his father. Hard to tell.

As his board of directors predicted, the station became an immediate drain on Turner's incoming cash. Irwin Mazo quit the company in frustration; so did Jim Roddey. Unable to stop the bleeding of cash, Turner was nearing defeat when he decided to take his case to his viewers—the few thousand that he had.

Turner went on the air live with a "Beg-a-thon." "Irwin and the others thought I was crazy, and in all fairness it looked pretty dark there for a while," Turner told writer Christian Williams, author of *Lead, Follow or Get Out of the Way.* "I had to actually go on the air in Charlotte and solicit loans from the viewers. I said it's a telethon—a telethon for me, because I need money to get the wolf away from the door. The telethon took in $35,000. . . . But you know what? I paid all those people back within three years. If I ever need money in the future, I know how to get it. I'll just go on TV and say, 'I'm Ted Turner and please send me some money. I promise to pay it back with interest.'"[8]

While Ted Turner was busy keeping his word, Rupert Murdoch was happily breaking his. The opportunity arose when he received a call late in 1968 from Baron Catto of Cairncatto, at the time employed by the investment-banking house of Morgan Grenfell. Lord Catto, knowing of Murdoch's newspaper-buying binge, alerted his longtime friend that London's *News of the World* was on the market. This was not a small piece of information, since the *News of the World* had the largest paid subscription base—slightly more than six million—of any newspaper on the planet.

Murdoch knew of the paper's major stockholders, the Carr family, headed by *News of the World* chairman Sir William Carr. He knew of their loss of wealth, their love of drink, and their absolute hold on the newspaper. What he did not know but would now learn from Lord Catto was that Carr's cousin Derek Ainslie Jackson—scientist, lover, and tax evader—wanted to unload his 25 percent share in the company. Jackson had once been married to Pamela Mitford, whose sister Unity was in love with Adolf Hitler. By the time Jackson decided to offer his shares in *News of the World,* he had made the first experimental determination of nuclear spin at Oxford, moved to Switzerland to escape British taxes, and married his sixth wife, while still friends with his first. Although his cousins the Carrs were willing to pay him the current market price for his stock, the wise professor wanted double that amount and placed his quarter share of *News of the World* on the open market.

Unfortunately for Sir William, Jackson found a bidder in the form of Robert Maxwell, a rogue publisher who was not above making life miserable for all around him. Maxwell was born Jan Ludvik Hoch in the Carpathian Mountains in Czechoslovakia, and proud to tell anyone who would listen that he did not have his first pair of shoes until he was seven. By 1968, he had not only several pairs of shoes, but also yachts, private planes, and homes around the world. He had made and lost several fortunes, and while no one was certain where his money originated, Maxwell usually managed to find it when he needed some cash. Jackson liked the sound of cash, and pledged his shares to Maxwell.

Moving to keep Maxwell at bay, Sir William Carr's bank bought shares on the open market, and the baron placed a call to Murdoch. Murdoch, openly salivating at the thought of six million subscribers, flew to England to launch his assault, summoning forth his best demeanor to use on the very British Carrs. After meeting with family members, Murdoch suggested the same sort of arrangement that Ted Turner would subsequently use so successfully with Rice Broadcasting: a reverse merger. Murdoch's News Ltd. stock would be transferred to the News of the World Group, which would issue enough new stock back to Murdoch to give him 40 percent of the company. Together Murdoch and Carr would have enough stock to outvote Maxwell, and *News of the World* would be saved from a fate worse than death.

Murdoch's only demand for such cooperation was to be named managing director of the News of the World Group. In return, he faithfully promised to keep Sir William in place as chairman for the remainder of his seven-year contract, and not increase his own holdings of the company beyond the 40 percent he was then arranging to receive.

A special stockholders' meeting was held on January 2, 1969, in the New Connaught Rooms on Great Queen Street, off Covent Garden. Murdoch had returned to England from Australia with Anna and their new baby daughter, Elisabeth, then several months old. Amid the gilded splendor of the 200-year-old meeting and convention site, the stockholders prepared to listen to both contenders for the company plead their cause.

Sir William, in extremely fragile health, appeared at the podium and gave a rambling endorsement of Rupert Murdoch, whom he described as upstanding, reliable, and conservative. Murdoch, who followed his peer to the dais, did not disagree, but rather indicated his eagerness to have Sir William remain as the titular head of the company.

For his part, Maxwell, looking like a used-car salesman in a too-iridescent suit, was openly booed as he stood to speak and lambasted the Carr family for failing to seize upon the opportunity presented by his cash offer. Frail and tearing, Sir William held up his hands and opened the floor to a vote with all the theatrics of Eva Perón. With sentiment on his side, Carr was hardly surprised when he carried the vote and Murdoch became the new managing director of the *News of the World*.

The following day, Murdoch arrived at his new office on Bouverie Street, around the corner from Fleet Street, to discover a gaggle of cleaning ladies drinking tea at the chairman's desk, apparently a local custom.[9] After dispatching them back to their duties with histrionics, he began a housecleaning of a different sort. In the weeks that followed, Murdoch fired reporters and editors, many of whom had been with the *News* for years. By the end of the month, he had made a move to increase his shares in the company by buying some of the stock held by Professor Jackson, who was still living in Lausanne, Switzerland, and still in need of quick cash. With the purchase of some of Jackson's shares, Murdoch owned nearly 50 percent of the company, despite his pledge to the contrary.

Murdoch's biggest lapse of integrity found its target in Sir William himself, who, after being allowed to recuperate for two months, was asked to retire. It mattered little that Murdoch had promised the patriarch of the Carr family that his position was secure for the length of his contract. There was no place for any hint of divided leadership in Murdoch's quest for control.

In another time, Carr would have taken on the Australian interloper. Now, too weak and too tired to fight any longer, he merely sighed and signed away his birthright and that of his family. For the first time in a hundred years, a Carr was not publishing the *News of the World*. The Sunday paper that had made its name being somewhat tawdry was now about to crank its standards *down* a few notches to breathe new life into an ancient form of journalism.

Murdoch hit his stride by the summer of 1969 when he gave the paper's editor, Stafford Somerfield, permission to publish a new version of the Christine Keeler story. Keeler, a rather naive prostitute with obvious charms, had a weeklong affair in 1963 with Britain's then secretary of state for war, John Profumo, a man she met while attending a dinner party at the Cliveden estate of Lord and Lady Astor. The married Profumo later lied to the House of Commons about the extent of his infatuation. Since such excesses are taken rather seriously in Great Britain, Profumo resigned in disgrace while Keeler ended up jailed for perjury. After her release, she sold her story to the *News of the World* for £23,000. Naturally, such *affaires de coeur* are substantial readership draws, and Keeler's tale was no exception. When the now older and wiser former call girl decided to reshape her story for quick cash, Murdoch via Somerfield was only too happy to accommodate by offering her $50,000 for her recount.

By this point, however, six years had passed—years in which Profumo had devoted his life to charity work and living down his indiscretion. When Keeler's dramatic retelling of the scandal found its way into the *News,* it seemed all of England took an affront while tripping over one another to buy copies of the paper.

"I believe [Profumo] has reclaimed his reputation so totally in the last few years," said the earl of Longford, former Labor Party leader in the House of Lords, "that it is quite revolting to think that some stale old stories are being published."[10]

Yet, Lord Longford's outrage was merely a precursor to the indignation Murdoch eventually would face. When defending the series of articles to BBC interviewer David Dimbleby, Murdoch said, "We can forgive Mr. Profumo. By all means forgive the individual; but you can't forget." At that point, Dimbleby quoted

Murdoch's own words: "People can sneer as much as they like, but I'll take the 150,000 extra copies we're going to sell."[11]

In a further effort to defend himself, Murdoch next appeared with interviewer David Frost on London Weekend Television's *Frost on Friday*. The resulting program placed Murdoch in a difficult situation, surprising for someone so determined to be in control. Murdoch's opening volley defended the ongoing serial by suggesting the story contained new material. Frost countered by mentioning Wayland Young's critically acclaimed book, *Profumo Affair: Aspects of Conservatism*, which had been published in 1963. Murdoch had never heard of it.

When Frost used a taped interview with Cardinal Heenan, head of Britain's Catholic Church, to criticize the content of the *News of the World*, Murdoch became hostile: "This easy glib talk that the *News of the World* is a dirty paper is downright libel and it is not true and I resist it completely. They wouldn't say it if it wasn't so successful."[12] A small line of perspiration began to form across Murdoch's brow. It caught in the creases of his forehead as he scowled, and remained there long after the interview was finished. His expression hardly reflected his anger at what Frost had put him through, the on-air challenges to his integrity. Murdoch, of course, would not forget. He never forgot a slight, imagined or intentional. For now, the skirmish was over with Frost the victor, but the war had only begun.

Murdoch moved about London in a summer of discontent. He felt unappreciated, scorned by pretentious aristocrats who clung to their pedigree with pompous authority as if pedigree still mattered. Murdoch knew that wealth was the only accurate measure of a man, and his wealth was compounding at a miraculous rate. Money was the very foundation on which superior people stood. Money allowed one to buy nobility. And influence. And power.

It was that ultimate goal, the earning of money, that pushed him into his next purchase—yet another British paper, albeit one without the lineage of the *News of the World*. The *Sun* was a new-comer on the Fleet Street scene, created in 1964 by the Mirror Newspaper Group as a vehicle to reflect the left-wing views of newly rich baby boomers whose antiestablishment leanings took life in the form of protest movements and the burning of bras.

That this generation of young, upwardly mobile men and women did not read the *Sun* came as no surprise to Murdoch, who remained steadfast in his belief that British readers wanted news to take their minds *off* politics, not preach to it. Such was the state of the newspaper in 1969 that Murdoch was able to gain control of the company with a down payment of less than $100,000.

"Mr. Murdoch deserves all credit for endeavoring to save a national newspaper from extinction, even if in a very different style," Hugh Cudlipp said.[13] Chairman of the International Publishing Corporation, the current owners of the paper, Cudlipp pointed to the $30 million loss the newspaper suffered during its eight years of publication.

Immediately after taking over the *Sun,* Murdoch wrote an editorial in which he promised, "The new *SUN* would still be a paper that CARES. The paper that cares—passionately—about truth and beauty and justice. . . . It will never forget its radical traditions. . . . It will never, ever sit on fences. It will never, ever be boring."[14] It was signed "Rupert Murdoch, Publisher."

On Monday, November 17, 1969, Murdoch published the first tabloid version of the paper and quickly proved himself wrong. In the weeks that followed, as the *Sun* struggled to find itself in the most competitive newspaper market in the world, what Murdoch "cared" about was attracting subscribers however he could. In predictable fashion, he reached down into the gutter and scraped its bottom for articles that were complemented by young women in various stages of undress. Exposed breasts made it into the paper by the third day. Just as predictably, subscriptions soared.

When the Murdochs and their two daughters returned to Australia to spend their traditional Christmas at Cavan, they were giddy with the joy that homecoming brings, augmented by a substantial increase in wealth. What should have been a relaxing holiday vacation, however, turned into tragedy with the disappearance of Muriel McKay, wife of Murdoch's vice chairman at *News of the World.*

Alick McKay discovered his wife was missing when he returned to his home at 20 Arthur Street in Wimbledon on December 29. The telephone had been ripped from the wall, and the contents of Muriel's handbag flung about with abandon. First McKay called the police, then he called Rupert Murdoch.

At 1 A.M. the following morning, McKay received a called from a man identifying himself as "M3," a member of the British Mafia, and demanding £1,000,000 in ransom for Muriel's return. In the days that followed, McKay pleaded for the return of his wife on the front pages of London's newspapers as well as on television. The police theorized that the kidnappers had mistaken Muriel, who had been driving Murdoch's Rolls-Royce during their absence, for Murdoch's wife, Anna. *She,* apparently, was the intended victim, much to Murdoch's horror.

Weeks went by, and despite more than a dozen calls and a trio of letters from the kidnappers, plus several letters from Mrs. McKay herself, the police were no closer to finding the missing woman. When a ransom drop was finally arranged, McKay and his daughter, Diane, were instructed to place £500,000 in cash in suitcases and, after following a labyrinthine route, leave them next to a minivan parked in a garage at Bishop's Stratford, a town in Hertfordshire in the rolling countryside just beyond London. Two London police officers, impersonating the McKays, made the cash drop, and the minivan was kept under constant surveillance.

Hertfordshire is regarded as one of the safest counties in all of Great Britain, a fact proven that evening as the bags remained next to the minivan untouched by passersby for over three hours, at which point a husband and wife by the name of Abbott noticed the unattended bags and called the police, who picked up the suitcases and took them to the local station. The detective watching the minivan, while not able to stop the interception of the bags, managed to note the number from a license plate of a blue Volvo that had repeatedly driven by the location.

XGO 994G, the plate, was registered to Arthur Hosein, a Trinidad-born Muslim who lived with his brother, Nizamodeen, at Rooks Farm, a dilapidated seventeenth-century house on 11 acres near Stocking Pelham in Hertfordshire. When the police raided the farm the morning following the ransom drop, they found the two brothers, as well as paper used for the ransom notes (one of which contained Arthur's fingerprints), but no Muriel Freda McKay.

The Hosein brothers were tried for kidnapping, murder, and blackmail in a three-week trial held at the Old Bailey, England's most important crown court, and found guilty on all charges. They received a sentence of life in prison for the crime. While Muriel's body was never recovered, such was the notoriety of the two brothers that their likenesses occupied a premiere spot in the Chamber of Horrors at London's Madame Tussaud's Wax Museum, and the pair was given an entire page in Great Britain's *New Murderers Who's Who*.

Murdoch and his wife felt real fear for the first time in their lives. Already paranoid about his vulnerability, Murdoch became doubly aware of his need for security. He hired bodyguards, had the children monitored, and resigned himself to the fact that life would never be the same. Anna had never liked London before; now she liked it even less. Her stomach pulled as if zipped closed. It was a feeling that lasted throughout the summer of 1970, into autumn, and beyond the cold rain of winter.

In Atlanta, Turner knew of neither Murdoch nor his private fears. Murdoch, however, *had* heard of Turner—not as titan of television, but rather as the surge of the yacht-racing circuit. Buoyed by his success with WTCG, which actually began to turn a small profit, Turner turned back to sailing determined to become the most famous captain on the open ocean.

In 1968, Turner purchased the 12-meter sloop *American Eagle* for $70,000 from entrepreneur Herbert Wahl and proceeded to sail it into history.* In his first two years of ownership, Turner sailed thousands of miles in the yacht with the flaming red hull, competing in the Caribbean and Europe as well as up and down the east coast of the United States. He was so successful in commanding the sloop, often in treacherous conditions, that he was awarded the 1970 Martini & Rossi Trophy as Yachtsman of the Year from the U.S. Sailing Organization.

The following year, as the Murdochs celebrated the birth of their first son, a boy they named Lachlan, Ted Turner intensified his efforts to sail in more races than any other captain had previously done. Jane Turner saw her husband so rarely that year that she placed the five Turner children in front of the television set on Sunday mornings, where they were able to see their father host a program titled *Academy Award Theater.* The show's title was a rather poor choice, since the old films being unreeled each week had neither won an Oscar nor apparently even been serious contenders. Turner had chosen the name himself, oblivious to the fact that the Academy of Motion Picture Arts and Sciences in Beverly Hills owned the trademark. He had other things to think about, namely sails and jibs, halyards and booms, and any number of other aspects to prepare to catch an elusive goal.

Murdoch's goals were a bit easier to understand and far easier to accomplish. He wanted to be seen as a savior of floundering newspapers who by sheer genius was able not only to rescue culpable institutions from demise but also to make a fortune in the process. If there be any doubters in England, he removed their arguments with the *Sun.*

---

* The *American Eagle* cost $300,000 to construct in 1964. Bill Luders designed the yacht for the Aurora Syndicate, and it was built by Luders Marine Construction. Wahl paid an additional $100,000 to outfit it for open-ocean racing.

The headline screamed in boldface across the top of the *Sun's* March 9, 1970, edition: THE SOAR-AWAY SUN TOPS 1,500,000. More than mere hyperbole, the headline spoke fathoms of Murdoch's skill. In less than four months of ownership, the newspaper had gained 600,000 readers, turning London's newspaper-heavy Fleet Street into a battleground as other publications struggled to compete.

Rupert Murdoch was having fun. His influence was felt in the headlines, in the layout, in the typestyle, in the photographs, and in the actual content of the stories that the *Sun* selected to run. BOY OH BOY, MAMA MIA, one headline read, announcing that actress Mia Farrow had given birth to twin boys. Inside that issue was a healthy portion of abridged news stories, crime profiles, excerpts from a book on extramarital love, and seven pages of sports coverage, a full quarter of the paper. And then there were the nudes—pictures of women whose ample breasts were not only their most identifiable asset but the newspaper's as well. So much so, in fact, that one critic dubbed Rupert "Thanks-for-the-Mammary Murdoch."

When not directly involved in the *Sun,* Murdoch was driving the workers at *News of the World.* The previous February, he summarily fired Stafford Somerfield, giving him a healthy severance package but no advance warning. He cut wages where he could, and where he could not he increased the workload. He invested heavily in television promotion of his product at a time when other newspapers were still limiting themselves to posters hung on newsstands.

"The ITA** went ape over 'Pussy Week in the *Sun,*'" said Graham King, Murdoch's head of marketing. "It was all about cats," but the ITA was as livid as the public was amused.[15]

"I've got a strong competitive urge," Murdoch understated. An aide clarified, "He finds out what his market is, what it wants and where the opposition can be hammered—and then he rips in

---

**The Independent Television Authority was the governing body of British TV and was charged with reviewing all television advertisements as well as awarding broadcast franchises.

like those Aussie soldiers charging across the Western Desert. All he lacks is a slouch hat and a bayonet."[16]

If Murdoch had actually carried a bayonet, it might have helped his cause. As it was, the mini–media magnate had been in the country several years and was either totally ignored or, worst, openly mocked by his established competitors. These men of elitist education and aesthetic taste looked upon those who dared challenge their dominance as something of a curiosity, and certainly not one to be taken seriously.

They referred to Murdoch as "Ned Kelly"—not a compliment in British literary circles (or any other for that matter).[17] Kelly was an Australian criminal–turned–folk hero who was hanged at the Old Melbourne Jail in 1880 for crimes that included robbing several banks and killing a trio of policemen. Murdoch hid his humiliation behind his drive to succeed, adding it to his growing list of slights, patiently stalking, always stalking, with the intensity of a jungle cat.

When Murdoch pounced next, all of England noticed, most particularly David Frost. London Weekend Television, the network that won the franchise to broadcast in London from Friday through Sunday nights, was in trouble. Frost headed the consortium that ran the company, and it was on his LWT program that Murdoch had experienced his humiliating interview. It came as no small surprise, therefore, when Murdoch bought his way into the company by snapping up the 7.5 percent of voting shares then owned by Sir Arnold Weinstock, managing director of the GEC (General Electric Company Ltd., no relation to America's GE). In return, he was awarded a seat on the board of directors.

Thus established, Murdoch surveyed the organization, or rather *dis*organization, and cringed. It was overstaffed and decaying in its own inefficiency. Moreover, the executive directors looked upon the station as a sacred cow whose very presence elevated the medium's impact on culture. They failed to grasp the fact that while it might have fed their egos to present programming heavily laced with classical music, plays, and the requisite educational documentaries, if no one watched, their mandate had failed. Worse still, they were going bankrupt.

It was horrifying enough for these seraphic pretenders to have admitted Murdoch to their board. That they should then have to prostrate themselves at his feet and beg him to redeem their transgressions was an act that qualified for martyrdom in their eyes. Yet they virtually pleaded with the man who published a newspaper appealing to the lowest of low to inject LWT with necessary capital and right its wrongs. Murdoch agreed, but on his terms, as usual: half a million English pounds tossed into the pot in exchange for 40 percent of the company. Not long after Murdoch's arrival at LWT, David Frost left the company and joined the BBC. It is amazing how comeuppance can broaden a sinister smile.

Ted Turner wasn't smiling, but that didn't mean he wasn't happy. It was just that with all the pacing and cussing, shouting and waving, it was hard to fit in a smile. During 1971, Turner sailed more than 12,000 miles in races that spanned the globe. The red hull of the *American Eagle* was nearly as famous as he was in some circles, having won, under Turner's command, the World Ocean Racing Cup.

The telephone in his office at WTCG was silent, the handset cord uncoiled into a limp pile of fettuccine after being yanked to its limit more times than anyone could remember. Turner fit business into his schedule to be sure, but often on the road as he traveled to catch the next regatta, climaxing with the 1972 Sydney to Hobart Yacht Race, which kept him away from home over Christmas as it had for the previous several years. Sailing, business, family—his priorities remained consistent.

It was to be a dramatic race, replete with high winds and rough seas. The *American Eagle* crossed the finish line in three days, four hours, and 42 minutes, eight hours faster than the previous year, and the second fastest time in the race's history.† After the race, in accepting his trophy, Turner leaped onstage and waxed poetic, calling upon nineteenth-century novelist Joseph Conrad and paraphrasing from the author's *Youth* and *The Nigger of the "Narcissus"*: "Ah! The good old time—the good old time—the good old time. Youth and the sea. The good strong sea, the salt, bitter sea, that could whisper to you and roar at you and knock your breath out of you. The crew of the *American Eagle* drifted out of sight. I never saw them again. The sea took some, the steamers took others. The graveyards of the earth will account for the rest. So be it! Let the earth and sea each have its own."†† [18]

For those who saw Turner as a hard-drinking braggart whose foul mouth and quick temper pierced even the thickest skin, this side of the unique sailor was a revelation. The other captains continued to talk about him long after he had left the Australian continent, not only for his recitation of classic literature, but also for the fact that he left behind the winning *American Eagle*, unwilling to pay to have her transported back to the United States.

Turner replaced the *Eagle* with a new yacht he named *Lightnin'*. The 27½-foot yacht was smaller and faster than the *Eagle*, and with it Turner won yet another Southern Ocean Racing Conference title. His most colorful race, however, preceded the conference, when Turner sailed in the Lipton Cup. With 300 yards remaining to the finish line, Turner was in the lead. That mattered little to the captain of a nearby tugboat who was

---

† At the time, the 73-foot maxi *Ondine*, owned by fellow American Huey Long, held the record, set 10 years earlier.

†† Conrad actually wrote in *Youth*: "Ah! The good old time—the good old time. Youth and the sea. Glamour and the sea! The good, strong sea, the salt, bitter sea, that could whisper to you and roar at you and knock your breath out of you." Conrad wrote in *Narcissus*: "The crew of the *Narcissus* drifted out of sight. I never saw them again. The sea took some, the steamers took others, the graveyards of the earth will account for the rest. Singleton has no doubt taken with him the long record of his faithful work into the peaceful depths of an hospitable sea. And Donkin, who never did a decent day's work in his life, no doubt earns his living by discoursing with filthy eloquence upon the right of labour to live. So be it! Let the earth and the sea each have its own."

pulling a barge out to sea, placing a taut steel cable between Turner and victory. Any other race captain would have changed course to maneuver around the cable. Turner, naturally, was not just any other race captain, and ordered his crew to continue at full speed directly into pending doom. When the tugboat captain finally saw the yacht and recognized his own danger, he immediately threw his engines into reverse, slowing the barge and slackening the cable, allowing Turner to sail on to victory and add yet another tale of adventure to his rapidly increasing portfolio.

Such tales of derring-do did not endear him, however, to the more fogyish members of the East Coast sailing community, who looked upon Turner as some sort of rogue. He did nothing to discourage such impressions; rather, he nettled their repudiation by referring to the members of the New York Yacht Club (NYYC) as "stodgy old twits."

His blackballing at the hands of the membership committee of the NYYC in 1970 was painful to Turner, though he sloughed it off at the time without comment. In 1973, however, he was eager for membership in the formidable club, but not for the cachet it delivered. Turner hated anything that reeked of pomposity. In this case, it was merely the requisite baggage he needed to have a chance to captain in defense of the America's Cup, the premiere racing event of the yachting calendar.

Commodore Bob Bavier, a past America's Cup defender (1964), submitted Turner's name for membership and argued for his acceptance.[‡] Bavier's craggy, suntanned face and bushy gray eyebrows commanded attention when he spoke, his large-toothed smile often camouflaging serious intent. He was serious when he demanded that his fellow yachtsmen approve Turner in spite of his image, which one member labeled as "an ass . . . no, no, not the whole ass, just the asshole."

---

‡ Editor and publisher of *Yachting* magazine, who died in March 2001 at the age of 82.

That Turner had just been awarded his second Yachtsman of the Year trophy certainly didn't hurt his cause. The NYYC counted many award winners among its legion. Bavier's endorsement gave the membership a final shove, and Turner received the news of his acceptance into the club in December 1973.

"I remember him telling me about the New York Yacht Club once," Turner said, speaking of his father. "How it was swank and ritzy and all. My father never would have dreamed of me being in that room. That I'd be a *member*."[19]

Rupert Murdoch knew of the New York Yacht Club, ate dinner there with members occasionally, and heard the conversation among the elitist group about the addition of Turner to its ranks. It was all part of the excitement of Manhattan, a place Murdoch had decided to call home. He had always loved the city, the throbbing energy that pulsed to its own rhythm without regard to the world at large. Noisy, smelly, dirty, wonderful. With Anna, Prudence, Elisabeth, Lachlan, and a new baby boy, James, in tow, Murdoch made the move as much to escape Great Britain as embrace America. Of course, he still had his English newspapers, at this point all generating a profit and amazing critics in the process. (The *Sun* alone now had 3.2 million readers.) It was, Murdoch felt, time to raise more eyebrows with the launch of a new weekly in the United States, a tabloid he decided to call the *National Star*.

Launching the same month that Time Inc. debuted its *People* weekly magazine, the *National Star* took aim at those who "find their dailies too intellectual." There were those who would compare it to Murdoch's British tabloids, though the paper could legitimately claim more genetics to the *National Enquirer*, a supermarket tabloid whose distribution it duplicated. *Time* magazine thought that Murdoch himself was far more interesting than his new paper, crediting the *Star* as being "written with zest." It is hard to determine whether *Time* was referring to the *Star*'s lead story on killer bees about to invade America—"They have already smashed their way through Brazil, Paraguay, Uruguay, Argentina, Bolivia and Peru"—or to the tsunami about to hit our shore—"If all the Chinese jumped up and down in unison, the vibrations would cause a tidal wave that could engulf America." Zest just doesn't get any better.

Those living in Texas already knew about Murdoch's love for breathless headlines and zippy copy, having been stunned into submission by the publisher's purchase of the *San Antonio Express* and the *San Antonio News,* the city's morning and afternoon papers, the previous month. He arrived in town with both barrels blazing, hitting the Texans between the eyes with headlines that touted BISHOP BARS GAY EX-MINISTER. It was small wonder that locals who labeled Murdoch the "Kangaroo" later called the *News* the "Rape Register" for its many stories on sex and crime.[20]

Murdoch took no notice of critics who claimed he was wallowing in his own slush, saying that he found it "very obnoxious" that American journalists "feel it's wrong to entice the masses into reading newspapers. The typical American journalism school is turning out journalists who feel that they should only be writing for the already enlightened, for the ten percent of the community that's most highly educated."[21]

The educational requirements for the readership of the *San Antonio News,* not unlike those of the *Star,* were apparently low, with pictures being a large part of the appeal. To work for either paper required a great deal of energy and tolerance and a certain amount of flexibility. As one journalist said, "It's a fun paper to work for. That is, once you get the ethical thing out of your mind."[22]

One story that the *News* managed to cover without hyperbole was the drama that unfolded during the 1974 America's Cup qualifying races. The four yachts entered that year were the *Mariner, Valiant, Intrepid,* and *Courageous,* with Turner helming the *Mariner* and Bavier, the *Courageous.* The *Mariner* was a new design from marine architect Britton Chance, who had conceived a unique shape for the 12-meter yacht featuring what he labeled a "fastback" stern. Despite logic that suggested the squared end of the yacht would create turbulence, Chance insisted that the *Mariner* had broken all performance records in the Davidson Laboratories test tank at the Stevens Institute of Technology, Hoboken, New Jersey.

When Turner began to sail the yacht, he discovered that it not only was slow, but it also pulled everything from banana peels to chocolate chip cookies in its wake. Turner was livid over the ship's poor design and blamed Chance for his poor performance in the trial runs. Colorful as always, he was heard to comment, "Damn it, Brit, even shit is tapered at both ends."[23]

The legendary ship designer returned the lip, but to a more impassioned ear—that of syndicate manager George Hinman, who, as a result, plucked Turner from the yacht and replaced him with Turner's race tactician and relief helmsman, Dennis Conner, age 28. Rather than stalk off in a sputtering fury as most had predicted, Turner conceded his defeat with stoic silence and accepted Hinman's offer to skipper the *Valiant*—the yacht least likely to become the Cup's defender.

After the trials finished with *Courageous* the victor, Turner retreated to a yacht that he had rented for friends and family, and drank. Eyewitnesses say that even as the liquor lit him from the inside as a candle does a pumpkin, he never railed against Britton Chance. True, there were some comments about Conner and his equal lack of success with the *Mariner*. And yes, Turner did mention something about the *Courageous* and the beauty of its lines, and that the yacht *wasn't* designed by Brit Chance. Nevertheless, considering his humiliation at being publicly ousted from the captain's chair in his very first America's Cup trials, he was nearly polite and surely poetic, quoting from Oliver Wendell Holmes' "The Chambered Nautilus."

"Leave thy low-vaulted past!" he shouted to no one in particular. "Let each new temple, nobler than the last, shut thee from heaven with a dome more vast, till thou at length art free, leaving thine outgrown shell by life's unresting sea!"

Squinting at the horizon and sweeping it like a searchlight, Turner fell silent, his large, tanned hands gripping the rail, kneading it like stubborn dough. The yacht rocked in the wake of a passing sloop. Turner looked thinner now, like a scarecrow leaking straw, his arms limp, his shoulders bent.

An early moon had risen in the Eastern sky, large and white against violet shadows pushing against heavy clouds that soaked up the last light of day. He had failed to win, but not to learn; his silence only a momentary respite in his world, which depended less on victory than on competition. He reminded himself of that and, inhaling a chest full of cool sea air, turned to his nervous guests, flashed his gapped Chiclet smile, and shouted, "Who wants a grilled cheese sandwich?" as if he were the happiest man in the world.

## FIVE

# Two Teams, a Tabloid, and Tears

*I've got a bunch of flags on my boat,*
*but there ain't no white flags.*
*I don't surrender. That's the story of my life.*

Ted Turner
Atlanta
Winter 1977

**D**orothy Schiff put down her cup of tea. The cup was classic Wedgwood, inherited from her father, Mortimer, but the tea was your standard-issue Lipton orange pekoe. Dolly, as friends knew her, hated to spend cash on exotic blends of Earl Grey or oolong; in fact, she hated to spend cash, period. She did like *receiving* cash, however, and on this particular day in 1976, she was getting a lot of it. Thirty-one million dollars, give or take a few pennies, for the sale of her beloved *New York Post* to Rupert Murdoch.

The *New York Post,* the nation's oldest continually published daily newpaper, was spearheaded in 1801 by Alexander Hamilton as a vehicle to spread his Federalist doctrine. At the time, the subscription rate was $8 a year, two weeks' wages for the average worker. The *Post*'s readers were hardly average, though, since they were the financial elite of their day—bankers, merchants, importers, investors.

By the time Dolly Schiff took control of the paper in 1939 literally for nothing from Philadelphia publisher J. David Stern, the *Post* was losing $4,000 a day. Luckily, Dolly herself came from a

107

long line of East Coast bankers, so she could afford the financial drain. More important, she wanted a vehicle in Manhattan to voice the policies of Franklin Delano Roosevelt and his New Deal, of which she thoroughly approved.

Installing her husband, city councilman George Backer, as editor, Dolly discovered three years later that the paper had actually *increased* in unprofitability, having eaten through $2 million of her personal capital as well as an equal amount of the paper's by the time her husband was ready to resign in frustration. Never a quitter, Dolly divorced George, married the *Post*'s managing editor, promoted him to editor in chief, and took over publishing the paper herself.

By 1976, Dolly had become an elegant New York institution, entertaining presidents, royalty, movie stars, and society's crème with the same kind of frugal budget she sprinkled on the notoriously underpaid *Post* staff. She also was now 73 years old, on husband No. 4, and ready to hand the newspaper's reins over to "another fool with too much money." Enter Rupert Murdoch, eager to claim the title, the paper, and the keys to the washroom for $31 million.

At that point, the newspaper had risen to a daily circulation of 500,000 but was still losing money, a famous prisoner in the shadow of the electric chair. News reports at the time quoted Dolly as saying that she wasn't selling the *Post* because of losses, but rather because changes in federal laws would have cost her heirs "prohibitive sums in inheritance taxes."[1] Years later she scoffed at such stories, bluntly revealing that her real reason for selling was that evening papers were losing money, and no one had been able to stop the flow of red ink—no one except, of course, Rupert Murdoch.

"We're both Pisces," she said. "I always knew he was waiting in the wings. He asked if he could come to lunch. I was ready."[2]

New Yorkers wondered, however, if *they* were ready for Rupert. As the competing papers ran stories of Murdoch's "sex and scandal" school of journalism, Murdoch pledged that he did not intend to alter the *Post*'s news format, or at least what he labeled the "essential characteristics" of the paper. "There will be more stories in the *Post* and they will be more tightly written, for I think many reporters tend to write too long," he said the day he took control. "But the *Post* will continue to be a serious newspaper."[3]

One New Yorker who was not convinced was Paul Sann, the paper's award-winning executive editor, who left his position after learning of the "Australian invasion." Murdoch assumed the position himself and settled into the *Post*'s offices on South Street, next to the city's old fish market.

Nine hundred miles south, Ted Turner had made his own major purchase by buying the Atlanta Braves baseball team for $10 million. Turner picked up the team from the Atlanta–LaSalle Corporation based in Chicago. "I'm doing this as a civic venture for the city and the South. I hope my television station and I can bring national championships to the Braves and all four Atlanta professional teams. Atlanta's got to have a winner," Turner said after signing the deal.[4]

The man who once said that "exposure to defeat is an important thing" had no need to remind his new team. Atlanta had finished the 1975 season seven games out of last place with 67 wins and 94 losses, and with attendance at its lowest since the Braves moved from Milwaukee in 1965. The town, indeed the entire state, that had come to expect *anything* from Turner watched and waited with anticipation for the Braves' new president to make his first announcement. A few rumors and several miscues aside, Turner remained uncharacteristically silent for four months before making a major announcement: the signing of pitcher Andy Messersmith for $1.75 million. Though Turner wasn't sure if Messersmith pitched right-handed or left-handed, he did know that he had signed what was labeled "a lifetime contract."

Messersmith had won 19 games the previous year for the Los Angeles Dodgers before declaring himself a free agent. When

Turner heard the news, he forged ahead and placed a personal telephone call to Messersmith's attorney, Herb Osmond. When Osmond did not return his call, Turner tried again. And again. On try No. 4, he lost his temper, shouted at the woman in Osmond's office who answered the phone, and still didn't get a response. Osmond had fielded offers from the New York Yankees, San Diego Padres, Pittsburgh Pirates, California Angels, New York Mets, Kansas City Royals, Texas Rangers, Chicago White Sox, and Los Angeles Dodgers. Turner finally telephoned and left a different number: $1.75 million. It got Osmond's attention.

"He'll never be traded. He'll be a Brave as long as I am," Turner said optimistically, a lump of chewing tobacco in his cheek. "Started chewing the day I bought the team," he added proudly, holding up a pouch of Red Man for the cameras. "Now somebody tell me, what the hell is a balk?"[5]

Turner, it seemed, had trouble understanding the game. He had no concept of a *backdoor slider, moon shot, painting the black,* or *twin killing*. And he could only guess what *in the hole* meant.[*]

If Atlanta wondered how its TV mogul owner was going to take to baseball, it quickly found out as the season opened. Turner made himself obvious, sitting in his box behind the dugout on aisle 105, though spending precious little time actually in his seat. He jumped, he hollered, he buried his head in his hands, a blur of constant movement. He had a microphone installed in his box to broadcast announcements to the crowd. And broadcast he did. On Memorial Day that first season, when San Diego scored six runs against Atlanta in the eighth inning, he picked up his microphone to announce: "Nobody is going to leave here a loser. If the Braves don't win tonight, I want you all here as my guests tomorrow. We're going to be in big league baseball for a long time, and one of

---

[*]A *backdoor slider* is a pitch that looks like it won't hit the strike zone, then breaks across the plate. *Moon shot* is an extremely deep home run. *Painting the black* is a pitch that lines over the edge of the plate. *Twin killing* refers to a double play. *In the hole* refers to the next batter up.

these days we're gonna start beating hell out of those guys who've been beating hell out of us."[6]

Earlier that day, he had taken part in a pre-game motorized bathtub race. On other occasions, he joined the ball girls in sweeping the bases between innings, added his weight to a mattress-piling contest, and participated in an ostrich-riding race, which he did not win. He also taped a commercial with his team, singing "Come on out and see the Braves at your Atlanta teepee."[7] He encouraged pre-game events in the stadium, including a mass wedding and amateur wrestling, changed the team's uniforms to a sexier cut, and for a while even added nicknames to the backs of their shirts, such as Bluto, Bird Dog, and Wimpy. He showered with the players, played poker with them, and ran sprints across the field, cheering and jabbering every stride of the way.

To see Turner at his most animated was to witness positive enthusiasm unleashed, a child at the North Pole. People shared in his energy, absorbed it as the sun itself, for there was a purity and innocence about it that made even the most cynical doubter smile. The virus that was Ted Turner's faith in the Atlanta Braves was contagious, and attendance began to mushroom. Thousands more came to each game until the Braves stadium was no longer a place of losers, but a clubhouse for fans united in fervor.

Watching Turner dance on top of the dugout roof, one might have thought he hadn't a care in the world. All motion, all energy, all passion directed toward the field. However, those stolen moments at the stadium took Turner away from a clandestine operation that few in Atlanta would have believed even if they knew it existed.

It had been four years since the last Apollo mission landed on the moon. Since that time, America's space program had been preoccupied with studying lunar samples, while commercial aviation had taken over the launching of private communications satellites. The first, Westar from Western Union, was sent into space in 1974. The next, Satcom I from RCA, was literally flung into orbit aboard a Delta rocket courtesy of McDonnell Douglas on December 12, 1975. While neither of those particular moments in history was given any thought by Ted Turner, they were carefully watched by Gerald Levin, vice president of programming for Home Box Office in New York. At the time, HBO was struggling to establish itself, having begun by distributing a pay cable service via microwave to a few assorted customers in Wilkes-Barre, Pennsylvania.

With the launch of the communications satellites, Jerry Levin saw the future. When on October 1, 1975, HBO went national for the first time with the Westar satellite transmission of the "Thrilla from Manila," the heavyweight match between Muhammad Ali and Joe Frazier at the Philippines Coliseum in Quezon City, television history was made. The dominant television networks were straddled with transmitting their signals through leased AT&T telephone lines. HBO took to the skies and on one single night changed the course of broadcasting.

While it took the world at large a number of years to realize what this meant, Ted Turner was a bit easier to convince. Of course, he did not know anything about Jerry Levin and had never heard of HBO. He did, however, know Andy Goldman, who worked in marketing at TelePrompTer Corporation, a cable service provider, and had convinced Turner four years earlier to allow his firm to carry WTCG on its service free. Andy liked the idea of being able to give his Alabama customers in Huntsville, Muscle Shoals, and Tuscaloosa some extra programming, and Turner liked the thought of saying to his advertisers that his station reached beyond Atlanta.

Having risen to vice president of TelePrompTer, Goldman phoned Turner with another suggestion. The concept was so simple even Turner could not argue with it: place his Atlanta station on Satcom I and beam it to every city in America. It was brilliant, it was unorthodox, and it was costly. The bill to purchase an uplink to transmit his programming to the satellite was nearly three-quarters of a million dollars. The cost of a transponder on Satcom I to beam it back down was another million—a lot of money for a man who had just purchased a losing baseball team for $10 million that he could not afford.

It took the better part of a year for Turner's team to raise the funds through individual contributions while attempting to keep their project a secret. That he was successful has more to do with Turner's ability to convince his own sales team of the concept's potential than anything else. That they took him seriously at a time when he was riding ostriches around Atlanta–Fulton County Stadium is perhaps the bigger surprise.

If there is a lesson here, it comes from Turner's refusal to be defeated. Despite appearances to the contrary, Turner had little in the way of operating capital and was dependent on the income from his billboard business, and WTCG to a smaller extent, to fund his dreams in both broadcasting and sailing. Yet, once convinced of the potential of the satellite, he was Alexander the Great attacking Darius III, Caesar crossing the Rubicon, Achilles battling Agamemnon.

In addition to his financial weakness, he faced a battle with the FCC, which forbade the same person to both own television product and distribute it. Through tireless maneuvering, and with the help of the Washington law firm of Pepper & Corazzini, renowned litigators of communications law, Turner established Southern Satellite Systems (SSS) as a separate independent company headed by Ed Taylor, a former vice president with Western Union's satellite service. SSS was to control the uplink service and be legally responsible for the distribution of WTCG-TV. Turner's resolve remained steady, and his determination barely wavered in the face of government scrutiny that boiled over from the FCC to the Internal Revenue Service and the Justice Department.

When FCC approval for the unique local station with a nationwide dream became a reality on December 17, 1976, it took only hours for WTCG to be beamed to the satellite and then across America. Though Turner coined the term *Superstation* to represent his channel, "The Little Engine that Could" might have been more appropriate, for while the station was available for national viewing, few cable services knew it existed. And the ones that did were far more interested in Elizabeth Taylor (who had just gotten married for the seventh time) than in carrying a station from Atlanta. Undaunted, Turner and his sales team blanketed the country one area at a time in a frontal attack on cable companies, even as baseball's Big Kahuna, Bowie Kuhn, worked to censure the Mouth from the South.

Kuhn, the commissioner of baseball, had been irritated with Turner for the "silliness" he brought to the national pastime. Turner pleaded ignorance. "There are plenty of books about how to play baseball, but not one about how to be an owner," Turner said. "I figured I'd do it my way."[8] His way turned out to be illegal, according to Kuhn, who suspended Turner for one year on January 2, 1977. Kuhn had taken exception to Turner's efforts to sign six-foot-three outfielder Gary Matthews while he was a free agent in October 1976. Apparently, Turner had a "small" conversation with San Francisco Giants owner Bob Lurie, for whom Matthews had played the previous five seasons.

"I ran into him at a cocktail party the night the World Series game was rained out," Turner said by way of explanation. "I had had about six vodka and tonics and I was feeling no pain. I told him that whatever the Giants would offer Matthews, the Braves would offer more. It was all in fun. I didn't mean that I was going to do it."[9]

Of course, he *did* do it, and therein, according to Kuhn, lay the problem. Turner offered Matthews a five-year, $1,875,000 contract, to which Kuhn responded that Turner had "recklessly disregarded all warnings."[10]

"I'm just thankful he didn't order me shot," Turner said, having to get the final word, twirling his cigar and flashing his trademark grin.

On exactly the same day, at exactly the same time, Murdoch was answering the press as well. He had been in charge of the *New York Post* for all of 10 minutes when he stunned Manhattan and several surrounding boroughs by making a bid for *New York* magazine and the *Village Voice,* as well as California's *New West* magazine, owned by the same company. It was an unfriendly takeover attempt that had *New York* magazine founding editor Clay Felker in a race to file a temporary restraining order suggesting that a Murdoch purchase violated antitrust laws.

Unlike Turner, who frightened people with his loud, unpredictable behavior, Murdoch frightened people with his ability to dominate and control. It did not help that he was Australian and a recent arrival in New York, and that his brusque energy often appeared to be Napoleonic in scope. "I'm very conscious of the feelings of writers and editors," he told the press, adding that it was "natural that they should feel a little uncertain."[11]

The writers and editors of *New York* magazine and the *Village Voice* were hardly uncertain. If anything, they were united in their opinion of what they saw as a Felker overthrow. In a signed statement, the editorial staff of *New York* magazine expressed their solidarity: "The current attempt to force a sale of the entire New York Magazine Company to a buyer who is unacceptable to Clay Felker, the founding publisher and editor of *New York* magazine, is a negative act that would undermine the strength, vitality and possibly the very existence of the publications of this company." The editors referred to Murdoch as "an Australian publisher with no ties to New York City or California, and whose standards—as reflected in most of his publications—are incompatible with those of the undersigned. We feel that this step would lead to the deterioration, if not the death, of the company and its publications."[12]

The editors of the *Village Voice* echoed the sentiment. "There is something called The Voice tradition. At its essence is editorial integrity and independence. Clay Felker respects this tradition and we at the *Voice* respect Clay Felker. Above all else, we are a writers' paper. Clay Felker has published articles he has disagreed with. He has protected writers from external intervention. This is a rare quality to find in a publisher anywhere in the world."[13]

Lest anyone think that he cared about the writers' sentiments, Murdoch was an uninvited attendee at an often stormy six-hour meeting of the board of *New York* magazine, armed with proxies representing more than 50 percent of the stock. Without pausing for pleasantries, Murdoch convened a special stockholders' meeting and proceeded to dismiss two of the board members from their positions—Harvard professor James Q. Wilson and Revlon executive Mary Joan Glynn—electing himself and his investment banker, Stanley Shuman of Allan & Company, to fill the vacancies. The outraged writers, artists, and editors, referring to themselves as "the talent package that is being bartered," called Murdoch "a man whose journalistic approach appears alien to us and whose commitment to our city is untested."[14]

New Yorkers appeared to be completely captivated by the publishing soap opera bubbling on their doorstep, and even the television networks found the brouhaha important enough to note. However, no one stopped to wonder why the Murdoch purchases were raising such dust. The *Post* had been limping uphill for years and was a well-written if uneven mélange of gossip, editorials, and left-wing political arguments. *New York* magazine was better written, but only because the city's power brokers, whose lifestyles it revealed in extraordinary style, demanded it to be. The *Village Voice* was a counterculture weekly consumed with covering New York's entertainment scene with a seriousness that suggested Broadway actually mattered outside of Manhattan. Even the most outspoken critics of the *Voice* had to find some delight, however, in its colorful classified ads section, which dominated the rear fifth of the paper.

That the nation as a whole would be interested in the absurdity of Murdoch's maneuverings in Manhattan became quite apparent when he was featured on the front covers of both *Newsweek* and *Time*. (The latter took the Murdoch approach by featuring him in a gorilla outfit atop a skyscraper, holding copies of the *Post* and *New York* magazine. AUSSIE PRESS LORD TERRIFIES GOTHAM, the strip headline shouted.) Rupert Murdoch had arrived.

By the time what seemed like the longest week in the history of Manhattan played itself out, the *Post* had a new editor, Edwin Bolwell (like Murdoch, an Australian import); the *Village Voice* had a new editor, James Brady (onetime columnist and vice president of the *National Star*); and Clay Felker, the man who had introduced Rupert Murdoch to Dolly Schiff, and whose employees had staged a walkout in his honor, had a fat new bank account (courtesy of his $200,000 severance package and the $1.5 million he received for his stock in the company). He was no longer frowning. Murdoch, too, seemed pleased with the outcome, for, in the course of several weeks, he had spent $51 million, bought two newspapers and two magazines, and generated the kind of publicity mere money could never buy.

He also effectively demonstrated that he did not particularly care who he trampled in his rush to expand. This was acquisition, not an exercise in grace and charm, and if others did not like his methods, Murdoch had a consistent response: "You don't like it, quit." He was not looking for friends and certainly not for praise. He was determined to make a profit, and let the bodies fall where they may.

Not to be outdone on his own turf, Ted Turner went shopping, checkbook in hand, and returned home with a National Basketball Association franchise, the Atlanta Hawks. For $4 million, Turner purchased 55 percent of a team that was headed out of Atlanta in search of greener grass. "You can't have an NBA championship if you don't have an NBA team," Turner said.[15]

Unfortunately for Turner, Atlanta's basketball players weren't any better at winning than its baseball team was. The Hawks had arrived in Atlanta from St. Louis, where they had their biggest success in the years 1957–61, winning the NBA title in 1958 by defeating the Boston Celtics. By the time the Hawks moved to Atlanta, however, those glory years were far behind them, with the team average less than .500 for much of the time. To run the team, Turner selected Mike Storen, the one-time commissioner of the American Basketball Association from 1973 to 1974. "It's really fun to sit down with your new partner," Storen said, "and learn he's been suspended for the good of sports."[16]

With his usual aplomb, Turner attempted to stir up interest in his newest ball club, though he was still slightly confused by the rules of the game. Under Turner, *officials* somehow became *umpires,* and *fouls* became *errors.* No matter. The fans, the players, the sportswriters lavished praise on Turner for his enthusiasm, if nothing else.

"Outnumbered five to one, there they were," Turner said. "Alexander the Great digging in with his famous phalanxes. Nine men deep, with swords of different lengths over the shoulders of the men in front. Oh, maybe it was five men deep. God, how could a guy carry a sword that long? Alexander the Great shocked them. Just like the Hawks. Goddamn. Go Hawks!"[17]

Turner applied the same unbridled excitement to taming Bowie Kuhn. He called on his league of fans to bombard Kuhn's office with letters of complaint and paid the members of Kuhn's staff a "finder's fee" to forward to Turner the names and addresses of the letter writers (who were later sent applications for Atlanta Braves season tickets). Friends in high places joined in the fight, including Georgia governor George Bushee, who attacked Turner's suspension as "the ultimate in punitive overkill, and nothing short of an outrage."[18] The Atlanta Chamber of Commerce called Turner "our city's cheerleader" and asked for a reprieve.

When Turner met with Kuhn to personally discuss his suspension, he addressed the man who was being paid $200,000 a year to supervise professional baseball as the Indian chief of the big leagues:

> Give us a way out of this thing, if you can, as the guy who is supposed to be the Big Chief of baseball. The little Indians. I am like the little Indians out in the West. You hear about the Big Chief back in Washington, the Great White Father who says, "You've got to move off your reservation."
>
> We kept moving the Indians back and back and back until they had to fight. A few of them had to fight. I do not want to fight.
>
> Great White Father, please tell me how to avoid fighting for what little we have left. The buffalo are gone. The white man came and killed off all the buffalo.
>
> They drove the trains through what we were told we would have—this land, you know? The Black Hills. Now this gold you want—the yellow metal—you want us to leave and go to the dust bowl of Oklahoma and these are our homes. We must fight for them.
>
> Please go back to the Great White Father, Soldier man, and tell him to please help us . . .
>
> I am very contrite. I am very humble. I am sorry. I would get down on the floor and let you jump up and down on me if it would help. I would let you hit me three times in the face without lifting a hand to protect myself. I would bend over and let you paddle my behind, hit me over the head with a Fresca bottle, something like that. Physical pain I can stand.[19]

Kuhn responded by issuing a formal suspension of Turner on January 25, 1977, "effective immediately from all management activities." In a three-page letter, Kuhn addressed Turner's unacceptable behavior, and the Great White Father told the owner of the Atlanta

Braves that he was "prohibited from managing or advising in the management of the affairs of the Atlanta Braves or engaging in any association whatever with any major league club or its personnel in absence of prior authorization from this office."[20]

When Turner received the news, he fell silent. His eyes lifted toward the ceiling as if they might float out of his head at any moment. "We'll just see about that," he said to absolutely no one. He then proceeded to call his attorney. The very thought of dragging the commissioner of baseball into a courtroom frightened Turner. "Scared me to death," he admitted. It also gave him a stage and a spotlight, two of Ted Turner's favorite things.

When Kuhn entered the courtroom of Judge Newell Edenfield in Atlanta on April 28, Turner saluted the baseball commissioner, causing the first of many bursts of laughter from the assembled press. While on the stand testifying to the circumstances surrounding his meeting with San Francisco Giants owner Bob Lurie, he gyrated, thrusted, squirmed, and dismissed questions from Kuhn's attorney, Richard J. Wertheimer, who persisted in suggesting that Turner was not being entirely truthful with the court. "After this is over, you keep that up, and you'll get a knuckle sandwich," Turner said, shaking his fist in Wertheimer's direction.

Kuhn was no less dramatic in his bid for the judge's attention, posturing himself for sainthood as he explained his reasoning. "It comes down to the ability, Judge, of our game to survive. We have come upon dangerous times. I sent out a whole series of directives against clubs contacting free agents prior to the deadlines we had set. I was trying to say, as loud as I could, that if there were violators, I would take strict actions."[21]

While Judge Edenfield deliberated, both sides went back to their respective corners—Kuhn to his presidential hotel suite, Turner to his seat above the dugout. For their part, the Atlanta Braves continued to lose games, and with every loss Turner became more frustrated. "The commissioner says the game is too complicated," Turner said. "Skippering a twelve-meter is complicated. Football is complicated. But my eight-year-old son plays baseball. How complicated can the game be? Let me tell you. The fans know how complicated this game is. One stood up in his seat and yelled at me, 'Hey, Turner! I can't stand this any longer.' I told him he only paid six dollars for his seat. I paid eleven million to sit two seats away and I'm not complaining."[22]

Not complaining? Turner did nothing *but* complain to employees, family, waitresses, cabbies, and Braves manager Dave Bristol—particularly to Bristol, until Turner finally ordered him to take some time off. "Take ten days," Turner said. "You scout the farm system. I'll manage the team."[23] Bristol left, but not to scout the minor leagues. Instead, he sidestepped the press and returned to his home in Andrews, North Carolina, where he rode his horses and pretended he was not disgusted and offended.

The following night, wearing the gray Atlanta road uniform with a large number 27 on the back, Turner shoved a wad of Red Man into his cheek and joined the team in the dugout at Pittsburgh's Three Rivers Stadium. The Pittsburgh fans were about as impressed by the sight of Turner in uniform as the Pirates were. Pittsburgh won the game 2–1, extending Atlanta's losing streak to 17 straight. Turner, of course, saw the loss as a sign of improvement. "We only lost by one run. Not too shabby"—*not too shabby* being a new catchphrase around the Braves dugout and televised on their scoreboard.

National Baseball League president Charles (Chub) Feeney was outraged when he learned that Turner had signed a management contract with the Braves and intended to head the team himself. Not since Connie Mack wore two caps had any team owner thought about managing a team, and Feeney snorted and huffed his way through a telephone conversation with Turner, first objecting to the fact that he wasn't consulted before Turner's latest assault on the fine institution of baseball, and then alerting the Atlanta Braves owner of rule 20-E. That piece of baseball law forbids anyone from managing a team in which he owns stock.

Now forbidden from managing and expecting his suspension to be reinstated by Kuhn at any moment, Turner fussed the way he always fussed—loudly and to the fans. From his seat on aisle 105, Turner, no longer in uniform but still screaming instructions, fumed publicly. "If you can't do anything else, make a lot of noise" was his motto. And that evening, with third-base coach Vern Benson managing the Braves, the team won—a major 6-1 victory.

When he returned to Atlanta the following day, Turner appealed Feeney's decision to Kuhn, who was still smarting from Turner's performance in the courtroom. As if to signal his intentions, Turner returned to Atlanta-Fulton County Stadium wearing number 27 again. He was on the field joining his players in batting practice and was appreciating the applause for a hit to second base when he was called back to the clubhouse. There he had a telegram from Bowie Kuhn read to him over the telephone. Though the telegram did not get immediately to the point, Kuhn's final sentence made his case: "Given Mr. Turner's lack of familiarity with game operations, I do not think it is in the best interest of baseball for Mr. Turner to serve in the requested capacity."[24]

After kicking over a trash can and slamming his fist against the hard wood of the clubhouse door, Turner telephoned Kuhn and, with enormous restraint and no mention of the Great White Father, asked the commissioner of baseball just *how* he was supposed to get experience if he wasn't allowed to manage his club.

"You get it in the stands, like the other owners. Why can't you be like everybody else?" Kuhn asked.

"Because I'm in last place!" Turner replied before hanging up the phone without admitting defeat.[25]

On May 19, 1977, Ted Turner's suspension was upheld by Judge Newell Edenfield in the Federal District Court of Atlanta, with the judge stating that Kuhn had the authority under the "best interests of baseball clause" in his contract. This time Turner did not object, though not for lack of fury. Rather, he had no more room in his schedule for baseball. June was sailing season, after all, and Turner could not ignore the call of the sea. The man who had no white flags on his boat was about to try again for the large silver cup with the word *America* written across its lip, and make headlines around the world.

S I X

# The Captain
# and the Carpetbagger

*Monopoly is a terrible thing—*
*till you have it.*

Rupert Murdoch
New York
October 1978

Ted Turner felt the bluster at his back, his jacket soaked with water, his eyes never leaving the extended mainsail, which strained against the wind like a child holding its breath. The sun had risen high over Rhode Island's Newport Bay, providing light but little warmth. It was June, but it felt like November. Even the seagulls knew spring was late this year, standing sentry, motionless, their feathers fluffed to trap even the smallest amount of body heat. Shouting over the wind, the cold, and the gulls, Turner was both anxious and excited as he ran the waves, read the very air that propelled him through the frigid water. As skipper of the *Courageous*, one of three 12-meter sloops competing in the elimination trials to defend the America's Cup, Turner was battling the best.

Sail maker Ted Hood, who had captained the *Courageous* to victory in the last Cup defense, was now skipper of the newest entry in the yachting contest, *Independence*. Sleek and fast, *Independence* was the favorite in the three-yacht competition, its state-of-the-art design scoring the highest in tank tests. The *Enterprise,* another new boat brought from the West Coast, was helmed by veteran sailor Lowell North. Each of the men used his own hand-crafted sails on his yacht, sloops that were equipped with every navigational instrument imaginable.

And then there was *Courageous*. The Olin Stephens–designed yacht was looked upon as last year's model, the also-ran in a field of designer labels. Both North and Hood considered the *Courageous* and her captain little more than window dressing. It was an impression that Turner quickly corrected when the America's Cup trials began in June 1977.

He used the frigid water and blustery weather against his challengers, reading wind patterns faster than their onboard computers, testing the competition in a game of skill. The sleek competitors *Independence* and *Enterprise* were ill equipped to handle 25-knot squalls. In contrast, it was Turner's favorite sailing weather. His 10-man crew was a seasoned team of athletes, each member volunteering his time for the sheer joy of this moment and performing nearly impossible feats of nautical dexterity. They knew Turner well and were confident of his ability to lead them through severe conditions. They were also used to his verbal abuse.

Their skipper's mouth, long on reputation and short on restraint, was on a nonstop tirade that began in June with the first trial run and continued through September. Even seasoned Turner watchers found that the extent to which the yachtsman allowed his colorful tongue to dominate the proceedings was extraordinary. As *Courageous* began to win in the initial races, her captain accelerated his commentary. Nothing was off limits; no racial slur, curse, or personal confrontation. It was Turner being Turner, after all. The people's choice was loud, crude, and vulgar, even in the most staid surroundings of Newport's exclusive clubs.

Bailey's Beach is a private club where the town's Spouting Rock Beach Association gathers to frolic, sun, and dine. Founded during the gilded age of the Astors, Vanderbilts, and Carnegies, the club was so prominent in the area that membership was limited to those whose blood was blue and whose wallets were full.

"Only the elite could bathe at Bailey's Beach," wrote socialite Elizabeth Drexel Lehr in her memoirs. "It was Newport's most exclusive club. The Watchman in his gold-laced uniform protected its sanctity from interlopers. He knew every carriage on sight, fixed newcomers with an eagle eye, swooped down upon them and demanded their names. Unless they were accompanied by one of the members, or bore an introduction from an unimpeachable hostess, no power on earth could gain them admission."[1]

On the first Saturday in July 1977, Turner and his mouth stepped into this den of decorum, sparking an incident that members still speak about in hushed tones some 25 years later.

"Turner and his wife were invited to have dinner here by this family from Atlanta," a Bailey Beach member said. "This couple was very *nouveaux riches,* very over the top. It was pretty obvious that Turner was bored, and struck up this conversation with some young blonde who was the date of one of our older members. Apparently, the conversation got tasty when Turner blatantly asked the woman if she had had sex with the old guy. No lead-in. Turner just upped and asked her. She wasn't at all shy about telling him that while they had slept together, she remained unfulfilled, shall we say. That's when Turner offered to do something about it, the story goes."

Turner disputes the details of the night but acknowledges he did speak with a "highly painted lady who was sort of attractive"[2] and asked to be seated next to her at dinner. When his request was denied, he left the party in a bored huff, leaving wife Jane behind and causing the Atlanta couple "social humiliation"—apparently something akin to rape in Newport. By the next month, the story had made its way into several national magazines, and Turner had written a letter of apology to John Winslow, president of Bailey's Beach. In the letter, Turner did not admit impropriety but merely alluded to the fact that his conduct "may have been bothersome to some of [the club's] fine members." Turner added that he had had "a couple of drinks too many" and begged Winslow to accept "his sincere apologies."[3]

While this was not the first and certainly not the last time Turner's mouth caused headlines, it took on added significance when, on August 30, 1977, Ted Turner was given the official nod by the selection committee to represent the United States in defense of the America's Cup. In the time-honored tradition, the selection committee, led by Commodore George Hinman, crossed the Rhode Island Sound to announce to the world that Turner had beaten the odds. It was not an easy moment for Hinman. He was, after all, the same man who had plucked Turner from the captain's chair of the *Mariner* three years earlier. Turner had outsailed the competition through a sustained mix of nerve, speed, instinct, and tactics. He had beaten Ted Hood's *Independence* so completely that the front-runner actually finished in last place. *Enterprise* was a distant second.

Hinman, in his New York Yacht Club dark blue sailing jacket and Nassau straw hat with the club's colors on its band, approached Turner without apparently noticing the cigar Turner held in one hand, the beer in the other, or the out-of-place engineer's cap on his head. Hinman was more concerned that an unexpected downpour had drenched him and the six other members of the selection committee. Yet, as the two men came together, the thunder stopped and the clouds parted, a stream of sunlight piercing the sky like life returning to a body. There, in the shadow of Mrs. Auchincloss' mansion, with its For Sale sign signaling the end of an era, Hinman announced with the unruffled air of *noblesse oblige,* "Gentlemen, congratulations. You have been selected to defend the America's Cup."[4]

Turner wiped tears from his eyes with the back of his hand, spilling beer in the process and barely missing Hinman's jacket. It had been a long fight and Turner had won, as he knew he would. "Everything I do is war," he said.[5]

For the first time in its 126-year history, the America's Cup was front-page news. The magnet that was Ted Turner pulled newspaper and television coverage from around the world. He attracted groupies who followed him from Bannister's Wharf across the cobblestones of Newport. They waited for him at Conley Hall, the English Tudor–mansion–turned–Salve Regina University dormitory, where the *Courageous* crew was housed. They stalked him at dinner and cheered him from the shore. Turner, as always, never disappointed the ever-increasing cult that buzzed about his person like flies on a picnic barbecue.

That *Courageous* was pitted against the Australian sloop *Australia,* captained by Noel Robins, held less interest to the press than Turner's continuing outbursts of quotable non sequiturs. "The primary purpose of the Cup," he told a reporter from *Yachting* magazine, "is to improve international understanding. The highest form of sportsmanship and goodwill is involved. We're ambassadors of the American way of life. That doesn't mean you don't race hard. You're respected when you're a hard driver or a winner. But many areas get warped."

The reporter instinctively waited. It would be only moments before Turner's philosophy lapsed into predictable controversy. "Part of the deal, of course, is to make love to foreign girls. That is one of the best ways there is to improve international relations. But, you know, you can't pick your nose and wipe the boogers on the blazer of the host commodore. It isn't done."[6]

His face was on T-shirts, posters, and mugs. He basked in the adulation like a child receiving praise from a parent. He pranced and preened, and then he delivered, winning his defense of the America's Cup with dispatch in four successive races. In a moment, Turner the sailor had become Turner the king, the hero of Newport, if not the nation. It might well have been his finest hour if Turner had but remembered his weakness for liquor. Instead, the yachtsman celebrated with beer, with champagne, and with aquavit.

The symphony of air horns that sounded his triumph joined fireboats that showered the *Courageous* with streams of water. Fireworks exploded overhead as Newport became a place of celebration and adulation. And still Turner drank. He drank through the applause and the shouts, he drank as he watched the crowds climb onto nearby rooftops for a better look, and he drank even as he reached shore and was lifted onto the shoulders of an adoring throng.

By the time Captain Turner reached the America's Cup press conference at the Newport Armory, he was barely able to stand, let alone walk unaided to the dais. The hall was cramped with cameras, lights, and reporters, most as eager to see if Turner would pass out as they were to hear any speech he might be able to deliver. As if on cue, in front of the cameras, Turner slid face first onto the floor, and it was that image of a prone, drunk hero that reached across America via CBS' *60 Minutes*.

When Turner finally rose to speak, "I love everybody in this room" was about all he could force his mouth to say—that and how much he loved the crew of the *Courageous*. While the New York Yacht Club fought off any attempt to suggest Turner brought dishonor to his win by celebrating himself into a stupor, the man himself remained unapologetic for his method of celebrating.

"Honestly, what am I going to say? A friend of mine was disappointed in me. He thought I'd missed my moment. My *moment?*" Turner wondered. "How the hell could I be profound? It was just a boat race. It was over. I had been away all summer. It was time to get back to work. I didn't even have time to make the *Today* show, and they wanted me bad. I have to work to earn a living."[7]

Making a living was also on the mind of Rupert Murdoch as he ran his own race against time. His battle was not with yachts or sails, but with the ever-changing winds of New York's Typographical Union No. 6 and the Newspaper Guild, which was threatening to walk out of contract negotiations even as Turner was celebrating in Newport.

It had not been an easy few months for Murdoch—or New York, for that matter. In 1977, the Son of Sam murders spread terror throughout the streets of Manhattan and Brooklyn, courtesy of a serial killer who used a .44 pistol and left an identifying note next to his victims. The murders began in 1976, when a teenage girl was shot to death and her friend wounded. By the following March, five more people had been shot, two fatally. In April, when two more random victims were killed, New Yorkers began to panic and in doing so created the perfect stage for Murdoch's special brand of journalism: heavy on hype, light on facts, with headlines blaring the sensational.

Murdoch ordered his reporters, including Steve Dunleavy, an Australian import fresh from the *National Star,* to capitalize on the tragedy, spinning the more gruesome aspects of the killings and stirring paranoia in the process. Accuracy was less important that sensationalism; corroboration was as absent as the killer himself. Given the media blackout that the New York police had placed on the crimes, Murdoch's *Post* resorted to fabrication. Not even organized crime was safe from the marauding news coverage when, on August 4, the *Post* suggested in its banner headline that the Mafia had put out a hit on the killer.

A week later, a young postal worker named David Berkowitz was captured and charged with the crimes. The *Post* saturated its front page with red ink to declare the murderer "CAUGHT!" despite the fact that he had not yet been formally tried. As news of the arrest spread through New York, reporters from the *Post* got Berkowitz's home address and broke into his apartment, photographing his bedroom and running the pictures in an exclusive feature.

When a *Post* reporter bribed a police officer to obtain a photo of Berkowitz inside his jail cell, the competition cried foul and a criminal investigation was launched against Murdoch and the newspaper. Although Murdoch spent an abnormal amount of time avoiding the spotlight, not even his political pull could sidestep the laws of New York. He was able, however, to escape prosecution in the case brought by special state prosecutor Roderick C. Lankler.

Freelance writer James Mitteager was not as fortunate. Mitteager, a former police officer, was accused of bribing Herbert Clarke, a corrections officer in the hospital prison ward, with $5,800 Mitteager had been given by *Post* metropolitan editor Peter Michelmore. Clarke, who was granted immunity in exchange for his testimony, admitted accepting the money and using a "spy" camera to photograph the sleeping Berkowitz. Charges were ultimately dismissed, and the picture of Berkowitz, which ran in the *Post* on December 2, 1977, was copyrighted by the paper.

The previous July, Osborn Elliott, New York's deputy mayor for economic development, lambasted the *Post*'s coverage of an electrical blackout in Manhattan, calling it a "disaster in itself." The *Post* had headlined its story on the daylong blackout 24 HOURS OF TERROR, labeling the outage as causing "the worst outbreak of rioting in the city's history." In a letter to the *New York Times* written shortly after the first big crisis Manhattan had suffered since Murdoch bought the newspaper, Elliott asked: "Are you proud of what your headlines produced? After reading your Friday editions, my conclusion—as a lifelong journalist—is that the disaster may turn out to be yours, not the city's."[8]

Mayor Abraham Beame joined the outraged when he singled Murdoch out at a news conference: "I am particularly saddened to see a fine old newspaper like the *New York Post* corrupted into a sensationalist rag by an Australian carpetbagger. He came here to line his pockets by peddling fiction in the guise of news." New York's first Jewish mayor, Beame had been targeted by the *Post* during the 1977 Democratic mayoral primary. Beame lost the primary to the *Post*-supported candidate, Ed Koch. "As a self-acclaimed kingmaker," Beame continued, "the man from Down Under has openly used his publications to wage political war and engage wantonly in character assassination. No New Yorker should take Rupert Murdoch's *New York Post* seriously any longer. It makes *Hustler* magazine look like the *Harvard [Law] Review*."[9]

The employees of the *Post*, caught in the shadow of Murdoch's questionable journalism, railed against their publisher in a joint show of discontent. Leading the way, noted *Post* columnist Robert Lipsyte walked off the job on September 27, 1977, citing "a lack of freedom to have opinions in counterpoint to the paper's policy."[10] That same day, 50 of the 60 reporters who worked at the newspaper echoed Lipsyte's complaint.

In a letter delivered to Murdoch by *Post* reporter Barbara Yuncker, the group complaint cited "disquiet over slanted news coverage," particularly during the Koch-Beame primary.[11] Murdoch reacted with despotical furor, rejecting the reporters' efforts to control the editorial content of the newspaper and exerting his own right to print whatever stories he cared to, edited to his liking. After a heated 45-minute meeting with Murdoch, Yuncker posted a notice on the employees' fourth-floor bulletin board announcing, "Anyone who questions Mr. Murdoch's integrity should find employment elsewhere."

All the reporters were members of the Newspaper Guild, and as such benefited from a negotiated job security that had protected them from layoffs in the past. With the arrival of Rupert Murdoch, however, union pacts were being revisited without regard to seniority or position. Murdoch, the onetime flag bearer for Marxism, was no longer a lover of the working man. For the publisher, unions had become a necessary evil, barely tolerated and certainly not encouraged. The reporters' letter of complaint provided Murdoch with an opportunity to express his own displeasure with the staff he had inherited from Dolly Schiff. He contended that the *Post* was dramatically overpopulated with workers who placed more importance on position than on production. When he announced his intention to reduce the staff by 35 to 40 percent, starting with those who were deemed "incompatible with the new management's publishing concept," the union immediately responded with charges of attempted union busting.[12]

As the disgruntled journalists and clerical workers met to decide their fate, Murdoch's pressmen and printers were meeting to discuss their own set of grievances. For all his displeasure with journalists he thought to be lazy, Murdoch considered the pressmen and their union to be "corrupt and intransigent and self-destructive." His passion for efficiency found itself wallowing in frustration when dealing with unions that dictated the number of people and the number of hours that each task required for completion. "American unions have taught their members to expect a great deal more than a day's pay for a great deal less than a day's work," Murdoch said.[13] His statement was a cannon shot into the belly of organized labor, and with it the unions began to unify into a defensive stance that braced itself for all-out war.

When Murdoch purchased the *Post,* he bought more than a newspaper. The venerable daily came boxed with a plethora of union contracts. They were contracts that Murdoch insisted "contractually mandated" that he employ twice as many workers at double the wages as his direct competition in Long Island and North Jersey; contracts that expired at midnight on March 30, 1978.

Murdoch, of course, was not alone in his fight to reduce manpower overhead. In his effort to cut wages and employees, he was joined by the other two dailies in Manhattan, the *New York Times* and the *Daily News.* All three were members of the Publishers Association of New York City, which was responsible for the actual negotiations with the Allied Printing Trades Council, representing the Newspaper Guild and eight newspaper craft unions.

As the countdown to the deadline grew increasingly nearer, Murdoch joined Walter E. Mattson, general manager and executive vice president of the *New York Times,* and Joseph F. Barletta, recently promoted general manager of the *Daily News,* for a private dinner at Christ Cella, the venerable East Side steak house. Both Mattson and Barletta had years of experience in labor relations and were well versed in labor law. Murdoch brought his own experience to the table, albeit more the seat-of-the-pants kind.

By the time the three men finished a dessert of New York cheesecake, a Christ Cella specialty, they had arrived at a decision. The exact specifics of that decision varied widely depending on who was asked. Murdoch insisted that the three executives had agreed in principle to force the union into cuts regardless of how long a threatened strike might last. Mattson, a large man with thinning blond hair and protuberant eyes, is said to have believed the trio agreed to make concessions only if the union compromised in its demands. Barletta, a soft-spoken attorney in his early 40s, sided with neither interpretation: "We agreed it was not wise to freeze ourselves in concrete."[14]

Though the specifics of the meeting have long been lost to history, the outcome caused the collective unions to strike the three Manhattan newspapers on August 9, 1978, effectively shutting down publication of the *Post, Times,* and *Daily News* for the first time in more than a decade. Murdoch was designated as spokesman for the troika, based on his familiarity with speaking before television cameras, and elected president of the Publishers Association. In the months that followed, each side remained determined to wait the other out, and in doing so began the most bitter labor dispute in New York history.

For the predominantly Irish Catholic members of the pressmen's union, the 1978 strike was a watershed event aimed at preserving the stranglehold workers had on the number of journeymen and apprentice pressmen needed to staff each press. In an age of automation and computerized typesetting and printing, these sacrosanct dictates were as anachronistic as the primeval ooze.

Though none of the newspapers was making great profits, Murdoch's *Post* was *losing* money. A lot of money. Murdoch would routinely inform anyone who would listen that the *Post* had emptied his pockets to the tune of $20 million in the two years since he had purchased it, and he intended to either make it profitable or stop publishing. For Murdoch, the choice was simple: cut costs dramatically. The pressmen knew that he intended to carry out his threats, given what had transpired with the *Post*'s news staff, and despite their public stance of obstinacy, the membership was clearly worried.

The head of the union, William Kennedy, was an overweight, cantankerous veteran of the grease and noise of the pressroom. He had worked for the *News* since he graduated from a Catholic high school in Brooklyn, and his loyalty was with the rank-and-file blue-collar workers who were his friends and family. Although Kennedy knew Mattson and Barletta well and felt at ease in his ability to intimidate through defiance, he was uncertain of Murdoch and uncomfortable with his presence at the bargaining table.

For his part, Murdoch savored his role as pot stirrer and made no secret of his intention to publish the *Post* with or without the pressmen's union. To prove his point, Murdoch flew in several dozen non-union laborers from his Texas newspapers and acquainted them with the equipment at the *Post*'s Manhattan printing facility. Far from a clandestine operation, he taunted the union with this trial run that managed to produce a mock *Post* edition with a fifth of the workers normally required under union dictates.

It was an extraordinary show of nonchalance on Murdoch's part, reflecting either enormous confidence or a solid bluff. In either case, Murdoch's ploy unsettled the union's rank and file, who began to put pressure on Kennedy to return to the negotiating table—and quickly. When no immediate talks were scheduled, Kennedy held a press conference and lambasted the newspaper's publishers for a strike he said was caused by "greed for profit."

The strike's impact was having its effect. Local television stations in Manhattan expanded their normal half-hour evening news coverage to 60 minutes, while newsstands settled for selling imported editions of the *Boston Globe* and the *Philadelphia Inquirer*. On the streets of Manhattan, young boys hawked copies of the *News World,* a dime-a-copy propaganda daily published by the Reverend Sun Myung Moon's Unification Church.

Not to be outdone, Murdoch invested in a new publication called the *New York Daily Metro,* published by a Yale graduate named Fred Iseman. Iseman had been a temporary employee at the *Times* when he found himself out of work on August 9 with the rest of the newspaper's staff. Spotting an opportunity to increase his notoriety as well as his bank account, Iseman met with Murdoch and proposed a rather unorthodox arrangement. In exchange for $150,000 in advance payments against the first editions of the *Metro,* Iseman agreed to publish a temporary newspaper that would be delivered to *Post* subscribers during the strike. At the end of the strike, Murdoch had an option to purchase the *Metro*. The key to making the arrangement work was to successfully keep Murdoch's name out of the deal. Murdoch would have remained the ultimate in silent partners were it not for a lawsuit filed by a *Daily News* columnist named Richard Brass. Brass had originally been Iseman's partner in the *Metro* before Murdoch's cash and coercion entered the picture. Once the *Metro* became an instant hit, Brass wanted his share of the pie.

Most of the staff for the *Metro* had been Iseman's friends at the *Times*. Their own conflict of interest at finding themselves on strike, yet working, was bad enough. None of them cared to explain how they had begun writing for a new newspaper while still under contract to the Times, with paychecks coming from Jeffrey Leist, then assistant treasurer for the *Post*. After Brass' lawsuit made the Murdoch connection public, a wave of indignation reverberated among the *Metro*'s reporters, most of whom claimed total ignorance of the *Metro*–Murdoch connection.

Murdoch once again waved away the controversy, saying his participation in the *Metro* was purely a courtesy to *Post* subscribers, whom he was desperate to keep from leaping to suburban non-union publications. He did not find it necessary to share the revelation that the *Metro* was making a profit of $30,000 a week, much of it finding its way into his pocket. At the same time, Murdoch was in the enviable position of having his other New York publications, the *Village Voice* and *New York* magazine, continue to reap the benefits of the strike with an increase in advertising revenue of several hundred percent.[15]

With his New York businesses escalating and his losses at the *Post* cut to the nib with the elimination of thousands of striking workers, Murdoch bided his time. In a rather amazing exercise, he appeared to be actively engaged in mediating while quietly going about his *other* business. When the union chiefs requested help from an arbitrator, Murdoch applauded the move, ostensibly in the name of speeding along toward a resolution of the strike. In actuality, he welcomed yet another element to stir the waters of discontent and muddy an already thoroughly unclear process.

Kenneth E. Moffett, deputy national director of the Federal Mediation Service, had been involved in overseeing the negotiations since the first day of the strike. His suggestions alternately incensed the unions and the publishers, with each side certain that Moffett was favoring the other. They did not change their opinion when Moffett asked Theodore W. Kheel to sit in on the negotiations, perhaps because Moffett found the arrival of Kheel a godsend. Kheel was perhaps the most famous figure in New York labor relations and had been instrumental in the settlement of the last major strike to hit the Manhattan newspaper industry.

While Moffett may have welcomed Kheel's involvement, Kennedy was less than excited by his arrival on the scene. Kennedy believed Kheel was likely to dictate terms to the union in an effort to bring the strike to an immediate halt. The publishers disliked

Kheel, if for no other reason than his ability to get union leaders to agree—usually on terms in excess of what the publishers would have offered on their own.

It was into this quagmire of disagreement and mistrust that Kheel stepped, or more correctly, leaped. He fashioned himself the hero and gave lengthy explanations to the press, his impeccably attired visage on display all the while. In doing so, he managed to take the spotlight away from Murdoch, who had begun to enjoy his position as the publishers' spokesman. That Kheel should now claim access to both sides as an independent gave the arbitrator a unique vantage point from which to express his presumably unbiased observations. Almost from the outset, Murdoch considered Kheel to be favoring the union position. Kheel had built his reputation on compromise, and compromise was not something Murdoch intended to allow. Murdoch could do nothing to eliminate Kheel from the process, however, since Kheel was sitting at the bargaining table with Moffett's blessing.

From the moment Kheel became privy to the particulars of the negotiation process, Murdoch made an effort to track the arbitrator's every step, expecting to uncover that Kheel was meeting privately with the union. To his astonishment, Murdoch discovered that Kheel was indeed holding private conferences, but with Walter Mattson of the *New York Times*. Murdoch, now certain that Mattson was attempting to arrange a private settlement that would leave Murdoch's *Post* and Barletta's *Daily News* at a disadvantage, demanded an explanation separately from each man.

Mattson and Kheel were longtime associates, having worked together on prior union negotiations, and both related the same story to Murdoch—one of comparing notes on the practicality of provisions in the publishers' demands for downsizing the union workforce. Though the explanation made sense, it reeked of intrigue to Murdoch, who envisioned elaborate scenarios of deception and betrayal.

Murdoch was quick to believe that others were capable of doing to him what he had done to others. Propelled by this paranoia, he called on his lares and penates to protect him from these imagined conspirators, all the while continuing to profit considerably from the strike fallout through his other publications. As president of the Publishers Association, Murdoch had little choice but to continue his dance with Mattson and Barletta, though as the weeks evolved, his enthusiasm pitched in waves of anticipation and disillusion.

He appeared on local television in September to make a public plea. To the astonishment of the staffs of both the *Times* and *Daily News,* as well as union members throughout the city, Murdoch asked members of the Allied unions to cross the picket line and return to work. It was Murdoch at his most manipulative, speaking for the publishers without their permission and challenging the unions with a backhanded compliment to "do the right thing." That his challenge should backfire surprised no one, especially Murdoch, though those intimately involved in the negotiations missed the point without exception.

Kennedy used the occasion to harness his increasingly desperate members to rally around the union in a show of solidarity. Mattson and Barletta looked upon the speech as provocation for members of the union to do exactly that at the expense of the very concessions they were hoping to achieve. Only Murdoch knew that he was working the room, playing both sides against the middle—in this case, Theodore W. Kheel. Murdoch's maneuver forced Kheel, the self-appointed advocate of prudent labor relations, to side with the unions out of a sense of fair and impartial negotiation, and in doing so played right into Murdoch's scenario, which saw the interloper as biased toward the union position.

Two weeks later, on September 27, with the unions refusing to budge at a negotiation table that still found Kheel acting as de facto arbitrator without results, Murdoch made his move. After meeting with Barletta to determine for certain that the general manager of the *Daily News* still had faith in Kheel's supposedly unbiased position, Murdoch instructed his attorney, Howard Squadron, to attend the next scheduled negotiation and "throw the bomb, throw the bomb."[16]

The "bomb" was Murdoch's unilateral withdrawal from the Publishers Association and the announcement of his intention to negotiate with the union representative on his own. No Kheel, no Mattson, no Barletta, and no Moffett. Murdoch and Kennedy, head to head. In yet another example of the quintessential Murdoch, the publisher opted to go it alone, not to get a better deal than the other publishers, but to get a *faster* deal. When he spoke with Kennedy later that day, he asked for nothing special. In fact, he agreed that the *Post* would go along with whatever contract the *Times* and *Daily News* were able to fashion—*if* the *Post*'s union employees would return to work immediately.

For New Yorkers, the move was a slice of déjà vu. How well they remembered that publisher Dolly Schiff had dropped out of the Publishers Association in 1963, right before the Easter advertising season, effectively ending a three-month strike against the *Post*. The *Post* had resumed publishing while the strike continued against its competition. Schiff's move, however, had a certain purity to its style. She knew that her paper could not survive without the advertising dollars she would reap from spring sales. It was a decision she had made without hesitation, the way a mother dives into a raging river to save her drowning child.

The *Post,* under Murdoch, was a different paper in a different time. There was to be no obituary of the *Post* if the union continued to strike. Murdoch had too much pride for that. This was not a mercy mission aimed at resuscitation. Rather, this was a calculated business maneuver designed to yield the most return while inflicting damage on the competition.

The day following Murdoch's "bomb," Theodore Kheel arrived at the mediation session and distributed photocopies of a poem by Robert Browning titled "The Lost Leader." Originally published in 1845 as part of Browning's *Dramatic Romances and Lyrics,* the poem begins, "Just for a handful of silver he left us, just for a riband to stick in his coat." Kheel labeled Murdoch "despicable," unaware that the publisher was only beginning to flex his power.

On October 5, 1978, the *Post* returned to circulation with the backslapping headline WELCOME BACK! The paper was 128 pages thick, three-quarters of which was advertisements from Manhattan's department and clothing stores. Speaking to A. H. Raskin, the award-winning labor reporter for the *Times,* Murdoch laughed at the irony of his situation. "Monopoly is a terrible thing," he said, "till you have it."[17]

Forty-eight hours later, Murdoch had assembled, edited, and published a Sunday edition of the *Post* that met with positive reaction and contained so many advertisements that the newspaper had reached the limit of its press capacity. It seemed as if Murdoch could do no wrong, unless one listened to Mattson and Barletta, who publicly attacked the *Post* owner for what they saw as tyranny disguised as resourcefulness. "In Murdoch's world there are no rules. His world is amoral," Barletta said.[18] A. M. Rosenthal, executive editor at the *Times,* said he felt that Murdoch "was a bad element, practicing mean, ugly, violent journalism."[19] To Kheel, Murdoch was little more than a traitor to his own: "In union parlance, Murdoch is scabbing. He's looking out for himself."[20]

The New York newspaper strike continued for another month until the *Times* and the *Daily News* negotiated a delicate peace and returned to the newsstands on November 6. As one editor later suggested, it was "payback time." In the advertising department of the *News,* managers began Project Bury Murdoch, aimed at stealing back the advertising clients Murdoch had acquired in recent weeks. It was a rather simple game, one that paid a bounty for each customer won back to the *News'* corner. The advertising sales reps at the *News* saw it less as a game than as outright war, and as such waged it nonstop over the weeks that followed. The extent of their success was obvious when Murdoch announced that the Sunday edition of the *Post* was ceasing publication after two months. The reason: lack of advertising dollars.

According to Kheel, Murdoch's defection actually brought the strike to a more rapid conclusion, for by caving in to union demands, Murdoch inadvertently increased the union's sense of power and therefore caused their resumption of serious negotiating. Kheel called it "clarifying the issues."

As Kheel was celebrating the successful conclusion of the 88-day strike, he learned that an exposé on his participation in several financial scandals was about to run in Murdoch's *New York* magazine. The article, written by freelance journalist Richard Karp, had originally been slated to run during the strike and had been postponed at Murdoch's request. When the article appeared in the January 1979 issue, it claimed that Kheel had been involved in business deals that were of such "questionable nature that he came close to serious legal difficulties and economic ruin."

Karp mentioned two financial cases. The first, involving the Stirling Homex Corporation, ended in the sentencing of brothers William and David Stirling on stock fraud charges. Kheel was said to have acted inadequately as a director of the company. The second, concerning the American Bank and Trust Company, concerned Kheel's involvement with David Graiver, who was subsequently indicted for banking-law violations.

Kheel denied any wrongdoing and pointed to a number of inaccuracies in the piece. He took out a full-page advertisement in *Cue New York* magazine, as well as one at the bottom of page 1 of the *New York Times,* describing Murdoch's efforts to retaliate against Kheel for his effective handling of the union strike. By that point, of course, Murdoch had long since moved on to other challenges and considered Theodore Kheel little more than a diversion to be played with, much like a cat smacks around a mouse before losing interest, leaving it battered yet alive in a corner of the room.

Murdoch had traveled back to Australia to pursue the controlling interest in the Channel 10 network from United Telecasters, eventually purchasing 48.2 percent of the stock for $19.2 million. When news reached the Australian Broadcasting Tribunal, the country's governing body of broadcasting launched an investigation into Murdoch's residency status. Current laws at the time limited ownership by "nonresidents" to no more than 15 percent of the stock in a broadcaster.

Although Murdoch was spending 90 percent of his time living in his elegant Fifth Avenue condominium in New York with his wife and children, he reacted to the investigation with typical perplexity. "I love Australia; I carry an Australian passport; my children are Australian; I pay taxes in Australia; and I have a home in Australia," he said, listing his primary residence as Cavan, his ranch outside of Yass, 200 miles from Sydney.[21] He had not visited the ranch in months. Yet, with the befuddlement of an ancient muse squinting as though attempting to spot some elusive concept in the distance, Murdoch blamed the investigation on "competing interests" who were determined to undermine his success.

Ultimately, Murdoch was successful in his bid for the national television network, then ranked third in Australia, though its reach was small compared to the ratings numbers being scored for Ted Turner's Superstation. WTCG-TV had been renamed WTBS for Turner Broadcasting System and was now reaching 43 of the 50 United States. For all his success in television, however, Turner still made the most news for his outbursts and for his triumphs on the sailing circuit.

In summer 1979, Turner had reassembled his *Courageous* crew aboard his 61-foot sloop *Tenacious* to race in the Fastnet, the toughest offshore sailing race in the world. Over the years, Turner had competed in the race several times and had previously won. The race, which gets its name from a rock off the coast of Ireland, follows a rhumb line from Cowes, on the Isle of Wight, through the Solent, a broad stretch of calm water between the island and the British mainland. The 605-mile course traces the southern England coast, past Plymouth, Falmouth, and the Isles of Scilly to Fastnet Rock, Europe's most westerly and loneliest outpost. Amid the desolation stands a 155-foot-tall lighthouse that is routinely pounded by some of the roughest seas ever measured.

The *Tenacious* set out with 305 other yachts on Saturday, August 11, 1979, in calm and unseasonably warm seas, with no suggestion that they were heading into the face of death. Turner, in his usual loud-mouthed commando style, was shouting orders to his 10-man crew, who functioned as a well-honed team. Among them was Turner's 16-year-old son, Ted Turner IV.

Midway through the race, as the *Tenacious* rounded Fastnet Rock on its way to Plymouth and the finish line, Turner learned from his navigator, Peter Bowker, that a fierce gale was heading toward the English Channel and would be upon them in six hours. For Turner, such news meant nothing more than preparing to throw a reef in the main, a No. 2 genoa to a No. 3 headsail, and assorted other maneuvers aimed at keeping *Tenacious* in the lead. As they continued to race, the southeasterly wind picked up to 60 knots. The night was black, shrouded by harsh, villainous waves rising 20 feet above the deck of the yacht. The rain drove shards of water against raw faces and hands as harnesses strained against a web of rigged lifelines. Still in the race to win, *Tenacious* was now in a race to survive.

Turner later recalled that as he stared out at the power of the sea, he thought 20 men would die that night. When the cold morning darkness gave way to a bright sun that rose over rolling seas of debris, Turner learned the truth of his statement. During the gale, 24 boats worth more than $5 million had sunk or been abandoned, and 17 sailors had died from drowning or hypothermia, plus four others on shore—the worst disaster ever to hit the sport of sailing.

Of the some hundred yachts that finished, Captain Turner and his *Tenacious* came in first. This time, however, as Turner jumped to shore, there was no gloating about triumph. The air hung heavy with tragedy, and even the victory of the moment could not alter the reality of death. As bodies were recovered in the largest maritime effort since World War II, Turner went man to man and hugged each member of his crew, ending with his own oldest son, who had weathered the storm without complaint. He was, after all, his father's son.

"Like any experience," Turner said, "whenever you come through it, you feel better. We were more afraid of being afraid than anything else. You always feel bad when your fellow yachtsmen drown. But you never can really be completely prepared for what nature has in store. We knew it was coming. We listened to the weather forecasts. But four people died on land, and how can you prepare for something like that—trees falling and walls falling?"[22]

While news of the disaster played out on television and in newspapers, the winning captain shrugged off the accolades of his peers for having led his crew to victory. Turner's mind had moved past the moment, and he was now obsessed with a new challenge. He had come up with an idea while watching the worried families of the Fastnet crews scour the news for information about their loved ones. Newspapers were, by necessity, always printing behind breaking headlines. Television was immediate, but only available at certain times.

"What would you think if you could turn on your TV and see news twenty-four hours a day?" Turner asked Asaad Omar. The

Yellow Cab driver knew he had Ted Turner in the back of his taxi, and looked in his rear-view mirror at the gap-toothed smile on the face of his eager passenger.

"Huh? Whaddaya think?" Turner asked again.

"No way," Omar answered. "It's always bad news. Who'd watch that?" the taxi driver shrugged.

Turner merely shook his head. *Only the entire world,* he thought. *Only the entire world.*

# SEVEN

# The Chicken Noodle Network

*I can't do news. I got too much other product
right now. And who wants news, anyway?
News is nothing!* Nobody *watches news.*

Ted Turner
Los Angeles
Fall 1977

To watch Ted Turner is to watch a dragonfly in flight. Dodging, weaving, moving without any visible means of support. A man in defiance of all things organized, polite, and predictable. A new breed of executive who approached business like a yacht race: Read the wind before it changes to harness the future.

It was in that special place of prediction and prophecy that Turner first imagined the Cable News Network. It did not matter that he never watched the news himself. Truth be told, he hardly watched television at all. What mattered was that in 1979, Turner saw an opportunity hiding within the media explosion called cable, and had the courage of his convictions.

At that time in television history, the three commercial networks were eagerly conforming to a time-honored tradition of what news should be. In the anchor chairs were Walter Cronkite and Harry Reasoner, Chet Huntley and David Brinkley, and a few others who held on to the heritage that legendary journalist Edward R. Murrow created in the infancy of TV. Thirty minutes

149

a night, expanded from 15 minutes in 1963 after years of persuasion, threats, and ultimately pure force.

For its part, cable television was primarily a service that allowed viewers to receive a TV signal in a remote area or additional channels without commercial interruptions. In 1979, the concept that people would *pay* to receive a television signal when they could still mount antennas on their roofs and get it for nothing was still a difficult mass sell. The major magnet of Home Box Office, followed by Showtime, pulled in viewers in sophisticated metropolitan areas, but for the remainder of the country, cable was the arena of polyester-suited bean counters who still thought their only source of income was in what they could collect from a monthly cable bill. The idea that they might make money selling advertising on a service that heretofore had no ads made no sense. It did not help that they heard it first from a man who was known for his crazy concepts.

By the time Ted Turner arrived in Las Vegas in May 1979 to attend the National Cable Television Association (NCTA) convention, he had made up his mind. He had scheduled a press conference to announce the launch of CNN, the Cable News Network, based on little more than a hunch and a hank of faith in the talent of a man named Reese Schonfeld. It did not seem to matter to the Mouth of the South that Schonfeld was under a binding contract with the Independent Television News Association (ITNA), an organization composed of independent television stations across the country that had joined together to receive a daily package of national news—most of it prepared by Schonfeld, who was ITNA's managing editor. He was smart and determined, and he knew just about everything there was to know about getting a news story on the air cheaply.

Schonfeld had met Turner at various conventions over the years, and each meeting seemed to be a little too much like the last. Turner would be a whirlwind of activity and sound, and Schonfeld would attempt to interest him in purchasing ITNA's news feed. The last time Schonfeld pitched Turner, he received what should have been his final rejection. "I can't do news. I got too much *other* product right now. And who wants news, anyway? News is nothing! *Nobody* watches news," Turner told him.[1]

To Schonfeld's surprise, the next time the two men talked, it was Turner who approached Schonfeld. Turner had an idea: Round-the-clock news. In-depth news, sports, business, weather, and entertainment. "It can't miss," Turner said. Of course, there was a good chance it *would* miss, and Schonfeld knew it. He also knew that Turner was offering him a chance to launch an entirely new form of television journalism. Schonfeld could get in on the ground floor, be a part of history.

If Turner was not such a good salesman, Schonfeld might not have agreed to travel to Atlanta for exploratory meetings. The fact that Schonfeld not only flew to Atlanta, but also agreed to leave ITNA for the opportunity to launch this concept Turner called CNN, proves just how great a salesman Turner was and is. Unfortunately, Schonfeld had only recently signed a one-year extension on his current contract—a contract Turner was only too happy to ignore as he nagged, pushed, and manipulated his first official CNN employee not only to attend the May NCTA conference, but also to bring along CNN's first on-air talent, veteran newsman Daniel Schorr.

The hiring of Schorr was Schonfeld's first official duty as president of CNN and one of his most difficult. Schorr began his career at the close of World War II as a foreign correspondent for the *Christian Science Monitor* before becoming a protégé of Edward R. Murrow at CBS News. The network remained Schorr's home for the next 23 years until CBS suspended him in 1976 for refusing to disclose the source of a confidential government document that he had exclusively obtained.

Schorr gained the respect of every working journalist by standing firm in his resolve during a subsequent investigation by the House Ethics Committee. The newsman said, "To betray a source would mean to dry up many future sources for many future reporters. It would mean betraying myself, my career and my life." When the House committee voted against citing him for contempt, Schorr refused CBS' offer to return to the network that had shown him so little support. Instead, he spent several years teaching and writing, and was thus available when Schonfeld offered him a role in the shaping of CNN.

Schorr knew nearly nothing of Ted Turner and even less about cable, but he loved the prospect of a regular paycheck, although he questioned whether Turner would be able to provide one with CNN. "At first blush," Schorr wrote in his memoirs, "not where a traditional newsman would want to spend his waning years, nor indeed, was I the kind of person who would appeal to a flamboyant media entrepreneur."[2] How wrong Schorr was. As it happened, he was *exactly* the kind of person Turner desperately needed to lend credibility to the start-up news service.

Amid the chaos and high-pitch energy of the Las Vegas Convention Center, Daniel Schorr was out of place. Certainly nothing he had ever covered during three wars and seven presidential administrations had prepared him for the unsophisticated theatrics and trailer-park vulgarity of the fishing series, wrestling shows, and travelogues being sold on the convention hall floor. Add the unbridled enthusiasm of Turner, desperate to sign a star on which to hitch his concept, and Schorr should have run for the hills. Instead, he went to Turner's penthouse suite at the Las Vegas Hilton, with its swag curtains and smell of stale smoke. There, in the same room in which Elvis once consumed fried chicken and fattening desserts, the venerable newsman watched as the tornado known as Ted Turner went into his act.

Turner talked about the three commercial networks. Said he saw them losing their audiences to video rentals and cable movie channels. Said he wanted to be the first to produce an all-news channel and all-sports channel. Said good morning to a young woman who sashayed out of the bedroom and out the front door. Said he wanted Schorr on CNN, but only if Schorr gave him an answer that very moment. "If not, forget it," Turner said between bites of breakfast. Daniel Schorr took two things away from the meeting: One, this was definitely *not* CBS. Two, he liked Turner's enthusiasm and wanted to be part of his team.

Schorr signed up with CNN that day after placing calls to his agent and attorney to get help structuring a contract that included the stipulation that Schorr would have no demand made upon him "that would compromise his professional ethics and responsibilities."[3] It was a clause so unusual in its scope that even today it is unprecedented. Yet, it was the only item that Schorr had insisted on to feel protected as a member of the Turner dog-and-pony show.

That afternoon, Turner made cable history by officially announcing the formation of CNN. At his side was Daniel Schorr, as promised, looking slightly overwhelmed behind his thick, black-rimmed glasses, staring out at all the media attention. Turner, of course, radiated in the glow of a clamoring press eager to learn about the network Turner projected as "the greatest achievement in the history of journalism."[4] As for Schorr, Turner introduced him as CNN's senior correspondent of the new network's Washington bureau and an instrumental player in the shaping of CNN. Although Turner was conspicuously short on details, he explained that CNN would showcase a two-hour daily newscast from 8 to 10 P.M. Eastern time, programmed as direct competition to the commercial networks' prime-time entertainment entries. In addition, thanks chiefly to Schonfeld's diligence, Turner was able to announce the signing of psychologist Dr. Joyce Brothers, medical reporter Dr. Neil Solomon, political columnists Roland Evans and Robert Novak, and astrologer Jeane Dixon as regular contributors.

What Turner did not mention was the fact that to finance CNN, he had attempted to sell half of his interest in the about-to-be cable network to Russell Karp, president of TelePrompTer, the largest cable service in the country. When that failed, he pitched the same proposal to former HBO exec Gerald Levin, now group vice president of video at Time Inc., HBO's parent company. Neither man had any faith in the high-risk network, even though both could well have afforded the cost with less apprehension than Turner could.

After discussions with Schonfeld, Turner had calculated that CNN's first-year start-up costs would total $20 million. With no other money readily available, Turner decided to sell his television station in Charlotte to Westinghouse for exactly that figure. Ironically, the station manager of WRET helped the decision along when he excitedly told Turner of his plans to run a week-long exposé on teenage prostitutes in South Carolina during the upcoming ratings sweep period.

"How many teenage prostitutes could you possibly have in Charlotte?" was Turner's incredulous response. It seemed the station manager had found five—conveniently, one for each day of the week—and intended to showcase the juveniles to steal the thunder away from his competition, which was running five nights on death row inmates. That was the day Turner decided to sell.

Although he needed money to fund CNN, and WRET was arguably a ready source of cash, it was not at the foundation of his decision to liquidate the station. Rather, Turner had changed, and could no longer morally support the type of programming WRET was broadcasting.

The transformation of Turner from an uncouth, womanizing loudmouth into an environmentally aware, womanizing loudmouth began as the first seeds of CNN were being planted. In pursuit of his interest in developing a 24-hour news network, Turner educated himself about world politics. Overpopulation, deforestation, and pollution were never a concern of Captain Courageous as he sailed in defense of the America's Cup. He never gave an ounce of time to raising the poverty level, fighting world hunger, or supporting the arts when he was constructing billboards in the swamps of Georgia. Now, suddenly, it *all* mattered, because he became aware of the extent to which those issues and a dozen more like them were hurting humanity.

Turner had never been the type to tiptoe when he could stomp. And stomp he did into the world of news, breaking stereotypes and demanding answers—to questions not only about how to produce a round-the-clock news effort, but also about why nobody had turned a bright spotlight on many of the issues he found waiting to be illuminated. The more Turner learned about the state of the world, the more he was driven to get CNN on the air.

Turner was not a convert as much as he was enlightened, though no amount of eye opening could change his overt personality. He remained at his best when challenged by long odds, and nothing he had done in his life equaled the risk he was taking now. Yet, as Turner sold others, he succeeded in continuing to sell himself on not only the need for a network like CNN, but also the financial bonanza it was going to be. At the moment, however, what money he had was leaving the coffers at an alarming rate, including $4.2 million for the Progressive Country Club—a one-time home for wayward Jewish boys, complete with its plantationlike, three-story brick clubhouse, Doric columns, and sweeping driveway—which would be the new home of CNN. The property had 21 acres in need of maintenance, homeless men living in the locker rooms, and a history that included some supposed Civil War battles that took place right on the front lawn.

If Turner was bothered by the outflow of capital, those around him saw little of his anxiety. Rather, he kept the energy high and the outbursts raging. While showing Schorr around the new CNN headquarters-in-the-making, Turner mentioned its Jewish history and joked that Schorr "should feel right at home here." He boasted that satellite dishes reminded him of a woman's breasts, shouted between offices instead of using the phone, and still talked with his cheek full of chewing tobacco.

Like a snowball rolling down a mountain, the momentum of CNN began to build, propelled by its own initiative and Turner's nonstop marketing of its potential. Schonfeld continued to hire staff, including two major executives. Burt Reinhardt, a veteran cameraman who had worked with Schonfeld in various capacities over the years, joined the team to run the news operations division. Ted "Mad Dog" Kavanau, a legend in newsrooms who had bounced around in local markets, took over as senior producer. Without committees, focus groups, or boards of directors to consider, the three men continuously bounced their ideas off of Turner, who remained an executive in motion, checkbook in hand, responsible for making every final decision.

The fragility of the setup became apparent in August 1979, when Turner left Atlanta to take part in the Fastnet race. Schonfeld was in Canada exploring a concept for an interactive newsroom set when he saw the report over the BBC's news feed that Turner was among those believed to have been lost at sea in the tragic race. Schonfeld knew better than most that without Turner there would be no CNN. It was hours before it was confirmed that Turner was not only alive and well, but also victorious. It was the type of story that CNN would have had on the air immediately. The irony of the situation was inescapable to Schonfeld; in the age of information, the need for a news network essential.

When Turner returned from England, Fastnet trophy in hand, he plunged back into his role as chief horn blower for CNN, taking to the road in a countrywide sweep to target cable systems still reluctant to join in his dream. In December, Turner attended the Western Cable Show, taking place adjacent to Disneyland, to announce CNN's first major advertiser—a 10-year, $25 million deal for Bristol-Myers to be the sole sponsor for health care news. The dollar amount, as large as it sounded in press release terms, was a small percentage of Bristol-Myers' total advertising budget. More than money, however, it represented a serious commitment to cable in general and CNN in particular.

Even as Turner was trumpeting his sales achievement, the buzz on the convention floor was over Satcom III. The RCA communications satellite, successfully launched only days earlier with all its 24 transponders dedicated to providing service for cable program providers—CNN among them—had disappeared into empty space. "We're searching the heavens," RCA vice president Robert Shortal said. "Other companies with satellites are searching the heavens. . . . We honestly don't know what happened . . . for all we know, it's on its way to Mars."[5]

On the *CBS Evening News,* Walter Cronkite waxed poetic about RCA's loss.

'Twas three weeks before Christmas
And down at the Cape
The SATCOM III satellite
Seemed in such great shape.

It was RCA's baby
That NASA would fling
As it happened
The one-hundred fiftieth thing

To be launched by a Delta,
A rocket so flyable
That's considered to be
Absolutely reliable.

And from somewhere in space
Comes the seasonal call
Merry Christmas, Goodnight
And you can't win 'em all.[6]

Wherever Satcom III ended up, it wasn't in orbit. It was permanently lost, and with it the hopes of several start-up cable services, their owners left wringing their hands and praying for a miracle that never arrived. Turner, as boisterous as ever, never missed a beat, bragging that he had taken the precaution of insisting that RCA provide a backup transponder on an existing satellite should the company be unable to provide one on Satcom III. He would have been less secure and far more aggravated had he realized that RCA had made the same promise to five other companies. Six companies all competing for the two empty transponders that RCA had left on Satcom I. In the end, RCA, in its corporate wisdom, decided that it would be unfair to choose among the six companies involved and therefore elected to keep the remaining transponders for itself. When Turner received the news, he was a very small bull charging an extremely large red cape. If the megaconglomerate thought the loudmouth from Atlanta was going to be intimidated by its size and legal influence, it was mistaken. Not Ted Turner. Not now or ever.

With his own lawyer in tow, Turner stormed into RCA's Manhattan headquarters and defiantly stood his ground, threatening, daunting, pacing like an angry victim. The smugness of the RCA executives was born in a place of irreproachability. Since Turner respected no boundaries, he pushed and shoved with the kind of coercion more appropriate to prison camps than high-rise suites. "I'm a small company, and you guys may put me out of business," Turner said. "But for every drop of blood I shed, you will shed a barrel!"[7]

Legally, Turner was actually in a weak position. While his contract did provide for a backup transponder, the contingency became effective only in the event of a successful launch. Whether the lost satellite qualified was questionable, though NASA insisted that its Delta rocket performed flawlessly and its part of the space shot was successful—the satellite was lost after NASA passed control to RCA.

Knowing that the entire fate of CNN rested on getting the transponder, Turner put on a show aimed at galvanizing his workers, who were largely unaware of the crisis. He walked the aisles, his determination shouting as loud as his words. He pounded desktops, slammed phone receivers, and pulled a gift sword off the wall, swinging it wildly as if commanding a charging cavalry. With five months remaining until the announced launch date of the news channel, it was no exaggeration. He was a general leading troops into battle.

At the time, the ragtag group making up the rank and file was a grassroots assembly of dedicated workers, the majority of whom were learning as they went. They had been recruited right out of college with little more than a promise of minimum wages and maximum exposure to live television. Schonfeld and his executives were teaching the new arrivals as much about the mechanics of remote feeds and story content as they were about budgeting on a shoestring and improvising on the fly. One CNN veteran called the team "a posse of mavericks—we didn't know what we were doing, and had no choice but to make up stuff as we went along. Yet, looking back at all those sixteen-hour days, and all the tears and frustrations and cold pizza, those were the happiest moments of my life."[8]

It has been said that Ted Turner is never happier than when he is facing an impossible challenge. In the case of CNN, every element of the network seemed to be running directly in the face of disaster. The chaos that was found in the basement of Turner's Tara—the name journalists had given to the old Progressive clubhouse—was expected, as workmen knocked down walls, strung cable, and made magic out of urine-stained walls and busted windows. The chaos that swirled around the remainder of the enterprise, however, was threatening to halt what Turner called the most significant achievement in journalism.

Regardless of Schonfeld's programming plans for CNN's lineup, the entire effort was mute if Turner failed to secure a means of transmitting the telecast. And getting a transponder on Satcom I would be moot if he had no money to pay for it—and he didn't. The sale of WRET had been held up by a coalition of black activists who wanted hiring concessions to be made at the station. Furthermore, the transponder issue had been thrown into the bureaucratic lap of the FCC, which was notoriously slow in making decisions. And the only thing that Turner had less of than money was time.

With his self-imposed deadline of June 1, 1980, fast approaching, the man who loved a challenge was staring down the throat of bankruptcy. "The whole deal is crumbling," he told his Washington attorneys at a lunch meeting in April. "And when it goes, it will take everything I've got with it. We haven't got a transponder and we haven't got the Charlotte money. The banks are calling in their notes on me, and the insurance company already has. I've got three hundred people on the Cable News payroll, and no money coming in to pay them. I just had to borrow $20 million to tide me over. The interest rate is twenty-five percent. Twenty-five percent of $20 million is $5 million a year, there's twelve months in a year, and that's $400,000 a month in interest. I can't pay it."[9]

Clearly, Turner was in trouble. In yet another swing of moods, he dove inward, an unnatural quiet surrounding a swirl of mental activity as he engaged in self-reflection. As outrage gave way to doubt, Turner remembered his father and the last moments of his life. There, deep in the memory of his father's failure, Turner found his strength. "Never set a goal you can reach, or else you'll have nothing to strive for," his father had told him. His father had neglected to take his own advice. Turner could not afford to repeat the mistake.

It was as if the sun came out, a door opening to clarity. Getting CNN on the air was no longer the goal, but rather just a small step in a larger plan. Reshape television and with it, the world. Renewed, clear-headed, and invigorated by the scope of his task, Turner pushed through his insecurity and projected confidence. Persistence was the key. If his motley team of untried students and temp workers were short on experience, they were long on energy, and he pushed them to perform beyond their own perceived capabilities.

He flew to Chicago to press the banks for more time on his loans. He flew to Washington to lobby the FCC for the essential transponder. He sold CNN to cable services, executives, and the man on the street. "I'm Ted Turner, and the world as you know it is about to change," he said over and over and over again.

Turner's own priorities had shifted for the first time in his adult life. Sailing, always No. 1, had now slipped into second place behind business. Family, of course, remained No. 3. Jane and the children were waiting as usual for any leftover attention that might be deflected their way. Little was. That much had not changed.

Operating on little food and even less sleep, Turner joined his employees on the front line in May as rehearsals began in CNN's new basement studios still under construction. Amid the sound of jackhammers, drills, hammers, and saws, and an opera of shouts, thuds, and ear-piercing squeals, members of CNN's first on-air team attempted to hone their skills. Remote feeds were cued and failed to show up onscreen, microphones went dead in the middle of sentences, photos failed to materialize until they were no longer needed and then refused to disappear. Schonfeld turned improvisation into a high art form with his trademark seat-of-the-pants style. The CNN president saw an organization in disarray, and even the slightest success was a cause for celebration.

Just three weeks before the planned unveiling of CNN, the FCC awarded the news network a temporary transponder on Satcom I. It was a six-month reprieve from a stillborn launch. In the same week, the FCC also approved the sale of WRET to Westinghouse, adding $22 million to Turner's bank account. The exhale of relief from Atlanta was heard across the continent.

In the newsroom, mud was still on the floor, walls had yet to go up, and the young employees were dealing with a lack of electricity and temporary toilets. There was to be no letup, and it became Ted Kavanau's responsibility to keep them from faltering. "I've been hearing that some of you have been saying among yourselves that this thing is not gonna work! That we're not gonna be a success," Kavanau said to the group as he stood on wooden crates. "Well, I didn't bring you here to fail. You will *not* fail! You will not fail because I will not *let* you fail! If any of you cannot work under those terms, leave the room! Right now!"[10] His look was that of a lion tamer daring the big cats to attack. No one in the newsroom moved, even to shift weight.

June 1 became known around the news set as either the Day of the Long Knives or the Day the Earth Stood Still, depending on who was speaking. Either way, the message was the same: no one knew what to expect when Ted Turner threw the ceremonial switch that bounced CNN's feed off the satellite. News anchors Lois Hart and Dave Walker, married onscreen and off, were assigned the first two-hour shift on opening night. They had moved to CNN from Sacramento's KCRA-TV, where they were extremely popular anchors on the local evening news. "The mantra that everyone chanted during those early days was 'Nobody's a star. The news is the star,'" Hart said. "Well, that was fine, but we all knew the real star was Ted Turner."[11]

On the afternoon of June 1, 1980, Turner, the real star, walked across the ground floor of the CNN building and attempted to remain calm. In five hours, his network, the "future of television," the "builder of world peace," the "most significant achievement in the annals of journalism" would be on the air—maybe. At the moment, he watched workers still stringing cable, movers still unloading desks, electric typewriters still being set up after the computer system failed to function, and he wondered. Being Ted Turner, he did not wonder *if* all the pieces would somehow magically fall into place. He *knew* they would. He just wondered *how*.

At 5 P.M. that evening, he was still wondering. Hart and Walker were in makeup, Kavanau was in the director's booth, Schonfeld was pacing, last-minute details pounding their way into short-term memory, interrupted only by the pain of a hernia he had suffered and left untreated.

Outside the building, a yellow-and-white tent had been erected on the newly planted lawn where a feast of Southern vittles and drink had been arranged for some 700 guests. Turner moved among them, shaking hands, smiling and loudly extolling the merits of cable, particularly to the Democratic congressman from Georgia, Wyche Fowler Jr. Conservative activist Phyllis Schlafly joined them briefly to praise motherhood and the American family. Dr. Joyce Brothers, pursing her lips, muttered about the need for population control to NFL commissioner Peter Rozelle, who appeared to be more interested in the food.

As the sun dropped low over the Atlanta skyline, Turner took a nervous look at his watch, another at the sky, and then walked to the microphone. The combined marching bands of the Army, Navy, Air Force, and Marine Corps, which had been providing music for the event, cut to a short fanfare. Inhaling a slow and deliberate draw of air, thick with humidity and the smell of lilacs in bloom, Turner stared out at the crowd and felt all eyes on him. CNN cameras recording the unfolding event caught Turner looking misty-eyed and slightly overwhelmed by the moment. A dream realized, the impossible conquered, the reality finally sinking in for the charismatic advertising salesman who just would not give up.

"I'd like to call our ceremonies to order," Turner said, squinting into the crowd. "We should be on the air at six o'clock, as predicted, but first we have a few statements from some visitors and some people who are with us." Tom Wheeler, president of the NCTA, labeled the launch "a telepublishing event marking a watershed in providing information."[12] After everyone applauded as if that made sense, Reese Schonfeld limped to the microphone in obvious pain and reminded those in attendance that it had been only "one year, twenty-two days, and seven hours since I received that fateful telephone call from Turner." It was impossible to fathom what Schonfeld had accomplished in that time. Even *he* had difficulty with the incredible scope of the achievement.

As the Reverend William Borders from the Wheat Street Baptist Church gave a blessing, Schonfeld said his own prayer. Turner, however, wasn't praying. In fact, he was hardly listening, his eyes focused on his watch and the second hand clicking toward 6 P.M.

Past a certain age, it is difficult to look at events in life with wonder. Excitement is buried under years of disappointment, packed tight with resignation. Ted Turner never acknowledged disappointment. Rather, he looked upon his defeats as opportunities to learn. Because of that, he never closed the bridge to childhood wonder, and walked across it once again this particular Sunday afternoon as he stood before the microphone once more.

Three flags rose high atop shining staffs. At the stroke of six, CNN's cameras caught the majesty of the moment as television screens across the country were transformed into the first signal sent over the first news network, and viewers heard Ted Turner's words: "One, [the flag of] the state of Georgia, where we're located; second, the flag of the United States, which represents our country and the way we intend to serve it with the Cable News Network; and over on the other side, we have the flag of the United Nations, because we hope that CNN's international coverage and greater-depth coverage will bring, both in the country and in the world, a better understanding of how people from different nations live and work, and hopefully bring together, in brotherhood and kindness and friendship and in peace, the people of this nation and this world."[13]

As the camera panned over the guests, their eyes raised to the sky, Turner read a dedication composed by his press department, seemingly unintimidated by the sentiment of the words. For once he dared not improvise his message. He had not risked toasting with champagne. No repeat of the America's Cup this day. This was a triumph to revere and share with history.

> To act upon one's convictions while others wait,
> To create a positive force in a world where cynics abound,
> To provide information to people when it wasn't available before,
> To offer those who want it a choice;
> For the American people, whose thirst for understanding and a better life has made the venture possible;
> For the cable industry, whose pioneering spirit caused this great step forward in communications;
> And for those employees of Turner Broadcasting, whose total commitment to their company has brought us together today,
> I dedicate the news channel for America—
> The Cable News Network.

With that, as Turner placed his hand over his heart, the military bands began to play the national anthem, and Hart and Walker assumed their positions in the electronic newsroom of the future. There was no transition from music to news, other than Turner's "We're on the air," followed by "at least I hope so."

*I'm David Walker . . . and I'm Lois Hart . . . now here's the news.* With those words, CNN marched boldly into history.

Some 1.7 million sets were able to receive CNN that day, far fewer than Turner's predicted 2.5 million. Those who watched the first few minutes saw a kaleidoscope of live satellite feeds from around the world, nearly seamless as they moved from one to the next, each anchored by Hart and Walker in Atlanta—poised, unflappable, professional, regardless of what surprises came their way.

President Jimmy Carter gave the anchors and CNN their first official scoop when he visited the hospital room of his adviser, civil rights advocate Vernon Jordan,* who had been shot in an assassination attempt. Though all the national news agencies had been given advance notice of the visit, only CNN broadcast the president's press conference live, interrupting the news network's very first commercial to accomplish the coup. Actor E. G. Marshall was midway through explaining the merits of Maalox ("There are so many medications for acid indigestion or heartburn relief...") when the video switched to Dave Walker, catching him as he was still introducing Carter. Slightly-rough-around-the-edges live TV, and cablecast hours earlier than the networks' affiliated news.

For all his melodrama and hyperbole about the launch, after the opening few minutes of the first hour Turner took his son Rhett and sought out a television set capable of receiving the Atlanta Braves, who were beating the Los Angeles Dodgers. Ironically, most of the sets in the CNN offices had yet to be wired for cable.

The day following CNN's debut, the nation's critics gave the fledgling network surprisingly mixed reviews. One said CNN stood for "the Chicken Noodle Network." In the nation's capital, the TV critic for the *Washington Post* wondered why CNN had not seamlessly switched feeds from Jerusalem to Los Angeles to New York and Key West (where hapless reporter Mike Boettcher was assigned to report on the Cuban refugee flotilla). While it was true that the network cut the president off midsentence to take a live feed from Israel, and Boettcher was caught picking his nose, unaware that he was on the air, the *real* news was that CNN did it at all.

"It was better than any sane man had the right to expect," Reese Schonfeld told the trade paper *Variety* (which misspelled

---

*Vernon Jordan later became an adviser to President Bill Clinton and was a central figure in the Monica Lewinsky sex scandal.

his name "Schonfield"). The paper, however, did appreciate the enormity of CNN's accomplishment. "Here was news—alive with all its wonderful technical warts, missed cues, field correspondents winging it, the President sweating during an impromptu news conference in Ft. Wayne, a live cutaway right smack in the middle of CNN's very first paid-for commercial, a live feed for refugee-packed Miami via an untested remote right out of the packing crate—and it all worked."[14] Well, sort of.

Turner leaped into the pool of critical comments, openly sparring with the naysayers who suggested that CNN was doomed even before its opening-day snafus. *Broadcasting* magazine went on record reporting that the network was expected to lose $2.2 million per month maintaining its seven domestic and three foreign bureaus, plus paying for feeds from the UPI film service. "It doesn't bother me that I'm committing almost all I have," Turner said. "Had I known I was going to fail when I started, I would still have done it because it needs to be done. Of course, I also think we'll make a fortune."[15]

The three commercial networks looked upon the start-up news service as a pale imitation of what they already provided for the American viewer. ABC News vice president Av Westin said, "We can't broadcast everything that comes in, but much of what we don't put on I'm not sure anyone would want to see. If you live in Kansas, do you really care about the comings and goings of ministers at a conference in Luxembourg?"[16]

"What kind of dumb question is that?" Turner rebutted. "Who is that guy anyway? *I* want to know about a conference in Luxembourg. I don't know about people in Kansas, but I'm sure they might want to know too."

CBS vice president Gene Mater suggested that at an annual budget of $30 million, CNN was spending less than a quarter of what CBS does on its news product. "Makes you wonder, doesn't it?" Turner asked in response. "We can cover the world news 24 hours a day for a year for the same price those pinkos at the networks spend to give us 30 minutes of news a day for three months. And they're laughing at me?"

When told by a reporter for *Home Video* magazine that CNN lacked focus, Turner exploded: "Wait a minute! Wait a goddamn minute! You think it lacks focus? What is focus, anyway? If you're live all the time, how can you have focus? Focus means that you know where you're going. You can't focus on something unless you know what you're focusing on! Focus is something a newspaper has, because there's a day to think about it. Or with a magazine there's a month. Whoever said that is a yo-yo."[17]

Amazingly, no member of the press seemed to realize the importance of the transformation that had taken place in communications. No longer would it be necessary to wait for information. Immediacy was the theme, and world news was the product. While looking at the tree represented by CNN, the international media had been blinded to the forest. On June 1, 1980, a window was opened on the world that all of us could see and hear.

At the moment, however, all eyes were focused on Turner the loud eccentric. *National Review* called Turner "a refreshing phenomenon—a dynamic Sunbelt go-getter who testifies to the survival of those entrepreneurial energies which even the federal bureaucracies now and then neglect to repress. He represents a gut-level rejection of socialist presumptions, and brings to his work a gambler's boldness, a set of first-class Southern wiles, and a baronial confidence in his sovereignty over that which is his. All of which is bound to madden any bunch of pinkos, anywhere. Good luck, Turner."[18]

Good luck, indeed. While most of his peers at the networks were quietly hoping he would fail, Turner never seriously considered the possibility. In speaking to a group of advertisers, Turner left no doubt that CNN not only was going to succeed, but that it was only the beginning of his plans to reinvent the way the world received its news. "I'm going now for the history books," he told them. "I'm swinging for the fences." Specifically, Turner said that he intended to be "in fifty percent of the homes in this country on January 1, 1985 . . . We're wiring the whole damn country, and we're gonna do it together. We're gonna make a ton of money. We're gonna do a lot of good. And we're gonna have a lot of fun."[19]

To any who still doubted, George Babick had a piece of advice. Babick, head of CNN sales in New York, suggested, "If Ted predicted the sun would come up in the west tomorrow morning, you'd laugh and say he was full of it. But you'd still set the alarm. You wouldn't want to miss the miracle."[20]

EIGHT

# Sign of the Times

*The man's charm is lethal.*
*One minute he's swimming along*
*with a smile, then snap!*
*There's blood in the water. Your head's gone.*

Journalist John Barry on Rupert Murdoch
London
Spring 1982

**E**nlightened. That's how Ted Turner saw himself: a newly
steeded warrior leading a disenchanted world into a new
age. By early 1981, he had uncovered the heavy hand of responsibility hidden within the credibility that launching a 24-hour
news service brought, and he willingly and unexpectedly
accepted the role he saw as uniquely his. Turner intended to save
the world, one CNN viewer at a time.

Through a different route and different politics, Rupert Murdoch found himself with a similar mandate. His audiences for
the most part were readers, not viewers. Regardless, he deemed
them in need of just as much guidance as the unwashed masses
Ted Turner hoped to reach. Murdoch's vision was centered less
on helping the world as a whole than on helping himself (which,
he postulated, would ultimately help the world through the
products and services he delivered). And whereas Turner found
inspiration in the liberal Left, Murdoch, the onetime Marxist,
had given up all pretense of being a supporter of the people and
moved politically to the hard Right.

171

That was not the case, of course, early on in Murdoch's career, when he had used the influence of his Australian papers to push for the election of Gough Whitlam, a Labor Party candidate for prime minister of Australia. As Murdoch's businesses quickly became more successful, however, he saw the folly of continuing to support a politician whose power base came from unionized workers. Murdoch did a rather remarkable about-face in the middle of Whitlam's first term, staunchly supporting his Conservative opponent, Malcolm Fraser.

His first major opportunity to play right-wing political matchmaker came in the form of an Iron Butterfly otherwise known as Margaret Thatcher. The head of Britain's Conservative Party, Thatcher was poised to take control of the British government at a time when the country's Labor Party had allowed England's unions to strike their way into a crisis of public services. Garbage piled up uncollected, transportation was repeatedly halted, medical care faltered, and newspapers were shut down. The latter got Murdoch's undivided attention.

Murdoch did not like politics per se. It was power that played a Sousa march in his mind, and politics, of course, led to power. Control the politician and gain the ultimate power. Driven and inexhaustible, Murdoch began a campaign in late 1979 to use his newspapers in England to ensure that Thatcher not only was elected to office but also was well positioned under his thumb. When Murdoch telephoned Thatcher and invited her to tea at his Sun offices on Bouverie Street, she was joyous in her acceptance and enthusiastic in her approach. She came and conquered, not over tea, but rather bourbon and water, which she drank while relaxing in a chair, feet on table, shoes on floor. Murdoch, unaccustomed to such familiarity at first blush, nevertheless managed to establish a dialogue that would have far-reaching ramifications. If she had any hope of winning, Thatcher needed to reach beyond the business class, with its sophistication and designer labels, down into the blue-collar *Sun* readership. To win and essentially transform the ruling house of Great Britain, she needed Rupert Murdoch—if not all of him, at least the part that controlled the *Sun*. In exchange for an endorsement from the paper, Thatcher was willing to play the political game of tit for tat.

She had been warned about Murdoch, a man the Conservative Party wisely compared to the rhubarb plant—the stalk incredibly nourishing, the leaves extremely deadly. By agreeing to accept Murdoch's endorsement, Thatcher was essentially accepting his as-yet-unmade demands, which were certain to be politically risky for her and financially lucrative for him. As the normally union-friendly *Sun* began to swing its weight away from the Labor Party to the capitalist Conservative, only the most politically naive missed the point. On Election Day, the *Sun*'s banner headline advised its readers to VOTE TORY THIS TIME. IT'S THE ONLY WAY TO STOP THE ROT. *Sun* subscribers heeded the advice, and on the strength of their votes pushed Margaret Thatcher into power.

With a newfound friend comfortably in power in England, Murdoch flew back to America intent on making similar inroads in Washington, D.C. Jimmy Carter's presidency was flagging, prompting Murdoch to set his sights on Congress, which, by no small coincidence, set its sights on him. Murdoch was drawn into a Senate hearing investigating the financing of Boeing airplanes by the Export-Import Bank. The planes were purchased by Ansett, the Australian domestic airline that Murdoch had acquired several months earlier as a by-product of his acquisition of Melbourne's 0 Network whose parent company owned both businesses. Murdoch's first decision as head of the airline was to postpone the order of a fleet of European-made Airbus 300 planes and purchase Boeing jets instead. Not that Boeing made a better product. In reality, an order from Boeing would actually take longer to be delivered, thereby increasing the cost to the airline in lost seat sales.

Murdoch's desire to buy American was motivated by his intention to elevate his importance and power in the United States. If Boeing was able to supply those jets with financing on equal or better terms than Airbus, Murdoch saw no reason not to utilize the purchase to brighten his own star in his adopted country. Although anxious to make the sale, Boeing had little control of financing purchases and directed Murdoch to its bank, Export-Import. That a meeting was arranged with Ex-Im on February 16, 1980, in Washington, D.C., had more to do with Murdoch's previously scheduled appointment with President Jimmy Carter at the White House than any particular request by Murdoch. It was, however, a convenience that would haunt him on the Senate floor three months later.

Murdoch was successful in convincing the Ex-Im banking officials to loan him money at 8 percent—an interest rate considerably lower than the bank might otherwise have offered, but equal to the deal that Airbus had quoted. When the Boeing order was placed and word leaked out in Washington that Murdoch had gotten a special financing arrangement from the bank, it was only a matter of time before journalists, and then the Senate, questioned whether President Carter might have played a part in the negotiations in exchange for an endorsement from the *Post*.

As the nation's capital swirled itself into a Charybdis over the possibility and Murdoch played into the intrigue by offering to testify in front of the Senate, the players assembled on May 12 and 13 to hear the whole truth and nothing but. That Murdoch told the truth that day is hardly surprising. After all, he had nothing to hide. What the Senate failed to grasp in its self-posturing was that Murdoch was on stage, performing for the honorable members of government with verve no less melodramatic than if he were on Broadway. What better way to introduce yourself to the Senate than by being exculpated by its most honored members. By the time Murdoch was finished with his testimony, in which he took exception to the overzealous theorizing by the media, he had hustled his way into the good graces of the Senate committee by complimenting them on their own efforts at maintaining high ethical standards.

"I want to say that you are a remarkable man, Mr. Murdoch," Senator William Proxmire said at the conclusion of the hearing. "We have had a lot of witnesses before this committee, but I was especially impressed with what a quick study you are. You seem to know a whale of a lot about an industry you've just gotten into. You are very refreshing, intelligent, and an effective witness, and responsive," the Democratic senator from Wisconsin added. As Murdoch left the Senate floor, he reminded himself yet again why he loved America—land of the free, home of the pushover.

Soon after his Senate appearance, Murdoch publicly endorsed Ronald Reagan for the presidency, certain that Reagan's brand of bellicose, hard-line rhetoric spoke to the ultra-conservative voters of America. Though Murdoch could not vote, he knew that a Republican in the nation's highest office was beneficial to his burgeoning businesses, and mandated that the Post editors produce stories slanted in favor of Reagan. It did not matter if not all the facts in the articles were accurate. It mattered only that Reagan was elected.

Proof that a victorious Reagan appreciated the help came in the form of a presidential plaque honoring Murdoch's unique contribution to the campaign several months after the presidential inauguration. Murdoch cherished the honor, though not for the reason Reagan might have thought. As always, all things centered on business, and he had very special plans for the fortieth U.S. president.

In January 1981, however, Murdoch was concentrating his efforts yet again in England, where he made an offer to buy the venerable Times, London's most celebrated newspaper, and one whose sundry editors became physically ill at the thought of Rupert Murdoch taking charge. Unfortunately for the traditional editorial management, the newspaper had been losing money for many years. That was not much of a crisis for the owner, Roy Thomson, a Canadian who in 1964 was given a hereditary barony and became known as Lord Thomson of Fleet for his ownership of any number of newspapers. For Thomson, publishing was a passion.

When Roy Thomson died in 1976, his son Kenneth inherited his title and leadership of the Thomson Corporation. Kenneth's passion lay more in making money than in publishing. After four years of watching profits spiral downward on the *Times* and its weekend sister newspaper, the *Sunday Times,* and enduring unsuccessful battles with the unions to allow modernization of the printing plants, he put both papers on the sales block. The *Times'* main attraction was its reputation as the British newspaper of record since 1785. That such a crown jewel should fall into the hands of a "sensationalist gossipmonger" was unthinkable— to all but Kenneth Thomson, that is.

*Sunday Times* editor Harold Evans and *Times* editor William Rees-Mogg attempted on their own to assemble a consortium of investors to take over ownership of the papers, but with little success. Although there was no shortage of would-be buyers, Thomson had set a bid deadline of two months and a week after he announced the publications were for sale. It was an impossible time frame for all but the wealthiest of investors.

By the close of business on December 31, 1980, four serious bids had been officially tendered from Associated Newspapers, publisher of the *Daily Mail*; Robert Maxwell, who had previously fought with Murdoch over the purchase of the *News of the World*; the Atlantic Richfield oil company, publisher of the *Observer*; and Rupert Murdoch—his the last of the offers to cross Thomson's desk. His bid was also the most challenging, for while Murdoch had a history of tolerating newspapers that continued to leak red ink as the *Times* might logically be expected to do, he was also the bidder most likely to interfere in the editorial content of his publications. "Professionally, everything Murdoch

touches turns to rubbish," said Jake Ecclestone, head of the *Times'*
journalists' union.[1]

Surprisingly, when Evans and Rees-Mogg evaluated the various bidders from an editorial standpoint for Thomson, both
men selected Murdoch as the least objectionable suitor. Evans
was initially adamant about the need to restrict the level at which
Murdoch had editorial control of the newspapers, though his
opinion was admittedly based on hearsay since he had never
actually dealt with Murdoch on a professional or personal basis.
Murdoch had heard of Evans by reputation as well, and even
before the decision was made over which bid Kenneth Thomson
would accept, Murdoch requested a lunch meeting with Evans to
discuss "a business arrangement."

Because Murdoch was a clear front-runner, Evans agreed to
meet, albeit with reluctance, given his rather scurrilous reputation among writers. In the course of the hourlong lunch, however, Murdoch was the ultimate seducer. Quiet, relaxed,
complimentary, he wooed Evans with a combination of intelli-
gence, charm, and guile to which Evans was completely defense-
less. The editor had come prepared to be intimidated and
unimpressed. Instead, he left injected with an elixir of Murdoch
magic: part truth, part promise, and all spun into an illusion
Evans desperately wanted to see.

With aversion suddenly tumbling down like the walls of Jeri-
cho, Murdoch was in a most remarkable position. Though still
going through the motions of being examined and questioned
by a team of government and publishing wise men assembled
for the specific purpose of vetting the would-be buyer of
Britain's most distinguished journal, Murdoch had essentially
won the newspaper, and on very economical terms. He had bid
a meager million pounds to enter the contest and had increased
his offer to 12 million several weeks later. Even the higher figure
was considerably less than the combined *Times* and *Sunday Times*
actually were worth. What made Murdoch's offer attractive was

his willingness to assume the newspapers' debts and his solemn agreement to give his employees editorial freedom.

In Evans' book, *Good Times, Bad Times,* he said Murdoch approached the vetting process like "someone visiting a friend in hospital, walking quietly, speaking softly." That was exactly how Murdoch saw the *Times*—critically ill and in need of emergency surgery to save its life. While Evans looked upon Murdoch's behavior as respectful and reverent, he completely missed his actual agenda: that of giving the board of mediators exactly what they needed to fill their bellies, with a pat on the back to seal the negotiations.

The fodder that Murdoch fed his vetters included the pledge that he would have no say in the editorial makeup of the paper or, for that matter, in the selection of the editors themselves. The extent to which the committee believed him is evident in the speed with which they approved the sale. The day following his private question-and-answer session, Murdoch was crowned the *Times* and *Sunday Times* owner-apparent. At a press conference to announce the deal, Evans and Rees-Mogg stood side by side Times Newspapers editor in chief Denis Hamilton, who dubbed the victor "one of the greatest newspaper executives in the world today."[2] Murdoch smiled in complete agreement.

Not all were as thrilled as Kenneth Thomson to discover that pending government opposition, Murdoch had added two more major newspapers to his growing collection. Among them were reporters for the *Times,* who met Murdoch for the first time on January 26, 1981, as he made an official visit to the newsroom. In answering their questions, Murdoch said, "I can sell myself to you as the least of the alternative evils. As regards the guarantees themselves . . . I think I have locked myself in, particularly with the power I have given [to the national directors] of absolute right of hiring and firing of editors and given them the right to be a self-perpetuating body. . . . What if I found a way of tearing up all those guarantees and fired an editor? The answer is there would be a terrible public stink and it would destroy the paper. . . . I get on with these people or I get out. Otherwise I would destroy what I am attempting to buy."[3]

It was a potent argument that found its target among the writers packed into the newsroom. None thought to question the reasoning set forth by the man who most certainly was to become their boss. Not one brought up the fact that Murdoch had made similar pledges to every newspaper and television network he purchased, only to swing the ax with the abandon of a lead guide clearing brush in the Serengeti. The *Times* surely would be no different, but for the moment Murdoch intended to play the role of savior. "I am not seeking to acquire these papers to turn them into something entirely different. They will remain editorially independent newspapers of high quality," he said.[4]

His unlikely ally in his efforts was Harold Evans, who began to write editorials not only backing Murdoch but also elevating his ethics to the point that sainthood was not entirely out of the question. "He is certainly now preferred to any of the other would-be corporate purchases because of his energy, his directness, his publishing flair and, above all, the commitments he has given on editorial independence," Evans wrote.[5] What Evans knew, and others did not, was that he was Murdoch's prime candidate to take over the editorship of the *Times* from Rees-Mogg, who had announced his intention to release the reins of the paper upon successful completion of the sale.

Murdoch, of course, had made much of his agreement to give up any say in the decision regarding the paper's new editor, and therefore moved with characteristic tact and determination to cast the illusion of impartiality at the first meeting of the *Times* board of directors after his purchase was approved. On February 17, 1981, the board met in London and was startled to discover that Murdoch had appointed a new member to their ranks. Sir Edward Pickering, who had worked at the *Daily Mirror* at the same time Murdoch did in 1953, had been brought out of retirement to fill a vacancy created by the resignation of a board member upon the sale of the newspapers. Murdoch was all innocence and culpability when informed by the board that they were responsible for new board nominations. He offered to dismiss Pickering if that was what the board demanded. It was in reality what the board wanted, but not what they collectively requested. Rather, they merely admonished Murdoch for his oversight and welcomed a man who Murdoch felt sure would cooperate with his dictates.

Rees-Mogg made an impassioned recommendation that Charles Douglas-Home, nephew of former British prime minister Lord Alexander Douglas-Home, be offered the editorship of the *Times*. Douglas-Home had worked for more than a decade at the paper in various positions and was a wise choice. Though rather unexceptional in personality, Douglas-Home had both the connections and education to handle the job, as well as the support of the *Times* staff.

After several board members agreed with Rees-Mogg that Douglas-Home was an excellent candidate, Murdoch took the floor and gave a sweeping endorsement to Harold Evans, labeling him the "finest journalist in England" and exactly the type of editor Murdoch needed to mold the *Times* into the paper of the future for all of Great Britain. It was classic Murdoch in the sense that it placed the responsibility of the newspaper's success not on Evans but on the board itself. Murdoch suggested that if he were denied his choice, his entire investment would be at risk. His entire rationale made no sense from a journalistic point of view, since Douglas-Home was an accomplished journalist who had demonstrated his business acumen on various occasions, as well as his ability to play politics when necessary.

Evans, however, had effectively edited the *Sunday Times* for more than a dozen years but recently had begun to coast on the reputation of the publication. What once was a fine newspaper that launched investigations into corruption and greed eventually settled into a rather predictable caricature of its former self, primarily due to Evans' lack of diligent involvement. Though he was a whirlwind of activity, his accomplishments appeared to be mostly behind him—until he was plucked from one pedestal and placed on another, courtesy of Rupert Murdoch.

Perhaps more amazing than Murdoch's selection of Evans as new editor of the *Times* was Evans' eagerness to work with Murdoch. In the course of a month, Evans had gone from Murdoch basher to supporter in print and in private, most likely because of Murdoch's promises for his future. That Evans believed those promises, given Murdoch's reputation with previous editors, was perplexing. "The man's charm is *lethal*," journalist John Barry later said of Murdoch. "One minute he's swimming along with a smile, then *snap!* There's blood in the water. Your head's gone."[6]

Nearly all the directors voting that day judged Douglas-Home to be the better candidate, yet they selected Evans for the job, less on his talent than on their desire to keep Murdoch happy and the *Times* alive. The bigger calamity was not that Evans would do a poor job maintaining the integrity of England's most famous newspaper, but rather that Murdoch would tire of the financial drain the publication would surely generate and close the *Times* down completely. With Evans confirmed, Murdoch had a sudden opening to fill at the *Sunday Times* and elected Evans' deputy editor, Frank Giles, for the position. Or rather, he once again *suggested* Giles to the board of directors, and they once again went along with his choice. Giles was a well-respected journalist and historian, having spent much of his career covering international politics. At the time of his promotion, Giles was nearing retirement age. As such, he was viewed by many as a stopgap compromise to head the *Sunday Times* since that paper, unlike its daily counterpart, was actually making money, albeit not a lot of it.

With the purchase accomplished and the executives in place, Murdoch returned to New York to watch the shakedown process that inevitably follows a change of ownership. The difference was that Murdoch openly courted dissension rather than harmony, pitting one executive against the other in a form of survival of the fittest. Other than seeing his businesses prosper and earn profits, Murdoch savored this part of the game. "He'd shake the trees and see what fell," said a writer who worked for Murdoch in both London and New York. "It was sadistic, but it worked. Those who were left standing at the end of the day were the best."[7]

Though Murdoch was unable to hire or fire journalists as part of his prepurchase agreement, his contract did not prevent him from tampering with the business end of the paper. He tore through the staff and began a wholesale firing of marketing and advertising personnel, removing longtime staffers, but never without a guilt-soothing salve of severance pay. He then turned to the reporters whose jobs were virtually guaranteed by contracts. The problem, as Murdoch saw it, was that there simply was too many of them—280 at first count. To maneuver around his own agreement and theirs, Murdoch offered a month's pay for each year of service to the paper for any journalist who willingly resigned. It made no difference to the new owner which writers left and which stayed. In a business based on profit, anyone is expendable, and nearly 30 took Murdoch up on his offer.

Unfortunately, the deal did not change the actual employee count by much. During the transition, Evans had brought over key players from the *Sunday Times* to help him at his new position. From Evans' view, the *Times'* readership had stagnated because of the very reputation that caused Murdoch to buy the newspaper. It didn't matter how respected a newspaper was if few people actually were bothering to read it. Within the first few months of Evans' tenure at the *Times,* radical changes took place. New typefaces began appearing in crisper layouts. Photos took on prominence, as did a conservative columnist hired to promote the views of Margaret Thatcher, whose administration was suffering under the nation's increased unemployment.

Murdoch celebrated his fiftieth birthday on March 11, 1981, in Australia at an elaborate party conceived by his wife and produced by a team of professionals who transformed Cavan with flowers and favors for family members gathered to pay homage to the man who had made them all extremely wealthy. Though Anna included fireworks and screened a film highlighting her husband's business achievements, it was Dame Elisabeth[*] who set the tone by toasting her son for his "wisdom."

Ted Turner would have argued that wisdom had nothing to do with Murdoch's success. If it had, he would not have had so many money-losing properties among his collection of newspapers, television stations, real estate, and airlines. Turner liked to think that *he* operated from a position of instinct, and it was a perception he presented for public consumption. In actuality, a great deal of pre-planning went into each of his seemingly snap decisions, a by-product of his training as a yachtsman and captain.

For a man who once said that "sailing is like screwing; you can never get enough,"[8] he informally retired from the sport at the end of 1980 after placing third in the America's Cup. His failure in the race was blamed less on his sailing ability than on his lack of concentration. Now more determined than ever to make CNN a success, Turner had far less time for his sports and sailing teams as well as his family, who continued to finish far behind in priority. Turner the Enlightened began crossing the country, preaching at every stop about the dire consequences of the world's lack of discipline in population growth, environmental concerns, and moral values. In what had become a familiar coda, he not only pointed to the commercial television networks for failing to respond to the disintegration of ethics and responsible behavior, but also alleged that the Big Three had actually caused many of the problems.

---

[*]Elisabeth Murdoch was awarded her title for her work with the Royal Children's Hospital in Melbourne.

"I've realized how unimportant materialism is. That's where this country is going wrong. We've become too materialistic and I think television is mainly responsible. Values and achievements are much more important than possessions," he said before taking on the challenge of correcting the problem himself. "There're a lot of wrongs that need righting. I won't stop and rest until they have all been righted—which means I probably won't stop and rest."[9]

And he didn't. In early 1981, Turner flew to cable conventions and advertising meetings and right into America's heartland in an effort to convince businesses that CNN was at the forefront of a boom in cable viewership. His news network continued to hemorrhage money at an alarming $3 million a month, with advertisers slow to pour cash into a business whose future was tentative at best.

Turner's problem centered on the limited access available on aging cable systems that often had fewer than 12 channels, all previously allocated to other networks. CNN fared better with newer systems that saw in CNN a public service guaranteed to please municipal authorities responsible for granting and renewing cable franchises. It was the newer systems that provided what little proof Turner had that cable would continue to grow during the remainder of the century.

That any advertisers believed his pitch was a strong testament to Turner's sales abilities. CNN soon managed to convince some 50 advertisers that having their message on an unproven network was worth the investment—even without ratings numbers to support Turner's claims of viewership. Since no ratings service had yet organized a system to monitor cable viewers, it was little more than blind faith that got companies such as Bristol-Myers and Procter & Gamble interested. "The cable viewer is different than the normal TV viewer," said Robert L. Turner, Bristol-Myers' director of media and program services. "He watches more TV, has a larger family, and is more upscale."[10]

Proving that point to others was a major obstacle for Turner, since demographic studies of cable viewers were as elusive as ratings. "The onus is on CNN to produce evidence that these homes are upscale," said William Tenebruso, senior vice president at Kenyon & Eckhardt Advertising, who remained unconvinced along with 90 percent of the country. Now, agencies were forced to rely on that most unpredictable of entries: Ted Turner's version of reality.

When it became obvious that the money being generated by WTBS would not cover the continuing losses sustained by CNN, Turner announced that TBS was considering a stock offer of one million new shares to finance company operations. Yet, with the announcement of 1981 first-quarter pre-tax losses estimated at $6.5 million for TBS, any thought of a new stock issue was abandoned, and Turner made no official statement on the situation—a rarity in itself. He did jump, however, at the opportunity to address the American Newspaper Publishers Association at its annual convention, telling the assembled publishers to "get in bed with the head of your local cable station owner. Be his best friend. Give him anything he wants," before adding, "and if you can, sell your newspaper. It's not that your newsgathering methods are outdated. Your communications methods are."[11]

Although Murdoch viewed any talk of the demise of newspapers as the ludicrous rantings of a deluded mind, he could not completely dismiss Turner's prophecies about the direction of television. Yet, where Turner saw cable, Murdoch saw satellite. "I don't see any fun in wiring a lot of homes," Murdoch said. "The way to make money is to buy a cable franchise and sell it quickly."[12]

It was a time when satellite service was an expensive proposition, with dishes costing tens of thousands of dollars, and networks the only buyers. Murdoch saw the potential of beaming signals directly into viewers' homes. No wires, less cost. "Murdoch sees around corners," one former aide said.[13] In this case, the future was more distant than even Murdoch predicted. It was enough to convince people that cable, which *was* in a limited number of people's homes, had a chance to compete against the omnipotent networks.

No one was more outspoken on the damage that commercial television was doing to media competition in the country than Ted Turner was. By late May 1981, in fact, he sued the networks along with the White House in the first of several far-reaching pieces of litigation aimed at opening up accessibility to the news. At the center of Turner's court case was CNN's exclusion from the network pool that routinely covered the White House. CNN head Reese Schonfeld pointed to so-called tight pools, in which only one television camera was allowed to cover an event, with the three commercial networks dictating the feed that was made available to other broadcasters. For Turner, it relegated CNN to a subservient status that was unacceptable if the news network was ever to be taken seriously. "The Constitution guarantees us equal access to newsworthy events in the White House," Turner said, "and by God, equal access is what we intend to have."

While the White House attempted to downplay its own role in any exclusion of CNN, the networks quickly countered Turner's claims by saying there was no merit to the suit. "Pool material has always been available to anyone wanting it, including the Cable News Network," an official release from NBC stated. "CNN has always gotten the material for charges far below cost. CNN just isn't willing to make the financial commitment to the pool."[14]

But Turner was not about to stop talking or fighting, as ABC found out to its surprise when it tried to book satellite time to transmit live coverage of Prince Charles' wedding in London, only to learn that CBS, NBC, and *CNN* had taken all available feeds. "Suddenly, ABC was reminded what the word *pool* means," Turner said, gap-toothed smile stretching from ear to ear.

In the months that followed, cable news generated a wash of publicity, beginning with CNN's hiring of ABC Chicago newscaster Sandi Freeman for its first prime-time interview hour, *The Freeman Report*. With the potential to compete successfully with the network's prime-time news hours as well as with ABC's *Nightline, The Freeman Report* represented a maturing for the fledgling cable service and the opportunity to attract highly visible political leaders to its programming day.

Though the networks continued to downplay the inroads that cable was having on the ratings, the trade media began to float rumors of competitive news channels being planned by ABC, CBS, and NBC. Of the group, ABC was the first to make it official with the announcement of a joint venture with Westinghouse Electric for a 24-hour news service called the Satellite NewsChannel. Without apology, ABC's video division, under whose auspices the service was formed, declared plans to "knock Turner out of the box." Unwittingly, the ABC challenge was exactly what CNN needed as proof that its concept was a hit.

Within weeks, Turner announced the formation of a second CNN offering, tentatively titled CNN II. The all-headline news service was structured to repeat news, weather, and sports every half hour nonstop. Turner leased transponders on Hughes Electronics' Galaxy I satellite and planned the launch of CNN II for January 1982, six months before the ABC–Westinghouse service was to be available. In addition, Turner pledged an advertising campaign budgeted at $80 million to launch the new network and buttress CNN. He announced the news in Boston while attending the sixth annual Cable Television Administration and Marketing Society convention. There, he told a standing-room-only audience, "Those no-good SOB's who are trying to sneak in the back door aren't about to put *me* out of business," as he flicked the ashes of his cigar into a coffee cup in the no-smoking ballroom of the Copley Plaza Hotel. He then walked over to a nearby piano and played a dirge for Group W Westinghouse. "It's a second-rate, horseshit operation," he claimed without making any effort to clarify. "The networks are in a state of panic. They're losing control of the news," he went on, suggesting that CNN had inflicted "tremendous damage" to the broadcast networks' ratings.[15]

Even as the networks stumbled over themselves in an effort to appear unfazed by the hyperbole and to dismiss a slight decline in ratings as attributable to CNN, there was genuine concern that their employee pool would be raided to fill some 500 new jobs generated by the two competing new cable news services. Compounding the situation, Turner expanded the reach of the original CNN to blanket all of Europe, Asia, and Australia. With the launch of Turner Broadcasting International under the presidency of Henry Gillespie, CNN was seen around the globe, allowing Turner to use the service to push his own issues and ideals across borders previously closed to all but signals such as Radio Free America.

Any doubt that Turner the man had taken on international political potency was dispelled when Fidel Castro invited the head of CNN to visit Cuba as his guest. Castro regularly watched the network via a satellite dish smuggled onto the island after CNN telecast Cuba's May Day parade in 1981—the first live television beamed from Cuba in more than 20 years. It included a speech by Castro, aired in Spanish but translated for American audiences. "I just wanted to let you know that I think CNN is the most objective source of news," Castro wrote in a personal letter to Turner, and issued an invitation for the media executive to visit his island at his earliest convenience.[16]

Turner accepted Castro's invitation in early 1982. He took a commercial flight from Miami to Havana on February 12, accompanied by three crew members, including a new girlfriend, Liz Wickersham, a onetime beauty contest winner and *Playboy* cover girl. Jane Turner, as always, stayed at home. On communist soil for the first time in his life, Turner approached the experience with naive exuberance. He smoked Cuban cigars, visited Havana's famed Tropicana nightclub, toured schools and factories with Castro as his guide, and caught a Cuban baseball game. The high-light of the four-day trip was a duck-hunting excursion on the south coast of the island—Turner, Castro, and their interpreters, wading in marshes and armed with what the dictator claimed were the only two shotguns in all of Cuba, poised to shoot endan-gered West Indian whistling ducks. Kill they did, with Turner's three ducks ultimately stuffed and presented to him as a gift from *El Presidente*.

Back in America, Turner faced the harsh assessment of right-wing critics who found his camaraderie with the Cuban leader to be glaringly un-American at a time when the Cold War was rag-ing in full armada. "I'm a very curious person," Turner said to a reporter from the *Atlanta Constitution*. "It was the first time I'd ever been to a communist country, and I was just interested in learning a little about how it worked. I just went down there as Citizen Turner," he said.[17] Perhaps. Yet, Citizen Turner returned a transformed man.

For the first time in his life, Turner found himself privy to unique information. He had gotten a glimpse into a world that no American diplomat had been allowed to explore, and he felt the need to use this knowledge to spread harmony among nations. "I'm the only man on the planet ever to fly on Cuba's Air Force One with their president and on America's Air Force One with our president. Look, this shows what I'm talking about," he said, pointing to a photo of the hunting expedition with Castro. "People are not all that different—all this killing and arms race is for nothing. Twenty-two attempts on his life by the CIA and I'm sitting next to him with a loaded rifle! Can you believe that? I could've shot him in the back."[18]

Of course, Turner did not shoot Castro in the back or any other body part. Rather, he convinced the Cuban leader to shoot a promotional video for CNN in which Castro said, "When there's trouble in the world, I turn to CNN."[19] It is difficult to imagine any network president being able to accomplish that coup, yet for Turner it was not even a hard sell. After all, he and Castro were two comrades, drinking tequila and sharing cigars, ogling women and feasting on barely cooked meat. "Castro's not a communist," Turner explained with an enthusiasm that surprised Reese Schonfeld. "He's like me—a dictator."[20]

The transformed captain of a new vessel had officially found his next calling: restorer of the world. What began as a notion piggybacked to his newest baby, CNN, now found shape in the form of public responsibility. "I'm here to serve as the communicator who gets people together. I want to start dealing with issues like disarmament, pollution, soil erosion, population control, alternative energy sources," Turner said.[21] It was a challenge that would eventually lead him into royal palaces and executive mansions, but not before putting him in direct competition with a man who had already gone that route, but for a very different reason.

Rupert Murdoch was notching his belt with political connections second to none in those industrialized nations from which he hoped to secure limitless wealth and influence. In a matter of months, however, the two executives would clash on an unexpected playing field, with the fallout from the battle destined to alter their lives and the lives of millions of people who would follow their lead.

# NINE

# Adolf Writes a Diary

*What's happened to the* Sunday Times?
*Rupert Murdoch has, for one thing,*
*with his talent for turning what he touches into dross.*

New York Times editorial
Spring 1983

It can be said of all great leaders that their stars must shine the brightest. Surely that was the case with Rupert Murdoch and Ted Turner, each man charged by the power he possessed, yet in constant need of the next fix to preserve his position. As the two media-moguls-on-the-make entered 1982, they found themselves in remarkably similar positions. Both men had emerged on the world stage, generating controversial headlines as they pushed their way into new arenas. Both men were at the helm of businesses losing millions of dollars. And both men were at the mercy of their own chief executives, who were attempting to bathe in the spotlight's glow.

Murdoch looked at *Times* editor Harold Evans and wondered how he could have been so wrong. The *Times* continued to bleed red ink, and rather than tightening his grip and ruling with a firmer hand, Evans started to panic under the stress of wearing the crown. Overwhelmed by the responsibility of publishing a daily newspaper, and vacillating in the tone and political posture it should assume, Evans was a Thoroughbred, locked in a stable and smelling the first hint of smoke and fire. In the initial two months of 1982, his movements became frantic, his memos convoluted, and his decisions based more on pleasing his boss than on publishing a newspaper. As a result, the *Times* lacked focus and missed stories, delivery deadlines, and readers.

The journalists looking to Evans for leadership instead found confusion, and began to form a grassroots effort to remove him in favor of their original choice, Charles Douglas-Home, whose time, it seemed, at last had arrived. Though aware of consternation within his ranks, Evans was far more concerned with what he saw as Murdoch's lack of guidance, including his refusal to grant Evans a definite editorial budget. In a variety of memos, Evans asked Murdoch for input, only to be lambasted by the News Corporation chairman in a return memo for his inability to make his own decisions:

> My chief area of concern about the paper is one I have raised with you several times: the paper's stand on major issues. Of course, it takes attitudes, but I fail to find any consistency in them, a thing a great newspaper must be seen to hold. Just what the position is, it is your duty to define, and it cannot be mine. But it must be defined with clarity and authority and even repetition.[1]

For months, Murdoch had been chafing at Evans' open criticism of Margaret Thatcher in favor of candidates from other parties. It had a profound effect on Murdoch's power base and was reflected in his own continued handling of Evans, who clearly was not following Murdoch's policies. Adding to the dilemma was the rising losses sustained at the *Times*. Oblivious, Evans continued to hire high-priced journalists in total disregard for Murdoch's effort to tame losses.

Economic analysts were not surprised, therefore, when Murdoch began to send signals to the newspapers' unions that costs had to be cut, and quickly. When the unions failed to respond—at least to Murdoch's satisfaction—he called a special meeting of top-level *Times* executives to inform them that he intended to close both newspapers if union concessions were not initiated immediately. With an impending sense of imminent foreclosure, investigative reporters from Frank Giles' *Sunday Times,* researching the details of Murdoch's losses, uncovered some startling news. Murdoch had transferred the rights to the titles *Times* and *Sunday Times* from Times Newspapers to News International, a division of Murdoch's News Corporation, essentially removing Times Newspapers' two most important assets, apparently in preparation to close the company.

The *Times* board of directors was alerted to the transfer, of which they had no previous knowledge. Baron Dacre of Glanton, Hugh Trevor-Roper, a ranking member of the board, announced that the removal of company assets was a "prima facie violation of the terms" of Murdoch's purchase of the newspapers and a "gross incivility."[2] Specifically, Trevor-Roper referred to the section of the parliamentary decree permitting the Murdoch purchase by stating:

> News International shall not without the consent of a majority of the independent national directors procure or permit anything to be done which shall result in Times Newspapers selling or otherwise disposing of any interest in the *Times* or *Sunday Times*.[3]

Outrage among *Times* employees reached fever pitch when Murdoch revealed he had told both Evans and Giles of his plans to transfer ownership of the titles, and both editors had approved of the move. He claimed he was totally innocent of any wrongdoing, suggesting that the transfer of the titles was for accounting purposes and that he in fact disposed of nothing, since he still possessed ownership of the titles.

Evans reacted with perceived confusion, claiming that he had not realized the impact of Murdoch's transfer, and in a dramatic show of innocence asked *Times* reporters to begin an internal investigation of their own, eventually publishing a story in his paper about Murdoch's breach of promise. It was not an act to win the publisher's praise. Rather ironically, the piece was used by Murdoch in his favor, for by allowing its publication, he was somehow deemed innocent by default. Evans was not so fortunate.

Mere days after Evans took his publisher to task for seeming impropriety, he found his own head on the chopping block. Murdoch requested Evans' resignation and was turned down by the defiant editor, who presumed that he could only be fired legitimately by the national board overseeing the newspapers' administration. In theory, he was right. Theory has little to do with life where money is concerned, however, and Evans quietly began to negotiate a severance package that might minimize the sting of his termination. He eventually settled for nearly $300,000 in cash and his company car without ever protesting to the national overseers, and was immediately replaced by Charles Douglas-Home.

As the Evans era at the *Times* was playing its coda, across the Atlantic in Atlanta, CNN president Reese Schonfeld was facing a similar fate, and for a similar reason. During his entire three years at CNN, Schonfeld had conducted business with an autocratic determination and strength. As the popularity of the cable network grew, so did Schonfeld's grasp on authority. Where he once cut corners, he now spent freely. Certain of his position and fed by its power, Schonfeld made the mistake of believing he was indispensable to both CNN and Ted Turner. He was incorrect on both counts.

In the early months of 1982, Schonfeld became involved in a struggle with Sandi Freeman's agent, Al Geller, over control of *The Freeman Report*. The interview series had been floundering in the ratings, and Schonfeld laid the blame on Freeman. Geller criticized Schonfeld for tampering with the guest lineup, which was changed frequently and at the last moment in an effort to keep the show topical. The set-to ended, as these things typically do, with a show of power and a sudden dismissal—in this case, Freeman's.

Schonfeld had not consulted Turner before making the decision. Nor did he bother to inform Turner when he hired television personality Mike Douglas at a salary of $1 million a year to front a Hollywood-based interview show. For all his skills at molding CNN into a legitimate and respected network, Schonfeld neglected to remember that the spotlight belonged to the network's owner. It proved to be a costly underestimation of Turner's ability to shed excess when he spotted it, regardless of the seeming worth to his empire. In May, Reese Schonfeld, the man who crafted CNN from a dream and a prayer, was fired. Though Turner kept him on in a consultation capacity, his presence on the CNN board was more figurehead than resource.

"You can't have a twenty-four-hour news network that's totally run by one person . . . and Reese wanted to make every decision himself. It just wasn't the kind of management style that was going to make the organization strong in the long run," Turner remarked about Schonfeld's firing.[4]

Turner appointed Burt Reinhardt as acting president of CNN, a logical choice since as head of CNN's news operations, Reinhardt had the necessary technical experience. What he did not have was a solid business and financial background. Both would have been beneficial, for as Reinhardt learned upon assuming the reins, CNN was nearly bankrupt. Checks were barely making it into the bank on Thursday to make payroll on Friday. CNN II, which had gone on the air as CNN Headline News, was under the control of senior producer "Mad Dog" Kavanau and was equally drained of funds. Viewers of both networks had no way of knowing that the electricity to the studios was about to be turned off for nonpayment of bills—and right at the moment that ABC-Westinghouse was about to debut its Satellite NewsChannel and give CNN its first real competition.

Suddenly, it did not seem to matter that Turner had renewed Sandi Freeman's contract and did not hire Mike Douglas. It mattered only that 24-hour television news was not able to pay for itself and was days away from having to fold its tent. Though desperate, Turner reacted in calculated fashion, taking a second mortgage on his house and requesting prepayments from certain advertisers. At best these were stopgap measures, though Turner regarded them less as survival tactics than as aggressive business maneuvers by a nimble executive.

In the first few months of Reinhardt's tenure, the lack of available funds colored every judgment, making the already cautious executive nearly apoplectic when a major decision had to be made. The situation became even more evident when the Satellite NewsChannel (SNC) went on the air on June 21, 1982. CNN Headline News, though in the market six months earlier, was instantly the underdog, being outspent and outviewed (SNC was available to 2.6 million subscribers, while CNN HN had less than half that amount).

Uncertainty reigned at both CNN and CNN HN, but never more so than on July 9, when a Pan American World Airways jet carrying 146 passengers crashed on takeoff from New Orleans International Airport. As producers searched the satellite feeds for video of the crash site, Reinhardt refused permission for a camera crew to be sent to the scene. Under Schonfeld, the policy was always move fast and pay later. With Reinhardt, it was a balancing act to keep the business afloat without alerting viewers to the seriousness of the fiscal situation.

SNC was immediately on the air with footage from its New Orleans–affiliated station. An SNC reporter was at the scene. CNN and CNN Headline News were left to deal with wire-copy reports and a telephone hookup from the spokesman at the airport. It was a humiliation that made Turner realize Scotch tape and safety pins were not adequate to save his Cable News Network from a major crash-and-burn.

What might have been a last gasp for anyone else became smelling salts for Ted Turner. He was a man reenergized as if by the fragrance of ammonia. He was alert, annoyed, and aggressive in his pursuit of a solution, one he felt was to be found within the cable industry itself.

Within weeks, Turner seemed to be everywhere. He appeared at cable companies, conventions, film markets, and industry shows. He had T-shirts printed with his likeness, bumper stickers made that advertised CNN Headline News, and buttons distributed that proudly proclaimed I WAS CABLE WHEN CABLE WASN'T COOL. He would stand and stretch himself out to his full height and begin flapping his arms as he wildly gestured to the audience that routinely gathered. Ted needed help, and he was not too proud, yet again, to ask for it. It did more than remind the cable operators that Turner had kept them in business. It showed that he was one of them, and they were not about to let him fail. Suddenly, channels that previously were filled with other programming opened for CNN. Advertisers joined the team effort and anted up. Banks rolled over loans and increased payouts.

Turner made TBS' worth appear to increase by using a ploy originated by billionaire Howard Hughes. Hughes was continuously placing his company on the market and having corporate entities bid on his business. While he never had any serious intention of selling, it provided a clear picture of how much the marketplace valued his worth. Turner played the same game, opening up bidding on Turner Broadcasting. At one point, 3M Corporation thought it had bought TBS for some $30 million, only to find its contract being used as leverage at Citicorp Bank to increase Turner's loan.

The subterfuge managed to fool the banks, the viewers, and ultimately SNC. As Turner Broadcasting stock continued to rise based on the optical illusion Turner had spun for public consumption, ABC stock was plummeting on the very real losses being generated by SNC. Sources estimate that in its first year on the air, the startup news network lost $60 million, with some insiders suggesting that the real cost was closer to $100 million.[5]

Even though ABC had far deeper pockets than Turner Broadcasting, the company also had to answer to its stockholders and explain why, with all its equipment, studios, personnel, and marketing prowess, it was spending more than double what CNN was to produce a similar product. Stockholders found that SNC, because of its connection with ABC, had been forced to use unionized workers and pay union wages. Furthermore, instead of operating scattered bureaus across the country, SNC depended on feeds from affiliated stations, necessitating the leasing of 10 transponders on the Westar IV satellite to accommodate delivery. That cost alone was eight times what CNN required, and became a rallying point for protesting stockholders.

In the end, ABC simply did not have the patience or the tenacity to battle a man like Turner. The network bureaucracy bristled at the thought of continuing to jockey its stockholders, adverse publicity, and the TBS propaganda machine, and began having internal discussions about shutting down its costly experiment.

For Turner, the thought that he had pushed a competitor into giving up was unacceptable. After all, Turner was a man who needed a crisis to energize him and drive him to succeed. Surrender gave him a victory but not a win, and because of it he made a move that amazed those both within and without his organization. In September 1983, Turner offered ABC $25 million for SNC. It was, of course, $25 million he did not have, but for Turner it was money well spent, if only so he could declare that he had bought out the competition.

As usual, however, the feather duster that Turner was wielding was less about cleaning house than about raising a smoke screen, even as SNC was signing off with the words "That's it for now. In fact, that's it, period. And now, Ted buddy, it's in your hands!" For those watching as the screen went blank and turned to static snow against black, few knew that Turner actually was still negotiating the last points of the deal. Across town, TBS controller Paul Beckham was finalizing the $25 million loan to pay for the acquisition. All the while, SNC was history.

*Forbes* headlined the deal with THE MOUTH OF THE SOUTH STRIKES AGAIN, quoting Turner as stating that "the SNC people were really worthy opponents. They did a good job."[6] It was an amazingly humble Turner basking in the glow of triumph. It was also a mood that wouldn't last long. "You know what we've shown?" he asked later in the piece. "That on a level playing field we can beat the networks in cable. CBS came after us with their cultural channel and lost maybe $40 million and they pulled out. RCA came in with NBC in their cable programming and they lost as much and pulled out. Now we've beaten a combination of ABC and Westinghouse. It cost them—we estimate—about $100 million. That was all they could take."[7]

In addition to putting SNC out of business, CNN and CNN Headline News were awarded SNC's slot on cable services around the country, effectively increasing CNN's reach by several million homes. Throughout what Turner liked to call the "bloody war," the one constant was the quality of CNN's broadcasts. Even in times of chaos and uncertainty, the news network performed predictably, and critics were nearly universal in their kudos.

As Turner took to basking in the glory that was CNN while continuing to lose millions of dollars, Rupert Murdoch had the opposite challenge: he was making millions by continuing to appeal to the lowest common denominator among readers. Nowhere did the effect seem more startling than at the *Sunday Times,* where a major publishing gaffe under Murdoch's direct control threatened to undermine the newpaper's credibility completely.

In early 1983, Peter Wickman, an agent for the German magazine *Stern,* contacted Murdoch with an offer to purchase the exclusive British rights to a property so confidential that Wickman refused to reveal even the subject without a written confidentiality agreement. Murdoch, always eager for a publishing exclusive, willingly agreed to the stipulation, and soon heard about Hitler's secret diaries.

The fact that there never had been the slightest rumor that Adolf Hitler had ever kept a diary did not affect Murdoch's consideration of the deal, which one historian labeled "the most remarkable find of a lifetime." And quite a lucky find at that. According to Wickman, veteran *Stern* journalist Gerd Heidemann had been told about the existence of the diaries by Konrad Kujau, a Nazi artifacts expert. Kujau, in turn, had gotten the diaries from his brother, an officer in the East German army who smuggled 60 volumes across the border into West Germany. Just how the diaries, alleged to have been written by Hitler between 1932 and 1945, came into the possession of Kujau was an even more remarkable tale.

According to Kujau, a plane carrying Hitler's personal effects had crashed in the historic town of Dresden on the Elbe River. The diaries miraculously survived the fire that destroyed the plane and the remainder of Hitler's belongings. They were rescued by an East German general who kept them hidden for the next three decades, only to be uncovered by Konrad Kujau's brother. The brother went to Konrad, Konrad went to Heidemann, Heidemann went to his editors at *Stern,* and the magazine went to the bank to withdraw 9.9 million marks (U.S. $3 million) to pay Kujau for the worldwide rights to the journals.

Murdoch was initially less interested in the authenticity of the books than he was in the cost to purchase the British rights. The knowledge that the competing *Daily Mail* was bidding for the diaries only increased his rush to cop the prize. Traveling to Zurich with longtime friend and Australian attorney Richard Searby, Murdoch inspected a single volume of the diaries, which were being kept locked in a bank vault, and received assurances that the journals were authentic. Unable to understand the German text and unfamiliar with Hitler's Gothic handwriting, Murdoch called upon *Times* board member Hugh Trevor-Roper, the very man who months earlier had accused Murdoch of "gross incivility," to examine the diaries and render his opinion. At the time, Trevor-Roper was the headmaster of Peterhouse College and author of the classic history of the Third Reich, *The Last Days of Hitler.* In 1978, he edited *The Final Entries 1945: The Diaries of Joseph Goebbels. Who better to authenticate the provenance of the journals?* Murdoch thought.

Trevor-Roper left the Zurich bank vault an excited historian. According to his statement, published on April 23, 1983, in the *Sunday Times,* Trevor-Roper said, "When I entered the back room in the Swiss bank and turned the pages of those volumes and learnt the extraordinary story of their diversity, my doubts gradually dissolved. I am now satisfied that the documents are authentic, that the history of their wanderings since 1945 is true; and that the standard accounts of Hitler's writing habits, of his personality and even, perhaps, some public events, in consequence have to be revised."

Just two days earlier, on the basis of Trevor-Roper's endorsement, Murdoch agreed to pay *Stern* $400,000 for the British rights to the diaries, and alerted Frank Giles that the *Sunday Times* would be breaking the news of the discovery in its next issue. Murdoch was anxious to beat *Stern* to publication and pushed his editor to expedite the announcement without regard to further authentication.

In America, *Newsweek,* which had also been bidding for the rights, decided against serializing the journals based on its belief that the diaries were forged. However, the magazine did run a 12-page cover story about the diaries with the sentiment "Genuine or not, it almost doesn't matter in the end." *Newsweek* felt that the discovery of the diaries and the perpetration of an elaborate forgery were equally newsworthy, and hedged its bets. Murdoch was not so fortunate.

When Giles published the front-page headline revealing the existence of the Hitler diaries, he had little time to gloat over his newspaper's scoop. The historian who only the previous day had declared his total belief in the diaries' integrity now found reason to doubt his judgment. On April 22, Trevor-Roper placed a call to Douglas-Home to vent his uncertainty, though he never telephoned Giles with the same apprehension. Incredibly, Douglas-Home did not pass the word along to Giles either, when there might have been an opportunity to limit the damage or even stop the story from appearing in its entirety. Giles did not learn of Trevor-Roper's change of opinion until he placed a congratulatory call to him to read sections of an advance copy of the *Sunday Times*. Only then did the editor hear that Trevor-Roper had sudden reservations. Ultimately, his second instinct proved correct.

*Stern* magazine editor in chief Peter Koch hosted a Hamburg press conference attended by Gerd Heidemann, and held up copies of notebooks bound in black imitation leather. Of the contents, *Newsweek* wrote that it "reeks of history . . . the most hideous years in human experience are described by the man who did so much to make them vile." Koch pointed to Trevor-Roper's endorsement of authenticity and that of Gerhard L. Weinberg, a University of North Carolina historian. Then British historian and journalist David Irving raised his hand amid the euphoria of self-congratulation to ask whether the documents had been chemically tested to verify their age. They had not. The press conference unraveled into a shouting match of accusatory remarks and defensive moves. Irving pushed, Koch retreated, and the entire Hitler diaries charade took on the image of an elaborately staged fraud.

While more questions were raised and tests were run, the results provided a confusing mix of corroboration and refute. First, Max Frei-Sultzer, former head of the forensic science department of the Zurich police, and Ordway Hilton, a handwriting expert, independently certified that the handwriting in the diaries matched samples of Hitler's own. Yet, subsequent chemical tests proved conclusively that the fibers in the paper were manufactured after Hitler's death, as were the ink and the binding. The covers of the diaries were made from leatherette first produced in the fifties, and even the ribbon attached to the wax seal was manufactured after World War II.

Perhaps most damning of all was the discovery that passages in the diary itself had been copied directly from *Hitler Speeches and Proclamations 1932–1945: The Chronicle of a Dictatorship,* edited by Max Domarus—a book not published until 1962. Armed with indisputable evidence of fraud, the German police attempted to locate Konrad Kujau, who was eventually arrested trying to flee the country. Kujau confessed to forging the diaries, then smashing the books with a hammer and staining them with tea to make them appear authentic. Further interrogation revealed that Kujau had been forging and selling Hitler memorabilia for so long that the *authenticated* writing samples used by both Hilton and Frei-Sultzer were Kujau forgeries as well.

Disgusted journalists at *Stern* held a six-day sit-in to protest the ease with which the magazine's management had been conned out of more than nine million German marks. Reporters at the *Sunday Times* were equally as outraged, while Giles, though embarrassed, pointed with pride at the 60,000-reader increase in circulation. The *New York Times* asked, "What's happened to the *Sunday Times*?" before offering the answer: "Rupert Murdoch has."[8] Meanwhile, Murdoch, grousing that it was "all Trevor-Roper's fault," was barely fazed by the entire brouhaha, saying only, "After all, we are in the entertainment business,"[9] further blurring the line between news and gossip.

The bottom line remained omnipotent for Murdoch, who found his profits rising due to the increased circulation regardless of the damage done to the reputation of the venerable *Sunday Times*. For Murdoch, it was a question of power, not accountability; money, not service. To his credit, he never claimed otherwise, his course never sullied by the temptation of rectitude. That this course should bring him into direct competition with Ted

Turner, newly righteous and self-proclaimed curator of the world, is one of those ironies of fate best left unexplained. That their first competition should take place out of the newsroom and on the high seas adds an even more Faustian cast to mere coincidence.

In the fall of 1983, the maneuvers that brought these two men to loggerheads began simply enough. With Turner in Atlanta and Murdoch in New York, on the other side of the world in Australia, planning was under way for the thirty-ninth running of the Sydney to Hobart Yacht Race and what looked like a battle for supremacy between two longtime rivals, England's Robert Bell and America's Marvin Greene. Greene was owner of the maxi yacht *Nirvana*, built in 1981 as the fastest 81-foot afloat. Bell owned *Condor*, a foot shorter but no less aggressive. Both men had been flirting with the uncontested first-place title since *Nirvana* was launched. The stage was set for one of these yachtsmen to claim victory.

In an effort to ensure a first-place finish, Bell hired Ted Turner to captain the *Condor* and bring his own team onboard—a package deal not unlike Turner's effort in the 1976 America's Cup. Over on the *Nirvana*, Greene was looking for investors to help him refit his yacht to ensure what he saw as certain victory. Enter Rupert Murdoch, always the gambler and eager to have an entry in the legendary Australian race. As it happened, Greene was entered in the race as a member of the New York Yacht Club, the same club that had taken great pains to distance itself from the drunken unpredictability of Turner during his America's Cup defense.

On December 29, the two maxi yachts answered the starter's gun along with some 70 other boats in spectacular Sydney Harbor, and began what was to become a nose-to-nose race for nearly the entire course. Three days later, as the two yachts moved past the Iron Pot Lighthouse at the mouth of the Derwent River for the final few miles of the race, Turner turned *Condor*, tacking across *Nirvana*'s path to take the lead. By sea rules, Turner had the right-of-way and had successfully maneuvered his way to the front. Unfortunately, he was also moving dangerously close to White Rock Head, a small land point jutting into the river. Turner called out to the *Nirvana* for clearance, a courtesy *Nirvana* was not about to give.

At this point, stories vary. However, one thing is certain. Just before White Rock, the two boats touched, sending the *Condor* into the point's sandbank. *Nirvana*'s crew, cheering at Turner's calamity, continued to sail toward the finish line. "Capsize" Turner, having more experience than most at moving yachts off coral reefs, submerged rocks, and, yes, sandbars, managed to get the *Condor* afloat and back on course, though not without losing five precious minutes. By the time *Condor* reached the finish line, she was just 182 meters behind *Nirvana,* but definitely in second place.

The day after the race, a protest jury was convened and ruled that the *Nirvana* failed to follow regulations. *Nirvana* was disqualified, and the race was awarded to *Condor*. That evening, at the official dinner celebrating the race, Turner accepted the applause of his fellow skippers with a speech aimed at the disqualified *Nirvana*'s poor sportsmanship. Moving beyond criticism to lambasting, Turner found his target in the form of Rupert Murdoch, who was at the time relaxing with his family at Cavan. That Murdoch had invested in *Nirvana* provided Turner with a flimsy reason to attack the publisher personally and professionally. A year earlier, Murdoch had met with Turner in Atlanta during the period in which Turner was pretending to be interested in selling TBS. Murdoch, unaware of Turner's subterfuge to establish his market worth, looked at CNN as a complement to his recently purchased majority interest in Satellite Television Plc, a European satellite distribution service that he renamed Sky. He anticipated being able to utilize CNN feeds on Sky as the basis of a European news service and was anxious to negotiate a buyout.

Turner was well aware of the potential that Europe held for a news service—particularly *his* news service. He fully intended to push his way onto and across that continent, and then move toward Asia, Africa, South America, and Australia. The difference between Turner's plan and Murdoch's plan lay in the form of delivery: Turner used satellites to get his signal to cable distributors; Murdoch wanted satellites to feed individual homes. That dichotomy would have a far-reaching impact in the future, but for now both men saw that goal as a distant promise.

As Murdoch quietly discussed his plans in a general sense, liberally splashing his dialogue with references to his growing empire, Turner found himself intrigued. Though he disliked the arrogance of the soft-spoken Australian, he nevertheless was curious to learn more about this man whose plans for media supremacy were not far from his own. Murdoch thought Turner an impostor, performing a role, always onstage. He refused to believe anyone could be that crude, loud, and obnoxious without an underlying scheme. He also knew Turner was deeply in debt and ripe for takeover. As the two men jockeyed for position, their initial conversation set the tone for all future confrontations. Neither man trusted the other; both saw threats on their scented territory, and each wanted to remove the other from the playing field.

After the Sydney-Hobart race and its resulting controversy, Turner saw an opportunity to do damage to Murdoch in his own country, not so much because he had a grievance, but because he wanted to make an impression. In his say-something-loud-enough-and-you're-bound-to-be-heard mode, Turner spoke of fair play and bullies, sportsmanship and cheating, while painting as unflattering a picture of Rupert Murdoch as possible without any concrete evidence.

That Turner chose this time to cast aspersions on Murdoch ignored the obvious fact that the Australian publisher was at home with his family, celebrating the holidays. Turner was unable to remember when the same could be said for him. Jane and the children were half a world away, spending another

Christmas alone at Hope Plantation, the 5,000-acre estate Turner had purchased several years earlier near Jacksonboro, South Carolina. Some said it was a marriage of convenience, except it was hardly convenient at all. Certainly not for Turner, who ignored his wife whenever they ventured out together and raged at her whenever they were alone. Unlike her husband, whose dimples only became deeper with age, Jane Turner had lost her flight-attendant good looks under the stress of a wandering husband and the loneliness of an empty life. When she did leave the house to attend a party or perhaps dine at a restaurant, Jane drank to excess. With her children now teenagers and spending increasing amounts of time away from home, Jane found the loneliness of Hope Plantation haunting and oppressive, and used it as an excuse to bury her insecurities in alcohol.

Seeing his wife deteriorate, Turner made an effort to work on repairing the marriage by agreeing to seek counseling with famed Atlanta psychiatrist Dr. Frank Pittman. Author of the best-selling book *Private Lies: Infidelity and Betrayal of Intimacy* and an expert in addressing adultery, Pittman worked with Turner in an unsuccessful attempt to reduce his need for paramours. In the process, Pittman prescribed the drug lithium to aid in controlling Turner's volatile mood swings, which often intensified during his fights with Jane.[10]

In addition to his open relationship with CNN staffer Liz Wickersham, Turner also became romantically involved with yet another blonde, J. J. Ebaugh, a commercial flier who eventually became Turner's personal pilot. Each woman knew about the other, and Jane knew about both of them as well as others, including prostitutes who found favor with her husband on his many business trips.

To his children, Turner's behavior was the stuff of mystery: explosive, temperamental, vindictive, driven, and typically absent. As his father had before him, Turner put his children to work picking weeds while dodging swamp snakes. He taught them to sail, and he taught them to hate. He also set an example that was totally at odds with his public campaign to remove sex and violence from television. It was an effort about to gain momentum in the years ahead, and set him on a path that would not only bring him to the brink of bankruptcy but also place him on a collision course with "that bloody Australian." Rupert's wholesome purity against Ted's uninhibited sexual exploration, Murdoch's gutter gossip against Turner's legitimate news—two men whose mandates put them at opposite ends of communication's moral code.

At age eleven, Ted Turner moved into his father's five-bedroom house at 3204 Abercorn Street, Savannah, Georgia.

The Savannah home where Ted Turner lived throughout high school and college and where his sister, Mary Jane, became ill.

Courtesy of The McCallie School, Chattanooga, Tennessee

## ROBERT E. TURNER

### SAVANNAH, GEORGIA

Enrolled September, 1950; Private Company F, '50-'51; Private Company E, '51-'52; Private Company D, '52-'53; Corporal Company D, '53-'54; Sergeant Company C, '54-'55; Captain Company E, '55-'56; Termite Football, '50; Mite Football, '51; Boxing, '50-'53; J.V. Football, '55; Sailing, '53-'56; Debating Team, '55-'56; Spanish Club, '54-'56; Georgia Club, '50-'56; Prefect, '52-'56; Neatest Cadet McCallie Regiment, '54-'55; Linus Llewellyn Award, '55; Holton Harris Oratorical Medal, '55-'56.

Ted Turner's senior photo and write-up upon graduation from McCallie preparatory school in 1956.

Turner *(seated, second from right)* joined the McCallie debating team in his junior year and quickly became recognized as the most talented member, winning the Tennessee State Championship as a senior.

Courtesy of: The McCallie School, Chattanooga, Tennessee

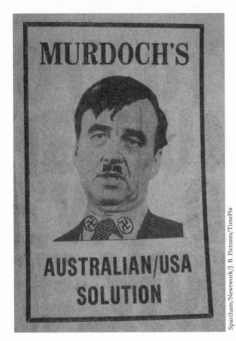

Poster depicting Rupert Murdoch as Hitler, regarding his attack towards unions, firing of 6,000 printers, and moving his papers away from Fleet Street, 1986.

Murdoch on the cover of *Time* magazine, January 1977 issue.

Queen Elizabeth II sitting with Rupert Murdoch at the *Times* monthly conference, 1985.

President John F. Kennedy meets with *Daily Mirror* owner Rupert Murdoch, 1961.

Rupert Murdoch with his wife, Anna, and their baby daughter, Elisabeth, at London Airport, 1968.

Rupert Murdoch with his family after receiving a Humanitarian of the Year Award. With him are: *(from left)* daughters Elisabeth and Prudence, wife Anna, and sons Lachlan and James, 1997.

Eric Gaillard/Reuters/TimePix

Will Burgess/Reuters/TimePix

Rupert Murdoch (age 70) and his wife, Wendi Deng (age 33), are seen arriving at a film premiere in Cannes, 2001. Deng is expecting their child in this photo.

News Corporation chief executive Rupert Murdoch and his wife, Wendi Deng, *(seated)* are joined on Sydney Harbour by sailing instructor Lyndsay Marwood at the start of the Sydney to Hobart yacht race, 2000.

Ted Turner with a look of determination while skippering *Courageous,* the yacht he would sail in the America's Cup, 1977.

George Silk/TimePix

© Bettmann/CORBIS

*Courageous* skipper Ted Turner holding a bottle and an admirer as he and his crew celebrate their victory over Australia. *Courageous* defeated Australia in four straight races to successfully defend the America's Cup, 1977.

Ted Turner sits with his family during the 1986 Goodwill Games in Moscow. The games, which he sponsored and founded that same year, were meant to represent the crumbling of the Cold War separation of East and West.

© Peter Turnley/CORBIS

Atlanta Braves owner Ted Turner *(left),* former President Jimmy Carter, and his wife, Rosalynn, cheer as the Braves take to the field for their first home game in the 1983 season.

Ted Turner and President Clinton at CNN headquarters, 1994.

Ted Turner and Jane Fonda at the 1992 tribute to Gregory Peck at the Lincoln Center.

Turner on the cover of *Time* magazine as *Time*'s "Man of the Year," January 1992 issue.

Turner Broadcasting System, Inc. president Ted Turner greets News Corporation chief Rupert Murdoch at the Center for Communications awards luncheon in New York City, April 11, 1994. Turner received the annual Communication Award at the event.

Turner Broadcasting Chief Executive Officer Ted Turner and Time Warner Chief Executive Officer Gerald Levin at the Turner Broadcasting and Time Warner merger press conference, 1995.

# TEN

# And Then I Bought—
# Oh, What Was the
# Name of that Country?

*I am eventually going to go broke,*
*but so is our federal government.*
*You operate at massive deficits every year*
*and keep smiling, and so do I.*

Ted Turner testifying before a
House Judiciary subcommittee
Washington, D.C.
August 1983

**W**hen Rupert Murdoch walked into the fourth-floor news-room of the *Chicago Sun-Times,* he entered as the enemy. Elegantly tailored and impeccably manicured, he looked around the room at the veteran journalists with their rolled-up shirt-sleeves and doubting faces and knew this was not going to be an easy sell. Chicago is known for its aggressive news coverage and the pit-bull reporters who provide it. Inheritors of the *Front Page* school of journalism, the reporters at the *Sun-Times* growled their dislike for the man who had bought his way into their news-room, and paid homage with scattered if disbelieving applause when he declared that he intended to leave the newspaper "sub-stantially the same." It was going to take more than an empty promise to convince this room.

Murdoch bought the newspaper for $90 million at the end of 1983 from Marshall Field V and his half brother, Frederick ("Ted"), a pair of very rich and very different siblings.* Marshall's main interest was in Chicago real estate; Ted's love was Hollywood.** One thing they agreed upon was their dislike for each other, which was intensified when Ted decided to sell his share of the *Sun-Times* to Rupert Murdoch, who offered far more than other bidders, forcing Marshall to sell his share as well.

Murdoch had gone through the newsroom drill with every newspaper he had purchased—the last time being just a month earlier with his fire-sale buyout of the *Boston Herald* for $1 million. Each time, he promised the same unwavering support for the journalists on the staff while insisting that the number of positions be reduced. Each time, he offered a window of opportunity for those who wanted to take early retirement and gain a substantial severance package. And each time, a number of reporters accepted the offer. In Chicago, there was a rush to take Murdoch's money. It was not that the writers needed quick cash. More likely, it was their nearly universal dislike for Murdoch's sensationalist form of journalism.

The newspaper's star writer, Mike Royko,† plastered his columns with negative opinions of Murdoch before jumping ship to the competing *Tribune*. "No self-respecting fish would be wrapped in a Murdoch newspaper," Royko wrote. "His goal is not quality journalism. His goal is vast power for Rupert Murdoch, political power." That he was right did not matter to Murdoch, who sued the writer when he defected, as much for publicity as for salve. Eventually, the lawsuit was dismissed.

Mere weeks into Murdoch's ownership, Royko's predictions began to come to fruition as Murdoch let it be known that he

---

*The Field brothers derived their wealth from the fortune founded by their great-great-grandfather, who founded Chicago's most famous department store, Marshall Field and Co.

**After the sale of the *Chicago Sun-Times,* Ted Field produced such movies as *Cocktail, Three Men and a Baby, Mr. Holland's Opus,* and *Runaway Bride.*

† Royko died of an aneurysm in 1997. At the time, his column in the *Chicago Tribune* was syndicated to more than 100 newspapers.

thought the *Sun-Times* was "dull." Excitement was what it needed, he suggested. "More color," he said. "Human interest, perhaps." When pressed for an example of a human interest story, he suggested running features on readers who had achieved success with their *Sun-Times* classified advertisements. "And the worst part was that he was serious," commented one reporter who subsequently and unceremoniously left the newspaper.[1]

In an effort to protect his interests against the corruption of hard-liners used to having editorial control, Murdoch shipped over a crusty fighter from Glasgow named Charlie Wilson to take the reins of the *Sun-Times* from former publisher James Hoge and restructure the paper. Hoge was a graduate of Yale; Wilson the school of hard knocks. He was, however, effective in conveying Murdoch's intentions and standing up against a rather effective ostracizing by the newspaper's employees. Wilson accepted few kindnesses and received none, but did manage to bring a credible work ethic to the newsroom. No reporter could fault Wilson's long hours or attention to detail, and during the months he grabbed the *Sun-Times* by the shirt collar, he shook loose an incredible amount of dry rot and deadwood.

When Wilson punched his way back to Great Britain, he was replaced by Frank Devine, a onetime editor of *Reader's Digest* who ran with the revisions Wilson had introduced, including more graphics, heavier emphasis on sports and crime, crisper type, and bolder headlines. Not the kind of headlines that Chicago had feared, necessarily. No HEADLESS BODY FOUND IN TOPLESS BAR.[††] Instead, Devine transformed the *Sun-Times* into a people's advocate, fighting against local corruption and old-boy politics while embracing Murdoch's right-wing conservatism, at least when covering Capitol Hill.

Although the *Sun-Times* did not overtake the competing *Tribune* in readership, it did improve its circulation handsomely

---

††An actual headline in the *New York Post*.

enough to carve a niche among younger and more impressionable Chicagoans. Similarly, the *Boston Herald,* while never a serious threat to the dominance of the *Boston Globe,* had a hard-core legion of readers who preferred its abbreviated style and modern layout.

As the fallout from Murdoch's two newspaper purchases continued to wash into his life like waves onto a beach, no one seemed more surprised than Murdoch himself by the intensity of opinion where his product was concerned. The most vocal critics were loud and negative and approached him with salivary excitement. Though the power that his papers bestowed on him was essential to his own growth, Murdoch remained dumbfounded by the energy put into attacks on him personally, never equating the two.

Adolph S. Ochs, famed publisher of the *New York Times* and the man credited with making newspapers "clean, dignified, and trustworthy," said that no man is big enough to own more than one newspaper. Ochs, who fought the yellow journalism of William Randolph Hearst and Joseph Pulitzer and won the battle for readership, would not have had anything nice to say about Rupert Murdoch. But then, Ochs came from a position of providing "all the news that's fit to print." By 1984, Murdoch was less newsman than power mogul. It was a subtlety the journalists in Chicago and Boston had yet to distinguish.

Of course Murdoch wanted his newspapers to make money, and his maneuvers with personnel and unions were specifically geared toward that objective. Unlike other executives, however, Murdoch did not see profit as the bottom line. Reporters who raged about his cost-cutting efforts as well as his style of journalism overlooked his real purpose: to influence, control, manipulate, and insinuate. Newspapers were merely the engine that drove the train.

Likewise, Ted Turner moved with surety to increase his reach and power. Having pushed an increasingly time-pressed America into consciously turning to television for its news, Turner next wanted to grab the nation by the scruff of the neck and awaken it to its environmental sins. He was joined in public by J. J. Ebaugh, who had moved into a secure position as his mistress du jour, and with saving the environment suddenly their top priority, the pair began to campaign for the creation of a foundation aimed at supporting conservation, recycling, and population control through television programming. The idea had originally come from Ebaugh with support from oceanographer Jacques Cousteau, to whom Turner had donated $4 million for a quartet of documentaries under Cousteau's *Undersea World* banner.

With typical speed and energy, Turner set about recruiting talent to spawn an environmental organization, including Cousteau's son, Jean-Michel; Lester R. Brown, founder of the Worldwatch Institute; Russell Wilber Peterson, onetime head of the National Audubon Society and governor of Delaware; and former president Jimmy Carter. The formal inauguration of the foundation, known as the Better World Society, took place in New York City at the venerable University Club, an Italian Renaissance palazzo on Fifty-fourth Street and Fifth Avenue, splendiferous in its gilt and marble excess, thus providing a regal setting for the launch.

On the surface, the Better World Society appeared to be a philanthropic organization aimed at kick-starting a long-overdue push for environmental reform. For the most part, that was an accurate depiction of its purpose. Hidden among its functions, however, was the spreading of Turner's own personal agenda for world reform, using the broadcasting community to disseminate his message as entertainment. In an effort to increase the sledge with which he hammered away at society's woes, Turner attempted to enter the major leagues by crossing from cable to broadcast television with a hostile takeover bid for the CBS Network. The David-versus-Goliath contest had all the elements of a Hollywood drama, complete with name calling, eye scratching, and clandestine meetings held in the dark of night.

The first hint that Turner had his eye on CBS came by way of an invitation he extended to CBS Broadcast Group president Gene Jankowski and veteran CBS News president Bill Leonard to travel to Atlanta and discuss the possibility of a "combined effort" between CBS and CNN.

CBS approached the meeting with visions of buying CNN and merging it with CBS News; Turner thought the meeting a fine way to open discussions about CBS investing in CNN as a minority partner, with his ultimate goal a complete takeover of the network. Since CBS had absolutely no interest in selling and Turner could not conceive of losing CNN, as soon as each side realized the other's intent, there was little to discuss other than the unseasonable humidity in Atlanta.

The favored corporate climate that developed during the early Reagan years began to yield fruit at the beginning of the president's second term in office. Nowhere was the impact felt greater than in the media community. When the ABC Network was courted and ultimately purchased by the smaller Capital Cities Broadcasting Group in March 1985 for $3.5 billion in stock and cash, the deal demonstrated to Turner the viability of his dream to own a network himself. When the FCC did not object to the sale and actually assisted in the transition, Turner saw his opportunity.

Another Southerner, Jesse Helms, the conservative Republican senator from North Carolina, formed a group called Fairness in Media and charged its members with the task of purchasing CBS stock. The ultimate goal: Take over the network and control its news—news that Helms felt had a liberal bias. Helms solicited support via a letter-writing campaign mailed to a million conservatives across the country.

> [If each conservative] shifts enough of his or her savings or investments to buy just 20 shares of CBS stock, we would have enough votes to end CBS's bias forever. . . .

> [CBS is] the most anti-Reagan network. . . . It's vital for
> us to put an end to media bias. . . . FIM [Fairness in
> Media] is counting on you to become Dan Rather's
> boss—by switching a portion of your investments to
> CBS stock. I am not giving economic or investment
> advice. The sole reason for this effort is to end bias at
> CBS Inc. You can buy stock in CBS by finding a stock-
> broker. They are listed in the Yellow Pages.

That Helms should attempt to control the thrust of news on CBS was more of an abhorrent concept to many than the idea of having Ted Turner at the network's helm. Radical in his bias against homosexuality, abortion, racial equality, arts funding, and aid to what he calls "foreign rat holes," Helms was the political antithesis of Turner. All of which made their meeting in early 1985 that much more fascinating. Turner contacted Helms to see if the two men could work together to gain control of CBS, with Turner's goal to program the network and Helms' goal to control the news. "It's no secret that I've wanted to acquire or be acquired by a network," Turner told the *Atlanta Constitution* in April 1985. "It goes back a number of years. I knew Helms wasn't going to leave the Senate to run a network if he was successful. And I suggested that I do have qualifications to run a network, and that was what my interest in meeting him was."

Philosophically, it was a pairing that was impossible to fathom, and Helms soon dismissed the prospect based largely on information about Turner's Better World Society and its announced intention of producing programming that advocated abortion, animal rights, sexual freedom, nuclear disarmament, and eco-feminism. Turner was fully capable of making a frontal attack on CBS without Helms in any case, and proceeded to instruct his attorney, Charles Ferris (himself a former FCC chairman), to inquire about FCC procedures in an unfriendly network takeover.

Thus alerted, CBS maneuvered its corporate posture in high dudgeon and reacted predictably as network chairman Thomas Wyman announced that there was "no financial substance" to Turner's interest in the network and that the mogul was "without proper conscience" to run a network. Typically unfazed, Turner lit another cigar. "Well, we'll just see who's the last one out of the pool," he responded, his grin intact and with enough mischief in his eyes that even Wyman admitted he was uncertain if he could prevent CBS from being put into play.

Daniel Schorr entered the arena by sending a letter to his former colleague at CBS, news anchor Dan Rather: "Dear Dan, Don't worry about Jesse Helms. I'm your new boss."[2] Ironically, the note was Schorr's swan song from CNN, for on March 8 he unexpectedly declined to sign a new contract, saying only that it was missing the clause stipulating that Turner would not require him to "undertake any assignments that would compromise his professional ethics and responsibilities." In commenting, CNN's Burt Reinhardt said only, "CNN is unable to come to terms on a new contract."

While Turner began to contemplate taking on several billion dollars in debt to pursue CBS, Rupert Murdoch was actively dipping into his own loan core to finance purchases totaling $565 million, with no new newspaper among his acquisitions. At the start of 1985, Murdoch had spent $350 million in cash to purchase the entire business division of Ziff-Davis, which included such trade magazines as *Hotel & Travel Index, Aerospace Daily, Meetings & Conventions,* and *Travel Weekly.* The purchase was unusual in that Murdoch had no experience in publishing trade magazines, and all the publications were earning healthy profits. "Travel is perhaps the most dynamic business in the world," he commented. "It has an enormous growth potential, and is a major strategic investment."[3]

Several months later, Murdoch stunned the Hollywood community with the announcement that he had bought a one-half interest in 20th Century-Fox Studios from its owner, Denver oil-man Marvin Davis. The studio that had given the world Shirley Temple, Marilyn Monroe, *The Sound of Music, Cleopatra,* and *Star Wars* was experiencing an earnings slump, and the resulting strain on funds had caused considerable friction between Davis (who had bought the studio in 1981) and Barry Diller, Fox chairman and the man charged with turning around the studio's fortune.

Davis, a large, imposing, and powerful businessman whose girth was outdistanced only by his ability to negotiate incredibly lucrative deals, was excited by the image that being a studio owner exuded but less than thrilled by the nonstop drain on his bank accounts. His working relationship with Diller, whom he had hired away from Paramount Studios, was aggravated by Diller's need for a stable foundation on which to rebuild the once-thriving enterprise. In Rupert Murdoch, both men found a soul mate of sorts. Davis liked Murdoch's ability to make an instant decision and generate cash; Diller liked Murdoch's appreciation of entertainment as a source of additional power for his growing empire.

Fox represented an opportunity to blanket the world in a way newspapers never could. While each paper Murdoch published gave him enormous local power in an isolated region, with a studio he gained the chance to reach across states, even across entire countries. The advantages intrinsic in film and television studio ownership—or, in this case, half ownership—were incalculable, and promised a ripe source of programming for his Australian television stations and growing European satellite network as well.

Murdoch gave the first indication that he was anxious to move into the entertainment field when he unexpectedly purchased 5.6 million shares of Warner Communications stock in mid-1984. Certain that Murdoch was planning a hostile run on the company to gain control of its studio operation, Warner chairman Steven J. Ross went looking for a white knight. He found him in the form of silent partner Herbert Siegel, who increased his own ownership of the $3.5 billion entertainment conglomerate to 29 percent, eventually buying out Murdoch (and yielding the Australian an instant profit of $41.5 million). That $41.5 million joined another $208.5 million as Murdoch's share of 20th Century-Fox.

As industry watchdogs mused about the personalities of Murdoch, Davis, and Diller, wondering aloud how many minutes it would take before the three executives had their first ego-inspired row, Ted Turner stole the headlines by announcing his planned takeover of CBS Inc. for $5.41 billion with no money down. In a rather daring scheme proposed by E. F. Hutton's mergers-and-acquisitions division, Turner intended to float high-yield, high-risk debt securities in combination with stock in TBS to cover the takeover. It was a deal that *Broadcasting* magazine said was given more credit "for brashness than for stockholder appeal."[4]

CBS' response was swift and predictable. Network chairman Wyman labeled the offer "grossly inadequate and financially imprudent" and predicted that Turner would bankrupt both CBS and Turner Broadcasting in less than three years if he were allowed to proceed. Additionally, Wyman suggested that Turner's offer failed to alert stockholders to the "exceptional degree of risk" they faced in funding Turner's junk bonds.[5]

If Turner had any thought of being taken seriously as a broadcaster, the barrage that the network set loose in response left no doubt that they considered him a dangerous outsider. "All that we and our audiences have gained from half a century of public service is at stake and we don't intend to lose," Gene Jankowski said in a closed-circuit feed to the network's affiliates.[6]

Turner dodged an increasing storm of controversy in his takeover attempt. At the same time, Murdoch was quietly preparing to take on the FCC himself, not in a bold maneuver to absorb

CBS, but rather in a friendly purchase of the Metromedia-owned television stations in seven large cities.‡ As usual, he had had no specific plans to buy TV stations in the United States, but "happened upon an opportunity."

Murdoch's opportunity came in the form of a high-level private cocktail party given on the lot of 20th Century-Fox at the end of March 1985. Barry Diller arranged the small event for John Kluge, chairman and owner of Metromedia, who had taken the company private two years earlier through an issue of junk bonds. Unfortunately for Kluge, the interest on the bonds was fast eating up his available working capital, and he saw a quick sale of the company's television stations as a way to generate immediate cash. Upon meeting Murdoch at the party in the conference room adjacent to Diller's elegant office, Kluge took a bite of goose-liver pâté on a wheat cracker and mentioned that he was thinking of selling his TV stations. Murdoch, passing on the pâté, said he would be interested in buying them—if the price was right. The price, Kluge said, was $2 billion in cash. Murdoch merely smiled and asked the waiter for a refill of his Perrier.

When Murdoch and the 70-year-old Kluge met the following day in Diller's office, junk-bond king Michael Milken joined them along with several other executives from the Drexel Burnham Lambert investment house. The price remained at $2 billion for the seven stations, though Kluge now said he was not ready to sell his outlet in New York and previously had promised the station in Boston to the Hearst TV group. For the remaining five stations, Kluge was asking $1.05 billion—still in cash.[7] Diller thought the figure unreasonable, and in truth it was substantially in excess of the value of the stations, or at least their value

---

‡ Metromedia was a large communications company that owned television stations in New York, Los Angeles, Chicago, Boston, Houston, Washington, D.C., and Dallas–Fort Worth, as well as 13 radio stations, a billboard company, a cellular telephone system, a television production company, and traveling entertainment shows, including the Ice Capades and the Harlem Globetrotters.

as individual stations. To Murdoch, however, the value in the deal was the opportunity to purchase stations in major cities across the country that could be linked into an ad hoc network, instantly giving them more significance to potential advertisers.

If Kluge had any doubts about how serious Murdoch was, they were erased when, the following week, Murdoch sealed the deal in Kluge's Waldorf-Astoria apartment in Manhattan. With a handshake, Murdoch agreed to buy *all* of the Metromedia stations, and promised subsequently to resell the Boston outlet to the Hearst group to fulfill Kluge's prior commitment.

The announcement of the sale of the Metromedia stations to News Corporation took place on May 4, just two days after CBS held its closed-circuit feed to ridicule Ted Turner's attempt to buy its network and its television stations in New York, Los Angeles, Chicago, Philadelphia, Boston, and San Francisco. While Marvin Davis was mentioned in the official release regarding the purchase, his involvement was not assured. Rather, Murdoch accomplished the purchase himself by assuming responsibility for the junk bonds previously held by Kluge, plus some $600 million in cash provided through open lines of credit from American, European, and Australian banks—and all this despite restrictions in the United States that limited station ownership to citizens of that country.

Other than his family, Murdoch's Australian citizenship was the only constant in his life. Now, suddenly, that too seemed to be quite expendable if there was power to be gained. By appealing directly to the Reagan White House, Murdoch did what Haitian boat people attempting to escape persecution could not: He found the door marked American Citizen and prepared to open it.

Even as he was in discussions with immigration in Washington, he appeared on his own Australian network espousing his loyalty to his native land. "I would very much like to remain an Australian citizen," he said, "because I have built what I consider a very big Australian company around the world. I would like to be seen as an Australian and as an American. I am not severing any links with Australia."[8] There was no mention of love of country or pride of birth. To Murdoch it was business, and as he sorted through the various regulations governing media ownership in the United States, he realized he had little choice but to become an American if he wanted to buy a network of television stations.

Since federal regulations also prohibited an individual from owning a television station and newspaper in the same city, Murdoch began to divest himself of properties that violated the law. The *Village Voice* was the first to go. Murdoch sold the *Voice* to pet-food giant Hartz Mountain Industries for $55 million, a $47.5 million profit over his purchase price. He had originally paid $75 million for both the *Voice* and *New York* magazine. Additionally, the recently purchased *Chicago Sun-Times* was put in motion in an effort to judge the level of interest. The paper was barely making a profit and was considered unlikely to fetch the $90 million Murdoch had paid. Knowing that he would also have to dump his favored *New York Post,* Murdoch began the application process for a temporary FCC waiver of its ownership rules while he determined if there was a legal approach around the problem.

The Murdoch welcome by the Reagan White House and FCC commissioner Mark S. Fowler was in marked contrast to the reception received by Ted Turner. Murdoch glided through the review process, flawed application and all, with a few wrist slaps for sloppiness, and won a two-year waiver on the ownership rules. Turner, waiting patiently to testify before the FCC to pitch his case for ownership of the CBS Network, was met with smoke screens and legal maneuvers. In a delaying tactic, CBS appealed to the FCC for a full hearing on the broadcast license transfers that were an intricate part of the Turner-planned buyout. With Turner paying legal fees and interest on borrowed fluid cash,

CBS anticipated that the slow arm of bureaucracy would do what the law alone could not: wear out its competitor before the real fight began. If this were an ordinary takeover battle, CBS would have been correct in its logic. However, as with all things Turner, there was nothing ordinary about either CBS' opponent or his tenacity.

Turner ordered his legal team to counter the CBS request for a full hearing with pleas to the FCC chairman to stop allowing broadcasters the opportunity to use the agency as armor against attack. Yet, even as CBS was attempting to throw up roadblocks to Turner's takeover bid, a series of petitions flooded across the FCC transom from such wide-ranging groups as the National Organization for Women to the United Church of Christ.

Countering Turner's claim for a speedy resolution of the takeover request, CBS fired back at the FCC, alleging "substantial and material questions of fact exist" in the TBS filings with the FCC and the Securities and Exchange Commission. Declining to state the exact nature of the factual inaccuracies, CBS pledged to reveal its case in a resubmission for a full hearing. It was a tug-of-war played out in the headlines of trade papers and newspapers alike, with no apparent movement on either side until an unexpected announcement by CBS made any FCC appeal immaterial.

On July 3, 1985, CBS Inc. announced its intention to buy back 21 percent of its own stock at $150 a share—at a time when the stock was actively selling at a $122 face value. The total package amounted to a $1 billion investment by the network and effectively stopped Turner's cash-poor junk-bond offering. With CBS calling its offer a "preferable alternative" and Turner rebutting that it was "a breach of CBS directors' fiduciary duty to the company shareholders designed to enrich and entrench present management,"[9] it appeared that in this skirmish, it was Goliath who knocked David flat. As the dust settled and everyone rushed to determine the condition of the rival executives involved, no one seemed to care that the outcome was far removed from the public interest CBS was mandated to serve.

In the end, a federal judge in Atlanta and the FCC both ruled that CBS could proceed with its share repurchase, scuttling Turner's bid in what by all accounts was a failure. While industry pundits prepared to bury Turner in columns and headlines alike, the irrepressible former billboard salesman proved yet again that his behavior was neither logical nor predictable.

Mere days from the throes of the war on CBS, with no official word that he had canceled his takeover bid, Turner stunned the Hollywood community by revealing his offer to purchase the legendary Metro Goldwyn Mayer Studios from owner Kirk Kerkorian. TURNER CAN'T HAVE LION, CAGE CBS TOO read the headline of *Daily Variety*.[10]

Never one to settle for announcing a single major play when two would make an even bigger impact, Turner also released the news that he had signed a two-year pact with the USSR State Committee to exchange news, sports, and entertainment programming. The deal included the production of an athletic competition to encourage peace "between Russia and the U.S., players and owners and for Lebanon, Israel, and the whole McGillicuddy." Turner dubbed it the Goodwill Games. Loosely structured among amateur athletic organizations, the games planned to award 70 gold medals in the contest, slated for summer 1986.

The announcement itself was something of a media event, staged by Turner to get maximum exposure through his own news outlets. With Turner stationed at the Waldorf-Astoria, Soviet officials from the sports authority Soyuzsport standing by in Moscow, world-champion diver Greg Louganis speaking from Phoenix, Arizona, and Western European reporters asking questions from London, the entire event was served up as a prelude to the 1988 Olympics, albeit on a smaller scale. Turner called the Russians "wonderful people"[11] and promised that the Goodwill Games would "make up for the Olympics." Turner was referring to the 1984 Olympic Games, which the Soviet Union boycotted in retaliation for the American-inspired stay-away from Moscow in 1980 over the war in Afghanistan. What Turner did not mention was how he planned to pay for the Goodwill Games, or, for that matter, how he planned to generate the necessary cash to buy MGM. Small details for a big thinker.

The actual infrastructure of the Goodwill Games was left to Robert Wussler, onetime president of CBS Television as well as CBS Sports, who had left to become senior executive vice president of TBS. It was Wussler who made 18 trips to Moscow, worked with Sergei Lapin, chairman of the USSR State Committee for Television and Radio, and hammered out the particulars. Yet, as complicated as the logistics were for staging such an event, and as optimistic as the Goodwill Games seemed, they were dwarfed by the enormity of the debt Turner had agreed to in jumping into the purchase of MGM.

Turner agreed to pay $29 per share for Kerkorian's 51 percent of MGM stock, for a total of $1.5 billion. To reduce that amount, Turner guaranteed to sell back the studio's United Artists film division, which Kerkorian had merged into MGM when he purchased UA in 1981. Removing the $470 million Turner negotiated for UA made the MGM purchase alone worth $1 billion plus change. For that price, Turner would receive the large MGM library—2,200 films that included such classics as *Gone with the Wind, The Wizard of Oz, Singin' in the Rain, Mutiny on the Bounty,* and *Ben-Hur,* plus scores of old television programs. In addition, the MGM package included the 44-acre studio complex in Culver City, California, and a film processing lab popular with off-lot producers as well.

At the time that Turner was attempting to absorb MGM, the studio had just hired David Gerber to head its television operations. One of Hollywood's most respected producers, Gerber's most recent project had been the CBS miniseries *George Washington,* starring Barry Bostwick, Jaclyn Smith, and Patty Duke, which won a Peabody Award. While the film division was losing money ($66.2 million in 1984), the television distribution arm, under MGM/UA president Larry Gershman, contributed $104 million in gross sales, thanks to *Fame, Kids Inc.,* and the *MGM/UA Premiere Network,* which once a month aired an MGM film over independent television stations.

To pay for his purchase, Turner turned to Michael Milken of Drexel Burnham Lambert—the very man who helped finance Murdoch's planned takeover of the Metromedia stations. By no small coincidence, Milken was also Kerkorian's investment banker. This tight-knit family of wheeler-dealers was still several years away from the junk-bond implosion that would ultimately send Milken to jail. For now, the mood was cautiously upbeat as TBS attempted to maintain an aggressive posture of confidence. Turner himself was so certain the deal would be successful that he flew to Alaska on a fishing expedition and disappeared into the ice caps of the Arctic without television or telephone to keep him advised. When he reappeared several weeks later, he was relaxed and excited about the prospect of taking over the helm of the studio that was formed in 1924 with the merger of Metro Pictures Corporation, Goldwyn Pictures Corporation, and Louis B. Mayer Pictures. He met with MGM executives and told them what he had spoken of publicly for years: he wanted to make "family pictures," movies like *Shane* and *The Right Stuff.* Ironically, neither film was from MGM.‡‡

Hollywood reacted like a petulant child, with one producer stating, "If [Turner] starts to let his personal convictions affect what pictures get made or what themes they have, he will drive the company into the ground."[12] Yet Turner had only to look to the late Samuel Goldwyn for support. It was Goldwyn who had

---

‡‡ *The Right Stuff* was produced by the Alan Ladd Company through Warner Bros., and *Shane* was a Paramount Pictures production.

said, "Public morality is a very important factor on the screen. I seriously object to seeing on the screen what belongs in the bedroom."[13]

On September 3, 1985, Rupert Murdoch looked out across a windless Manhattan night, alone and unconcerned about morality. He caught the stillness of the evening, drawing in the dry air in heavy sighs of resolution. Caught in the glare of downtown streetlights, his face was thick and hung in ropes of flesh and wrinkles, a blotchy pink and white, like rumpled chintz. This was his last evening as an Australian, and Rupert Murdoch reflected on his life. It was a momentary pause in the manic pace that had become his reality, and when he caught himself becoming even briefly sentimental, he immediately closed the portal and pretended a part of him was not dying.

The following morning, Murdoch dressed in a dark suit, plain tie, and starched white shirt, having given thought to each element of his appearance. He wanted this day to be observed in a subdued, almost reverent way, without the intrusion of the newspapers that had made him his fortune, or the reporters they employed. Like a rosary processional, the Murdochs left their Fifth Avenue co-op, Rupert first, followed by Anna, Elisabeth, Lachlan, and James. The family entered two waiting limousines—Anna and the children in the lead, husband and father following—and snaked their way through midtown traffic to the federal courthouse in lower Manhattan where, at exactly 10:55 A.M., Rupert Murdoch became a citizen of the United States. In that afternoon's edition of the *New York Post*, he was pictured shaking hands with the honorable Judge Shirley Wohl Kram, surrounded by his smiling family.

In Australia, Murdoch's mother, Elisabeth, attempted to deflect the impact of his lost citizenship by claiming, "The whole affair has been blown out of all proportion. Rupert's affection for his home country is in no way affected by this. He's still very fond of Australia and I very much hope one day he'll be back here. If Rupert had not achieved so much, nobody would be taking any notice, would they?"[14]

Dame Elisabeth was far too astute not to realize the basic fallacy in her logic. Clearly, her only son was willing to do whatever it took to maintain and increase his power and achievements, including forsaking his country. The point did not escape *New York Times* columnist William Safire, who asked, "Isn't it true that his main reason for becoming a citizen is simple greed and lust for power?" Safire argued that someone, anyone, "should remind him that allegiance means loyalty, sometimes passionate loyalty."[15]

Murdoch's loyalty, of course, was clear and evident. He was loyal to himself and to his family (who remained Australian citizens). Later his wife, Anna, would say, "I realized then how strong his ambitious drive was,"[16] as if his behavior during the previous 18 years had given her no clue.

With the citizenship issue resolved, Murdoch had cleared the final hurdle. Now in control of the Metromedia television stations, he began to formulate plans to launch a fourth television network to compete with ABC, CBS, and NBC. "They are hated in Hollywood because they call all the shots," he said, referring to production companies that were at the mercy of the networks' ratings-related quick-cancellation policy. Murdoch planned instead to offer independent stations "strong original programming" in exchange for five minutes per hour of advertising time on their outlets. Networks typically reserve eight minutes of each hour for national advertising sales. Independents would be free to sell the three minutes of advertising per hour themselves, increasing profits. "We expect to be welcomed with open arms," Murdoch said.[17]

Gilding his comments in the glow of expectation, Murdoch was anything but assured of an easy acceptance of his idea for a new network. It had been tried in the past (most recently, Paramount had made an effort to form the Paramount Network) without success, yet success was what Murdoch desperately needed. While News Corporation was still generating overall profits despite the drain of the *New York Post* and the *Boston Herald,* the billion-dollar debt load Murdoch was assuming with the purchase of the Metromedia stations was staggering. Since the stations alone were not generating enough profit, Murdoch was counting on a successful national network to pay off his loan. Failure would necessitate issuing more News Corporation stock, diluting his majority ownership to the point where he might eventually lose control.

A similar situation was facing Ted Turner as he relied on his own junk bonds to finance his much-ballyhooed acquisition of MGM. Confident in his ability to sell off portions of his purchase to raise immediate cash, Turner was relying on the long-term value of the MGM film library to generate the profits needed to reduce his debt. Ted the Terrible, as those on the MGM lot began to call him, had one advantage over Murdoch. With the successful junk-bond issue by Drexel Burnham Lambert, Turner owned *all* of MGM. Murdoch owned only *half* of 20th Century-Fox, which did not sit well with a man used to being in total control.

Murdoch resolved the Fox ownership issue in late September 1985 by taking on $325 million more in debt and buying out Marvin Davis' interest in the studio. As part of the negotiations, Davis kept ownership of certain Fox properties, including the Pebble Beach Country Club, a half interest in Colorado's Aspen Skiing Company, and 2.7 acres of the studio lot that fronted Century City's Avenue of the Stars, on which Davis planned to build a high-rise office tower. Though the final terms were easy to define, the negotiations were acrimonious and rife with nit-picking, and included a last-minute deal to provide office space on the Fox lot for Davis' son, John, who was just beginning his career as a film producer.[§]

---

[§] John Davis went on to produce such hits as *Predator, The Firm, Grumpy Old Men, Doctor Dolittle,* and *Behind Enemy Lines.*

As 1985 came to a close, Murdoch and Turner were months away from owning competing studios within five miles of each other on Los Angeles' westside. Two long and arduous paths had brought these men side by side, yet they were separated by opposing ideologies, styles, and ethics. Each was determined to build the dominant global media empire and manipulate the way the world interacted and related in commerce, entertainment, and information. Both were on parallel courses that set in motion changes in communication that were about to alter history, and affect every human on the face of the earth.

# ELEVEN

# A Dash for Freedom, A Race for Goodwill

*I've never done anything like this before.*
*It's like a sailboat racing in a hurricane.*
*It's like being in an airplane in a storm.*
*You buckle your seat belt.*

Ted Turner on buying MGM Studios
Atlanta
March 1986

**A**spen Mountain is not the tallest peak in the United States, but the grandeur it projects makes it seem that way all the same. Perhaps it is because the town of Aspen is so small in contrast, its antique brick buildings butted up against the mountain at the head of Roaring Fork Valley, a glittering jewel of architecture, nature, and the extremely rich who call it home. At Christmastime, Aspen becomes starlight as hundreds of white lights festoon the village in decked halls burning Yule logs. Here, in this land of privilege and excess, Rupert Murdoch looked out across Aspen Mountain and made a decision.

In a life spent battling the high costs driving the newspaper industry, Murdoch always came to the same conclusion: he was being victimized by the unions. From Australia to Great Britain to America, union printers and the excessive wages they earned were bilking hundreds of millions of dollars from his businesses, while those same workers were making the day-to-day operations of his company a management nightmare. Staffing rules coupled with work restrictions to make budgets and schedules nearly irrelevant. In December 1985, Rupert Murdoch decided that it was time for a new order of business—one based on cost efficiencies and technological advancement, free of the constraints of the old union boys.

The mood in England had been slowly moving against labor loyalties, in large part due to the politics of Prime Minister Margaret Thatcher, with continual consoling by Rupert Murdoch. The Thatcher-embraced Employment Act of 1980 set the stage by making it illegal for British unions to participate in sympathy strikes. It was a remarkable piece of legislation that transformed the working landscape by stopping unassociated unions from striking a business in sympathy with those legitimately on strike because of failed contract negotiations. With the threat of public and private shutdowns no longer an issue, industry leaders, Murdoch among them, began to take back control of their businesses.

Thatcher reinforced her anti-union position through the Employment Act of 1982 and the Trade Union Act of 1984. Under these new laws, unions were prohibited from staging flying pickets, in which thousands of protestors surrounded plants and effectively prevented the orderly conduct of business. In addition, companies were given the authority to fire striking union members *en masse* on breach-of-contract grounds. (In 1981, President Ronald Reagan had used a similar law in the United States to discharge 11,359 striking air-traffic controllers and replace them with non-union labor.)

Braced by the new laws, Murdoch began to reevaluate his options in controlling costs and was convinced that the answer lay in building a new printing plant—one capable of handling all of his British newspapers in a single location. Thus inspired, in 1984 he authorized the construction of a large, high-tech facility in the district of Wapping, not far from the Tower of London. The area itself had a rather colorful history, having served as a port for hundreds of years. In the sixteenth century, pirates and other rovers of the sea were hanged in Wapping at low tide, their remains left "until three tides had overflowed them." Warehouses later replaced squalid housing in the district. To the remaining residents of the area, Murdoch's plant represented the final desecration of the architecture of the historic landscape, and its construction in the mid-eighties met with protests from homemakers and blue-collar workers alike.

Murdoch had knocked down a number of decaying though architecturally fascinating warehouses to build a $140 million concrete eyesore that resembled a high-security prison. Labeled Fortress Wapping by the locals, the new plant sat near a small bend on the Thames River between the financial districts of the city and Canary Wharf. Originally, Murdoch had planned for it to replace the outdated facilities of the *Sun*, which were barely able to keep up with increased circulation. The new plant never opened, however, after the Society of Graphic and Allied Trades (SOGAT) and National Graphical Association (NGA) unions pressed for new hires at increased wages, forcing Murdoch deeper into a now all-too-familiar corner.

Pressed to respond, he reacted with aggression hidden under a blanket of calm. In a move as risky as it was unprecedented, Murdoch pledged to do what no publisher had accomplished in more than 200 years of British journalism: break the print unions and free his newspapers from their stranglehold of inefficiency and featherbedding. The secret operation about to take place at the Wapping plant was a clandestine plan as complicated and logistically intricate as any military invasion. Within the walls of Wapping, Murdoch constructed a war room whose mission was to computerize the typesetting and printing processes. With the help of $10 million in equipment and software from Atex Media Solutions, a subsidiary of Eastman Kodak Company, Murdoch began revolutionizing the process by which his newspapers went from journalist to typesetting to printer to delivery truck. At the time, the Atex system had been in use for nearly a decade in the United States. In a matter of months, he had brought in technicians, computers, presses, electronics, and more, all under a cloak of secrecy so tight even his top executives were unaware that the Wapping plant was being transformed into a state-of-the-art facility unlike any in England.

As work continued around the clock, Murdoch's chief negotiator, Bruce Matthews, pursued contract talks with union leaders, who remained blissfully unaware that it was an elaborate ruse to bide time. Ironically, the longer the talks were extended, the more demanding the union became. Union members, well aware of the publisher's billion-dollar debt and his need for a continuing cash flow to satisfy interest payments, wrongly assessed their competitive position and voted to authorize a strike against the News International papers. In a further display of arrogance, they promised to make good on their threat if Murdoch's negotiators did not agree to the union demands—and quickly.

Obliged to explain the activity at his Wapping plant, Murdoch announced that he intended to launch a new daily newspaper, the *Post*, and print it at Wapping. The news was met with an official notification of the unions' intention to include all of the *Post*'s printing staff in its ongoing labor negotiations. Indeed, a union would be involved at Wapping, but it would be neither SOGAT nor NGA. Instead, Murdoch took a page directly from Eddie Shah, a bulbous, philistine publisher and Thatcher supporter.

As Murdoch was building the Wapping plant, Shah attempted to start a national color broadsheet similar in content and appearance to America's *USA Today*. He built a printing facility from scratch using the latest in computerized typesetting and color printing equipment. With dreams of satellite printing stations and electronic distribution, Shah negotiated with England's Electrical, Electronic, Telecommunications, and Plumbing Union (EETPU) to install and operate the equipment at the plant. While his newspaper, *Today*, was not successful,* his

---

* *Today* was eventually taken over by Murdoch's News International, and ceased publication in 1995.

method of sidestepping the powerful SOGAT and NGA unions was. Murdoch hoped to duplicate that triumph by negotiating a secret contract with the EETPU at Wapping.

That Murdoch was able to come to terms with the EETPU while continuing to equip the Wapping plant, without compromising the integrity of his overall scheme, stands as testament to his determination. Nowhere was that determination evidenced more than with his continuing eagerness to accrue debt when his future income from publishing was uncertain.

And so, as Murdoch stepped out into the air that night in Aspen, his mind was an entire orchestra playing a rumba beat. His thoughts drifted to newspapers—always newspapers—Australian, American, British, and the excitement about to unfold because of the decision he had just made. In the distance, he heard the crunch of tire chains against packed snow as he squinted, then glared, across the lake of lightbulbs that electrified this most perfect spot on earth. The sky, cold and silvery as fish scales, competed with its own spectacle of stars. Murdoch knew his world was about to change. He knew the incredible risk he was about to take; knew that he loved the risk, for it made victory that much more exciting.

If he had had a choice, he would have waited a little longer, stretched out the game, played the victim for a few more weeks. However, an unfortunate leak had forced his hand. Days before, a small article in the *Morning Star*, a daily printed by the Communist Party, had hinted of his plans. *Okay then*, he thought, *bloody good*, a smile cracking his lips and allowing the steamy vapor of his breath to drift toward the mountain.

The article was about a letter from balding, bespectacled Geoffrey Richards, a partner in Farrer & Company, Murdoch's law firm headquartered in Lincoln's Inn Fields. The letter had been meant for the eyes of Murdoch's negotiator Bruce Matthews only. That all of London, or at least those who found time to read the *Morning Star*, should see it was a bit of an inconvenience.

Richards logically and dispassionately spelled out the systematic measures that would enable News International to fire all its contracted union printers, down to the last man. "The cheapest way of doing so would be to dismiss employees while participating in a strike or other industrial action," Richards wrote in part. "The idea is to catch as many employees as possible in the net."

Leaving the rustic opulence of Aspen behind, Murdoch flew to London in January 1986 and proceeded to take direct control of the transformation of the British printing industry. He had decided to print *all* his papers at Wapping in a combined effort of monumental scope. For the first time, British journalists' fingers would rest on computer keyboards rather than upright typewriters, writing stories that would be electronically sent to editors and then to the composing room. Of course, his plans presumed that Murdoch's team of reporters would come to Wapping to work—trampling over union picket lines, if need be.

The National Union of Journalists (NUJ) was perhaps the weakest labor organization in all of England. Its members were largely male, rowdy, educated freethinkers who had become journalists in order to dig for the truth. Group involvement was never part of the lifestyle in a profession where secrecy and scoops made or broke careers. As the first whispers of Murdoch's plans began to waft their way from Wapping back to Fleet Street, the NUJ was quick to side with the printers, whose indignation sent them blindly into the trap, striking Murdoch's newspapers on January 24. Overnight, nearly 6,000 union printers were out of work.

Seeking to help the reporters find the path to sanctity, Murdoch placed temptation upon the altar of decision by offering each journalist a raise of 2,000 pounds per year plus company-sponsored private health insurance in return for joining the move to Wapping. While NUJ made feigned overtures of solidarity, the reporters themselves wasted little time in pledging their troth to Murdoch. Given that the alternative would have been immediate dismissal, the wisdom of their choice seemed obvious.

At the *Sun*, editor Kelvin MacKenzie rallied his reporters. "Because where we had been on the end of blackmailing, bullying, every single pay round, every single piece of technology that was introduced into the world, we tried to introduce into this building—every single time there was a threat that if we didn't turn it away they would shut us down. In a minute-by-minute industry, when they've got you by the balls, you've got to listen. Well, [the union printers] haven't got us by the balls anymore. The situation is simply this . . .the only people that matter anymore are the journalists . . . there can't be papers without journalists and with this in mind, we are now going to make this momentous step from Bouverie Street down to Wapping. . . I personally want every single one of you, including those who are ideologically at the opposite end of the pole from me. . . . I want every single one of you at Wapping."[1]

At the *Times*, Charlie Wilson (who, after his stint at the *Chicago Sun-Times*, had replaced Charles Douglas-Home as editor) shouted support to his journalists with, "The storm has broken tonight."[2] At the *News of the World* and the *Sunday Times*, votes were taken and the counts tallied. In all, only 60 reporters quit on principle; the rest packed up their files and asked for directions to the warehouse district.

For the printers, the sinking feeling of betrayal mixed with outrage as they also made their way to Wapping to join the picket lines outside the increasingly fortressed plant. On January 25, 1986, Murdoch labeled it a "dash for freedom" as the journalists and editors were trucked through the picket lines in armored buses supplied by the police. As the level of hostility rose with the passing days, then months, desperation replaced reason, the printers' jobs gone along with the machinery they ran. "Fleet Street is one of the great bastions of Luddism," said a senior government official in *Time* magazine. "The print unions, which have rejected every attempt to adapt to the future, are now washed up on a very lonely shore."[3]

Inside the compound, the printers would have been lost in a world of Atex computer terminals, "F" keys, and high-tech composing systems. They weren't alone. The reporters who made it safely to their new desks found inputting their stories far harder than writing them. Notes on the use of the new keyboards were posted alongside leads and contact numbers.

As frustration among the picketers mounted, Margaret Thatcher's Tory government called in police backup in an effort to control the angry crowds. The picketers' numbers swelled into the thousands. Adding to the growing tumult, several hundred police on horseback maintained their own vigil, barely able to stem the hostility.

Murdoch refused to show any sympathy for the striking workers, never failing to mention in interviews the wage gauging that had existed among their ranks for decades. "We have been giving in to the unions for years, and finally we snapped," he said.[4] As a gesture of conciliation, Murdoch offered to donate the former *Times* printing plant to the union with the suggestion that they start their own paper. It was a haughty bit of facetious advice, given the competitive situation in the British newspaper world. When the unions turned down his offer, Murdoch reverted to compensation as a form of salve. The union leaders listened dispassionately to Murdoch's pledge of 50 million pounds in severance pay. Still refusing to accept the inevitable, union leaders turned down Murdoch's money as well, effectively delivering the publisher a perfect ending to his labor dispute. According to Murdoch, he offered the unions more than any other publisher would have in similar circumstances, and was now relieved of any responsibility for residual hardship they might suffer.

Unfortunately, union leaders did not see it that way, nor for that matter did their membership. They responded by hurling rocks, bottles, lightbulbs, and smoke bombs at the police and security protecting Fortress Wapping. As delivery trucks attempted to leave the plant filled with newspapers, the picketers circled the vehicles and blocked their movement, shouting chants of hatred at their former boss. Signs on the outside of the plant read: DANGER! UNLAWFUL ENTRY PROHIBITED. IF YOU TRY TO BREACH THE SECURITY MEASURES, WHICH INCLUDE BARBED RAZOR WIRE AND SPIKED WALLS, YOU COULD SUFFER SERIOUS INJURY. As the mob surged forward in unity, none of them seemed to care. The black steel fence bulged under the pressure of the shoving horde. It was after midnight before riot police were able to restore order, with several hundred picketers and a few dozen police injured as a result.

Prime Minister Thatcher backed Murdoch completely. "Mr. Murdoch is trying to get rid of restrictive practices which should have been got rid of years ago, and to protect the future of some of Britain's most distinguished newspapers," she said.[5]

The strike did not officially end until mid-January 1987. During that time, the printers who were unable to work within their trade continued to picket, albeit on a reduced scale. The steam that drove the printers faded with any hope that they had of regaining their jobs. In the final negotiations, the printers were awarded 60 million pounds, a pittance to Murdoch, whose print workforce had been cut from 5,500 in 1985 to 570 in 1987. His British newspapers were generating 2 million pounds per week in income, and it was suggested that he would save 50 million pounds annually due to the change. Even his enemies within the Labor Party admitted that his actions had forced the industry to move ahead with the times and into the computer generation.

"The financial world, the industrial world and a whole lot of the rest of the world are impressed that we've been able to change the industrial environment in Fleet Street. And of that we're very proud," Murdoch said.[6] "I feel like a man who has been in a life sentence and has just been freed. I feel wonderful."[7]

In Atlanta, Ted Turner was keeping a close watch on Murdoch's union battles. Turner was decidedly anti-union, and had pushed hard to keep CNN from becoming unionized shortly before he fired Schonfeld. But his interest in Murdoch's effort was less about politics than about profits: the more money Murdoch made, the more he would have for Turner.

Backed against a wall in his effort to buy MGM/UA, Turner had made a quiet offer to sell a 49 percent interest in CNN to Murdoch for a nonnegotiable price of $300 million. The same offer was sent to Viacom as well as the NBC Television Network, with each answer virtually the same. Each of the parties found the idea of owning CNN exciting. Owning less than *half* of CNN, however, was not. Each intended to reject the offer had Turner not changed his mind and pulled the entire deal off the table.

As if on cue, while Turner was grasping for an influx of cash to make his studio dream come true, CNN came into its own as a dominant network. The first sign came with the hiring in mid-1985 of Mutual Radio Network commentator Larry King to replace Sandi Freeman, whose contract was not renewed. King had been a local broadcasting celebrity in Miami, Florida, before moving his interview program to Washington, D.C. Within weeks of his June 1985 initial broadcast from the capital, King had eclipsed Freeman's ratings, and *Larry King Live* soon became the most popular program in the entire CNN lineup.

Yet it took a national disaster to demonstrate the unique value of having a network focused on news 24 hours a day. On the morning of January 28, 1986, the *Challenger* space shuttle was launched from the Kennedy Space Center at Cape Canaveral. It was a bitterly cold Florida morning, and for those 550 reporters at the press site, this was another routine assignment—so routine, in fact, that the only national crew televising the launch live was from CNN.

The networks, long accustomed to successful launches of the shuttle, had relegated the event to page 2 news, mentioned in passing on evening newscasts—little more. Then, of course, the unthinkable happened. A little over a minute into the flight, the shuttle was swallowed in an enormous fireball, its two solid rocket boosters corkscrewing across the sky, followed by entrails of billowing plumes of frozen vapor.

President Ronald Reagan, watching the launch on CNN from the White House, reacted with what he called "stunned silence." Within minutes, the three network channels had interrupted their regular programming to show the last tragic moments of the flight, over and over and over. For those first few all-important seconds, however, it was only CNN correspondent Tom Mintier, covering the liftoff, who put the disaster into words and, ultimately, in perspective. Across Europe, Asia, and Australia, word of the disaster was spread using CNN footage. Finally, the world realized what Ted Turner had been promising since the moment CNN went on the air. His Cable News Network was the "first electronic equivalent of a wire service," according to *Variety*.

Even as the world was literally beating a path to his door, with competitors outbidding one another in an attempt to have exclusive rights to CNN's news coverage, Turner had his eyes on the future, restlessly maneuvering through the global financial markets to acquire MGM/UA. Turner's lust for the studio was so strong that he overlooked what most analysts saw as an outrageously high purchase price for the legendary film facility. The latest negotiation still called for Turner to pay $1.5 billion for the studio by giving Kerkorian $20 a share in cash, plus one share of TBS preferred stock—stock that Turner guaranteed would pay dividends of 14 percent interest. The deal was a calculated risk for Turner, who seemed rejuvenated by the threat of failure. Should he be unable to pay cash dividends in 1988, his only alternative would be to pay Kerkorian with TBS common shares, which would dilute his own control of TBS, or worse, cause him to lose it entirely to the former MGM owner.

No one believed more in Turner than Turner himself, and he leaped at the opportunity to prove the naysayers wrong once again. Even though everyone at MGM knew that Turner intended to sell off various portions of the studio to pay off his excessive debt, when he arrived on the lot for his first tour as owner, he swaggered into place, his Rhett Butler role-play intact.

Turner's acquisition of the most famous movie studio in the world was a career highlight. While the creation of CNN took more creativity, energy, and salesmanship, and its impact on history would be far-reaching and impressive, the MGM/UA purchase was the realization of a seemingly impossible dream. Walking through the gates of MGM, Turner raised his arms wide and screamed *"Awwwlriiiightt!"* In the Irving Thalberg Building, named after the original creative force behind the earliest MGM hits, employees hung from nearby open windows, applauding the arrival of their new boss, catching a glimpse of his dimpled cheeks and gap-toothed grin, and wondering what the next several months would hold. Few could have guessed what Turner had in mind.

When he made his first announcement as the new head of MGM, Turner put Hollywood producers, writers, directors, and stars on notice that there was a different type of executive in town. The man who now owned some of the most famous movies in history unveiled his plans to colorize a select group of pre-1950 theatrical releases, among them the Academy Award–winning *Yankee Doodle Dandy, Captain Blood* with Errol Flynn, *Father of the Bride* starring Elizabeth Taylor, Humphrey Bogart's *The Maltese Falcon* and *High Sierra,* and *Dark Victory* starring Bette Davis. (Some of these films were Warner Bros. and RKO releases, acquired when MGM bought UA in 1981.)

"To change someone's work without any regard to his wishes shows a total contempt for him, for the director and for the public," writer-director Woody Allen said. His was only the first of a stampede of outrage over the process that director John Huston likened to "washing flesh tones over a da Vinci drawing."

The legendary director Billy Wilder was even less kind. "Those fools! Do they really think that colorization will make

*The Informer*\*\* any better? Or *Citizen Kane*† or *Casablanca*? Or do they hope to play off some of the old stinkers by dipping them in 31 flavors? Is there no end to their greed?"

Turner was amazed at the reaction from Hollywood, refusing to listen to any suggestion that colorizing a film was tampering with art. "Women put on makeup, don't they? That's coloring, isn't it?" he asked. "Nothing wrong with that. Besides, when was the last time anyone took photos in black and white? I know, Ansel Adams—but he's dead, too."[8]

On *Larry King Live* on Turner's own CNN, guests Burt Lancaster and Jimmy Stewart ripped into the new owner of MGM for the "pathetic logic" that allowed him to tamper with perfection. Watching from Atlanta, Turner later told King he was devastated. "Those guys are two of my favorite actors, Larry," Turner admitted, though when King suggested Turner respond with equal time, he timidly declined.

The politics of Hollywood washed into Washington via Robert J. Mrazek, the representative from New York's Third Congressional District, who tacked a bill creating the National Film Preservation Act onto Interior Department funding legislation. The Mrazek bill was eventually amended by legislation introduced by Representative Sidney Yates of Illinois, who succeeded in getting a disclaimer added to altered films that reads:

> This is a colorized version of the film originally distributed in black and white. It has been altered without the participation of the principal director, screenwriter, and the other creators of the original film.

---

\*\* John Ford produced and directed *The Informer* in black and white and won the 1935 New York Film Critics Circle Award for best director. Turner colorized the film and eventually released it on home video, only to later discontinue sales. Ironically, original black-and-white versions of the film are still available in video release from Turner Home Entertainment labeled "In Magnificent Black & White."

† Turner was prevented from colorizing *Citizen Kane* due to a stipulation in director-star Orson Welles' contract that forbade any outside tampering with the finished film.

Although the collective indignation over the proposed bastardization of film classics continued to build, Turner was too busy to hear much of the noise. Three months after the close of the MGM sale, Turner found himself struggling to keep up with the million-dollar-a-day interest payments. Publicly, he was extremely lighthearted about his debt, even to the point of enlarging it. "Two billion dollars I owe!" Turner told *Sports Illustrated* writer Gary Smith. "Actually, it's closer to one point nine, but I like the sound of two billion better."[††]

Turner's mother, who happened to be riding in the rear of the car during the interview, leaned forward to ask, "Oh my. How much did he say?"

"*Two billion,*" Turner responded. "No individual in history has ever owed more."[‡]

"Oh Ted, I get a headache thinking about it," said his mother. "Well, you're honest, you'll try to pay it all back, I know."

"Here's my picture in today's paper, Mother. Do I look worried?"

"Oh Ted, you're so full of the dickens. I just wish you had time to come to my house for dinner. It seems like the only time I talk to you anymore is in a car, driving from one place to another."

"Sorry, Mother," Turner answered. "I've got to go."

Turner was racing to catch a plane back to Los Angeles, where, under mounting pressure from his accountants, he agreed to split up portions of MGM, selling the studio's motion picture and television production wing, its home entertainment group, and its name and lion logo *back* to Kerkorian for $300 million, far less than he had paid three months earlier for those same items. In addition, Turner sold the studio lot in Culver

---

[††] Turner combined his MGM debt with the $64 million he paid to buy 75 percent of the Omni Hotel complex in downtown Atlanta as the new enlarged home for CNN and TBS, plus the $35 million in start-up costs for the Goodwill Games, and $6 million for his sixth estate—this one in Florida.

[‡] At the time, Rupert Murdoch's debt actually exceeded that amount.

City, California, and the MGM film laboratory to Lorimar-Telepictures, a television production company responsible for such hits as *The Waltons, Dallas, Falcon Crest, Knots Landing,* and *The Love Connection,* for $190 million.

Days later, Turner was on the move again, this time flying to Moscow to oversee the July 1986 debut of the Goodwill Games. His arrival in the Soviet Union at the Sheremetyevo International Airport was itself a hammer-and-sickle ego boost, with Turner greeted like an arriving head of state. "We can best achieve peace by letting the peoples of the world get to know each other better," Turner proclaimed. "Not only will the participants compete together in the spirit of good sportsmanship, but the audiences worldwide will see the harmony that can be fostered among nations."

The $100 million games, assembled in a year and a half since their announcement, were bleeding red ink thanks to mediocre ad sales, but Turner looked upon the athletic competition less for its potential profits than for its potential humanitarian benefits. "These people are *people,*" Turner said, referring to the Soviets. "So we've got different political systems, so *what?* That's just like saying all the Jews should be dead, you know, because they don't believe the way we do." The Cold War and its nuclear threat hung heavily on Turner's mind. "A nuclear war is only gonna happen once. I'll tell you, just stand back from it and look at it dispassionately, like you were an extraterrestrial being that was flying over this beautiful planet, and you'd say that we're mad. M-A-D."[9]

By contrast, around Atlanta Turner took great pride in his frugality, driving an aging Toyota Cressida with a CNN sticker on one end of the rear bumper and one instructing HONK IF YOU LOVE MOVIES on the other. In Moscow, frugality was for peasants. The Communist system of government, which prided itself in enforcing universal treatment for every citizen, routinely broke its own rules by separating the "haves" from "have nots" through grand accommodations and transportation for the former. While in the Russian capital, Turner traveled in a chauffeur-driven limousine, slept in the city's finest hotel suite, and tipped in dollars "'cause you can't buy anything with those rubles or rubies or whatever they call their money."

Turner started professing a fondness for Russian politics: "Communism is fine with me. It's part of the fabric of life on this planet."[10] He did not, however, particularly like the food. He never ate potatoes, a Russian staple, and could not stand *borscht*. He had his fill of caviar the first night, and never developed a taste for vodka. When he discovered that the Soviets had yet to open their first pizza restaurant,‡ Turner ordered 100 deep-dish pies from an Atlanta Pizza Hut franchise and had them shipped to the Soviet Union on KLM Royal Dutch Airlines. Because Russia does not permit the importation of meat, all the pepperoni was removed from the pizzas before the imported pies cleared customs.

As Soviet general secretary Mikhail Gorbachev opened the Goodwill Games with vague references to the "lurking catastrophe" and the "dangerous race toward the abyss," those watching in the half-filled stadium stands seemed more interested in waiting for their cue to hold up large flip cards to form a picture of Lenin's face. Even as athletes from 70 nations marched into the competition, flags and arms waving, politics was not far from the scene as Soviet camera crews left the athletes to show more flip cards in the stands, now displaying a picture of an American cruise missile superimposed by a giant red X.

Any goodwill hoped for on the field failed to materialize as the games began. The Russian athletes dominated the Americans to such an extent that accusations of drug use stole the headlines. "He's souped up," pole vaulter Earl Bell said of Soviet competitor Sergei Bubka, who won the event with a world-record

---

‡ Pizza Hut opened its first Russian franchise in Moscow in 1990. It is now the second-highest-volume Pizza Hut in the world. Paris is the first.

leap of 19 feet, 8¾ inches.§ "It all comes down to the doctors," said fourth-place finisher Mike Tully. "It may be they've figured a way to get around the drug testing." Runner Carl Lewis added, "The Russians just cheat." To Lewis, who had won four gold medals in the 1984 Olympic Games, it didn't seem to matter that Ben Johnson, a Jamaican from Canada, outran him in the 100-meter to take first place. "They'll try to help anyone beat us," he said.[11]

Only hours after the games began, Soviet dissidents Olga and Yuri Medvedkov were arrested and jailed for their anti-Communist views. The incident was widely reported in American newspaper and television reports, though not on CNN despite the availability of cameras and crew. Stuart Loory, CNN bureau chief in Moscow, excused the oversight by claiming no video was available to accompany the piece.

When not in the stadium stands watching the games, Turner was giving interviews, joking with the athletes in the locker rooms, awarding medals, and always talking. He was the kid, and the candy store was open. As if to prove the point, he made certain that his entourage—all 85 of them—shared his excitement. Included were his wife, Jane, his five children, his former girlfriend Liz Wickersham and current girlfriend J. J. Ebaugh, and Jimmy Brown.

Fifteen days later, as the Goodwill Games ended, Turner was $28 million dollars in the hole, world peace was just as tenuous, and critics were laughing themselves into hernia operations after viewing the televised product. *People* magazine said that Turner "started his Goodwill Games in Moscow with all the enthusiasm of Mickey Rooney and Judy Garland putting on a show in the barn, but with half their resources."[12] *Sports Illustrated*'s William Taaffe wrote, "TBS may be full of goodwill, but 129 hours of multievent television is too daunting a task for a network still in knee pants," adding that the entire production was "painfully inept."[13]

---

§ In the years following the first Goodwill Games, Sergei Bubka repeatedly went on to break his own world records. He currently holds the record for the highest indoor jump at 20 feet, 1¼ inches, set on July 31, 1994.

Turner dismissed the criticism as missing the entire point of the effort. "This wasn't about making money. My main concern is to . . . build up a global communications system that helps humanity come together. Money isn't everything, man. Jesus Christ didn't make money; neither did Martin Luther King."

Countering what he saw as the growing hostility of Americans toward Russia, Turner had one final message to send to the world before leaving the land of beet soup and potato vodka. "In the U.S., we're saying things like, 'They're an evil empire and a bunch of bums,' and we don't even know them. To keep from blowing ourselves up, isn't this worth a shot?" he asked. "Can't hurt," he answered, adding, "And not just ourselves. What about the elephants?"[14] And with that he snapped shut his final suitcase and headed to the airport to fly to Africa, land of the elephants, for a hunting safari.

Back in Los Angeles, the smog seemed to have settled permanently on Pico Boulevard at the entrance to 20th Century-Fox. A brown wash of particles hung as if draped across the sets from *Hello, Dolly!*, their deteriorating facades visible from the street as Rupert Murdoch made his way onto the lot and into the office of studio chairman Barry Diller. Diller and Murdoch had established a comfortable working relationship—the aggressive head of Fox wielding a free hand to mold and fashion the studio in his image, with Murdoch wise enough to give Diller the financial support that Marvin Davis had not.

The perpetually tanned and demonstrative Diller, who had gotten his early Hollywood credentials working for ABC Television, where he developed the concept of made-for-TV movies, was using Murdoch's six Metromedia stations (plus an additional station purchased in Boston[§§]) to form the core of what the press was billing as a "fourth network" to compete against NBC, CBS, and ABC. It was an ambitious concept even for Murdoch, and the

---

§§ Murdoch bought back the Christian Broadcasting Network's Boston outlet WXNE-TV for $28 million dollars in 1986, and changed its call letters to WFXT-TV.

chances of success were slim. Ever since the late seventies, the networks' share of television viewership had been dropping from 90 percent to 75 percent of American households. Their lockjaw grip on TV audiences had been frayed by the emergence of video-tape, cable, and an ever-growing number of independent stations, each tugging at the same finite number of viewers.

Diller's concept for making the Fox Network a reality was dis-engagingly simple: deliver alternative programming that was judged too risky, crude, or controversial for traditional networks. Diller's first effort was a late-night talk show to star comedienne Joan Rivers, a popular fixture on NBC as the regular substitute for late-night champ Johnny Carson on the *Tonight Show.* When Diller first mentioned Rivers to Murdoch, he had no idea who she was. Yet it did not matter to Murdoch if she was known or even funny; it only mattered that Diller thought she was power-ful enough to launch his network.

The announcement of the *Late Show Starring Joan Rivers* took place in early May 1986 in the formal sculpture garden of Fox TV's Los Angeles affiliate KTTV. The assembled television press snacked on breakfast canapés and coffee, unaware that Rivers had been reduced to tears nearby. The comedienne had arrived moments before the press and was desperate to speak with Johnny Carson, hoping to break the news of her defection from the *Tonight Show* to him in person. Carson, however, had already been informed by NBC president Brandon Tartikoff and refused to speak to Rivers. The resulting hysteria brought Diller and Jamie Kellner, his newly hired Fox Broadcasting president, racing to the side of the new network's first star, and the pair remained by her throughout the course of the press conference.

"Joan Rivers has brought a real sense of adventure and audac-ity to television," Diller said. Little did he know the extent of the adventure and audacity that Rivers and her show soon would bring to the studio. When the *Late Show* premiered on October 9,

1986, it was carried on 95 stations reaching 85 percent of American homes.

Hit by a sluggish economy, the three traditional networks were struggling with layoffs, management changes, and continuing belt tightening. Murdoch pitched Fox Broadcasting to potential advertisers as the cornerstone of a global network that included his Sky Channel in Europe and Network Ten stations in Australia. In response, the Gillette Company signed a $4 million agreement to air a coordinated campaign across the continents. It was, of course, a natural extension of Murdoch's method of doing business. The Australian-turned-American headed an Australian company headquartered in New York with newspapers and satellites capable of reaching every corner of the globe.

The international base was also reflected in Murdoch's unique method of refinancing his mounting debt. Rather than issuing preferred shares of News Corporation that could be converted into common stock in the company (typical but also highly dilutive to Murdoch's majority control), he went to the Euromarket with another offer altogether. Two hundred thousand shares of nonvoting preferred stock in News Corporation that could be converted into common stock in Reuters Holdings, the British-based international news service in which Murdoch held a 9 percent stake. It was a bit of global hocus-pocus that was unheard of but not illegal.

Turner was facing a similar financing dilemma to pay off the high-interest junk bonds that paid for his purchase of MGM Studios. Turner's approach, however, was more predictable, though surprising nonetheless. In a move that was as remarkable for its timing as it was for its structure, Turner announced he was stepping aside from the day-to-day management of TBS and assigning the responsibility to a five-man management committee composed of veteran TBS executives. The quintet consisted of Robert Wussler, TBS executive vice president and former CBS network president; Jack Petrick, executive vice president and general manager of WTBS, charged with handling the MGM film library; William Beins, Turner's longtime CFO and vice president; Gerald Hogan, Turner's vice president of advertising; and Terence McGuirk, vice president of special projects, who oversaw legal and cable matters.

Media analysts were skeptical about the legitimacy of the announcement, with most suggesting it was little more than subterfuge created to impress the financial community. "He would never even let the five go out and have a beer together, let alone run the company," said one.[15]

Turner's agenda became apparent several months later, when on January 13, 1987, the media mogul made an open appeal to cable industry leaders to save his company from falling into "enemy" hands. In this case, the enemy was Rupert Murdoch, and rumors were rampant that he intended to gain control of TBS. "We had enormous value to the cable industry," Hogan said. "The worst thing that could happen to them would be that we'd sell something to Murdoch."[16]

Tele-Communications Inc. (TCI) president and CEO John Malone captained the meeting of cable executives from ATC, Cox, Continental, United, and Warner, who listened quietly while Turner solicited an influx of quick funds. Lots of funds. Half a billion. In exchange, Turner was willing to part with one-third of Turner Broadcasting. Although it was not an instant sell, it was hardly a difficult decision for Turner's major customers. What was good for Turner ultimately was good for the cable industry. With their self-interest in mind, the cable companies passed the hat and publicly rescued Turner from being devoured by debt.

Turner would later say that the buyout was only one of several options he had available to him. Clearly, it was the most synergistic, yet when the final agreement was announced on June 3, 1987, it was painfully obvious that Turner the maverick had been roped and tamed for $562.5 million. In exchange for the cash,

Turner transferred ownership of 37 percent of TBS and gave up 7 of 15 seats on his board of directors to the cable interests. He also agreed to put any expenditure that exceeded $2 million up to a vote of the board, with a four-fifths majority needed to proceed. Tamed and roped.

All the public scrutiny that Turner's business maneuvers generated between the end of 1986 and the dawn of 1987 managed to deflect attention from the reality of his life. Unbeknownst to all but his closest confidants, Turner's personal world was collapsing around him and became the focus of much of his energy.

The dramatic turn of events began soon after Turner arrived in Africa for his post–Goodwill Games hunting safari. Botswana was an emerald swirl as the fertile Okavango River delta flowed toward the Kalahari, papyrus poking toward the hot summer sky like arms cast to their creator in worship. As Turner's sons Rhett and Beau took photographs of wild game, their father hunted lions, eager for a trophy to bring back to Atlanta. Drinking heavily and sleeping only sporadically, Turner was stunned to hear from his safari guide, documentary filmmaker Rick Lomba‖, that Turner's romance with J. J. Ebaugh was finished. Turner was completely unaware that Ebaugh was upset over Turner's indulgence of his wife during the Goodwill Games. Ebaugh left Moscow and flew to California into the arms of a podiatrist whom she had known for several months.

Upon returning to Atlanta, Turner reverted to form and launched a sales campaign to win back the woman he credited with opening his eyes and mind to the "precarious condition of the environment." With the five-man team supposedly in charge of TBS, Turner concentrated all his effort on J. J. It took several months and multiple pledges of devotion, but in the end,

---

‖ Rick Lomba was an eco-activist best known for his film *The End of Eden,* which focused on elephant culling and population control in Kenya. In 1994, he was mauled to death by a male tiger while filming an animal rescue operation at the Luanda Zoo in Angola. He was 44 years old.

Ebaugh believed Turner when he said, "I can't live without you."[17] So too did Jane Smith Turner, his wife, who announced her separation from her husband and her intention to seek a divorce after 22 years of marriage.

In September 1986, while Jane remained at their Florida plantation with her three children, Turner moved with J. J. into a small home in Roswell, Georgia, on the northern banks of the Chattahoochee River. The same month, his Cable News Network moved into new headquarters in the Omni Hotel, which was renamed the CNN Center.

For Turner, the uncertainty of his future played on his mind, affecting his emotional stability and confidence to the point that conducting daily business became nearly impossible. Not even the quick influx of financing could placate his anxiety or put an end to his increasing insomnia. For the first time in years, Turner thought about his life—and his death. The specter of his father's suicide haunted him. A mounting nervous energy played a fitful tune, threatening to explode in temper as release. And then, just as unexpectedly, he received news that made his business problems irrelevant—news so dreaded that Ted Turner fell to his knees in prayer.

# TWELVE

# For Richer or Poorer, in Sickness and in Health

*What is a newspaper?*
*You cut down a tree, mash it, make paper,*
*deliver it by truck to somebody's house,*
*then another truck takes it away—*
*and every stage requires fuel!*

Ted Turner
Atlanta
August 1987

The telephone call was unexpected, like autumn mushrooms springing from a cloak of dew. *Moscow calling. There has been an accident. Ted Turner has been seriously hurt. Ted Turner IV.*

The news struck Ted Turner III with uninvited urgency, the kind that delivers an adrenaline surge followed by nervous nausea. The kind that Turner had experienced few times in his life, but never with this intensity. What followed was a frantic exercise in international diplomacy to learn the details of a near-fatal wreck that smelled of booze and excessive speed. With CNN's Moscow bureau acting as the go-between, the news trickled back to Atlanta. *Ice-slick roads. A night of drinking in a Moscow bar. A CBS cameraman at the wheel. Head-on crash. Iron streetlamp. Both men in a Moscow hospital. Face crushed. Internal bleeding. Jaw wired shut.*

For the man who was used to controlling each aspect of his life, from home to business to romance to press, the injury of Turner's eldest son was an emotional watershed. His skin the color of boiled ham, his nerves dancing to a staccato rhythm, Turner moved through one day to the next with helpless abandon. Inexplicably, he did not fly to Moscow to be at his son's side, but rather waited to receive the all-clear from the Russian doctors before sending an air ambulance to transport Teddy to Atlanta's Emory University Hospital, one of the nation's leading acute care teaching facilities. There, specialists immediately began to reconstruct Teddy's face, which had been cracked and battered beyond recognition.

Little in Turner's world prepared him for the arbitrary hand of fate. His mandate had always been control: as a sailing captain, as an executive, as a husband, and as a father. Forced to admit his vulnerability, Turner reacted with characteristic impulsiveness, charging forth and gathering the troops—in this case his family members—to rally around Teddy.

The family fix was little more than a stopgap, however, for as soon as Turner was assured that his son was responding to treatment, he redirected his energy toward his next order of business: the launching of yet another cable channel, Turner Network Television, to broadcast films from his newly acquired MGM library as well as major events—"Things like the Rose Bowl Parade and the Kentucky Derby, the Indianapolis 500 and the Olympics," said Turner. "And yeah, the Academy Awards. Let's get that too," he added, apparently unaware that the show was contracted to ABC.

It was then that Turner discovered that although he owned the entire MGM library, he did not have clear television rights to the films. Among the movies that were not available for broadcast were two of the biggest: *Gone with the Wind* and *The Wizard of Oz*. Those rights had been licensed to CBS for 20 years.

"When Turner discovered that CBS owned the rights to air *Gone with the Wind*, I think he was shocked," said CBS Broadcast Group president Gene Jankowski. "He came to us and began to negotiate to get the films back. As it happened, we had already made back what we had spent on *Gone with the Wind* in just the first few telecasts, so [CBS Television president] Bud Grant did the deal that gave Ted Turner back the movies he was determined to own outright. Of course, it cost him several more million."[1]

Exhausted at the end of his perpetual workdays, Turner had begun to spend evenings resting on the pull-out sofabed in his penthouse office at Atlanta's new CNN Center rather than make the drive back to his Roswell home. His trademark drive seemed to be faltering along with his ability to exist on little sleep. In its place were mini-naps and long periods of inactivity. Concerned about his health, Turner began to consult Atlanta specialists, though initially he was found to be in remarkable shape. It was only after he continued to complain of a lack of energy that further tests were done and a diagnosis rendered. Turner had chronic fatigue syndrome, a condition that surfaced in the early to mid-eighties, the cause of which has yet to be identified.

Unwilling to bend to his health, Turner made few compromises in his schedule, which often included traveling for weeks at a time, with meetings and speeches in multiple states. *Sports Illustrated* writer Gary Smith watched as Turner made appearances on CNN's *Larry King Live,* NBC's *Tonight Show,* and CBS' *60 Minutes*; spoke at Yale, the Africa Travel Council, the International Radio and Television Society, and George Washington University; and met with the Motion Picture Association of America over eggs, the president of Volkswagen over croissants, his investment brokers at Drexel Burnham Lambert over burgers, MGM executives over club sandwiches, and the head of Ford Motor Company over a chef salad. He also had two dinner meetings at the film studio, attended an Atlanta Hawks basketball game, and got up at 4:15 A.M. to do a live satellite feed to Cannes, France. All in a seven-day period.

Turner's girlfriend, J. J. Ebaugh, was so concerned he was working himself to death that she threatened once again to break off the relationship if he did not slow down. Although

Turner agreed to the ultimatum, it did not necessarily translate into a less crowded schedule. Business meetings were canceled or postponed only to be replaced by kayaking, hunting, and skiing trips. It was a schedule Turner himself labeled "impossible." Yet it continued.

Rupert Murdoch's own manic pace was hardly helped by his determination to launch a fourth television network while continuing to build his media empire. Should anyone doubt his intention to refuse to rest on past achievements, Murdoch saturated the press with notices of intended acquisitions as well as series launches to such an extent that his name became linked with projects as widespread as experimental farming and space exploration.

The truth was no less amazing or diversified. Murdoch first leaped over the Pacific with his first purchase in Asia, paying $300 million for Hong Kong's leading English-language daily, the *South China Morning Post*. Unlike the ailing newspapers he had bought in the past, the *Morning Post* had earned $21 million in net profits the year before. Jumping back to America, Murdoch paid yet another $300 million, this time for Harper & Row Publishers, which pleased his wife, Anna, who had moved from raising the couple's children to writing novels, despite her husband's repeated mockery of her attempts. "Rupert never saw the need for me to have an independent career," Anna said a decade after publishing her first novel, *In Her Own Image*, in 1985. Her writing career didn't fly far from the nest, however. *Image* was published by William Collins Sons & Co. Ltd., the British publishing house in which Murdoch had been quietly picking up shares and now owned 42 percent interest.

For several years, Anna had been struggling for her own independence, pushing to emerge from under her husband's dominance and fame. She enrolled at Fordham University and later received her Master of Arts degree in literature and mythology from New York University. When *In Her Own Image* was published, it gushed with romance. Set in the desolate bush country of Australia's New South Wales, the novel told of a woman who lived on her daughter's sheep ranch, a place of long-buried secrets about to be flushed into tormented reality. It was the type of story that Harper & Row might find acceptable and well structured, though its prose might have been too innocent for its plot. More than a few critics pointed out the coincidence that Murdoch bought an American publishing house just as Anna was preparing her follow-up novel. He purchased it for an amount that left industry analyst Ed Atorino, managing director of Smith Barney, "flabbergasted by the high price."[2] Perhaps no one was more flabbergasted than Harper & Row executives, who had been entertaining a bid from competing publisher Harcourt Brace Jovanovich for 30 percent less.

Amid talk of synergy between authors and Fox Television, and a bottomless well of creative ideas, the real clutch behind the drive to buy Harper & Row was Ian Chapman, chairman and CEO of William Collins. It was Chapman who alerted Murdoch to Harper & Row's availability and pushed for a quick buy of the publisher, whose authors ranged from Mark Twain and Aleksandr Solzhenitsyn to Colleen McCullough, author of *The Thorn Birds*. Once put on the scent, Murdoch concluded the deal in two days with a handshake.

It was Murdoch's favorite kind of acquisition: quick, spontaneous, and without complications, three words that did *not* manage to enter into his latest Australian acquisition. For that purchase, he needed patience and extraordinary determination. Murdoch found both in what journalists reported was a "grudge purchase"—the return of Australia's *Herald* and *Weekly Times*, the newspapers his father once ran so superbly, to Murdoch family control.

While Murdoch was busy telling anyone who would listen that he had an "emotional attachment" to the newspapers, and most bought into the argument that he was finally getting back at the company that did not treat the family well at the time of his father's death, there was a far more fundamental purpose behind the acquisition, one that escaped notice at the time: reduce News Corporation debt by spending money.

In what later appeared to be a sleight-of-hand straight from Houdini, Murdoch bid $1.6 billion for the assets of the Herald Group after a seven-week struggle with Australian media baron Robert Holmes à Court, who had stubbornly refused to part with his 15 percent ownership of the company. Following a last-ditch Perth–New York telephone negotiation, Holmes à Court finally agreed to part with his shares, but only after Murdoch agreed to transfer ownership of Melbourne TV station HSV-7 and a group of West Australian newspapers that were once under the Herald Group umbrella.

The deal served Murdoch well in camouflaging his true agenda: that of moving around stock ownership in a clever shell game. In acquiring the Herald Group, he made a cash payment to one-third of the company's shareholders. To the remaining two-thirds, Murdoch issued News Corporation shares or convertible stock. Those shares went to a variety of Australian newspapers that held the Herald stock—Queensland Press Ltd., a Brisbane corporation; Advertiser Newspapers in Adelaide; and Davies Brothers, headquartered in Hobart. Each of those companies was actually a subsidiary of the Herald Group. Essentially, Murdoch was giving the stock back to himself, thereby gaining assets without diluting his ownership percentage in News Corporation. The presto-chango stock swap was made legal by a convenient change in Australia's media laws governing ownership of newspapers.

Murdoch's debt, of course, took another giant step forward, increasing by another billion dollars, which the banks eagerly advanced based on the worth of the *Herald*. It was the ultimate pyramid scheme: taking on more debt to buy more companies in order to increase assets, allowing one to take on more debt. It required Murdoch to remain in constant motion both physically and mentally as he jetted between his international holdings, which were now spread over four continents.

His business plan did not allow for a major investment of time, his rarest commodity, in any one venture, however. Yet, by mid-1987, the ever-changing challenges of establishing Fox TV as a fourth commercial network were demanding major attention, led by the drama being created backstage on the set of the *Late Show Starring Joan Rivers*. Since its debut in October 1986, the *Late Show* had been struggling to attract guests that would keep an audience. NBC's *Tonight Show* was threatening to boycott any guest who appeared on Fox, and while the show never truly carried through with that threat, the suggestion alone was enough to intimidate many Hollywood stars. Compounding the tension on the Rivers set was a building dissension between Fox executives and the star herself.

Rivers had been placed in a rather impossible position. As Fox's first star, she was charged with representing the fledgling network as well as attracting other talent into the fold. Rivers responded by doing what she did best: being outrageous and controversial and skating on the edge of good taste. Fox had spent millions constructing a studio home for the comedienne, complete with a five-room dressing suite, a comfortable green room for visiting guests, and a stage dressed with designer furniture exuding an image of understated elegance.

Diller had promised Rivers that he would give the show time to build, and signed her to a three-year contract presumably with that purpose in mind. He oozed camaraderie, pledged assistance, and ultimately turned his back on the entire program. Fox had bought a star whose reputation was built on personal assault. No one was immune, including the star herself. Yet, the more Rivers drew on her legacy of scathing humor and Jewish guilt, the more the general viewing public turned the channel to NBC. Diller, in an effort to stop the hemorrhaging of viewers, immediately demanded that Rivers' husband, Edgar Rosenberg, an executive producer of the program, stop interfering in the show, initially attempting to have him banned from the set. Rosenberg was Rivers' lifeline, soul mate, and best friend, and Rivers took any assault on her husband as a direct attack on her.

Courtney Conte,* a veteran field producer and highly respected problem-solver in Hollywood who joined the show as an assistant to its original producer, Bruce McKay, now ran interference between Fox executives and Rivers. Conte had been attacked by the studio for supporting Rivers, and the star believed he was a mole for the studio. Line producers began rotating through the executive suite with the regularity of new moons. Morale on the set plummeted, taking Rivers' energy level along with it.

With the series running into a multi-million-dollar deficit, Fox attempted to tighten the purse strings at the same time it wanted to expand its audience. The most symbolic example was found in the removal of the refrigerator containing sodas and water for crew and guests. Installed in its place was a Pepsi machine selling a variety of beverages "at cost." The production staff, in full defiance of the studio, refused to use the machine and blanketed it with often rude messages directed at Diller and Murdoch, who found the Pepsi machine an "inappropriate vehicle for employee disputes."

By the first week of May 1987, Diller gave up on the *Late Show*, convinced that every effort had been made to salvage the unsalvageable. The death knell for the talk show sounded on May 12 in Manhattan at a meeting of Fox executives at Murdoch's office. Reviewing the falling ratings for the series, Murdoch shuffled through the various Nielsen markets and ordered, "Buy her con-

---

*Conte went on to become vice president of production at Carsey-Werner Productions and was involved in the creation of such comedies as *Roseanne, 3rd Rock from the Sun, Grace Under Fire, Cybill,* and *Cosby* before being promoted to co-president and head of production for Carsey-Werner-Mandabach.

tract out now." No remorse, no reflection. "If we're going down, let's cut our losses and try something else."[3]

Three months later, Rivers' husband, depressed over the show's failure, committed suicide in a hotel room in Philadelphia. The comedienne received neither flowers nor condolences from Murdoch, who chose to ignore those seeking to hold him even partially responsible. He was busy preparing for the start of the fall television season, as his fledgling network now had its first full-fledged hit in *Married . . . with Children*. It was a show that would eventually set the tone for the fourth network. The comedy, starring Ed O'Neill and Katey Sagal, pushed boundaries and knocked down walls right along with America's perception of acceptable levels of gratuitous sex and senseless violence. *Married . . . with Children* debuted in April 1987 and went on for a run of 10 years, to the continuing frustration of those who longed for a higher order of sitcom taste. Yet the show, whose original working title was *Not the Cosbys,* found its audience among the same viewers who snapped up Murdoch's sensationally headlined newspapers in the checkout lines in supermarkets.

Fox wanted young America, Fox wanted reality. With *MWC,* they got both. Young America watched the program, and the reality was that Mom and Pop America were none too happy about it. In Michigan, one housewife, Terry Rakolta, became so incensed by the image of a television series that showcased a shoe salesman who scratched his crotch and had smelly feet that she sent letters of protest to every advertiser on the program. Though her previous campaigning had been limited to country clubs and the boards of a number of Detroit museums, Rakolta's letter writing achieved results that surprised even her. Coca-Cola president Ira C. Herbert responded with a personal apology, saying he was "corporately, professionally and personally embarrassed."[4] She appeared on ABC's *Nightline* to proclaim that the Fox show was "consistently offensive" and "exploited women, stereotyped poor people and is antifamily." Unfortunately, her comments attracted so many viewers to the program that for a while, *MWC* was Fox TV's top-rated show.

The popularity of the program did not stop Fox from losing $59 million in 1987, about the same amount that Murdoch made by trading foreign currencies among his various international companies. In fact, business was so good in 1987 that the corporation made $600 million in profits—albeit with $4.6 billion in debt. Even so, Murdoch showed no sign of ending his shopping spree. In September 1987, he acquired 14.7 percent of the British conglomerate Pearson PLC, whose holdings included the *Financial Times* as well as Royal Doulton China, and later increased his ownership to 20 percent.

He was a rich man, a press baron with homes in five cities and businesses across the world. The master manipulator of stocks and corporate holding companies, his string of finances so complicated only a few of his accountants knew his real worth. Murdoch reached a milestone by being ranked eighth on Forbes magazine's list of the 400 richest men in America in October 1987. He was worth $2.1 billion according to *Forbes,* which calculated his fortune based primarily on his stock.

Unfortunately for Murdoch, between the time he made the list and the moment the issue was published, the Dow Jones average plunged a record 508 points and brought the Australian markets down with it. On Black Monday, October 19, 1987, Murdoch's fortune dropped $1.7 billion overnight. As copies of *Forbes* were being delivered to newsstands across the country, the Commonwealth Bank in New York City was placing a lien on Murdoch's Manhattan penthouse at the corner of 88th Street and Fifth Avenue.[5]

Although many major players on Wall Street had taken a beating, Murdoch's was worse than most, with News Corporation's stock price plummeting by more than half. For a less seasoned mogul, such news might have spelled disaster. For Murdoch, it served to motivate him to play a game of real-life

Monopoly with recharged enthusiasm. If cash was in short supply, Murdoch's audacity was not, particularly where the FCC was
concerned. Even as the market was vacillating, Murdoch moved
his attention away from net worth to confront the FCC's cross-
ownership rules that forbid a company or individual from owning a newspaper and television station in the same city. While
Murdoch had received a two-year temporary waiver of the rule,
allowing him to keep the *New York Post* as well as the *Boston Herald*** when he bought the Metromedia stations, those waivers
were about to expire, and Murdoch still was not eager to sell.
Pushing the limits of legal tolerance, he placed his faith in Washington lobbyists and an organization called the Freedom of
Expression Foundation, whose $300,000 annual budget relied
heavily on Murdoch's Fox Broadcasting for financing.

Since buying the *Boston Herald,* Murdoch had managed to
turn the newspaper around, and bragged that it was now making
a profit for the first time in nearly a decade. The *New York Post,* by
comparison, continued to lose more than a million dollars a
month, and while Murdoch had indicated his willingness to part
with the financially draining newspaper, no suitors came calling.

In November 1987, the Freedom of Expression Foundation
petitioned the FCC to eliminate or modify the rule. It was a step
openly supported by President Ronald Reagan, who long held the
position that the FCC "needlessly regulated our telecommunications industry."[6] For a moment, it appeared that Murdoch was
actually maneuvering his way once again through the government
regulatory system, as he had for years in Australia. He had not,
however, counted on the tenacity of his enemies in the Senate,
including Edward Kennedy, the senior statesman from Massachusetts, whom Murdoch's *Herald* routinely referred to as "Fat Boy."

In mid-December 1987, Kennedy, sensing payback time, had
a conversation with fellow Democrat Ernest Hollings of South

---

** Murdoch sold the *Chicago Sun-Times* for a $60 million profit in 1986.

Carolina, who quietly inserted an amendment into the omnibus year-end spending bill that effectively prevented the FCC from loosening its 12-year-old television/newspaper cross-ownership restrictions. Although Kennedy refused to admit that the amendment was aimed specifically at Murdoch, he had no choice but to acknowledge that Murdoch was the only owner of both a newspaper and television station in any U.S. city. "Now he can keep his newspaper or he can keep his broadcasting station, but he can't keep them both. That's the law," Kennedy said.[7]

Murdoch was in Los Angeles when he received news of the amendment. He channeled his resources into discrediting the law as well as the senators behind the revision. It was time to call in favors and call on friends, including Charles Z. Wick, a member of the Reagan cabinet and head of the U.S. Information Agency. Wick, who would later become a member of the board of directors of News America Holdings Inc., a division of News Corporation, began to stir support for Murdoch among Reagan Republicans.

An outraged Murdoch went on CNN's *Crossfire* and told co-host Pat Buchanan, "We're keeping the *Boston Herald* in spite of Senator Kennedy." The *Herald*'s editor ran a front-page story headlined KENNEDY'S VENDETTA, and *Herald* columnist Howie Carr asked, "Was it something I said, Fat Boy?"[8] Even the *Wall Street Journal* took sides, writing, "This furtive operation stinks to Ouagadougou of a tyrant's way of shutting down critical newspapers."[9]

While his attorneys appealed the amendment in federal court, Murdoch began to hold meetings with potential buyers for the *Post*. He made no secret of his displeasure in having to dispose of the newspaper that he loved despite its lack of profitability. "You might [someday] get the *Post* scratchily in the black," he said, "but never get rich on it." Rather, he held on to the *Post* primarily for "a position of influence—I hope for the good."[10]

Despite a favorable ruling by the U.S. Court of Appeals on February 11, 1988, which agreed with Murdoch's argument that he had been targeted individually for punishment by the Hollings amendment, there seemed to be little doubt that Murdoch ultimately would be forced to divest himself of the *Post* and the *Herald*. In an effort to ease the way for a *Post* purchase, he issued an ultimatum to that newspaper's union, insisting on immediate concessions amounting to $24 million over three years, including across-the-board wage cuts, the elimination of jobs, and a wage freeze for the entry-level worker. According to Murdoch, the unions had until February 19 to accept his proposal, or he would simply close the paper and dismiss the staff.

The leading bidder for the *Post* was New York real estate developer Peter Kalikow, who had offered Murdoch $37 million for the nearly bankrupt newspaper—a deal that on the surface seemed excessive until it was discovered that the offer included the *Post* building, itself valued at $35 million. Rumors floated around Manhattan that Kalikow's actual motive was to convert the *Post* building into condominiums. It was not such a far-fetched concept when one considered that Kalikow previously had tried to evict 1,338 tenants from a block-long set of apartments in an attempt to build four luxury residential towers. Throughout the negotiations, Kalikow insisted that he intended to continue publishing the *Post* for at least a year, a pledge Murdoch accepted.

When the *Post* was finally sold in early March to Kalikow, Alexander Cockburn, writing in *The Nation*, refused to believe it, likening the move to Dracula selling his coffin. "The *New York Post* gave Murdoch his public profile in the United States," wrote Cockburn, "and provided the fulcrum of his political influence. Before he bought the paper, in 1976, he was just another scuffler, putting out *The Star*. Now that he's given it up, he'll be just another tycoon, nourishing dreams of a fourth network, calling up Fox executives to get the ratings and the latest box-office receipts."[11]

While Cockburn was in the basement checking the coffin, Murdoch continued to pursue his case in the U.S. Court of Appeals. In early April he emerged triumphant, gaining a ruling that the Hollings amendment was unconstitutional since it was aimed solely at Murdoch. Despite Murdoch's smile as he spoke to the press and subsequently held up a copy of a *Time* magazine headline that read TABLOID KING KO'S CONGRESS, he essentially had won the battle, but lost the war. With his favored *Post* sold, Murdoch was a media monarch without a crown—a newspaper in America's most important city.

Amid a plethora of press announcing his demotion among his New York publishing peers, Murdoch began spending more time in California, where he was seen speeding his red Lotus along the twists and bends of Stone Canyon Drive in Bel Air at dawn, heading toward Fox Studios, where his continuing presence was less than welcomed by studio head Barry Diller. The power play that had existed between Diller and former Fox owner Marvin Davis, and had been eased by the sale of the production facility to Murdoch, began to reemerge from the dust of memory and would eventually play heavily into studio politics.

In April 1988, however, Murdoch had more immediate challenges. To consolidate his growing book publishing division, he merged his William Collins entity with his newly purchased Harper & Row to form HarperCollins, positioning it as a major player in hardcover publishing as well as textbooks. Also, in order to facilitate the sale of Fox television programming in Europe, Murdoch leased four transponders on the privately owned Astra satellite from the tiny country of Luxembourg for his Sky Channel service. In addition to the four channels of programming, Murdoch pledged to launch a news channel "modeled on Ted Turner's Cable News Network" as well as a sports channel.[12] "The European public, particularly the British, have been deprived of choice and advertisers poorly served by existing stations," Murdoch added, pledging to spend $650 million on programming.

At New York's Waldorf-Astoria, Ted Turner leaned forward and had the news whispered into his ear. "Humph . . . $650 million. Hell," he muttered between teeth clenched in a smile as he walked to the microphone and prepared to officially announce the launch of his TNT network to the gathered press. "I was an eye-tre-preneur for a good number of years," he said in his best Huey Long voice. "And I enjoyed it enormously. But today is not a good time to be small. So, I went big. . . . You might have heard I bought a studio." Scattered applause filled the ballroom. "And then I sold some of it to pay for it." Laughs from journalists, their mouths full of free lunch. "But I kept the movies, a billion dollars' worth to put on TNT." Take that, Rupert Murdoch. $650 million. . . . Humph.

For Turner, it was almost like the old days: entertaining a crowd with outspoken remarks, cracking jokes, talking ad lib. When a critic asked about the preponderance of reruns, Turner blurted out, "Life is really like a rerun, don't you think? At least for some of you who have been married twenty years or better."

It was a brief glimmer of the old Turner, the outspoken propagator of ethnic slurs and malapropisms, free to make his own decisions and speak his mind. Not so anymore. This was the new Turner, ruled by a committee of cable operators, a Turner displaced by economic shortfalls and a lengthy divorce. The loss of wife Jane had left Turner $40 million poorer and emotionally shaken. "He never really thought Jane would ever leave him," a friend in Atlanta said. "They had been through so much, built the family, the business, and no matter how he behaved, how he caroused, Jane was always there to take him back. Now what she wanted was the money and the Kinloch Plantation in North Carolina."

With J. J. Ebaugh waiting, reassuring, guiding, indulging, Turner had someone to fall back on: a young, exciting, adventurous new "Jane" who had enlightened him to the damage being done to the planet and the need for environmental controls and cleanup. Where Jane Turner was subservient and malleable and lived in the shadow of her famous husband, J. J. was driven, impulsive, and outspoken. So outspoken, in fact, that she confidently gave an interview to *Atlanta* magazine soon after Turner's divorce became final. When the article appeared in November 1988, it had the tone of a woman triumphant—"The Woman Who Tamed Ted Turner," the title suggested. When asked about eventually marrying the playboy of the Western world, she blithely said, "He'll do whatever I want. He gave up $40 million and a whole harem [for me]. That's a hell of a lot."[13]

For a man used to being the captain, they were hard words to acknowledge, let alone read. Seeing the article in print, Turner reacted like a caged tiger, pacing the room not in anger but in contemplation. The situation in which he found himself was of his own making. What he had done could be undone, Turner knew, and he set about unraveling the relationship that most of his friends were certain would lead to marriage.

"He lived for romance," Ebaugh said. "He's a King Arthur type—if he could be anyone, it would be King Arthur. Ted has set about unifying the world, like Arthur did, and all the virtues he lives by are the virtues of the Knights of the Round Table. That song Lancelot sang all the time, Ted goes around singing. You know, the one from *Camelot*—''tis I, 'tis I, *c'est moi, c'est moi.*'"[14] By the time Ebaugh discovered that the song is about one man's devotion to himself, the relationship had ended Turner style, by telephone.

Though the romance had ended by the beginning of the new year, Ebaugh remained at Turner's Roswell home and continued to work for him at CNN. "He's very demanding, extremely demanding," Ebaugh said. "He's very busy, very driven, but wonderful. After all those years, I don't have any complaints at all."[15]

Those same words, different accent, could have come just as easily from the mouth of Anna Murdoch. "It's hard for Rupert to slow down, relax," she said. "He says, of course, that he loves his work, so why slow down." From Anna's perspective, her husband was actually working more, not less, as the responsibilities of his latest acquisitions became apparent.

The man who would be king of all Australia's media found his purchase of the Herald Group to be an antipasto of disturbing loose ends. Forced to divest himself of the Brisbane *Sun* and his father's legacy, the *Adelaide News,* to escape antitrust charges from Australia's Trade Practices Commission, Murdoch worked the government's last nerve through a complex buy-back arrangement with the newspapers' editors. The deal called for the journalists to buy both newspapers with Murdoch-arranged financing, and rent the newspapers' buildings from him. Additionally, the two papers would continue to be printed on Murdoch-owned presses. While the move was required, according to Murdoch, to keep both newspapers from collapsing under the cost of complete autonomy, it was nevertheless an inadequate explanation to the watchdog politicians overseeing trade.

Even more disturbing were the rising losses at the *Herald*—more than $10 million during the first year of his ownership. Despite efforts to Murdochize the headlines, design, and content, the Melbourne mainstay was still disappointing in terms of circulation and advertising sales. John D'Arcy, a onetime accountant and the newspaper's managing editor, was summarily dumped in November 1988, even though he had been a supporter of Murdoch's purchase of the Herald Group. Unusually ruthless even by Murdoch's standards, the firing of D'Arcy evidenced a growing desperation on the part of the publisher to begin to make money on his acquisitions, many of which were drowning in ever-increasing amounts of red ink.

To the onlooker, Murdoch still remained the dominant, globe-trotting publisher. In January 1989, as Anna Murdoch coordinated another extravagant birthday party for Murdoch's mother, Dame Elisabeth, at Cruden Farm, Murdoch confidently pledged to increase his financing of the Institute of Birth Defects at the Melbourne Royal Children's Hospital, a favorite charity of his mother's. A month later, he offered $450 million cash for the remaining 58 percent of William Collins Sons & Co. that he did not own, and prepared to fly via the Concorde to London to launch his new four-channel Sky Channel satellite service.

Yet, all of his purchases, including the 20th Century-Fox Studios, suddenly seemed to be insignificant baubles on a chain of gold compared to his acquisition in August 1989. For an astronomical $3 *billion*, Rupert Murdoch became the owner of the most circulated paid weekly magazine in America, *TV Guide*. Megapublisher Walter Annenberg, who inherited the *Daily Racing Form*, the handicapper's bible to Thoroughbred horse racing, from his father and built *TV Guide* from the basement up, smiled all the way to the bank. As industry observers wondered aloud about Murdoch's ability to pay off the debt assumed by his acquisition of *TV Guide*'s parent, Triangle Publications, and joked about the mock headline BINGO BARON BUYS BOOB TUBE BIBLE, others suggested that Murdoch planned to taint *TV Guide*'s coverage to favor Fox Broadcasting programs.

Walter Annenberg curdled at the prospect. "There must be an arm's-length relationship between *TV Guide* and the networks," he said. "Mr. Murdoch is too intelligent to do anything as stupid as that. The very idea of it is inane and stupid. Do you suppose the man would pay that money and jeopardize the value of the property?"

No, came the answer from his rival networks, all of which were collectively holding their breath and hoping not to turn blue with envy. No one, however, was jealous of Murdoch's incredible debt load, now at $7.6 billion.

"Murdoch is financing his company through short- and medium-term revolving credit lines at thirty major banks around the world," a Murdoch ex-banker told *Fortune*. "It's next to lunacy."

"All it would take is for one company to fail—just one—and Murdoch's house of cards will fall quicker than a soufflé in an igloo," said an investment analyst at Chase Manhattan, one of Murdoch's lenders.[16]

For the publisher himself, the talk was discouraging. Year after year, he had demonstrated his agility at finessing bankers; for decades, he had turned nearly bankrupt newspapers into thriving publications. He reassured the doubters, rejected the numbers, and pledged autonomy for the magazine that both ABC and CBS called their "most important tune-in medium."[17]

Only when alone, the darkness that precedes dawn cloaking him with silence, did he pause to evaluate the honesty of his critics' comments. Only then could he bring himself to wonder why they refused to listen—why his efforts to convince found more doubters than supporters. Only then did he dare to admit the reality of his fear—that they might be right.

# THIRTEEN

# Brother, Can Ya Spare a Dime?

*Fortune favors the brave.*

Rupert Murdoch
London
April 1989

There would be no more excuses, no more justifications, no more explanations from Rupert Murdoch about his business practices or his brand of journalism. After a life spent on the outside fighting for credibility, the media mogul had had enough. He was no longer content to be the unpopular cousin who wasn't invited to the party and pretended it didn't matter. At this very moment in early 1989, Rupert Murdoch demanded respect. He had proven himself repeatedly, and now, he decided, others would have to prove themselves to him.

The cause of this transformation was less a need to prove a point than it was the realization that News Corporation had grown so large that, with $4.35 billion in revenues, it was the third largest media company behind the recently merged Time Warner* ($8.7 billion) and Bertelsmann–Doubleday–RCA Records ($6.2 billion). Murdoch had literally bought himself into the exclusive club of major publishers.

---

\* On March 4, 1989, Time Inc. and Warner Communications Inc. announced plans to become Time Warner Inc. in a stock swap.

His effort to deliver a CNN-type news service in Great Britain via his Sky Channel was dependent on his potential to cast a large footprint from the transponders he had leased on the Astra satellite, as well as his ability to sell an entire nation on spending a few hundred pounds to install small receiving dishes on individual rooftops already teeming with antennas. Murdoch based his pitch on Hollywood and the films he had stockpiled through licensing agreements with Warner Bros. Studios, his own Fox Studios, and the production companies Orion and Touchstone, a subsidiary of Disney.

Having spent $45 million to develop Sky Television and another $90 million on film rights, he placed enormous faith in the future of direct broadcast television. It was a confidence borne as much from his need to skirt the local newspaper/television cross-ownership regulations as from any clairvoyance into the future of broadcasting. Since Murdoch's satellite signal did not originate in England but rather in Luxembourg, the same laws that governed a broadcast signal did not restrict his. Plus, his investment in British newspaper publishing was secure.

The ultimate success of Sky, of course, was totally dependent on sales of satellite dishes. Despite an extensive and costly advertising campaign, mainly in Murdoch's own papers, dish sales were meager. Murdoch then launched a word-of-mouth campaign by *giving* away the $350 dishes to a number of homes in various neighborhoods and offering to rent dishes to their friends at a loss. And while dishes began to make their way onto rooftops all across London and its suburbs, those losses continued to mount at an alarming pace.

For the media mogul, his Sky News channel alone warranted the expenditure, if only for the influence it generated internationally. Just as Turner had found in America, the power base of a news organization translated into enormous influence throughout Europe. Though Murdoch's reach was small and aimed at Great Britain, it actually blanketed eight countries, all in one small corner of the continent. And like CNN, Murdoch's fledgling news channel received a surprise boost from a breaking news story that transfixed much of the world.

In June 1989, the crush of the student revolt by army troops in China's Tiananmen Square was carried live across the European continent. While CNN provided on-the-spot coverage, Sky offered continuing updates. Extensive coverage of the revolt and the subsequent crackdown was exactly what the students were counting on. News was being made because of the coverage, and the point was hardly lost on Murdoch, who commented that "watching the events in China on CNN was the most amazing experience; it was an extraordinary moment in history, to know that what was happening in China was happening in part because we were all watching it."[1] Unfortunately for Murdoch, few were watching it on Sky Television.

Despite the exorbitant amount of money Murdoch was pouring into the start-up network, the satellite service was failing to keep either viewers or advertisers interested in its four channels. Typically, feature films would have been Sky's biggest draw if Hollywood had not complicated the situation by insisting that Murdoch scramble the signal to protect it from being received by bootlegged dishes.

Pushed to get Sky into service before the competing British Satellite Broadcasting (BSB) system, Murdoch reached into his back pocket and tapped a small, unused subsidiary he had been talked into investing in several years earlier. For under $4 million, Murdoch had grubstaked an Israeli enterprise that was attempting to develop an encryption process, initially for military use. Adi Shamir, a professor at the Massachusetts Institute of Technology, had invented the process based on mathematical algorithms and had approached Murdoch's technology guru, an Australian named Bruce Hundertmark, about licensing the invention.

After a considerable amount of explanation, Hundertmark convinced the publisher that encryption technology had a future.

With Murdoch's money and the marketing savvy of an American Israeli named Michael Clinger, Hundertmark formed News Datacom as a subsidiary of News Corporation. Though the company was officially based in Hong Kong, its research division was located in Israel, and it was there that Hundertmark came up with the concept of making the technology easily transportable through the use of a single-chip Smart Card. By 1989, Hundertmark's confidence and familiarity with the encryption process made headlines when it was incorporated into VideoCrypt, an elementary form of scrambling based on Shamir's algorithms, used by Sky to safeguard Hollywood product from being stolen out of midair.

Stumbling and bumbling into business, Sky Television was good at only one thing: making Murdoch's money disappear, and disappear quickly. The company was hardly alone among his businesses, of course. Fox Broadcasting had lost $20 million the previous year—a tiny amount only when compared to the $100 million that Sky had sucked out of the Murdoch accounts. Adding to the loss were interest payments due on Murdoch's debt that totaled nearly $300 million in the last half of 1988.

With its stock prices suffering due to its large debt obligations, News Corporation appeared to have little choice but to sell assets to raise capital. In typical fashion, however, Murdoch paid no attention to the predictions of financial analysts. Even if the market was ripe for such a move, he was not in the mood to sell any of his fledgling assets, convinced of their long-term profitability. Instead, he elected to form a new company, Media Partners International. Critics called it "Son of News." And his financial advisers called it the perfect place to dump his debt to make News Corporation look like a reasonably leveraged company. All legal, yet an early version of creative accounting that would later hit its peak with the Enron Corporation and the corporate scandals of 2002.

Regardless of where Murdoch buried his debt, it was not about to vanish quickly. News Corporation, under any of its reworked names, owed $4.8 billion to 146 banks stretched across four continents. An additional $1.2 billion was held in securities with maturity dates ranging from 3 to 10 years in the future. Just keeping track of the various payment schedules kept an entire division busy.

Longtime friend Richard Sarazen, who had been Murdoch's chief financial officer for 10 years and had been given carte blanche to find the funds necessary for Murdoch's impulsive purchases, found himself taking the responsibility for the money squeeze and debt payments that were barely being serviced in late 1989. Like the proverbial magician pulling a rabbit out of a hat, Sarazen did what he had been doing for years: arrange a short-term loan, this one in the amount of $750 million, to pay debts as they came due. Unfortunately for Sarazen in particular and News Corporation as a whole, the magic failed the following June when that loan came due.

Murdoch was able to pay off only a third of the amount, with $500 million about to default. Word of News Corporation's tenuous financial condition was about to splash across the front pages of business journals everywhere. With hat in hand, Sarazen begged the banks to roll over the debt for three months. To the loan officers, the request was a red flare shot up into the sky. While they reluctantly agreed to Sarazen's request, the nervous tension moved like static on polyester sheets. News Corporation had long been the darling of the financial sector. Banks had rushed to accommodate Murdoch based on his reliability, a track record unbroken for 20 years. Even when his businesses lost money, his debt payments were consistently met—until now. Suddenly, Murdoch's empire seemed too scattered, spread thinly into so many countries with so many subsidiaries that Murdoch himself was no longer able to play watchdog over them all.

As Sarazen scrambled to line up alternative financing and Murdoch became more aware of the extent of his problem, various elements of News Corporation's businesses started to misfire, one after the other. Sky Television, already his largest financial drain, found itself facing additional competition with the arrival of BSB. Having won the original franchise for commercial-direct satellite-to-dish service from the Independent Broadcasting Authority in 1986, BSB limped into service in April 1990 and divided the already small number of customers eager to try the new technology. After BSB debuted, it was losing between seven and eight million pounds a week. It was little comfort to Murdoch to see his competitors struggle knowing he was losing two million pounds a week himself.

With a 15-month head start, Sky should have been poised to dominate the market and quickly put BSB out of business. Instead, both companies found themselves struggling to compete for a shrinking consumer base. As losses continued to mount, BSB chief executive Anthony Simmonds-Gooding spoke publicly and often about his well-funded operation, pointing with pride at everything from the amount spent on programming to the cost of paintings on the office walls.

The banks funding Simmonds-Gooding's operation found his pontificating as disturbing as his excessive spending, and threatened to cut off cash to the company if sales of home dish units did not improve. Smelling wounded prey, Murdoch met with BSB's consortium of owners to discuss a buyout. In truth, he was no better equipped than BSB to continue to bleed millions of pounds weekly. The only hope for survival for either company was in a fusion of assets.

In November 1990, Murdoch announced a merger of both satellite services, with the name British Sky Broadcasting (BSkyB) surviving the cut and Murdoch clearly in charge. One of Murdoch's first acts was to remove Simmonds-Gooding and take over his extravagantly furnished office at BSB's old headquarters in Battersea. Eventually, all the BSB offices would be dispersed throughout Sky's far less opulent Brentford headquarters. For the moment, however, Murdoch was far more con-

cerned with finding a way to stop the losses raping the coffers of
News Corporation. To his credit, he did not try to assign blame
for his failing satellite subscription service, least of all to Richard
Sarazen, who had recently been promoted to senior executive
vice president. Sarazen was never enthusiastic about the purchase to begin with. Murdoch did hold Sarazen accountable for
the lack of continuing financing, however, and shortly before the
merger, he had relieved Sarazen of his CFO position to clear the
way for some desperately needed emergency resuscitation.

To all the world, News Corporation was a thriving media
conglomerate. The press lavished praise on Murdoch's inexplica-
ble ability to stay one step ahead of technology while keeping the
wolf at bay. Murdoch had managed to turn much of publishing
on its head by giving the public what it actually wanted instead
of what the more educated journalists thought it deserved. And
he did it at the expense of other publishers. In fact, when Time
Warner was formed in early 1989, *Business Week* headlined the
story KEEPING UP WITH THE MURDOCHS.[2]

Yet the image of the master of money, corporations, unions,
and employees had a flip side that was all too fragile. Murdoch
the manipulator was ultimately at the mercy of those who gave
him his power—the banks that financed his buying sprees. And
the banks were no longer amused by Murdoch's act. Part of the
trouble was that the banks had at last figured out how Murdoch
performed his magic. In June 1990, just before his promotion to
senior executive vice president, Richard Sarazen had revalued
News Corporation's assets upward of three billion Australian
dollars, based on little more than his need for higher valued
assets. While such a move is illegal in the United States without
documents supporting such claims, in Australia it is not only
allowed but also accepted. Sarazen had done it often. The difference this time was that the banks were watching—closely.

As pieces of his domain began to crumble, Murdoch spent
each and every waking moment putting out fires and shoring up

foundations that were dissolving around him. Dry sand falling into a hole. He would later say he felt like a toad attempting to escape the spikes of a harrow.** He quoted Kipling to a group of Japanese bankers: "The toad beneath the harrow knows exactly where each tooth-point goes."[3] The difference, of course, was that Murdoch had no clue when he would be fatally stepped on by any number of increasingly impatient banks.

In late September 1990, Sarazen was replaced by his deputy, David DeVoe, a 40-something accountant who had been in his former post all of nine months. Where Sarazen was dynamic and charming, DeVoe was meticulous and dry. It was therefore largely up to Murdoch to lure major lenders into rolling over billions of dollars in debt as it came due, while DeVoe attempted to organize the various pieces of the incredibly complex financial picture. To help DeVoe, Murdoch's largest creditor, Citibank, assigned a young vice president named Ann Lane to oversee the creation of a business plan for News Corporation that would allow it to rise above its debt load.[†]

Murdoch first met Lane in the company of Citibank vice chairman William Rhodes at Manhattan's La Côte Basque, the restaurant that lent its name to a chapter in Truman Capote's novel *Answered Prayers*. Where Capote saw ladies who lunched and gossiped, Murdoch found La Côte Basque to be an elegant and reserved meeting place where he felt comfortable and pampered. There, under French artist Bernard Lamotte's 50-year-old murals of the port of St. Jean de Luz, Murdoch talked turkey and ate *cassoulet toulousain*.

"I needed to be convinced that he was serious about putting his corporate finances in order and was willing to listen and act on the recommendations we made, and was willing to do whatever was necessary to sell this package," Rhodes later said. "He

---

** A harrow is a sharp-spiked implement used for aerating soil.

† John Evangelides, an executive director of Samuel Montagu & Co., the merchant bank representing Midland Bank, handled the European end of the business plan.

had the right attitude and he knew what he had to do to get his house in order."[4] What Rhodes asked Murdoch to do was essentially be available around the clock to cajole, explain, and satisfy the questions of a growing number of bankers, most of whom had never heard of Rupert Murdoch and were uncertain what News Corporation produced.

Ann Lane had a far more specific job: corral the various companies that formed divisions of News Corporation, generate a cohesive business plan that illustrated their synergy for future profits, and present the plan to the various banks that held the paper on Murdoch's debt. Unfortunately, when Lane opened the Pandora's box of documents that purported to list News Corporation's various outstanding loans, she uncovered a labyrinth of startling complexity. She had approached this latest assignment fresh from untangling the finances of real estate mogul Donald Trump, and presumed that *that* experience would prepare her for anything. What Lane uncovered, however, was a hodgepodge of due dates, interest rates, codicils, buyouts, rollovers, transfers, and syndicated refinancing packages unlike anything she could have predicted. Further complicating matters was Murdoch's wanton practice of obtaining financing for his own personal use under the guise of official News Corporation business—approximately, according to Lane's estimates, $450 million.

To locate the origins of the various loans was difficult enough. To uncover which banks currently held the contracts was even worse, since the originators of the loans had syndicated them out to smaller banks to spread the risk. Lane spent months merely calculating the exact amount of Murdoch's indebtedness and then structuring a business plan, known as the Dolphin Memorandum, that she felt might eliminate much of the company's overdrawn status and bring debt into a responsible percentage of total income.

The working mantra of the memorandum's debt override agreement was "We are what we are" and "Nobody gets out." It was a basic admission that the 146 banks determined to hold Murdoch's debt were in their predicament together. "Nobody gets out" meant that all banks had to continue to roll over Murdoch's debt in order to allow the company to remain in business at least long enough to pay back the banks. "We are what we are" was a blatant acceptance of culpability, with each bank accepting responsibility for its piece of the corner in which News Corporation had carefully painted itself. Each bank remained responsible for its existing loan agreement with no changes.

The plan was workable from Citibank's perspective. As the principal lender, it had the most to lose should Murdoch default on any payments. It also had the most to gain—$150 million as a flat fee for Lane's rescue operation.[5] What made the charge fascinating from a business perspective was that while News Corporation was the target of the reorganization, it was the banks that were being saved. Yet, to save themselves, the banks had to loan Murdoch even more money—$600 million in short-term loans to keep his spiderweb of businesses from collapsing.

The Dolphin Memorandum had an Achilles' heel at its very foundation: no bank could cash out. The plan was workable, even brilliantly conceived, if indeed all the banks fell into place. One after another, that is precisely what occurred. Murdoch's charm, his calm, polite reserved tone, built confidence in bankers who had grown to trust his ability to transform the media world. To witness the process, Murdoch had called his elder son, Lachlan, to his side, pulling him from Princeton, where he was a philosophy major studying the theories of Immanuel Kant and Georg Wilhelm Friedrich Hegel. Lachlan later said the struggle was so debilitating that one night, walking home from the office with his father, "I wanted to put my arms around him and hold him up."[6] Still, bit by bit, one bank at a time, the pieces fell into place. A flow chart on the wall in Murdoch's New York office kept track of their progress, with the names of banks changing from red to purple and eventually to green as each accepted the rescue plan—until December 6, 1990, when a bank in Pittsburgh said no.

Murdoch often has recounted the story about that bank's loan officer, who told David DeVoe he was unsure of News Corporation's ability to pay its debts; so unsure, in fact, that he was willing to put the entire company into receivership to ensure that his bank received at least a portion of its debt. The bank was owed $10 million, pocket change to Murdoch in previous years. If he attempted to pay off the bank, other banks in the all-for-one debt override agreement would insist on getting paid as well, causing a domino effect that would have repercussions far beyond a bankrupt News Corporation. It exposed the fundamental weakness in Lane's plan, a plan that was weighted in value for those banks, like Citibank, that had the most to lose. Pittsburgh National Bank, having been brought into the News Corporation loan through an Australian bank that had syndicated its debt to a variety of smaller financial institutions, was a minor cog in the scheme of things. Yet, in true weakest-link fashion, it was in a position to bring Murdoch to his knees.

Philip Townsend, Murdoch's butler at his London flat, later told the story of watching his boss nervously telephone the White House to ask for help from President George Bush. The great media mogul had been reduced to begging, and though the nation's commander in chief took the call and listened, Bush was unable to give counsel or intercede. Little in Murdoch's curriculum vitae prepared him for groveling, but if necessary, he was fully prepared to do what it took to save his empire. Groveling included.

As anyone knows who has had to deal with a bank from a position of weakness, there are few moments in life that make one feel as insecure. For the mogul who could talk to kings and heads of state, advise presidents and control lives, it was a humbling, frightening experience. With his options expired and his company within a day of declaring bankruptcy, Murdoch placed a telephone call to Ann Lane and admitted that after all the effort to consolidate, cajole, and coerce, after all their success at convincing bank after bank to extend loans and forgo payments, he did not see how he could get the bank in Pittsburgh to cooperate. "I don't think I'm going to get there with this bank," he said to Lane.[7] He was finished.

No one realized the extent of his misfortune more than Ann Lane. She had been at this precipice before, but not at this height and not with this much at stake. After ending the conversation with Murdoch, Lane called for reinforcements—the banking version of the artillery—in this case, John Reed, chairman of Citibank. It was her trump card, held for emergencies, when mere arm twisting and outright begging failed.

Reed, too, had played this part often. In this case, however, one of the largest media corporations in the world would be forced into receivership, sold off newspaper by newspaper, right down to the last satellite dish. While Rupert Murdoch would not be totally out of business, what remained of his empire would be unrecognizable compared to its current structure, with hundreds of thousands of people affected.

The final verdict on the loan rollover belonged to the head of the Pittsburgh bank. As far as Reed could assess, the bank remained unconvinced that Murdoch was in firm control of his empire. It was a sentiment shared by the media mogul himself. When Murdoch arrived in London at the law offices of Clifford Chance, Citibank's attorneys in Great Britain, he was shown into a conference room, feeling much like a convicted killer being strapped into the electric chair. The stage had been set for a last-minute reprieve—one chance to survive and an incalculable number to fail.

Murdoch was to place a personal call to the president of the bank in Pittsburgh to plead for time. Lane coached him on his approach, and as he dialed the number, she backed away, knowing Murdoch was now alone. His company, his future, his life. In a scene that might have been right out of a melodrama on Fox, Murdoch attempted to keep his voice steady as he asked to speak with the executive officer. He felt his hand shaking and pressed the receiver tightly to his ear, wondering if anyone had noticed, hoping that they hadn't.

When a voice came on the line, Murdoch began to speak, only to realize he had not gotten through to the bank president's office at all, but had instead been transferred back to the loan division. Back to the same officer who had denied the loan rollover to David DeVoe. Stunned, Murdoch spoke in short bursts, trying to appear casual as his world proceeded to crumble. Ann Lane nervously twisted her fingers, a thin layer of sweat making them cold and damp. She sucked in air, more from instinct than intention, her mind now braced for failure.

She hardly heard Murdoch introduce himself, and was replaying the scenario of the past few months over and over in fast motion in her mind, looking for the mistake, analyzing the map for the wrong turn. "Yes, yes, we would be happy to do that," she heard Murdoch say before he hung up the phone seconds later. She watched helplessly as the air drained from his body like a collapsing balloon.

"*Phew,*" was the only word Murdoch said at first. He turned in his chair and then stood to look at the worried faces across the room. "I need a drink," he said. Then a smile slid his lips apart, and his tired eyes crinkled in triumph. The Pittsburgh bank had agreed to extend the debt. The loan officer had suggested he would come to New York to learn more about News Corporation. He wanted to meet Murdoch in person. He had said, "We don't want to be that difficult."[8] Then it was over. News Corporation would live for another day, yet Rupert Murdoch and his company would never be the same.

In skirting disaster, Murdoch had little choice but to agree to free the reins of control. In that, he joined Ted Turner, who had suffered the same fate at Turner Broadcasting. The irony, of course, was that both men borrowed heavily to keep from diluting their ownership and relinquishing control, only to end up relinquishing control anyway.

Turner absorbed the ego-shattering reality of his predicament through a series of diversions that kept him out of the office and in the spotlight with a new romance. A major romance with a major star. Jane Fonda.

The Fonda-Turner matchup had heads shaking in wonder when it first became apparent that the two were serious. For Fonda, it was a rather whirlwind courtship, even by Hollywood standards. No sooner had she announced her divorce from husband Tom Hayden in 1990 than she found herself being pursued by Turner. Never known for subtlety, Turner turned on the charm, Southern and otherwise, only to find himself just one of many admirers. The most serious competition came in the form of Italian soccer star Lorenzo Caccialanza, a muscular specimen attempting to break into acting. Presumably that only strengthened Turner's resolve, and after several months the couple that Fonda herself described as "just friends for as long as it lasts" were spotted at Tiffany's, and not for breakfast. Turner purchased an opal-and-diamond engagement ring and slipped it onto her finger on her birthday, December 21.

In the meantime, Rupert Murdoch had been taken to task by a documentary that aired on Britain's Channel 4. Titled *Empire,* the program accused him of irregularities in his handling of News Corporation shares through his own subsidiaries as well as excessive use of tax havens. While Murdoch attempted to dismiss the charges made by reporter Christopher Hird (a former investigative reporter for Murdoch's *Sunday Times*), the show caused News Corporation stock to plummet 20 percent in a single day. According to the program, while Murdoch's maneuvers were not illegal, any change in the current laws could "upset a delicate balancing act that is already testing his bankers' nerves as never before."[9]

Adding to Murdoch's woes, his accountants were forced to wipe $6 billion from the company's balance sheets to comply with U.S. regulations regarding valuation of assets. "This has been a chastening experience," Murdoch told Peter Bart in *Variety*. "There have been, shall we say, some unpleasant moments."

The extent of Murdoch's understatement was illustrated when he added, "I have always felt my specialty was operating a media company. I did not think I would spend three months of my life in constant dialog with bankers." Yet, he seemed hopeful. "There is not a single division of this company that won't be operated more efficiently."[10]

Though he came dangerously close to losing his entire empire, Murdoch emerged a victorious if slightly haggard man. He celebrated the former by traveling to Australia for Christmas and actually forgetting about business for more than a week. As for the latter, once he was confident that News Corporation was on steady financial footing—at least for the foreseeable future—Murdoch allegedly underwent plastic surgery to remove some of his celebrated shar-pei wrinkles. According to butler Philip Townsend, Murdoch left a bottle of pills next to his nightstand labeled "To be taken on the morning of surgery." The pills had been prescribed by a leading British plastic surgeon with offices on London's Harley Street, famed for its private medical facilities. The official explanation for Murdoch's hurried visit to the doctor came from Anna, who said he was having some "tests." She later added that if anyone should ask, Townsend should say that the Murdochs were "away for a couple of days."[11]

Indeed they were. The pair turned up next at a rather posh country hotel in the Lake District called the Miller Howe, where Murdoch remained in seclusion, shielded behind dark glasses and surrounded by vistas of Lake Windermere and the Langdale Pikes. The hotel's owner, eccentric TV chef and author John Tovey, attempted unsuccessfully to meet with Murdoch, and his famous guest was reduced to making business calls in the hallway, since the bedroom wasn't furnished with a telephone. Though the physical evidence of a facelift was never overtly obvious, Townsend nevertheless maintains it not only took place but was buoyed by treatments with the hair colorant Grecian Formula 16.

Ted Turner needed neither surgery nor hair color to feel young. He had Jane Fonda, who had gone from movie sex goddess in *Barbarella* to successful fitness guru, making time in between for that controversial visit to Hanoi. Critics eyed the pair with suspicion, but there was little doubt that Turner found Fonda to be wonderment, the ultimate trophy wife who came complete with her own trophies—two Academy Awards, to be exact. Not that Turner was even aware of their existence. While first showing Fonda around his 125,000-acre Montana ranch on horseback, he brought up marriage, then said he knew she would not want to give up her career—"at least until you win an Oscar." It was left to Fonda to explain her best actress wins in *Klute* and *Coming Home*.[12]

Turner merely smiled at the faux pas, but then, he had been smiling a lot lately. He smiled when he took Fonda to Russia for the premiere of *Gone with the Wind* (some 52 years after its debut in America). He smiled when she took him to the Oscars. He smiled as he showed off his homes in Florida and the Carolinas, including St. Philip's Island near Beaufort, South Carolina. And he smiled when he publicly announced their engagement in 1990 on Fonda's birthday.

They were together three weeks later when, on January 16, 1991, America went to war. Even before White House press secretary Marlin Fitzwater announced that the United States and its allies were attacking Iraq, whose forces had invaded Kuwait the previous August, Americans were watching the war live on CNN, the only U.S. news crew permitted into the country. Operation Desert Storm, as the offensive was known, became required viewing across the country, with CNN's Peter Arnett reporting from the Hotel al-Rashid to America and 105 other countries around the globe.

It had been 10 years since CNN first went on the air. Ten years in which the news service was playing catch-up with the three commercial networks and their expansive bureaus and expensive anchors. Now, in the heat of battle, in the center of a conflict so charged with danger and patriotism that for weeks Americans could not pull themselves away from the sight of the green night-vision scope and tracer bullets, CNN reigned.

The news network not only succeeded in getting its signal out of Baghdad, but it also put a personal face on a war that had no winners. We became familiar with names like Scud and Patriot and Iraqi foreign minister Tariq Aziz, but most of all, Americans became familiar with the horrors of war as interpreted by CNN. Although the commercial networks broadcast special coverage and extended news programs, they had lost this war of the airwaves by being exactly what they had been structured to be: aloof, detached, too-coiffed anchors safe behind a desk in a studio. Compared with CNN, they were remote talking heads that were somehow removed from the real world of bombs and land mines and night sorties.

Even when the networks managed to get their anchors to Kuwait and dress them in bush jackets as if costumes might fool viewers, the public continued to perceive that CNN was broadcasting the real war, the whole story. CNN remained in Baghdad, broadcast an exclusive interview with Saddam Hussein, and dared to question whether the targets being attacked were actually schools, hospitals, and factories manufacturing baby formula, as Saddam claimed. It created a flood of charges from the conservative press that CNN was being used by the Iraqi government to deliver its own message.

While CNN was the first to admit that remaining in Baghdad came at a price, the controversy over CNN's extended coverage managed to overlook a far more outrageous sin. The American government, under the guise of a military blackout, clapped a lid on information reaching the American people. As the commercial networks were spoon-fed newsfeeds, CNN continued to make its own headlines and infuriate President Bush, who nevertheless continued to watch its coverage.

The crisis in the Persian Gulf reminded viewers that CNN filled a unique void. In a world ever more dependent on instant communication, there was no better source of facts than the Cable News Network. Most believed that what CNN telecast was the truth, or at least one version of the truth. They sucked it in, hyperventilating on the round-the-clock coverage and getting their next fix of war news day and night.

When the war ended a month and a half later, the major networks, having lost money on their commercial-free coverage of the crisis, began to tighten corporate belts in every division, particularly news. CNN, in contrast, announced its intention to open more bureaus in the Middle East, accurately sensing that the war was far from over. The 153 CNN staffers in the region were told to remain in place, with CNN proposing to open bureaus in Beirut, Amman, and Damascus.

As Turner was ordering his troops into expansion mode, Murdoch had been forced into a humiliating retreat. Though his immediate banking worries had been pacified, his debt load had actually expanded, including the $600 million in funds he needed to borrow just to allow News Corporation to pay its bills. And while official statements from News Corporation's spokespersons suggested that the company had no plans to sell any assets, offers were being quietly made for various Murdoch-owned media. When word of a deal finally surfaced, it came as little surprise that the amount of the first sale came to exactly $600 million.

K-III Holdings, the investment partnership controlled by Kohlberg Kravis Roberts & Company, the New York financial firm famous for megamergers and takeovers, came up with the cash to buy *New York* magazine, the *Daily Racing Form, Seventeen,* and *Premiere.* Even in debt, Murdoch staunchly refused to sell *TV Guide,* the magazine whose purchase got him into his financial dilemma. Ironically, the magazines he *did* agree to sell had to be pulled from his grasp. "I don't do it happily," he said. "But the whole point of this exercise [is] you've got to swallow a big dose of realism."[13]

For Rupert Murdoch, the wallowing in humility continued for the remainder of 1991. He maintained watch over his finances and kept his wallet in his pocket, passing up acquisitions he later termed "irresistible—well, nearly irresistible."

Ted Turner was named *Time*'s Man of the Year for 1991, and told the magazine's editors, "I'm not going to rest until all the world's problems have been solved." He received word of the honor a week after marrying Jane Fonda at his 8,100-acre Avalon Plantation. The ever-resourceful Fonda wrote the wedding vows herself (predictably leaving out the word *obey*) and pinned up her own hair with freesias. She announced her intention to give up her film career by telling *Time,* "Ted Turner is not a man that you leave to go on location."

She was right, of course, as was Rupert Murdoch when he said, "Fortune favors the brave." Turner had been brave for much of his life; Murdoch too. But both men would have to call on their renewed inner strength and determination as they challenged convention and manipulated fate in the months ahead. Their individual maneuvers conducted in the name of business would set them on a collision course that would alter the way America viewed itself and, ultimately, the way the world viewed them.

# FOURTEEN

# Saving the Planet, or Owning the World

*In global catastrophe circles,*
*[Ted] Turner is a hero.*
*One man with a nationwide cable network*
*is worth a hundred John Denvers with guitars.*

Esquire magazine
February 1991

"**I** can identify about half the birds," Ted Turner told a gathering of members of the National Audubon Society. "But not all of them. I have trouble with the warblers and the sparrows and the goddamned sandpipers. And seagulls. They all look the same to me." Turner had come to Chicago to explain the facts of life to this group of conservationists whose organization's stated mission was to "conserve and restore natural ecosystems, focusing on birds and other wildlife for the benefit of humanity and the earth's biological diversity." He was about to give them an earful of vintage Turner mixed with enlightened Turner, with a dash of a New Age Rhett Butler thrown in.

Enlightened Turner: "I have gotten so worried—I mean, you know, between underwriting Cousteau and Audubon and National Geographic programs and worrying about the arms race and worrying about the population explosion, worrying about poverty and the Third World, worrying about deforestation, worrying about the oceans, worrying about the rivers, the streams, the lakes—I'll tell you, I worry so much I literally, the last five years, have spent half my time sick—I mean, physically ill."

Vintage Turner: Midway through an interview following the speech, he turned to a photographer taking pictures as he talked. "Five minutes, that's it. I won't be able to talk with you snapping at me. Five minutes."

New Age Rhett Butler: "People have got to be less selfish and work more for the general good. There has to be an emphasis on the quality of life, rather than the quantity of life: your relationships with your family, your relationships with your friends. . . . You can have lots of fun. Make love more, not less. But use birth control."[1]

The man who was just as eager to bed a strange woman as he was to sail around the world had transformed himself into a crusader for clean air, clean water, and clean living—up to a point. "No use going crazy about that," he said, making sure everyone knew that population control had nothing to do with abstinence. "Just be wise."

In the past, wisdom and Turner were not easily linked. Yet, with the economic turnaround of WTBS (thanks in no small part to the movies Turner purchased via his MGM acquisition) and the newfound respectability of CNN, the Mouth of the South had become more introspective. He wanted to leave his mark, he said, not so much for what he bought or created, but for what he changed. And at the moment, Turner wanted to change everything. "We've got to rebuild the whole world," he said, adding that it had to start at home in America. "The United States is generally looked at by the rest of the world as a bunch of pigs. And when you look at us, we are. We use ten times as much as the average citizen of the rest of the world, and maybe seventy to eighty times as much as anyone in the Third World."[2]

If the habits of the slovenly United States left Turner embarrassed, it did not change his business goal of cashing in on its riches. Remaining high on Turner's list of priorities was the takeover of one of the commercial networks. After his failed bid for CBS, Turner's thirst to change the tint and scope of American programming had not diminished. He still referred to the networks as "the three blind mice"[3] for their failure to see that their programming was providing less than positive role models. He continued to threaten to make another run for ownership even though his board of directors, who controlled his spending, was convinced it would be a waste of money. Yet Turner persisted, introducing the concept at each board meeting.

He did manage to convince the board to launch a three-month test of the Airport Channel, a specialty station beamed exclusively into the waiting areas of airports in Atlanta, Dallas, and Chicago. Even more aggressive was his push to create a private advertising-supported entertainment-and-news network to run exclusively in McDonald's fast-food restaurants across the country. It would be aimed at young males and children who made up the majority of the eatery's customer base, because Turner wanted to take advantage of his acquisition of Hanna-Barbera Productions, creators of such hits as *Yogi Bear* and *The Flintstones,* for $320 million. In addition, Turner proposed using the 3,000 half-hour cartoons in the Hanna-Barbera library to launch Cartoon Network on cable. He also envisioned his Check-Out Channel positioned at checkout stands in some 5,000 grocery stores, and his Transit Channel in underground subway systems.

During much of 1991, Turner was absent from his Atlanta headquarters, preferring to run his business from the seclusion of his Flying D Ranch in Bozeman, Montana, where he had moved with Fonda soon after their marriage. The main ranch house was finished in mid-1991 and included a reflecting pond for his wife. "I wanted it special for Jane," he said. In this case, "special" meant 14 acres of glassy water mirroring the Spanish Peaks, a mountain chain that ran across the property. Turner had the top of the mountain shaved so that the entire peak in all its grandeur would be reflected in the pond when viewed from any angle.

That specific alteration was a marked deviation from Turner's strict rule that the property was to be left in its natural state. To achieve that goal, he pulled up the barbed-wire fence installed by the cattle rancher who sold him the place, and auctioned off the equipment and herds that grazed there. In their place he imported bison, the type that had roamed on the grounds hundreds of years before, and allowed the pastures to return to native grasses. It was a move that peaked the ire and curiosity of local ranchers.

"I'm going to have the biggest bison operation in the world," Turner said, "and I'm going to show you can do something compatible with nature and still make money doing it."[4]

To the amazement of many in Bozeman who looked upon Turner as the ultimate interloper, his donation of the Flying D Ranch to the Nature Conservancy was as unexpected as it was controversial. When he deeded the ranch, it became the largest preservation easement in the entire Northwest. Sandhill cranes, bald eagles, coyotes, elk, and deer were protected from poachers and hunters—except Turner, who, though sealing off the property to outsiders, continued to hunt for his own pleasure.

By banning outside hunting on his property, he closed off hundreds of acres of land used for years by Montana's hunting groups. "Screw you, Teddy," said one neighbor, reduced to poaching. "I'll shoot an elk on your land whenever I want and you, too, if you get in my way."[5] It was big talk from a small man about a visionary he had no interest in understanding.

What was easily understood, however, was that this Montana newcomer had changed Planet Earth. All the ranchers had satellite dishes, receiving their news instantly, like the rest of the world. An earthquake in Chile? Turn on CNN. Revolt in Russia? Bernard Shaw was reporting the news seconds after the feed was received. CNN had become a worldwide party line that could no longer be denied even by the most isolated.

Dictators and despots found their worst crimes made public by journalists equipped with microwave dishes. Diplomatic efforts began to be conducted over CNN as heads of state relayed their positions via satellite servers. To those men and women, it mattered not so much that the world was watching, but that a select few who could change politics—and the world—were.

Perhaps nowhere was the impact of CNN felt more immediately or with such force as it was during the Soviet Revolution in 1990, when Party conservatives made a dramatic bid for power. General Secretary Mikhail Gorbachev was forcibly detained at his country retreat in the Crimea and placed under house arrest by Defense Minister Dmitry Yazov. As a state of emergency was declared throughout the Soviet Union, the masses across the country turned to CNN. Over the next three days, the population witnessed the first instant revolution in history. Because of Turner's infiltration of Moscow with the first Goodwill Games, CNN's camera operators had made contacts that rivaled the Kremlin's own. Footage of protests from around Russia was televised not only across the world, but within the country itself. Though the generals attempting the coup took over official Russian television, they were powerless to stop CNN's satellite coverage of the conflict. Russians in Latvia, Armenia, Lithuania, Moldavia, Estonia, and Belarus were able to see Boris Yeltsin, who had been chairman of the Russian Supreme Council, stand atop a tank with a variety of other leaders to pledge support of Gorbachev and call for an end to the coup.

As Turner watched the unfolding of events on his own news network, he wept openly. Not only did he consider Gorbachev and Yeltsin to be his friends, but he considered *all* Russians to be his friends. The man who started the Goodwill Games to bring peace between the two world superpowers was now instrumental in influencing the outcome of an entire country's future. When the coup ultimately failed and Gorbachev returned, albeit briefly, to power, he gave credit not only to his friends in politics but also to CNN's coverage of the revolution.

Rupert Murdoch disliked Turner's love affair with the Soviets almost as much as he disliked the fact that CNN had turned out to be such a successful enterprise. It did not help, of course, that Fox Television had an agreement with CNN to provide its domestic and international news coverage, an agreement Murdoch announced he would terminate at the expiration of the current contract in late 1992. He wanted to allow Fox stations that opportunity to build their own news departments, and pushed for news that reflected "American ideals." Ideals, certainly, that would closely mirror Murdoch's conservative views.

The Fox Network had been growing steadily since its launch, but even with a 28 percent increase in audience share, it remained a distant fourth in the ratings. It was hurt in part because Fox had yet to program a full seven-days-a-week schedule, a situation Murdoch promised to remedy by 1993.

His concern prompted a permanent move from his apartment in New York to a Beverly Hills estate in 1991. For Fox head Barry Diller, having Murdoch underfoot and watching over his shoulder was a personal affront, and one which industry observers predicted would not be tolerated by the autocratic Diller for long. In fact, to the amazement of most, Diller withstood Murdoch's supervision for nearly a year, much of which he devoted to developing Fox Television and preparing to leave the studio. Such major moves in Hollywood are rarely done on impulse. In this case, given the $13 million yearly salary involved (some $10 million more than Murdoch himself received), it took extended introspection. Nevertheless, in February 1992, Diller resigned as head of Fox Inc., intent, he said, on being his own boss.

It was yet another example of Murdoch getting his way. Diller had essentially served his purpose, gaining respect for Fox Studios and launching Fox Television, and now Murdoch believed he could handle the operation better than anyone. Diller was philosophical about quitting Fox and highly complimentary to his former boss, helped along by a $34 million settlement agreement. But later he said, "I often had to fight the desire to join people who were worshiping the Sun God. It's a hard fight. He knows it and he's quite good at using it. The problem is that Rupert and his employees always see the relationship differently. Rupert's force of personality, charm and seduction is so great that they convince themselves his attention is given forever. In fact, it's a loan. The point is that it really is *his* company and he runs it as an extension of his fingertips."[6]

Diller had not been off the lot one day when Murdoch had taken over his office, called in the redecorators, and began removing what he labeled "fences between the divisions." For Murdoch, a healthy exchange of ideas held far more importance than the confrontational style that Diller employed. As for Fox Television, "I've been overseeing it very closely over the last few months," he said. "I guess I'll be making more direct decisions, although we've got a very strong team here."[7]

While Diller repeatedly refused to discuss his own plans for the future, he was anything but tight-lipped about his ex-boss. "Rupert Murdoch and I have no disagreements. I would say that if you're going to work for somebody, work for him. He's the best. Straight, supportive, honest and clear. . . . He's been involved in Fox activities since its inception, and that's not sweet rhetoric. I own two million shares of stock [valued at $52 million] and I'm holding on to it."[8]

Though Murdoch made it clear that he intended to become involved in every aspect of the corporate structure at Fox, he devoted an inordinate amount of time to developing Fox News as a viable entity. In Murdoch's mind, news and entertainment were intertwined. Just as he felt that newspapers' fundamental responsibility was to bemuse, so too did he expect broadcast news to sparkle with show-business gloss. To ensure that his new news division came wrapped in a cellophane of flash, Murdoch promoted Steve Chao, a Harvard graduate who had honed his skills at the *Enquirer* and developed reality programming for Fox Television, to president of Fox News Service.

Chao, who had made his mark at Fox with such programs as *America's Most Wanted, Cops,* and the late-night dating show *Studs,* was eager to spring into the executive ranks with a reputation. Deciding that controversy was the quickest route to notoriety, Chao proceeded to decorate his new offices with stained diapers and excrement. Though the decor was make-believe, his intent was real, as evidenced further when, during meetings, he propped his feet on Murdoch's desk for effect.

What might have been a stellar career imploded in controversy mere months later during a conference of Fox executives, their wives, and a hundred or so invited dignitaries. They had traveled to Snowmass, Colorado, in 1992, to discuss the place of television in current society and to hear a panel of speakers, among them Steve Chao. Chao's need to put on a flamboyant show overcame what remained of his common sense. As he began to speak, a young man with a blond ponytail entered the room and swaggered to the front of the hall. There, next to Chao, he proceeded to strip—not in the style of an exotic dancer, down to a G-string amid gyrating hips, but more like a model exposing himself for art students in a figure-study class. Naked and proud of his endowment, the stud struck poses as Chao continued to speak.

"Pay attention, Anna!" Chao shouted at Murdoch's wife, who had allowed her mind to drift toward the spectator sport. Among those in the audience waiting to hear a pin drop were then Secretary of Defense Dick Cheney and his wife, Lynne, chief of the National Endowment for the Humanities. While it was classic Chao, it was more than Murdoch intended to tolerate. The man was fired several hours later and removed from the conference and, ultimately, the Fox lot.*

---

* Chao went on to form his own production company, eventually becoming president of USA Cable, a division of USA Networks owned by Barry Diller.

Chao aside, Murdoch's devotion to the development of a news network found life at that year's meeting of Fox affiliated stations. Labeling his effort "a return to old-fashioned enterprise," Murdoch pledged to create a news network that would link "almost umbilically" the "dissemination of news and entertainment for the good of us and our viewers." His approach would pay little homage to the Edward R. Murrow school of news or even CNN for that matter. "Forget about what the competition is doing," he told his collected affiliates. "Forget about the 95% of AP wire information. Without reinventing the wheel, it is possible to radically improve the program. The talent must be different and not broadcast news: the talent must be real journalists and real characters."[9]

The affiliates who left the meeting impressed by Murdoch's enthusiasm and drive missed the point. They absorbed the mood of the man without hearing the message he was delivering: News is entertainment. It is not about politics or murder or corruption in business. It's about getting people in front of their television sets and keeping them there. It's about the bottom line.

That was what Murdoch meant when he said he wanted to radically improve the program. What he did not say was that while he was improving the program, he would be twisting the content—not enough to be dishonest, but enough to push his sermon of conservative values and big-business ethics. The power that news delivered to its manipulator would be incalculable. For now, the push was on to create the framework, to outline the division, to inspire the troops.

In lieu of a blueprint, Murdoch took his cue from CBS News, hiring its onetime president Van Gordon Sauter** to replace Chao as president of Fox News Service. That Sauter took the position reflected his desire for lucrative employment more than his belief that Murdoch was serious about delivering unbiased, quality news.

---

** Sauter served as president of CBS News from 1982 to 1983 and as executive vice president of CBS News from 1983 to 1986.

If Sauter had wanted to know what was expected of him as head of Fox News, he had only to pick up a copy of Murdoch's *Sun,* dated August 21, 1992. On the cover, bosoms flailing and in full color, Sarah Ferguson, the duchess of York, was having her toes sucked by her American boyfriend, John Bryan. The photo itself would have been evidence enough had it not been the exclusive providence of the *Sun*'s archrival, the *Mirror.* When the *Mirror* purchased the British rights to the photos from its Italian photographer and launched an expensive advertising campaign to announce their release, Murdoch authorized the same-date publication of the same photo, easing around the copyright laws by printing the photo as it appeared on the cover of the Spanish magazine *Hola!,* which was in turn published on the front page of the *Sun.* "The lawyers tell me we're okay," Murdoch told a writer from *Forbes.* "We were reporting the news."[10]

Four days later, the *Sun* carried as news the tantalizing transcript of a taped telephone conversation between Princess Diana and an unidentified man who was decidedly not His Royal Highness, Prince Charles. In the United States, this news was carried in the *National Enquirer.* Van Gordon Sauter never made the connection.

Even with his spending power reduced to the nub by the rigorous controls of his funding banks, Murdoch found the money to purchase the Spanish network Antenne-3 and announced plans to fill its programming with dubbed versions of Fox product. He also stepped up the cross-pollination of Murdoch assets by buying Fox films for his BSkyB customers to watch. His direct involvement in the long-range planning for BSkyB resulted in the first-ever profit stance for the satellite service, which inched into the black in mid-1992. This, coupled with an improved profit margin at Fox Studios due to the box-office success of the film *Home Alone 2,*[†] meant that Murdoch was able to begin reducing his debt load in advance of his bank restructuring arrangement.

---

[†] *Home Alone 2* earned $103 million in theatrical release alone. It was the second-highest-grossing film in 1992, behind Disney's *Aladdin.*

It was a remarkable turnaround, but no less so than the one experienced at Turner Broadcasting, where net income in 1992 was $105 million based on revenues of $1.7 billion. In four years, Turner managed to double his business sales, declare a stock dividend for the first time since 1975, and make more profit than *any* of the three big broadcast networks.

"I've been through a lot of campaigns," Turner said at the start of 1993. "I'm only 54, but I've already got the mileage of a 150-year-old man. I'm like a New York City taxicab that has three drivers driving twenty-four hours a day seven days a week."[11]

Turner credited his rebound to long workdays and the fact that he owned the majority of his programming. "We control more of our own software than any other programming entity in the world," Turned said.[12] The same film that airs on WTBS was a likely product for TNT. Videos in both black and white and colorized versions were packaged by Turner Home Entertainment.

"We're really in the business of remarketing product," said Scott Sassa, president of Turner Entertainment Group and one-time publicity chief under Murdoch at Fox. "We buy as much software as we can, and find as many ways to get it out there as we can."[13]

"It's like the modern chicken farmer," Turner added. "They grind up the feet to make fertilizer, they grind up the intestines to make dog food. The feathers go into pillows. They use every bit of the chicken. Well, that's what we try to do over here with the television products."

Yet, even as Turner Broadcasting was climbing toward record numbers, Turner had a vision that allowed for unlimited future growth by continually adapting CNN for various cultures in varying parts of the world. It was a challenge assigned to Tom Johnson, former editor of the *Los Angeles Times,* who took over as president of CNN on the eve of the Gulf War. "The criticism that CNN has been a U.S.-based network with a U.S.-based content and focus is an absolutely valid criticism," Johnson told *Forbes* in

1993. "We are reaching out to internationalize this network as aggressively as we know how."

Johnson's plan was to regionalize the look of CNN International for various areas of the world, with U.S. content amounting to no more than 30 percent of the total coverage. The reason for his mandate and Turner's enthusiasm was simple enough. Money and power were the rewards that continued to drive TBS, with an improved environment and better education high on the list of benefits usually mentioned in the next breath. Despite television's acceptance in the United States and Western Europe, it was just beginning to emerge in the international marketplace.

The massive population of Third World countries stood poised to become the next television generation some 50 years after the TV revolution had conquered the United States. In the years between 1987 and 1992 alone, the number of television receivers jumped 50 percent. As television sets became available, so did the news they endlessly beamed forth. News that linked nations, where boundaries meant nothing and information was the only political party that mattered. When Communism collapsed in Eastern Europe, Lech Walesa, the Polish shipyard worker–turned–president pointed to a television set and said, "It all came from there."

Money and power. Power and money. Rupert Murdoch on the West Coast (when he wasn't in New York or London or at his home in Aspen) and Ted Turner on the East (when he wasn't on his Montana ranch or any of his other eight properties) had plenty of both, yet not nearly enough by their own calculations. At the start of 1993, both men laid the ground work to correct that situation, albeit from polar-opposite approaches.

Turner, always the visionary, placed his faith in new and untapped markets, reworking the old until it was fresh, and opening frontiers through friendships. Not that all his visions were totally clear. Just months after launching the Check-Out Channel, Turner shut off the signal. Servicing television monitors and hearing checkers' complaints was not his idea of a cash cow. Likewise the McDonald's Channel, which only slowed traffic in a place known for speed.

Murdoch, always the businessman, sniffed out new ventures through acquisition. Good businesses having bad luck were particularly vulnerable. As for friendships, they had no place in his game plan unless they served a temporary purpose.

The year following his takeover of Fox proved that point well. After firing Fox News head Steve Chao, Murdoch also found it necessary to remove the top executives at Fox Films and Fox Television—or rather, convince them not to stay. As one Hollywood mogul told *New York* magazine, "He doesn't see much value in individuals. Each of us has a weak spot, and this is Rupert Murdoch's weak spot. He's not a person who admires people."[14]

If that statement needed further clarification, any confusion over Murdoch's allegiance to employees was settled when he surprised New York City and the FCC by offering to repurchase the *New York Post* in 1993 in a fire-sale rescue that resonated with told-you-so's.

Peter Kalikow, the real estate developer who had bought the newspaper from Murdoch in 1988, had seen it continue to suck away at his finances until he was forced into bankruptcy in mid-1991. Rumors began surfacing that the *Post* was actually run by members of the Mafia, allegations officially leveled by District Attorney Robert Morgenthau, who charged a number of *Post* employees plus various members of the Bonanno crime family with an assortment of crimes including bribery and extortion.

Just as the *Post* was breathing its last, an angel appeared in the form of investor Steve Hoffenberg, who promised to inject cash into the newspaper in exchange for ownership. What at first seemed like divine intervention soon turned into the deal from hell when Hoffenberg was arrested for fraud in a suit brought by the Securities and Exchange Commission. Hoffenberg would later be sentenced to 20 years in prison.

Unable to fulfill his promise to save the *Post*, Hoffenberg turned to his friend Abe Hirschfeld, a once penniless immigrant-turned-wealthy parking lot king, who agreed to take over the *Post*. Hirschfeld then promptly fired its editor, columnist Pete Hamill, who at the time was the most respected journalist working at the newspaper. In a style somehow befitting the *Post*, Hamill refused to leave, publishing an issue on March 16 headlined WHO IS THIS NUT? that devoted 24 pages to lambasting its new publisher. Hirschfeld, it seemed, had a history nearly as long as the *Post*'s, which included a 1977 conviction for falsely imprisoning a city employee who had refused to give him a permit for a parking garage.

The *New York Times* carried an editorial saluting the *Post*'s journalists. *Newsday*'s Pulitzer Prize–winning writer Murray Kempton prayed for the *Post*, where he once was employed, in print:

> The besieged *New York Post* staff, depleted in numbers, pillaged by marauders, and captained at the breach by the last romantic, who is Pete Hamill, has turned desperately at bay, loaded all guns from its diminishing stock of newsprint, and volleyed defiance. . . . May God be good to them and find them a savior.

Small wonder that when Murdoch arrived on March 23, 1993, to rescue the *Post* from itself, the staff gave him a standing ovation. His pose, however, was less savior than curmudgeon. "I'm not here as some fairy godmother to pour some more money into the paper," he lashed out. "We have to find a way to at least break even."[15] Among the methods slated to be tried was a restructuring of the advertising rate card, a firm determination of target readers, and another new editor, Hamill having refused to remain at the paper under Murdoch.

One person Murdoch did not push aside was Massachusetts' Edward Kennedy, his old nemesis from the Senate. It mattered little that Kennedy had forced the issue that pushed Murdoch to sell the *Post* in 1988. Now Murdoch needed the senator's cooperation to get the newspaper back. As one Murdoch supporter said, "They're both older, and they may need each other down the road."[16] It also helped that Kennedy was up for reelection the following year.

While Murdoch was able to gain control of the *Post* for a quarter of the $38 million Kalikow paid him for it, he also had to pledge up to $7 million in accounts receivable to Hoffenberg, and Hirschfeld would be refunded most of the $2.5 million he had sunk into the newspaper during the 18 incendiary days he owned it.

Now that Murdoch had gotten his favored newspaper back, he was not about to take any chances with its turnaround. Though his workload at Fox had grown after Diller's departure, Murdoch thought nothing of spending 16-hour workdays toiling at the regenerated *Post*, and rented an apartment nearby. Ken Chandler, the British-born editor of Murdoch's *Boston Herald*, was named editor for the transition to help his publisher buoy the *Post* up for the rough weather ahead.

The restructuring of the *Post* went on for months, as did Murdoch's fight to keep the newspaper and his Fox television outlet in Manhattan. In the end, he won on both fronts, a living testament that rewards are paid to the persistent. By the time Murdoch was officially given the FCC's blessing three months after his return to the *Post*, he had reluctantly moved on to concentrate on other areas of his burgeoning business. Even so, he would always stop in at "the paper," as he called it, to once again roll up his shirtsleeves and, if only for a moment, relive the glory days of newspapermen with ink-stained fingers and clattering keyboards.

What eventually *did* pull Murdoch far afield from his first love was an opportunity to invest in the Far East, an area he saw filled with endless potential. His first foray into the Asian market had been his purchase of Hong Kong's *South China Morning Post*. At first glance, the prospects for an English-language daily

in a city that was 97 percent Chinese seemed poor. It was one reason why Murdoch's purchase price of $300 million appeared
ridiculously high to industry soothsayers at the time.

In the years following, however, he capitalized on what he saw
as the *Morning Post*'s biggest asset: its classified ads. While the area's
other newspapers were beating each other into submission with
exclusive news coverage, Murdoch allowed his news team to freely
steal from his other newspapers and fill out the editorial with wire
coverage—anything to provide a wraparound for the breadwinning
classified advertisements. His sales team tripled ad sales and doubled ad rates, returning a net of nearly 50 percent. In 1993, the *South
China Morning Post* hit a record page count with a Saturday edition
that carried 142 pages of advertising and 16 pages of editorial.

The *Morning Post* also alerted Murdoch to the potential of the
region. He studied the culture, made friends with government
heads, visited the elders, and recruited the smartest and youngest
talent. The years of homework served him brilliantly when
another opportunity presented itself in the area—this time in the
sky and with a far greater reach.

On July 26, 1993, Murdoch was granted a waiver by the FCC to
keep his cherished *New York Post*. The celebration within the *Post*
editorial department, however, took place without its elusive chief
leading the backslapping. The media mogul was half a world away,
signing the paperwork to buy 64 percent of a satellite TV concern
called Star whose footprint not only blanketed all of Asia but also
cast its shadow across the sea to the Eastern Mediterranean. For
$500 million, Murdoch bought into the future—*his* future, to hear
him tell it. He was buying potential, pure and simple, betting once
again that his instincts would place him at the forefront of commerce and communications in the most heavily populated arena
in the world. *Star TV*. Even the name was fabulous.[††]

---

[††] Despite the success of the *South China Morning Post,* Murdoch sold his majority share
in the newspaper in October 1993 to pro-Beijing businessman Robert Kuok to help
finance his Star TV purchase.

Yet, in this most culturally diverse region of the world, the complexities of programming such a beast were incalculable. The expanse was home to the oldest religions in the world. Whole civilizations rose and fell under the Asian sun, the followers of these civilizations still existing, tucked away in far-off corners that had essentially remained untouched for thousands of years.

For Murdoch, the challenge was the prize: make Star TV work as a thriving, massive communication vehicle reaching across continents and cultures, and gain a dominance no one else on earth could touch in terms of viewers, influence, or control. The Australian–turned–Ugly American wanted to own the region, cosmically speaking. He wanted Star TV to be the first, the biggest, the only satellite service to extend from the rice paddies of Anhui Province to the Hall of Boundless Happiness in the Lama Temple of Beijing.

That most programming comes from America is understood around the world, except in China, which had followed its own course without regard to popular trends. Murdoch's key to success would likely be found in appealing to the younger generation of Asia with enough youth-oriented programming to get them to purchase the Star TV service. At the same time, a majority of time-honored features and documentaries would be provided to keep the older population from exercising veto power. The sensitivities of the region notwithstanding, it was a delicate balance that needed to find its center quickly, before criticism of its Western programming could outdistance its traditional merits.

Murdoch may have been leading the pack, but he had only a whisper of a head start. The Hong Kong conglomerate Wharf Holdings Ltd. was set to launch Hong Kong's first cable system. Warner Bros. was actively seeking a partner in Chinese-language programming. Home Box Office, a Time Warner pay cable network, was on cable systems in the Philippines, Thailand, Singapore, and Taiwan.

Because Star TV already carried the BBC World News Service to its viewership, the roadblocks were in place against an easy CNN break into the market. Even so, Ted Turner was as eager as anyone to find the niche that granted him entry, and pledged to spend $15 million to open production facilities in Tokyo for English-language news and information programs. In addition, Turner joined a "loose consortium" with HBO, ESPN, and the Discovery Channel to sell what he called a "program neighborhood," grouping together shows of like interest.[17]

With programming in the American market reaching the saturation level, the untapped Asian market had long held the promise of the future. Until this moment in history, government controls restricted access to the point where no progress of any kind had been achieved. With satellite transmission ignoring borders, cultures, politics, and the military, those restrictions suddenly collapsed into a tangle of raw nerves and payoffs.

The World Bank estimated that Asia would continue to outpace the rest of the world by two to one. The business that accommodated that growth and complemented its progress would be the business that won the grand prize. Murdoch intended to succeed in Asia as he had in most other parts of the world—through instinct, connections, and detached ruthlessness.

Yet the land of the rising sun was not like the rest of the world. Its cultures, its religions, its pace were not Murdoch's, nor Turner's for that matter. Both men, however, placed so much belief in its long-term importance that they simultaneously put into motion changes that would reverberate throughout their empires, and from which only one would emerge the winner.

# F I F T E E N

# He Did *What?*

*At the beginning, the thing that motivated me was adventure.
I just wanted to see if I could do it. And then, later on,
when I got all these networks, then I said,
"It's really important that some broadcaster really cares
and it's just not going for ratings all the time."*

Ted Turner
Los Angeles
July 1994

Ted Turner looked every bit the part. Dressed in the gray wool of a Confederate officer, his polished brass buttons gleaming in the afternoon sun, Turner tugged nervously at the edge of his jacket and sang "I wish I was in the land of cotton" under his breath. He was on the lush green plain that was the Gettysburg battlefield, his face smudged with mud and his scabbard slung low around his waist, ready to make his official acting debut. This Civil War buff, this lover of the South, had arrived to do a cameo in his own $20 million filmed version of the decisive battle in the War Between the States.

Five thousand extras wandered in organized fashion, preparing for director Ronald Maxwell's cue to launch the next scene. The camera was focused on Turner. In his role as Colonel Waller Tazewell Patton (great-uncle of General George S. Patton of World War II fame), the media magnate had but to raise his sword and help lead the South into Pickett's Charge, the final gruesome end to the slaughter at Gettysburg. As Turner said his

313

single line, he was amazingly at home, a study in confidence, a man at ease with his hobby.

He had bankrolled the picture for his Turner Network Television channel, only to later decide to release it first as a feature film. He also agreed to appear in the role to experience the reality of battle. It was a time when men still fought for honor face-to-face, and watched one another die with respect and courage. "A noble time," he later called it. "A noble film."

Before the film premiered in October 1993 in some 100 theaters across the country at four hours and 18 minutes, much of the talk was of its length. That was before anyone had seen the film. Leaving the theater, audiences rarely mentioned how long they had sat in the darkened auditorium; rather, they emerged swept up in the intensity of a battle that defined America. On one field, where 158,000 men fought and 43,000 were killed, there was no need for romance or subplots or any melodrama concocted in a Hollywood script conference. In *Gettysburg*, the war was the star, supported by the wills of men who might otherwise be friends.

There was something of Turner in those Confederate generals and, ironically, something of Murdoch on the Union's side. Each man was able to galvanize his troops to work long hours under extreme conditions, often without question for the good of their respective companies. Turner's employees had followed him in his early days based on little more than faith in his vision; Murdoch's employees found his lead to be charged with the energy of change. In each case, as the companies prospered and became larger and their leaders became more inaccessible, that loyalty flagged in direct proportion.

Neither man, despite their wealth and decades of combined experience, showed any indication of slowing his workload or reducing his schedule. Sixteen-hour days were routine, many of those hours spent traveling or on the telephone, each leader armed with artillery that would soon be aimed at each other.

*Gettysburg* was distributed by New Line Cinema, an independent film production and distribution company that Turner had purchased in 1993 for $500 million from its founder, Robert Shaye.* Turner had successfully talked his board of directors into allowing the acquisition, along with another—Castle Rock Entertainment,** for which Turner paid $150 million. Turner had long wanted to own more Hollywood film production units for exactly the reason he purchased MGM and Murdoch acquired Fox: a continuing supply of films to program on a growing number of television outlets. With New Line and Castle Rock, Turner bought respect, clout, and a small slate of quality product.

Murdoch was feeling none of his competitor's respect. He was still fighting an uphill battle with those who saw him as the purveyor of cheap sensation. Yet, his most unnerving challenge presented itself much closer to home. It did not come in the form of a business deal, newspaper acquisition, or television coup. This was personal, a private confrontation, in which Murdoch welcomed a new member into his family. His daughter Elisabeth had fallen in love with a man named Elkin Pianim while attending Vassar College, from which she later graduated with a degree in business. Quiet reserve and affection marked the couple's extended courtship, during which Pianim went to work for the Rothschild Investment Bank in New York, and Elisabeth moved to Australia for her first job in television at the Nine Network. The long-distance separation heightened the romance, and when Elisabeth announced their engagement in 1992, she expected her parents to share her joy.

---

* New Line was started by Shaye in his Greenwich Village apartment. One of the first films he distributed was the 1968 version of *Night of the Living Dead*. Later, the company specialized in art films, including Lina Wertmuller's *The Seduction of Mimi*, Orson Welles' *F for Fake*, Bertrand Blier's Oscar-winning *Get Out Your Handkerchiefs*, R. W. Fassbinder's *Despair*, Bill Forsyth's *Gregory's Girl*, and Whit Stillman's *Metropolitan*.
** Among Castle Rock Entertainment's feature films are *When Harry Met Sally . . .*, *A Few Good Men*, and *The Shawshank Redemption*. Castle Rock also produced the *Seinfeld* television series. The company was formed in 1987 by five media moguls, including director Rob Reiner and former Fox executives Alan Horn and Martin Shafer.

What made this news difficult for Murdoch was not the fact that his daughter was in love, but that her fiancé was black. The son of a jailed Ghanaian politician and economist, Pianim was tall and good-looking, with an eager smile and a business drive that Murdoch would eventually come to appreciate. For now, however, the notion of an interracial marriage weighed heavily on his mind.

Murdoch has never been characterized as a racist, though his London *Sun* had often been accused of an anti-black bias. He was merely conservative and had an image of life in which blacks and whites each had a place—just not together, and certainly not married. To have it foisted on him by his own daughter was a shock, even with the couple's lengthy courtship. The pair had been dating for years and a marriage proposal had never materialized until now.

At Christmastime 1992, Elisabeth had grown tired of waiting for a serious commitment from her long-term beau and issued Pianim an ultimatum that resulted in an engagement ring. Gone was any thought of an official Murdoch protest as father gave his blessing, albeit with the uneasy feeling that accompanies all parents when they sense a complex time ahead. His mother, Dame Elisabeth, remembering the time, said, "When my children were young, I would have found [a mixed marriage] difficult. No doubt I would have had to accept [it], but difficult. Now all that is changed, and I know that Elkin and Elisabeth can overcome any difficulties."[1]

While Anna handled the plans for the elaborate wedding as she had for Prudence's 1985 marriage to investor Crispin Odey,[†] daughter Elisabeth continued working, taking various jobs in television unrelated to the Murdoch empire. After continued public outcry, Pianim's father, Dr. Andrews Pianim, was released

---

[†] Odey was a young stockbroker when he married Prudence, and rejected any help from the Murdoch family in his business. In 1991, he opened Odey Asset Management, and by 1994 was the highest paid executive in England. His salary that year was $35 million. His short marriage to Prudence ended in divorce.

from prison after spending nine years isolated from public view. Soon after, he flew with his Dutch wife, Cornelia, to visit the Murdochs in California. They were appalled to learn of Pianim's treatment at the hands of Ghanaian president Jerry Rawlings. According to letters Anna and Rupert wrote, they found the respected Pianim, at one time the acting principal secretary of the Ministry of Finance and Economic Planning for Ghana, "calm and dignified." He was, Murdoch felt, "a good man."

That opinion had not changed by the day of the wedding, when the Ghanaian contingent showed up in colorful traditional dress at St. Timothy's Roman Catholic Church, a few blocks from 20th Century-Fox Studios. Also attending the service were former president Ronald Reagan and his wife, Nancy. The evening reception was held at Murdoch's Misty Mountain estate, where the guests dined on caviar pie.

This was a time of closure for Murdoch. As the bride and groom waltzed to Stevie Wonder's "Ribbon in the Sky," Elisabeth's father had the satisfaction of knowing his financial house was in order. Unbeknownst to all outside of the immediate family, Murdoch had arranged to buy out his three sisters' shares of News Corporation stock, held under the family's Cruden Investments. With the exception of 10 percent remaining in his mother's name, Murdoch now owned all of his family's 32 percent of the business, assuring an easy probate of his estate when that moment arrived. Given the volatility of the stock, it was still consolation for the man who remembered his own fate at the time of his father's death. As he watched with pride at the party unfolding around him, Murdoch felt content, perhaps even happy. He had done things well.

His biggest problem was with the Fox Network's languishing station count. While ratings continued to improve on the backs of such huge successes as *Beverly Hills 90210* and *The Simpsons,* the number of stations committed to carrying Fox programs was still small compared to ABC, CBS, and NBC.

Murdoch approached the problem as he did most: by digging deep into his wallet. In this case, he thought that the universal appeal of sports might provide the answer, and stormed the office of the National Football League with an offer of $1.58 billion for a four-year contract to carry NFL Sunday afternoon games on Fox. The games had been a CBS Network franchise for more than 40 years. With his signature on a contract, Sunday afternoons and the NFL belonged to Murdoch.

Like Turner, Murdoch was reinforcing that product was king. Though he could not buy the NFL outright, he could borrow it for an afternoon every week in the fall. Station owners across the country took note of Murdoch's confidence in his affiliates. Even if the Fox Network was an illusion spun of confidence and hyperbole, as many critics had accused it of being from its inception, there was suddenly a very real look about the place. Though the NFL was a franchise in decline, it was authentic, all-American, basic stuff that spelled *foundation* to stations who began to look at the fledgling network as competition for the first time. For Murdoch, that alone was worth the overpayment.

It was a time in America, indeed the world, when the Internet was a little-understood technology that promised everything from interactive communications to interlinked business opportunities. To gain a baby foothold in the technology, Murdoch invested $12 million to buy a small Cambridge, Massachusetts–based company called Delphi Internet Services. Delphi was an Internet service provider (ISP) and was positioned to be a window on the Net through which many who opted to use the technology were supposed to navigate.

Murdoch himself had long held that the only interactive technology he cared to personally utilize was the telephone. That did not, however, keep him from eagerly jumping into the arena when an opportunity presented itself. He had come to do business in Massachusetts for another purpose altogether. The man who had gone to such great pains to purchase the *Boston Herald* and even greater pains to fight the FCC to keep it now agreed it was time to sell. He had been offered a reported $20 million for the *Herald*, a considerable profit over the $1 million he had spent to purchase the newspaper from the Hearst Corporation in 1983. And this time, Murdoch was selling only the newspaper, not its Harrison Avenue headquarters, which the *Herald*'s new owners would now lease from the media magnate. Murdoch sold the *Herald* to Patrick Purcell, publisher of that newspaper as well as the *New York Post*. Purcell also served as president of News America, the publishing division of News Corporation, a position he relinquished with the closing of the sale.

Murdoch's eagerness to divest himself of the newspaper came as Boston's Channel 25, WFXT, came on the market. WFXT had been sold when Murdoch bought the Metromedia stations to comply with FCC cross-ownership rules. Though he had sold the station, Murdoch had maintained options for its repurchase— options he now intended to exercise.

The *Herald* deal was consummated via a handshake on January 18, 1994, one day after a catastrophic earthquake hit Los Angeles. On *that* day, Murdoch began conducting business from his Mercedes coupe when he discovered the phone lines were down both in his home and on the Fox lot. "It was an earthquake, not a hurricane," he said, as if everybody were doing business from their cars that day.

Murdoch had important calls to make to China, where the government had taken exception to a comment he had made in a speech in London. Addressing, quite on the record, 300 members of the British media and government, he had essentially bragged about his success with BSkyB. It did not matter that most of the channels he had added to the satellite lineup were repeats of old movies and television series. Murdoch had a point to make. "Technology is galloping over the old regulatory machinery. Information-hungry residents of many closed societies [can now] by-pass state-controlled television."[2] The comment was heard like a cannon shot over in China, and the reaction was to seal off access to the very dishes that could receive Murdoch's signal.

"I announced all our new channels in Europe," he later said. "I said governments can't stop news from getting in. It's the end of authoritarian government. All commonsense clichés. My enemies in China immediately frightened the propaganda ministry into considering an edict saying individuals can't have satellite dishes."[3]

That Murdoch could pick up the phone and reach the Communist leaders in China was no more surprising than his ability to turn the situation somewhat in his favor without leaving the front seat of his car. Eventually, the answer came in dropping the BBC News from his Star service beaming across China. The British had long been critical of China's human-rights record, and its posture was particularly offensive to Jiang Zemin, China's president since 1993. By replacing the BBC News with a Mandarin movie channel, Murdoch sidestepped a potentially explosive issue in the name of profit and at the expense of ideology.

"All the dishes in the world are made in China! Their own figures show 300 million homes get our channels—a music channel, an old Chinese movie channel. . . . China's like the Industrial Revolution in Europe 200 years ago,"[4] Murdoch said. With a population estimated at 1.5 billion, the potential of China seemed limitless as long as its government was placated.

In the Far East, however, potential and reality had proven to be enormous divergent points for any number of American companies that had attempted to penetrate the Chinese market. For Murdoch, the challenge was not simply to blanket the vast country with an invisible satellite signal; the real trick was to make money doing it. In 1994, Star was generating all its income from advertisers on its stations, though the amount of disposable income in China was so small that few advertisers bothered.

The exact same situation existed in India, another hope for Star. As in China, India's population was exceedingly poor, and the country was crisscrossed with cable services called *dish wal-*

*lahs,* which served as few as 50 homes. Conservatively, some 20,000 dish wallahs were operating in the country, essentially stealing Star's signal and making small profits in India's most densely populated cities.

Programming was the key to uncovering the hidden potential of the region, according to Murdoch, with the universal appeal of sports programming supplying the quickest return with the fewest cultural risks. Just as the NFL held the promise of furthering the Fox Network's popularity in the United States, Murdoch invested in the new NFL World League, a relaunch of a failed concept from 1991, with six European teams hoping to begin playing by April 1995.

Ted Turner was hardly unaware of the promise that the Asia/Pacific region held, and made a highly publicized fact-finding visit to the area at about the same time. Closely watched by his handlers, who feared his typical foot-in-mouth blunders, Turner made it out nearly unscathed, although his comment about not being able to find a good Chinese restaurant in China left many in the area perplexed but unfazed.

He hurried back to America to launch what he thought was going to be one of his most popular cable channels—Turner Classic Movies. Hosted by the *Hollywood Reporter*'s Bob Osborne, TCM had a less than auspicious start, launching with only one million subscribers (TNT, by comparison, started with 17 million). Still, Turner was enthusiastic about its long-term prospects and staged a glamorous launch party right in the middle of New York's Times Square. There, surrounded by the likes of Hollywood legends Arlene Dahl, Jane Powell, Celeste Holm, and Van Johnson, Turner pulled a ceremonial lever to switch on his newest movie channel. High above Times Square, a giant television screen flashed to life—a little too brightly, however, for two New York cabbies. More interested in the show than the road, they crashed head-on just a hundred feet away from the platform where the stars were smiling down at the curiosity seekers.

Also in New York that day, Rupert Murdoch responded to the hoopla with a dry "Rather unnecessary, isn't it?" Yet another Turner channel attempting to squeeze yet another penny from what Murdoch termed "the same old films." He actually wanted the old Turner back. The one who got drunk and said whatever he felt. The one who took chances. The maverick mogul. Murdoch surmised that the man who founded CNN was now content merely to repeat himself. "Sad, really," Murdoch said without giving it much more thought.

There was little doubt that Murdoch loved competition. He rolled around in it the way a dog scratches its back in the sand. It was his fun, the game he played to keep himself from getting bored. And when he sensed the playing field was shrinking, he pouted, much the way a small child does when denied the last chocolate on a dessert tray.

He would get his chance to play again the following month, thanks to a comment made by Michael Milken to another billionaire, Ronald Perelman. Milken had made several billion dollars himself since advising Turner to buy MGM, then got into trouble with the Securities and Exchange Commission, served 22 months in jail, and was now forbidden to actively trade stocks again in his lifetime. That did not, however, stop him from giving his friends advice, Ron Perelman among them.

Perelman was the arrogant billionaire owner of Revlon and a dozen other companies, including a majority share of New World Communications, a company that produced television shows (*The Wonder Years, Crime Story*) and owned 12 TV stations across the country. Milken's concept was an interesting one. Not only would it fill Perelman's pockets with money, but Perelman would not have to give up anything in the process.

The plan was simple enough: Ask Rupert Murdoch to invest $500 million in New World Communications, and in return offer to switch the affiliations of all 12 New World stations to the Fox television network. Because Murdoch would not be buying the stations, but rather purchasing a minority ownership of New World, he would not be in conflict with FCC ownership regulations. And because Perelman was not selling the stations, he would get $500 million for switching loyalties, plus a ready outlet for New World shows. When the concept was explained to Murdoch, he took mere minutes to accept the deal, and less than two weeks to finalize the arrangements.

When the announcement was made in mid-May 1994, the television world was stunned by the fallout from the Murdoch deal. CBS, at the time the ratings leader in prime time, lost eight station outlets in Dallas, Detroit, Atlanta, Cleveland, Tampa, Phoenix, Milwaukee, and Austin. *Time* magazine headlined the deal MURDOCH'S BIGGEST SCORE and quoted an industry source as claiming the arrangement was the "greatest realignment of affiliations in the sixty-year history of American broadcasting."[5]

Both Murdoch and Perelman, rather new to the television game, were astounded by the aftershock that rolled with a defining force through Hollywood and New York. Howard Stringer, president of the CBS Entertainment Group, labeled Fox "a purveyor of downscale sitcoms and titillating soap operas."[6] Actually, they were far more. With the Perelman stations, plus another 38 that had joined Fox since Murdoch acquired the rights to the NFL, the Fox Network would soon be broadcasting on 188 stations across the country, putting it within striking distance of the other networks, which had around 215. "No one in their right mind can ever say 'the three traditional networks and Fox' anymore," said media analyst Paul Schulman. "Everybody should refer to them as 'the four networks.'"[7] And nearly everyone did.

When the Fox station owners met in Los Angeles in June, Murdoch addressed the group in triumph. "There is a moment in time," he said, "when the opportunity presents itself to leap forward and achieve great success. There is no doubt in my mind that that moment is now for Fox. We intend to seize this moment and propel our network forward to the forefront of American broadcasting."[8]

For Turner, the words resounded with self-adulation. It was, he thought, the bragging of a foolish man. Better to do the work and let the results speak for themselves than boast about a future that might never be. Turner had learned that lesson himself and now found the knowledge had moved him into a different place in life. He felt wiser, enlightened. He rather liked placing himself in the position of sage. In previous years, viewers around the world had tuned in to CNN in near-record numbers, even without the benefit of a national crisis. This time, it was plain morbid curiosity as the world devoured hours of news coverage of the 1994 murder of Nicole Brown Simpson. Former football star O. J. Simpson's erratic behavior helped keep viewers addicted to their televisions, unable to pull themselves away from the continuing coverage of the horrible tragedy and the melodrama unfolding around it.

The Fox Network was not able to benefit from the crime, since it had yet to develop a news broadcast of its own, and was left borrowing from CNN and other sources for newsbreaks. "Anything that makes trouble for [Murdoch] I'd love to see," Turner commented. "Because he makes all the trouble he can for me. I personally like him. He's an interesting person. And I know he'd like to have CNN, so I have to worry that he'd like to eat me."[9]

Turner's latest imbroglio with Murdoch reached its peak during ongoing negotiations to have CNN placed on Murdoch's Star satellite service. Star attempted to place conditions on what and how much news coverage CNN could beam into China and India, citing "cultural sensitivities." CNN balked and declined Star's offer, further heightening the logomachy between the men.

In an interview in London's *Financial Times,* Turner noted that Murdoch was 10 years older than he, and that "if the actuarial tables are right, he'll be dead ten years before me, and I'll have ten years of peace and quiet."[††]

Murdoch, finding humor in the discord, sent Turner a note. "Dear Ted: Let's have lunch before it's too late. Rupert."

As light and mischievous as Murdoch's response sounded, the two men were political opposites who had each made a full swing in their views. Turner, the early conservative, had grown more liberal and enlightened with age; Murdoch, the young left-winger, had shifted hard to the right as his businesses grew.

Standing as a glaring example of the difference between the two men, Turner's 1994 Goodwill Games took place in St. Petersburg, Russia, in late July. The world was now a far different place than it was when the first games were held in Moscow in 1986, the Cold War having assumed its place in history. For that, Turner gladly claimed a stake, however small. He relished the concept of world peace, making allies out of enemies, and envisioned a time when countries played out their aggressions on an athletic field. Murdoch looked upon the Goodwill Games as Turner's folly, an unnecessary reason to cast $40 million into the wind. For Murdoch, it was about business; for Turner, it was about humanity.

From the Goodwill Games to conservation to population control to the environment, Turner had skewed so far left that he had gone off the trail completely and was charting an entirely new frontier. A small bout with skin cancer only served to propel the Samaritan to an even purer place. The cancerous lesion on his lip was quickly treated through surgery, though it was said by friends to have awakened in Turner a "closer association with purpose." One goal he remained determined to reach was owning a U.S. television network. Since his failed attempt to take over CBS in the mid-eighties, Turner's thirst had only grown, his desire festering like an old wound, the infection spreading more each day. During the latter part of 1994, the network of choice

---

[††] Only seven years separate the men's birthdays.

was NBC, third in the ratings and looking to secure a monetary partner, if not a new parent. Had Turner not been restrained by his board of directors, he would have made a direct assault on NBC in damn-the-torpedoes fashion. But there were many on the board who found his addiction to network ownership lacking in sound business sense, chief among them Time Warner, which controlled 20 percent of TBS' voting stock.

Having tried and failed to convince Time Warner head Gerald Levin that owning NBC would prove synergistic with the other TBS properties, Turner took his campaign to the public via a speech delivered at Washington, D.C.'s National Press Club and broadcast nationally over C-SPAN.

"I'm being clitorized by Time Warner," he shouted, comparing his treatment to female circumcision. Suddenly, Turner was white-hot, stomping the floor, shouting, beating the podium as if anyone in the room might miss the point. "Time Warner wants to go out and try and get a network of their own, but they're holding me back from doing so. And it just isn't right. I had this deal worked out to acquire NBC, a little over a year ago, for about $5 billion—a billion in cash and a billion in preferred stock, and $3 billion in debt, which would have been no problem to finance. And I went to Time Warner with that, and they said no. It's just not right."

Rambling and dodging, lurching back and forth before the microphone, Turner was a moving target eagerly unloading his pain. "And now I have to compete with Rupert Murdoch, who has his own studio, who has his own broadcast network, and who now has his own cable network. And so I have to fight with one hand tied behind my back. It's like fighting a war without an air force. All you've got to do is look what happened to Poland to know how that works, and what happened to Iraq, and what would have happened to Haiti."

The old Turner had resurfaced, spitting mad and ready to bop the next Time Warner executive he saw. "It means I'm going to have to sell out. I'm going to have to put my company up for sale. That's the only way to resolve this thing, if I can't resolve it peacefully with Time Warner. . . . And you know who would be the buyer of our company?" he asked. "Rupert Murdoch would. I mean, he outbid everybody for the NFL. Rupert Murdoch is the only one who can do it. The rest of them are astute businessmen. They can't match a madman. . . . There's a thin line between madness and brilliance. . . . In fact, the most dangerous kind of competitor is one who is a little mad. You know?"

The audience understood. Even Rupert Murdoch got it. And with that, Ted Turner went back to his Montana ranch, watched his bison, and sulked.

Of course, Murdoch was having his own problems. Internet problems. As the world's media giants rushed to find their way in cyberspace, Murdoch found himself confused. "For older people like myself and my company, it will be a new and more competitive world," he said.

He did not understand computers or Web sites or ISP or e-mail. He was uncertain about downloading and uploading and found himself longing for the newsroom. *That* he understood. With Delphi, Murdoch had moved into the Internet. He established Fox Interactive. In Europe, News International had a New Media division to place his newspapers online and in digital format. His HarperCollins division had its own New Media division for electronic books. And *TV Guide* was creating *TV Guide On-Line* and *TV Guide On-Screen* in association with the country's largest cable company, John Malone's Tele-Communications Inc. And while it all sounded very current, very high-tech, Rupert Murdoch was uneasy. Extremely uneasy.

"I wish I was a scientist or a physicist. There's so much to know. The biggest challenge is getting an education on all this stuff," he told a reporter from *InterActive Week,* an industry newspaper to which he did not subscribe.[10]

The latest metamorphosis of Rupert Murdoch had him well positioned to take advantage of the age of information. While others had leaped into the industry at the first turn, Murdoch, by either caution or design, waited to see how the various players positioned themselves in an uncertain but growing marketplace. When he eventually merged onto the Information Superhighway, it was already crammed with racers speeding toward an unknown future. What scared Murdoch was that he had no roadmap to guide his way.

Newspapermen like Murdoch were a different breed, a club of insiders who worked their sources and knew their turfs, funneling information onto a page. Now the club was gone, replaced by an online network whose purpose was to spread information to the widest audience—bits and pieces scattered like buckshot across the world and landing in unfamiliar places.

At a time when his empire stretched over five continents, when he counted 120 newspapers in his fold, plus a publishing house with 40 imprints including the world's largest producer of Bibles, Murdoch postured like a man in control and a visionary with a plan for the future. In truth, there was no plan, no concrete vision, only incredible gambles made on instinct and based on opportunity.

The greatest gamble, however, was still in the future, one that would place him on a direct collision course with Ted Turner. Two men, each brilliant in his own way, restrained by their convictions and convinced of their purpose, armed to change not only the way the news reached the world, but also the bias with which it was spun.

# SIXTEEN

# Walking on the Potomac

*Power? What power? I have no power.*
*No more than any American.*
*This myth that I have some influence*
*up there on Capitol Hill is baloney.*

Rupert Murdoch
Washington, D.C.
January 1995

The violet shadows of predawn were shattered by an explosion so white-hot it lit up the sky like daylight and sent shards of blazing metal raining down on the mountainous landscape of Xichang, a forbidden city within South China. Soldiers from the People's Liberation Army stood frozen, unable to believe it had happened again. A second Hughes Apstar-2 satellite had failed to reach orbit on the back of a Long March 2E rocket that had roared to life only seconds before. This time, however, it show-ered death on 6 villagers and injured another 23.

When NBC learned of the tragedy, it did not mourn the deaths of the innocent, but rather grieved for the loss of a satel-lite that was supposed to give life to its CNBC network and SuperChannel across the Far East. Seemingly undaunted, it took NBC less than three weeks to negotiate transponders on Rupert Murdoch's Star satellite service for its stations. Simultaneously, NBC dropped its legal action against Murdoch, a complaint it had brought before the FCC months earlier. It was a very convenient coincidence.

The network had joined with the National Association for the Advancement of Colored People (NAAPC) in allegations that Fox misled the FCC about the extent of its Australian ownership when it received approval to purchase its six Metromedia stations in 1985. The NAACP had questioned the purchases, albeit 10 years after the fact, when it awakened to the knowledge that the Fox Network was attempting to grab as many television outlets around the country as possible to increase viewership, with the purchases funded by News Corporation. The NAACP stance was that allowing a foreign company to throw big bucks at small stations unfairly prevented minority entrepreneurs from competing.

Washington media attorney David Honig agreed to take the case before the FCC. He was later joined by NBC, who enlarged the scope of the investigation to include the possibility that Murdoch intentionally deceived the FCC about the foreign ownership of his Fox stations. At the time he was granted permission to purchase the original six Metromedia stations, Murdoch listed News Corporation as owning 24 percent of the voting stock of Fox Network owned-station group. The remaining 76 percent was owned by Barry Diller and Murdoch, then a newly sworn-in American.

NBC's sudden about-face in light of the Xichang incident did little to derail the FCC investigation. If anything, it stirred the pot of contention even more vigorously due to its timing. "The light bulb has just gone on that the guy is so integrated, he has so many ways to win, that the networks are by comparison pretty narrow companies," said Steven Lerman, a Washington media attorney.[1] Among those ways to win were the 42 million homes in 53 different countries that Murdoch could reach in Asia through Star TV, as well as his newspaper and magazine empire, which stretched across five continents.

The pressure brought by the FCC hit its peak in January 1995, when Murdoch was questioned for nearly three hours about his ownership position and motives in dividing up the Fox voting stock. "Either your people can't read, don't understand English or understand instruction, or you have a witch-hunt in this," Murdoch lashed out in uncharacteristic anger.[2] He clearly sensed the danger he faced: the very real possibility of losing his Fox ownership rights.

As dramatic a challenge as the FCC investigation was, it was not the only pressure being brought by Washington on the media magnate. In mid-January, details surfaced of a two-book deal between the Murdoch-owned HarperCollins publishing house and newly installed House Speaker Newt Gingrich—a deal worth $4.5 million to the veteran politician. The contracts were signed two weeks after a meeting Murdoch held in the offices of the then Speaker-to-be. The meeting was short and pleasant, and according to both men, no book deal was ever discussed. Rather, they talked about the recent elections that had swept Republicans into a controlling position in both the Senate and the House. "The most insignificant meeting in the history of the world" is the way Murdoch lobbyist Preston Padden labeled it in *Time*. Insignificant perhaps, but not unnoticed.

By the following month, details of the contract had been leaked to the press, and the new Speaker was forced to give up all but one dollar of the advance and agree to accept only actual royalties on sales of the books. It had, as investigative journalists pointed out, a "familiar smell." They were referring to Murdoch's habit of mixing politics with business in a way that was as helpful as it was blatant.

They had only to look as far as England to find an example in Margaret Thatcher. Murdoch made no secret that she was a close friend, or that she had consulted with him from the very start of her campaign for the office of prime minister. It was, in fact, after another famous "short meeting" late in her career that

Thatcher approved Murdoch's purchase of BSkyB, overlooking some rather stringent regulations that her own home secretary found "not technically legal." After she was pushed from power in late 1990, HarperCollins signed Thatcher to write her memoirs for a reported $5.4 million, a figure that made Gingrich's deal look sickly by comparison. As one critic later said, "If Gingrich was being bribed, he was being under-bribed."

After Murdoch's move into China through his Star TV deal, the Basic Books division of HarperCollins pledged $1 million to Deng Maomao, the youngest daughter of Chinese leader Deng Xiaoping, to write her father's biography. The deal allowed the *New Yorker* to quip, "Deng Maomao may or may not be China's Newt Gingrich, but Rupert Murdoch is definitely China's Rupert Murdoch."[3] *Deng Xiaoping: My Father* was later described by the *New Yorker* as a "turgid, barely literate piece of propaganda."

In an effort to distance himself from the growing swirl of controversy, Murdoch contended he had no idea that Harper-Collins was even negotiating with Gingrich at the time of their meeting. Gingrich said he had no idea that Murdoch owned HarperCollins. Both men were reported to have made the comments without a hint of a smile.

In Atlanta, Ted Turner turned off his speakerphone and sat in silence. He had just received word that his latest effort to buy a network—in this case, NBC—had been scuttled, this time not by Time Warner but by the head of NBC's parent company, General Electric. Jack Welch, GE's chairman, wanted to maintain control of the combined NBC-TBS venture, a condition Turner could never accept. Turner took on an injured silence as though in deep mourning. Though he did not know it at the time, it was the death of a dream and, like any death, demanded as deep a mourning from those who have lost.

Convinced that Time Warner had a negative impact on his efforts to convince NBC to sell on his terms, Turner offered a billion dollars to Time Warner head Jerry Levin to buy the conglomerate's 20 percent of TBS voting shares. Levin wanted $1.6 billion, citing the improvement in TBS' market value, largely due, of course, to Turner's own efforts.

It was with similar irony that Rupert Murdoch approached the dais at the Waldorf-Astoria Hotel ballroom to receive the International Radio and Television Society's Gold Medal Award for his "contribution to media around the world." There would be no mention of the ongoing FCC investigation or the potential multi-million-dollar fines that were likely to be levied should he be found guilty. This was a dinner of celebration, where tables sold for $10,000 each and the money funded educational programs to give "up-and-coming communicators the realities of the business world."

Murdoch had the look of an injured soldier—dour, wan, and prone to sporadic outbursts as if reliving a bad nightmare. He was not happy with his chosen country, which had apparently decided to punish him for, what, breaking some regulation that was put into place to protect our free airwaves from commercial exploitation by foreigners? Clearly, it did not apply to him.

As the clock ticked forward on the investigation and more depositions were taken, Murdoch grew angrier with each passing day, pulling political strings like a master puppeteer. It was an all-or-nothing gamble that might have gone either way. In truth, the FCC was trapped by its own ignorance of the facts, and by a man far more adept at playing the game than the FCC was, despite the fact that the FCC wrote the rules.

At an April 1995 hearing, the FCC issued a statement saying News Corporation's interest in Fox Inc. had indeed violated foreign-ownership restrictions and recommended a complete restructuring of the company. The decision made it appear as if Murdoch had broken the law and was about to be punished, but it was an illusion far grander than any on one of his Fox TV shows. What the FCC's recommendation did *not* say was that there was reason to bring the case before a public hearing. Essentially, the commission was deciding Murdoch's fate as a private matter.

It did not seem to matter that News Corporation had been 74 percent over the ownership limit for a decade. What mattered was that no one could find any proof that Murdoch had attempted to hide the fact. While camouflaging his corporate ownership structure under wire photos of his hand raised to God, taking his oath of allegiance to America, Murdoch had announced it for all to hear, if they had their ears to the ground. No one did. They were too busy looking at where he was pointing—directly toward the future of the Fox Network.

FCC chairman Reed Hundt, a Clinton man, was in favor of following the staff's recommendation and forcing Fox to restructure. Commissioner James Quello thought otherwise. Quello liked Fox, liked the concept of a fourth network, and liked the fact that Murdoch made it work despite the constraints of the marketplace and the incredible odds. Andrew Barrett and Rachelle Chong, the two other FCC commissioners, seemed to be favoring Quello's position.

In the hearing room of the FCC, Murdoch was seen holding his wife's hand and occasionally whispering into her ear, while daughter Elisabeth, accompanied by her husband, Elkin Pianim, was passing around baby pictures of their newborn daughter, Cornelia. Elisabeth and Elkin had just returned from California, where they were looking over their new business. Daddy Murdoch had loaned his younger daughter $35 million to purchase two television stations of her very own. Both NBC affiliates, the stations were located in Salinas/Monterey and San Luis Obispo.

Murdoch was given 45 days to convince regulators that it was in the public interest for Fox to maintain the status quo. It was 35 more days than he needed. Moving into action, Murdoch

danced and played around Washington, making his first appearance at the White House Correspondents' Association dinner on
April 29, 1995. Sitting next to New York Republican Alfonse
D'Amato, Murdoch had only to bring up the subject and allow
D'Amato to do his campaigning. "I think [the investigation] is
*terrible*," D'Amato groused to the others within earshot. "It's a
political vendetta," albeit one going in Murdoch's favor.[4]

The following week, Georgia Republican and HarperCollins
author Newt Gingrich picked up the ball and passed it to Jack
Fields, the Texas Republican who chaired the telecommunications subcommittee to which the FCC reported. Fields made it
known that he would make life unpleasant for the FCC if Murdoch's business was harmed in any way. In the meantime, he quietly called for a repeal of *all* foreign-ownership restrictions as
part of a telecommunications regulation overhaul.

While Washingtonians positioned themselves carefully on
the fence, Murdoch returned to business as usual, announcing a
four-year, $2 billion deal with MCI Communications. The
money bought MCI 13 percent of News Corporation stock and
an agreement from Murdoch to allow MCI the electronic distribution rights to News Corporation's books, movies, and television programming. He announced the move at the National
Cable Television Association convention in New Orleans, where
he managed to steal the spotlight from Turner for a second con-
secutive year. (At the previous convention, Murdoch announced
his sweeping purchase of New World Communications.)

Turner, who was now introducing himself as Jane Fonda's
Last Husband, spent most of his time in New Orleans looking
over his shoulder. The rumor circulating on the convention floor
was that Murdoch intended to use his newly found $2 billion in
cash to buy out Time Warner's share of Turner Broadcasting.
Naturally, the rumor had its start with Murdoch himself. "I
made a joke about buying CNN just to annoy Ted the other day.
He gets a bit excited at times," Murdoch smiled.[5]

In May 1995, Murdoch invested in a weekly Washington magazine he labeled the *Weekly Standard,* the only weekly conservative journal in the nation. (The others, the *American Spectator* and *Commentary,* were monthly, and the venerable *National Review,* biweekly.) From the start, the *Standard* was destined to be Murdoch's personal voice at the foot of the American government, either tickling or biting depending on the administration. Victor Navasky, publisher of *The Nation,* questioned just how deep any criticism might cut. "Murdoch has never been shy about proclaiming his allegiance to the bottom line," he said.[6]

The following month, with equal enthusiasm, Murdoch announced his $5.3 million investment in the *People's Daily,* the Communist Party's newspaper in China. Labeling the paper "the ideal partner," Murdoch apparently had succeeded in getting the attention of China's ruling party by introducing cash into the equation. The *People's Daily* and Murdoch were each 50 percent owners of the Beijing PDN Xinren Information Technology Company, specializing in electronic publishing and online databases.

The $5.3 million was pocket change compared with the $347 million Murdoch gave to Hong Kong billionaire Li Ka-shing's company Hutchison Whampoa and to Li's son Richard (founder of the technology investment firms Pacific Century Group and, later, Pacific Century CyberWorks) through his private Genza Corporation for the remaining 36.4 percent of Star TV that he previously did not own. Keeping it all in the family, Murdoch installed his older son, Lachlan, the recent Princeton graduate, as the deputy director of Star. In addition, Murdoch found the time to arrange a deal allowing him to build four television studios in Tianjin, a co-venture arrangement with the Tianjin Sports Development Corporation. He also got permission to supply Star TV's pay-movie channel to hotels in China.

In the same week, Murdoch concluded a deal to purchase broadcasting rights to Rugby Union matches in South Africa, New Zealand, and Australia for $500 million. Previously, he had acquired the United Kingdom rights to broadcast Premier Soccer League games on BSkyB. Days later, he spent half that amount to join Brazil's media powerhouse Globo in a venture to bring direct-to-home satellite service in Latin America. It was a busy July.

The purchases were outdistanced by a gift, however. On the last Friday of the month, the FCC formally forgave Murdoch for his sins, ruling that the "public interest would not be served by a more extensive restructuring of Fox." This prompted local scribes to comment that the man did indeed "walk on the Potomac." In putting the entire issue behind him, Murdoch's only comment on the matter was, "Despite the best efforts of our commercial adversaries and political enemies, our good name has been restored. It is never easy to prove one's innocence, but the FCC has authoritatively concluded that we told the truth and that we reasonably relied on good faith in our understanding of the law as it existed in 1985."

In the media world, it was as if the moon had suddenly swung through Scorpio. No sooner had the dust settled over an empty Murdoch grave than Disney announced its purchase of Capital Cities/ABC Network for $19 billion, and Westinghouse wrapped up a deal for the CBS Network, paying $5.4 billion.

Turner watched as the networks changed hands, and he briefly attempted to halt the CBS sale with a counteroffer, only to find that a cash shortage once again preempted his bid. "It was a frustrating time for Ted," talk-show host Larry King later said. "He wanted a television network in the worst way, but could not convince the right people that he could run it successfully.

"Remember," King continued. "This is a man who could charm anyone . . . anyone. I remember once in 1989, my contract at CNN was up and my agent brought me two great offers. One was from Roone Arledge, head of ABC News, who wanted to give me a show following *Nightline*—a version of *Larry King Live* on ABC. Another was an Oprah Winfrey–type show from King

World. I called to tell Ted that I had gotten these two great offers. I wanted to get his blessing.

"When I told him about the shows, he said to me: 'Say good-bye Ted.' That was it. 'I want to hear you say, *goodbye Ted,*' he said again. Well, there was something in the way he said it. I just couldn't do it, and I told him. I really loved being at CNN and didn't want to say goodbye. And that was when he gave me some great advice. He said that he couldn't match the other deals, but that nobody should ever take a job just for the money. It was good advice."[7]

Turner would have done well to take his own advice. Soon after the CBS/Westinghouse deal was concluded, he announced his intention to merge TBS into Time Warner in a deal initially worth $8.5 billion in Time Warner stock. It was a merger that would create the largest communications conglomerate in the world. Media watchers were astounded by the speed with which the deal was seemingly structured, and equally amazed that Turner, for all his effort at building an independent organization, would subsume his ego to that of Time Warner head Gerald Levin. Just as surprising was John Malone's intention to go along with the merger. Malone, chairman of Liberty Media and president and CEO of cable TV giant Tele-Communications Inc. (TCI), owned 21 percent of TBS from his purchase of stock during Turner's MGM money crunch. He agreed to convert his shares into 8 percent of Time Warner without any say in the management of the company.* By comparison, Turner was positioned to receive 10 percent of Time Warner voting shares, have two seats on the board, and apparently still run TBS.

On August 19, 1995, Levin and his wife flew to Montana for lunch at Turner's Flying D Ranch. They were picked up at the local airport by star chauffeur Jane Fonda, while Turner nervously paced through the kitchen watching lunch being prepared.

---

* Malone's stock was to be held in a trust, with his voting proxy held by Levin.

That it was a turning point in his life was certain. Less obvious
was whether he was making a wise decision.

Those closest to the negotiations insist that Turner had
decided to sell his businesses after seeing ABC and CBS swallowed up by large conglomerates. He was convinced that only the
largest players would survive in the world market, and Turner
was nothing if not a survivor. "Ted is an extraordinarily smart,
adept player," Peter Chernin, chairman of Fox Filmed Entertainment, said at the time. "He's successful because he's a buccaneer
rather than a corporate type. He's got real vision, is tremen-
dously entrepreneurial, and is willing to take enormous risks."[8]

Still, the idea of Ted Turner working within a corporate
structure as the No. 2 man felt strangely foreign, a round peg
punched into a square hole. "It's not like he's going to be out
running errands," Robert Goldberg said. Television critic for the
Wall Street Journal, Goldberg had long been a Turner watcher and
had cowritten a biography of the legend. "The hard part for him
won't be being number two to Time Warner chairman Gerald
Levin, but being part of a corporate culture like Time Warner's.
He's always been a quintessential outsider; when he was a kid, he
named his boat Pariah."[9]

The merging of Time Warner and Turner Broadcasting was
the big-bang approach to success. Size is strength, the move suggested. Yet, to realize the benefits of combining those in control
of distribution with those in control of programming would take
a delicate balance of skills that neither Time Warner nor Turner
had previously shown. Time Warner, itself only a six-year-old
company, was still attempting to manage the shakedown process
of that merger and remained a gangly, unmelded behemoth.

When Turner and Levin met the press in September 1995, to
announce that the boards of their two respective firms had voted
to merge, Levin clasped Turner's hand, raised it in victory, and
called him his new best friend. It was obviously a spontaneous
gesture, if the dropped-jaw look of surprise on Turner's face was

any indication. He had no trouble rebounding, however, as he played to the roomful of journalists who all wanted to know *why*. "I don't feel like I sold the company," Turner responded. "I'm going from like a 23 percent owner of Turner Broadcasting to a 10 percent owner of a lot bigger, more powerful, stronger company. I'm tired of being little all the time. I want to see what it's like being big for a while."[10]

Big? Think GIGANTIC. At the press conference to announce the deal, page after page of type listed the proposed combined holdings. Under film: Warner Bros., Castle Rock Entertainment, New Line Cinema, Turner Pictures, Hanna-Barbera, and the MGM/United Artists film library. Under television: Home Box Office, Cinemax, the WB Network, and cable systems serving 11.5 million homes, plus CNN, CNN International, Headline News, Turner Network Television, WTBS, Cartoon Network, CNN Airport Network, and Turner Classic Movies. Under publishing: *Time, People, Money, Sports Illustrated,* Warner Books, Turner Books, and Book-of-the Month Club. Under music: 50 record labels, including Warner, Atlantic, and Elektra. Plus Six Flags theme parks, the Atlanta Braves, the Atlanta Hawks, and World Championship Wrestling.

Just looking at the list made Turner smile. He was vice chairman of it all. Later, he hummed as he strutted down the street, arm in arm with his former movie-star wife. "Life is good," he said to no one in particular, smiling at strangers, hugging babies. "You only live once!" he shouted, waving to a black couple in a Yellow Cab. "I felt it was time to put some muscle on the bones," he added before disappearing around a corner, leaving a vapor trail in his wake.

# SEVENTEEN

# You Call That News?
# *This* Is News

*Sometimes you're treated like the skunk at a tea party.*
*But that's the fate of anyone who challenges the status quo.*

Rupert Murdoch
Washington, D.C.
February 26, 1996

So Rupert Murdoch was human after all. The 64-year-old had nearly removed his right index finger in an accident aboard the 78-foot *Sayonara,* the yacht owned by Oracle Corporation chairman Larry Ellison, which was competing in trial runs for the famed Sydney to Hobart Yacht Race. Murdoch the deal-maker, the media king, the scourge of all things literate, had caught his finger between the main sheet and the mainsail boom. He needed some emergency plastic surgery to make certain his check-writing hand remained functional.

The operation was such a success that during the three-day exercise, not only did Murdoch help Ellison win the 1995 race, but he also managed to take his turn at the grinder, galley, and helm. While Murdoch later remarked that his duties were mainly to act "as a bit of ballast," the experience did nothing but increase his love of competition and remind him yet again of the thrill of victory.

A day after the race, Murdoch and his finger (now bandaged to the size of a casaba melon) returned to his life made up of details. He soon added roughly a billion more when he made official what he had hinted at in November 1995. He was launching an international news service to compete with CNN. Yes, he knew the risk; yes, he had the financing; and yes, America was ready for—no, *needed*—an alternative to CNN. "We think it's about time CNN was challenged," Murdoch said in a speech to Boston businessmen, "especially as it tends to drift further and further to the left. We think it's time for a truly objective news channel." Without giving details (Murdoch felt no need to tip his hand), he pledged that the station would arrive full-blown on cable systems across the country by October 1996. Though the announcement was small, the task ahead was enormous, yet it was not the only major bit of business to keep Murdoch working long into the night.

In late January 1996, MCI successfully bid $682.5 million in an FCC auction for the last remaining orbital slot with full coverage of the continental United States. The company immediately joined forces with Murdoch to announce the formation of a direct broadcast satellite (DBS) service with the ungainly name of American Sky Broadcasting, or ASkyB. The name, of course, was drawn from Murdoch's British service, BSkyB, which had just signed its five millionth customer and projected annual profits of $382 million in the year ahead. With start-up costs amounting to $1.2 billion, half of which was coming directly from News Corporation, the pay TV service was poised to "reinvent the way Americans receive their television," according to Murdoch.

Despite his leadership in the European DBS arena, Murdoch was years behind in the space race in America, where there were already several DBS services in the market, such as fledgling operations Hughes Electronics (DirecTV), Hubbard Broadcasting (United States Satellite Broadcasting Company, Inc., or USSB), AlphaStar, PrimeStar, and EchoStar, which had lost to MCI in the latest round of bidding. Yet, as Murdoch pointed out, each of those firms was jousting for the same home market. For its part, ASkyB proposed to incorporate business clients within its marketing plan by including business information services among its projected 200 channels.

MCI's involvement with Fox continued to deepen when Murdoch sold his Delphi ISP to the telecommunications giant in another stock swap that presumed to show MCI's continuing commitment to the information explosion. Murdoch found the Internet as mysterious as it was potentially lucrative, and by passing Delphi off to MCI, he sidestepped potential losses without cutting loose the technology completely. DBS, however, was something he understood and championed, even if others questioned the economic possibilities.

Ted Turner had little faith in the future of DBS, with its 21-inch rooftop dish and a signal affected by weather. He had even less for the Fox News service, declaring at a cable television convention in Anaheim, California, that he was looking forward "to squishing Rupert like a bug." It was the opening salvo in a snicker campaign that found its fuel in competition but sucked its oxygen from opposing ideologies.

The glove slap that Turner delivered across Murdoch's face was returned at the end of February 1996, during a standing-room-only extravaganza at the National Press Club. It was intended to be a press conference to announce Murdoch's plan to donate an hour of free television to the political candidates the night before the November presidential election—10 minutes per candidate on 10 politically charged issues.

When it came time to promote his new 24-hour news service, however, Murdoch reminded the reporters in the crowded room that Turner had referred to him as "the Schlockmeister" for his programming content at Fox Broadcasting. "To this, I guess, I must plead guilty," he said. While absorbing the scurrility, he let fly with his own mud, saying, "We [at Fox] do, however, draw the line at professional wrestling and brown-nosing foreign dictators. You'll have to turn to Ted's channels to see that. I'm reminded of something Disraeli said to a colleague: 'It's true that I am a low, mean snake. But you, sir, could walk beneath me wearing a top hat.'"[1]

As the media scrambled to report the quote and pick apart the growing feud between the two men, a comment Murdoch made following the put-down received almost no press despite its implications. While discussing plans for his Fox News service, he lamented what he saw as a "growing disconnect" between those who provided the news and those who watched it. To Murdoch, it was a question of "values." He pointed to a recent poll conducted by the Times-Mirror Company, publishers of the *Los Angeles Times, Baltimore Sun, Hartford Courant,* and New York's *Newsday*. According to Murdoch, the poll suggested that while 40 percent of those questioned considered themselves to be conservative, only 5 percent of the media identified themselves as such. "In that gap, there is opportunity," Murdoch pledged.[2] Opportunity to tip the scales toward a conservative posture, a Murdoch stance. No squished bug, Murdoch.

Not content with bridging America via a satellite network, Murdoch planned to spread across Europe as well, joining with three potential competitors in an alliance to design a digital television network in Germany. The entire contract between Murdoch's BSkyB, Germany's media group Bertelsmann, and France's pay TV giant Canal Plus and media group Havas was only five pages long. Murdoch had negotiated it with his usual aloof passion and intense speed in only 19 days. He had devised it all while on a stroll in London's Green Park. The sprawling lawns and mature oaks, once home to duelists defending the honor of ladies fair, were not far from where Murdoch signed the deal over grilled salmon at the Ritz Hotel. He had come to London to help welcome his daughter Elisabeth to her new position as program director at BSkyB. She had arrived in town fresh from the sale of her two California television stations for a $12 million profit. Like father, like daughter.

Not all the Murdoch offspring found comfort in working for Papa, however. Murdoch's younger son, James, had quit Harvard during his senior year a few credits shy of a degree to open a record company in Manhattan called Rawkus Entertainment with two high school friends, Jarret Myer and Brian Brater. James moved into a Tribeca loft squeezed between a porn shop and a falafel stand, and proceeded to sign such acts as Whorgasm, Plastique, Poppa Bear Kool Breez, 7 Universal, and Motorbaby to contracts. When James released Whorgasm's first (and only) album, *Smothered*, he sent a copy to his father, who was not certain how to appreciate the industrial-metal rock music and lyrics of "Scream Motherfucker," "The Truth Puts Me to Sleep," and "Tell Him to Get a Bigger T.V."

Meanwhile, Ted Turner and Jerry Levin had begun a whistle-stop national tour of the Ted and Jerry Show, an act aimed at selling the merger of Time Warner and TBS to stockholders across the country. The initial reception to the pair was mixed, with the cerebral Levin finding it hard to relate to his outspoken and outgoing partner. Compounding their mission was an uncooperative Federal Trade Commission, which took exception to Tele-Communication Inc.'s (TCI) position in the merger. As the FTC analyzed the merger, it became increasingly apparent that TCI, the nation's largest cable operator, and its head and chief shareholder, John Malone, were making money from both sides of the merger—its 21 percent stake in TBS, plus a heavy investment in Time Warner.

At the National Cable Television Association convention in May 1996, Turner and Levin made a joint appearance of unity and strength despite the FTC posture, while Murdoch stole the majority of the cablers' interest by flashing gold in the faces of their corporate heads. Offering to pay cable systems $10 to $11 a subscriber to unlock channels across the country, Murdoch grabbed even Time Warner programmers' attention, saying, "It is business, after all." He seemed to be doing most of it, including promoting the new Fox Kids Network, in partnership with *Mighty Morphin Power Rangers* creator Haim Saban.

Deals with Murdoch, however, were beginning to alter depending on the climate of the moment, particularly in Europe, where his efforts to expand his global satellite service had taken a detour. The perfectly laid plans of his Bertelsmann/Canal Plus/Havas coupling in Germany had dissolved when Murdoch calculated that the pace of his partners was progressing too slowly for his own master plan. He dropped the trio via a written termination of their agreement, but not before secretly testing how he might be received by Leo Kirch, the son of a small-time winemaker who had grown into Germany's leading media magnate through drive and political connections. Murdoch and Kirch had similar operating styles: quick to make decisions and answering to no one. In this case, Kirch's answer was yes.

Upon first hearing of Murdoch's deal with the Bertelsmann/Canal Plus/Havas group, Kirch had reacted with typical ardor and contemplated launching his own service, linked to his pull within the Bavarian government. In what proved a dizzying waltz, Murdoch went from one partner to the other, finally lighting on Kirch as much for whom he could influence as for what he might be able to contribute. "Clearly these are strange days," said Herb Granath, head of Disney/ABC International Television, who looked at the Murdoch–Kirch deal and added, "Alliances in Europe are being made and unmade very quickly."[3]

It has been said that the difference between billionaires and millionaires is that millionaires take holidays. That was proven over the Fourth of July holiday, when media power broker Herb Allen once again hosted his annual executive retreat in Sun Valley, Idaho, and once again Rupert Murdoch put in an appearance. Disney's Michael Eisner was there, triumphant over his Cap Cities/ABC purchase; so too were Barry Diller and Jerry Levin. An early arrival to Sun Valley that year was New World's Ron Perelman.

Perelman had been pestering Murdoch for months to buy the remainder of New World Communications and take the business out of his portfolio. A skilled negotiator and as determined as any man when he wanted to buy or sell, Perelman was an irritant, the rash beneath the waistband, the mosquito that buzzed long into the night when the rest of the world was sleeping. Murdoch, of course, was just as determined. He had gotten what he needed from the New World stations. Owning them outright would add nothing. It would, however, give him crowing rights over a trophy that no individual had ever managed to achieve: ownership of 22 television stations, including every top 10 market except San Francisco. Disney's ABC Network owned only 10 of its stations; NBC, 11; CBS, 14. None generated the 35 percent coverage of the country that Murdoch could claim by adding New World's outlets to Fox's own.

The deal to buy New World was struck over corn on the cob and burgers—a deal worth $3 billion in Fox stock to Perelman and infinitely more to Murdoch. The day it was announced to the press turned out to be ripe with stories. The FCC had given its OK to Time Warner and Turner to join in a merger then worth $6.3 billion (the value of Time Warner stock had decreased since Turner originally discussed the sale). One small catch: Time Warner cable service had to carry a news channel to directly compete with its own CNN.

The press suggested that Murdoch was clearly in the lead position to have his Fox News Channel picked for the assignment, with NBC/Microsoft's just-launched MSNBC a distant second. The journalists had no way of knowing that Murdoch had moved directly from talking with Perelman on Herb Allen's front porch to cornering Jerry Levin on the lawn, remnants of corn on the cob still in his teeth. Murdoch upped the reward for Levin's assurance that Fox News would have a home on Time Warner's Manhattan cable service. He offered to pay $25 a subscriber for the all-important New York audience. All this before fireworks lit up the night sky over Allen's estate. The Fourth of July, a time when billionaires do not rest.

They don't rest on Labor Day either. It was over that weekend in September 1996 that Jerry Levin made his fateful trip to Turner's Flying D Ranch to determine what exactly his vice chairman would do to earn his salary. According to documents filed with the SEC at the time, Turner was slated to make $23 million in compensation over a five-year period, including a base salary of $700,000 a year. In addition, he had deferred compensation of $350,000 per year, plus as much as $3.6 million in annual bonuses. By design, Turner's pay equaled Levin's, and his bonuses were 90 percent of the Time Warner chairman's.

After thrashing out their differences, which according to Turner were many, the executives mutually agreed that Turner would be in charge of CNN, TNT, WTBS, Cartoon Network, and Time Warner's HBO, Court TV, and interactive division. Although he would have an office in New York, his principal base of operations would continue to be in Atlanta, on the twelfth floor of one of CNN's dual towers. His penthouse apartment occupied the twelfth floor of the tower directly opposite.

Turner further agreed in writing to keep his mouth shut. According to the 200-page prospectus sent to stockholders of both TBS and Time Warner, Turner needed "prior written consent," signed by the entire Time Warner board, before he could even propose a "merger or other business combination," or encourage a transaction that might involve a "change of control," or announce or instigate "any meeting of the stockholders," or even comment privately about such matters if his comments would "force Time Warner to make a public disclosure."[4]

While it all looked fine on paper, taming Turner and keeping him caged was certain to be a task for Levin and his multitude of underlings, many of whom had begun their careers working for Turner and still felt a certain allegiance to the visionary. For all of a week, it looked to Time Warner that confining Turner within his contractual limits would be its biggest challenge. Then Jerry Levin took a walk in the rain to see Rupert Murdoch, and life as he knew it changed completely.

When Time Warner announced its intention to freeze Fox News off Time Warner's Manhattan cable service in deference to MSNBC, it awakened a sleeping lion in Murdoch that soon was doing public battle with Time Warner and Ted Turner. Calling in political favors and launching an attack in the *New York Post,*

Murdoch threatened and chided and exposed until the very skin that held the skeleton of Time Warner together became raw with anger and indignant with abuse.

Turner likened Murdoch to Hitler, and Murdoch's *Post* said Turner "must be off his Lithium again." Time Warner cable blocked ads for Murdoch's upcoming Fox News; Murdoch blocked Warner Bros. station WBTV from BSkyB. Roger Ailes, head of Fox News, pulled New York mayor Rudy Giuliani into the grudge match, with Giuliani promising to run Fox News on the city's public access channels on Time Warner cable and reexamining Time Warner's Manhattan franchise. Time Warner president Richard Parsons labeled Giuliani's interference a violation of the First Amendment and promised a court fight.

Lawsuits were filed, depositions were taken, and as usual Turner spoke his mind, this time about Murdoch's influence peddling. His new word for the man: *scumbag*. Murdoch jabbed back, fencing a no-show zone around Ted and Jane as they sat in Yankee Stadium watching the Atlanta Braves lose to the hometown team. Jane Fonda had joined in the attack, pointing to Murdoch's hiring of Giuliani's wife, Donna, as a reporter on Fox TV's local outlet. Giuliani labeled Fonda's shot "cheap," and by association Fonda as well.

When the Fox News Channel finally went on the air Monday, October 7, 1996, it carried the tag line "We report. You decide." The thrust of the news service was unbiased reporting and presenting the complete picture. Critics reported that despite its claims, Fox News had not found a way to reinvent the news. Rather, it merely added to the saturation level. Newzak. Televised wallpaper.

Less than a year after it was conceptualized and six months after it began preproduction, Fox News was a reality: round-the-clock headlines plus evening news hours, with such hosts as *20/20*'s Catherine Crier* and *Inside Edition*'s Bill O'Reilly. Viewers

---

* Ironically, Crier began her broadcast career on CNN. She was co-anchor of *Inside Politics,* a daily examination of the 1992 political process, and *The World Today,* the premier evening newscast. In addition, she hosted *Crier & Company,* a live, half-hour, hard-news talk show.

around the country tuned in out of curiosity, and the more conservative among them stayed.

The mood of the broadcasts was slightly edgy, laced with Murdoch's tabloid journalism. Co-anchors Louis Aguirre and Allison Costarene reported that the pope *might* have Parkinson's disease. Fergie *might* be under a suicide watch. Clinton *might* have won the televised presidential debates.

Time Warner president Richard Parsons resigned as chairman of New York's Economic Development Corporation citing "recent events." Mayor Giuliani labeled it "harassment" if he was required to testify in the Time Warner/Fox News lawsuit. And Manhattan federal judge Denise Cote placed the entire debacle on hold until the case was deliberated.

For Murdoch, the issue was one of trust. He had gotten Levin's word via a handshake. For Turner, the issue was one of responsibility. Murdoch had little and Fox News had none. Frank Rich, writing in the *New York Times,* asked the question that many were thinking. "How do New Yorkers pick a dog in this fight?"

Certainly, Murdoch was correct in assuming that when his attorneys called on October 20, they had news concerning his Time Warner suit. Still in Sydney following the annual News Corporation stockholders meeting, Murdoch was eager to rejoin the battle for cable coverage in all-important Manhattan. What he found himself facing in its place was a warrant issued by Israeli investigators who wanted to question him about income tax evasion.

Murdoch was stunned long enough to realize that the charges were anything but a joke. They had been leveled against his News Datacom Research division in Jerusalem, the subsidiary that made his Smart Cards for BSkyB decoding. A minor cog in a major business machine to be sure, but enough to bring down the entire conglomerate if the charges proved even remotely true. In the weeks ahead, as the Manhattan cable wars played themselves out to a predictable conclusion, Murdoch found himself drawn into the kind of intrigue more likely found on Fox TV than in the life of the conservative businessman.

Catching wind of the charges, Turner took little time before assigning guilt. "The man moves his money around like peas under a cup," he said in Atlanta. "He doesn't give any of his money away, and the Israeli government is looking into his finances."[5]

The case against Murdoch unraveled into an amazing story of corporate greed and subterfuge, in which he turned out to be the victim rather than the manipulator. Murdoch never could be accused of paying taxes agreeably, and certainly no more than necessary. His offshore businesses of corporate divisions were structured for exactly that purpose, yet provided the perfect screen for would-be theft.

According to the lawsuit Murdoch filed in February 1996 and another he filed in October, Michael Clinger, the marketing guru originally hired by Bruce Hundertmark to be his partner in News Datacom, had developed his own business-within-a-business by controlling the supplier used to make Smart Cards for Datacom. The lawsuit alleged that Clinger, through a series of offshore holding companies in the Channel Islands, owned 60 percent of Phoenix Micro Inc., a Guernsey firm that made the decoding cards that Murdoch used in his pay TV satellite services. Due to proprietary codes and exclusive manufacturing techniques, Phoenix Micro was able to lock out competitors for the production of the cards long after Hundertmark and Clinger had been bought out of Datacom by Murdoch.

With Clinger controlling Phoenix and Phoenix the sole source of Smart Cards, Clinger allegedly was able to charge a price far in excess of the cards' actual manufactured cost. According to the News Corporation lawsuit, Clinger was pocketing about $1.50 from each of the more than 19 million cards made. Leo Krieger, a close friend of Clinger's and an accountant at Datacom, had knowledge of the scam yet kept the details to himself until the day tax investigators came rapping at his door with a warrant for his arrest, charging him with evasion.

Krieger, looking to prove his innocence, exposed his former friend's exploits while carefully sidestepping self-incrimination. It did not help matters that Krieger was having a rather torrid affair with Clinger's ex-wife, the leggy Israeli socialite Niva Von Wiesl. The affair had ended Clinger's marriage, and as a result he began a campaign of harassment against the pair that ended with Krieger's arrest.

Armed with tapes of bugged telephone conversations, Krieger plea-bargained his way into News Corporation's good graces by agreeing to testify against Clinger in exchange for his freedom and some $312,500, discounted from his original asking price of $1 million. Unwilling to rely only on Krieger's testimony, Murdoch's attorneys hired the private investigation services of Argen Ltd., which tracked Clinger and his money through a series of banks in Liberia, Panama, and the Netherland Antilles.

Once Clinger received word that News Corporation was digging into his finances, he ordered his own attorneys to approach Murdoch, threatening to expose information proving that Datacom was guilty of tax evasion. When Murdoch rebuffed Clinger, the Israeli tax office, otherwise known as *Mas Hachnasa,* moved in. Ultimately, Murdoch and Datacom were found innocent of any wrongdoing, and Clinger was found guilty of defrauding 30 million pounds from Murdoch's assorted businesses.[6] Yet, in October 1996 that verdict was several years and millions of dollars in litigation away.

Murdoch was disturbed by his perceived guilt at the time of the investigation, and appalled at the release of a book by former *Sunday Times* editor Andrew Neil. In it Neil wrote:

> When you work for Rupert Murdoch, you do not work
> for a company chairman or chief executive: you work
> for a Sun King. You are not a director or a manager or

> an editor: you are a courtier at the court of the Sun
> King—rewarded with money and status by a grateful
> king as long as you serve his purpose, dismissed out-
> right or demoted to a remote corner of the empire
> when you have ceased to please him or outlived your
> usefulness. . . . The Sun King is all that matters.[7]

In the style to which he had grown comfortable, Murdoch said nothing about the book in public, though to selected friends he commented that he found it bitter and disappointing.[8] He was particularly obsessed with the term telephone terrorism, which Neil used to describe Murdoch's "weapon of choice." He found it rude, but he never disputed its truth.

Murdoch was spending hours on the phone as 1996 came to a close, attempting to lasso an increasingly far-flung empire and finding much of it spiraling out of his direct control. With his own worth now pegged at $3.6 billion, Murdoch seemed to be working harder than ever to maintain a position he had worked years to achieve.

The Time Warner cable fracas was no closer to reaching a conclusion and, if anything, took a negative turn for Murdoch when, on November 6, Judge Denise Cote ruled that Giuliani's efforts to nudge Time Warner to carry Fox News violated the cablecaster's First Amendment rights to control its own pro-gramming. Taking the ruling further, Cote said that Giuliani's efforts were inspired by a desire to give "special advocacy" to a political supporter, and the city government's threat to review Time Warner's cable franchise in light of the Fox News blackout amounted to illegal pressure tactics.

Murdoch continued to grumble about the right to compete and monopolistic conduct—this from the man who had pulled the BBC off Star TV in Asia and was the only entrepreneur in the United States allowed to own a newspaper and television station in the same city. Undeterred, Murdoch continued to press his suit against Time Warner in the name of free speech, and promised to take the case to the Supreme Court if necessary.

While lawyers wrangled over the Constitution and its impact on cable TV, Murdoch took another hit, this time to his DBS dreams. His ASkyB alliance with MCI, which seemed such a sure thing just weeks before, came to a crashing conclusion the day following Judge Cote's decision, when MCI head Bert Robert alerted Murdoch that the company could no longer afford to fund its share of their partnership. With MCI out, Murdoch faced mounting costs: a still-unpaid bid for the FCC license fee, a satellite, a launch, programming. Unwilling to absorb the high start-up charges on his own, Murdoch went in search of another partner, casting his net wide to attract a company that was willing to risk hundreds of millions of dollars on an unsure investment.

Murdoch pointed to his success with BSkyB while downplaying his continuing losses on Star TV and the money he had previously committed to start-up services in Japan, South America, and Mexico. Investors found his terms restrictive, the risk excessive, and the potential too small. In desperation, Murdoch turned to the company that nearly outbid MCI for the ASkyB orbital slot—EchoStar.

Founded in 1980 by Charles Ergen, a rogue salesman of large 12-foot satellite dishes, EchoStar Communications launched its first digital satellite in December 1995. Selling its channels under the name Dish Network, it had reached 100,000 customers in its first four months of broadcasting. From its base in Colorado, EchoStar was wobbling into prominence in the field, chasing the rainbow created by DirecTV, the industry leader.

For Murdoch to travel to Denver and sit across a desk from the kicked-back Ergen was a little like Custer setting up an appointment with Sitting Bull. They were natural enemies attempting to conquer the same territory. Yet meet they did, and on February 24, 1997, they announced a partnership that shocked investors and press alike. In a deal worth $1 billion, News Corporation had acquired 50 percent of EchoStar, the No. 3 satcaster. A reworked

ASkyB, renamed Sky Television, was to be a joint venture, with Ergen president of the company, Murdoch chairman.

Ergen later said that despite the initial surprise, the partnership made sense. "News Corp. made sense as a strategic partner because they brought things other people couldn't—satellite capacity, programming content, worldwide expertise. They know more about DBS than anybody, and they brought capital. We made sense because we got them in the marketplace today, as opposed to a year from now. It's certainly an equal partnership, and it's certainly complementary."[9]

Preston Padden, the newly appointed head of global satellite operations at News Corporation, projected that Sky would eliminate the competition. "Our goal is to come to market with a television product so superior, and a consumer proposition so compelling, that a substantial number of 70 million households stop writing their checks to their current service—usually cable— and start writing them to Sky."[10]

It was a war cry aimed directly at cable companies around America. Ted Turner's buddies. The John Malones of the world. And the very people who were currently putting Fox Television in 100 million homes around the country. Essentially, one side of the business was pitting itself against the other in a fight to the finish.

*Newsweek* headlined the deal RUPERT'S DEATH STAR, and the nickname stuck. Cable companies around the United States renamed EchoStar "DeathStar." Murdoch was stretching yet again, pushing the limits of government regulation as he promised to combine local networks with movie channels, pay-per-view, weather, and news. Five hundred channels in all. Either it was the future, or it was nuts, depending on who you asked.

"It was a brilliant, bold move that does what Rupert always tries to do—change the basic competitive battlefield," said industry analyst Michael Garin, co-founder of TelePictures (which had previously merged with Lorimar and bought the MGM studio lot from Turner).[11]

To cablecasters around the country, it was mutiny. Murdoch, the man who had just lashed out at Time Warner for keeping Fox News off of its Manhattan system with threats that it would kill his network, was now attempting to bury his allies. "It made no sense. It was sheer stupidity on the part of Murdoch, who seemed blinded by this need to show he could predict the future," a Time Warner executive said.[12]

Larry King asked Turner if he was shocked by the EchoStar merger. "The man's beginning to think he's invincible," Turner responded. "But was I shocked, no. Nothing he does surprises me because he just turned sixty-six and he's running out of time. He's got to do it quickly before he passes on. As hard as he works, you know, he could have a stroke or a heart attack at any time. This nice man could trip and fall . . . a hundred stories. . . . I'm wishing for it. Hoping for it."[13]

The sentiment was echoed by cable operators who failed to understand the motives of the executives who seemed to be on divergent courses. In New York, where the litigation continued nonstop to force Fox News onto Time Warner's Manhattan cable service, the merger seemed particularly oxymoronic. That summer of 1997, Time Warner's Jerry Levin found space to put on Fox News, agreeing with Murdoch that it was of value to his customers. The two had met, ironically, sitting in the same chairs in which they had made their handshake deal the previous year—at Herb Allen's July Fourth retreat. They laughed like the old friends they were not, agreeing to let the past remain in the past.

Hardly surprising, given the needs of their conglomerates, each dependent on the other for services around the globe. It did not matter what the courts were saying, or the critics, or the politicians for that matter. Slapping each other on the back, the deal was struck for their own economic interests. In the end, only the public got squished like a bug.

# EIGHTEEN

# The Sky Is Falling

*I want to be the hero of my country.*
*I want to get it back to the principles*
*that made it good. Television has led us,*
*in the last twenty-five years, down the path of destruction.*
*I intend to turn it around before it's too late.*

Ted Turner, quoted in *Citizen Turner*
New York
1995

There was an undeniable mystery about the man. Cold, calculating, a hardened geode that remained unopened, hiding mineraled teeth and a sparkle that was hinted at but never really seen in the business world. Anna Murdoch had seen her husband's passion, of course, though not lately. Lately, he was absorbed in what could be seen only as passion of a different sort, one far removed from romance, yet passion nonetheless. Murdoch wanted to lace the globe with satellites that individually and together would blanket information to the world in a chenille of his own making.

Oh, Murdoch was known, of course. The public Murdoch in his crisp shirt and business suit. The congenial and polite Murdoch, who could lean forward in his chair, blow into his cheeks with calculated thought, and share a piece of juicy gossip. The feisty Murdoch, who reacted with hurt and amazement when cornered with an obvious bit of legislation that spoke directly to his behavior and usually not in agreement.

It was to the last Murdoch, the one controlled by government mandate and regulation, that much of the communications world was looking in 1997. He had come out blaring promises about Sky Television that included his intention to rebroadcast the signals from local network affiliates that stepped directly on FCC must-carry rules and copyright laws. Although it was true that the regulations were in a state of flux, the rights of networks to determine who carried their own programs seemed rather straightforward.

If Murdoch had only *that* goal to deal with in his promising Sky business plan, it might have been obtainable through the labyrinthine routes of government committees, lobbies, and political pressure. Unfortunately, his grand scheme to bring the new New World to the old New World was falling apart, or more appropriately, being ripped apart along with his agreement with Charles Ergen of EchoStar. The word around town was that DeathStar was dead.

The challenge that faced Ergen was basically how to operate as CEO of a company he was not being allowed to run. One major issue was encryption technology. Murdoch wanted to use his own through the now-maligned News Datacom. Ergen favored his system, developed through a Swiss company. And while that issue was a tough one, in which both men remained immobile, it apparently was only the start of a long list of items that Ergen wanted and Murdoch did not—or perhaps it was the other way around. It was hard to tell, since neither was talking. Certainly this much was known: Murdoch was unhappy in the deal, Ergen threatened to sue, and Sky Television was again without a bird in orbit. Then, on May 1, 1997, Murdoch's problems deepened when onetime lobbyist-turned-global executive Preston Padden walked off the job, having been moved to Denver along with other former ASkyB personnel to work with Ergen and found the association impossible.

Murdoch had recently had a similar fallout with Leo Kirch in Germany, with both men dictating terms of their arrangement and neither wanting to allow any decrease in control. The breakup of BSkyB's alliance with Kirch's digital TV service was minor compared to the situation Murdoch faced with a broken Ergen alliance.

"The Sky is falling, the Sky is falling," critics larked almost as a rejoicing. The mighty had fallen, or at least stumbled rather publicly, and cable execs across the country were secretly pleased, even if none went on record to declare it for fear that the mighty might soon fall on them. As it happened, their fear was not misplaced. Murdoch, in his rush to save face and restore legitimacy to his tarnished domestic DBS scorecard, opened discussions with PrimeStar Partnership, a small dish network owned by an amalgamation of cable companies as a complement to their cable service. Among those companies were John Malone's Tele-Communications Inc. and Jerry Levin's Time Warner Cable.

To understand the extent of Murdoch's determination to achieve DBS parity in the United States was to witness the media mogul placing a call to Ted Turner and asking for his help. The same Ted Turner who was pictured in a straitjacket in Murdoch's *New York Post*; the man who only weeks before had compared Murdoch to "the late Fuhrer"; the man being sued by the man doing the suing.

While the actual conversation was short (Turner advised Murdoch to call Jerry Levin), the reality of the moment underscored Murdoch's belief that even your enemies could be your business partners if they had something you need. Murdoch needed PrimeStar, and to get the renegade satellite service he had some major fence-mending to deliver. In the annals of classic business maneuvers, this one might stand at the top if Murdoch was not also involved at the very same moment with an even more unlikely negotiation.

The man who had turned exposed breasts into a sales tool for tabloid fodder had begun discussions with televangelist Pat Robertson, who had called for a boycott of advertisers on Murdoch's heathen Fox series *Married . . . with Children*. Murdoch wanted to buy Robertson's Family Channel, the station that had begun life as the Christian Broadcast Network but changed its name in 1989 to attract more viewers. While *Time* magazine pointed out the logic of the partnership, it could not help but add, "Now all it has to do is pass muster with God."[1]

It had been a month of convenient bending of loyalties. Not only had Murdoch waved the white flag at Turner and broke bread with Brother Robertson, but he also had switched political loyalties in England, advising the *Sun* to back Labor Party liberal Tony Blair against the Margaret Thatcher–aligned John Major. This was, of course, the same *Sun* that, when Major was first elected on the heels of its endorsement, headlined IT WAS THE *SUN* WOT WON IT. With the wind blowing decidedly Labor in the current British political climate, however, Murdoch wisely decided to back Blair and ended up on the winning team yet again.

China, as well, saw Murdoch eat crow in an effort to improve his marketing stance in the Far East. No longer was he threatening to spread the word of truth through his satellites at the expense of "totalitarian regimes everywhere." Now Murdoch saw the wisdom of allowing China to exist with its Tiananmen Squares and human-rights violations. "Western companies like News Corp. have much to learn about doing business [in China]," he said. "[We] need to pay special attention to China's unique cultural heritage."[2] Talk about turning the other cheek for profit.

In the final two weeks of May 1997, Murdoch flew to Tokyo to give that speech, stopped in Sydney to see his son Lachlan, who was now the publisher of Murdoch's *Australian,* jetted to New York to meet with Levin at Time Warner, got challenged to a boxing match with Turner, lunched with Pat Robertson to seal his $1.9 billion bid for the Family Channel, headed to Colorado to talk with John Malone about a $1.1 billion swap for a 30 percent stake in PrimeStar, and ended up in Los Angeles to oversee his $31 million bid to acquire the Los Angeles Dodgers baseball team.

All before receiving the United Jewish Appeal's Humanitarian of the Year Award from Henry Kissinger back in New York at the Waldorf-Astoria on May 29.

The humanitarian in Murdoch had been cleverly left hidden while the businessman was never more obvious. In folding his DBS operations into PrimeStar, Murdoch kept his hand in the American market without falling deeper into that black hole of debt. He was set to become the largest shareholder in PrimeStar in exchange for giving the cablecaster its 28 high-power frequencies in space. Moving Lachlan from Star TV over to his Australian publishing division gave his older son some needed experience in that area of the conglomerate. At about the same time, younger son James moved into the New York offices to oversee News Corporation's new music division while keeping his own company, Rawkus Entertainment, intact.

The purchase of Robertson's Family Channel was brilliant. Not only did it give Murdoch a ready-made delivery service for his Fox Kids product, but it was also financed by his Fox Kids Worldwide and Haim Saban's Saban Entertainment, splitting the load to shuttle the billion dollars in debt away from News Corporation. In negotiating the deal, Robertson and his son initially wanted to value their shares of the company higher than those of other shareholders, until the resulting outcry from his investors forced Pat to see the evangelical light. Though the more holy members of the group expressed concern that Murdoch might turn their wholesome network into something akin to Porn-Again Christian, Murdoch already had his Fox Network for that, thereby assuring a continuum of apple pie, home, and hearth, as well as Robertson's *700 Club*. It also put Murdoch on a collision course with the Disney Channel, which had already scented the same turf minus the ministry.

It was not just Disney's family fare that was being targeted. Eager to optimize his sports franchise as much as possible, Murdoch joined with John Malone's TCI to bid $850 million for 40 percent of Cablevision's Rainbow Sports Network, to compete directly with Disney's ESPN service inherited along with the studio's ABC Network buyout. With the Cablevision addition, Fox Sports had access to 55 million homes, 17 National Basketball Association teams, 12 National Hockey League teams, and 20 major league baseball clubs. In addition, the purchase yielded Murdoch the extra bonus of a 20 percent ownership in Madison Square Garden, the New York Knicks, and the New York Rangers.

In contrast, over the same time period Ted Turner found his business economizing. Now under the thumb of a debt-ridden Time Warner Inc., Turner arrived at work to discover that nearly a thousand staffers had been cut from his divisions alone— among them his own son Teddy, whom Turner informed one night at dinner, "You're toast." To hear him discuss it, it was the single most difficult part of the transition from owner to employee. "When I spoke to Jack Welch at GE years ago," Turner remarked to the American Society of Magazine Editors, "he said he could cut thousands of people, and he was smiling. That's not me. My father always told me: 'If you can find gainful employment for people who are good workers, that's how you build up a stronger society. When you let somebody go, that's something like a funeral.'"[3]

The downsizing at Time Warner came at a time of personal wealth for Turner, and the issue weighed heavily on the man who always considered himself one of the boys. His wealth had more than doubled, with his current worth valued at just over $3 billion. Though not the richest man in the United States, he suddenly became known as its most generous when his conscience convinced him to donate $1 billion to the United Nations over a 10-year period.

Turner dropped the news of his unexpected gift into a speech he was giving in 1997 at a United Nations Association dinner in New York, having made the decision just two nights before. In the nine months since he had decided to sell his companies to Time Warner, his assets had increased the amount of his pledge, and as he told reporters after the dinner, "I'm no poorer than I was at the start of the year." While his accountants and advisers scrambled to find a way to painlessly donate $100 million per year over a decade and perhaps even turn it into a tax advantage, Turner placed the American wealthy on alert. "I'm putting every rich person in the world on notice that they'll be hearing from me about giving money," he said.[4] "I'm setting the standard for gallantry."[5]

Six years prior to his pledge to the United Nations, Turner had set up the Turner Foundation, with $150 million earmarked for more than 300 environmental and population-control causes. The foundation donated $7 million annually, most of it generated by interest on the principal. In addition, Turner had announced in 1994 that he was giving $25 million each to his alma maters, Brown University and McCallie School, plus another $25 million to the Citadel, where he had sent his sons. The schools received $1 million in cash apiece, spread out over the years 1994 to 1998. The remaining $60 million was placed in three charitable trusts in the form of stocks, with the various schools paying Turner interest on their shares and the actual principal untouchable until his death.[6]

Turner's gift to the United Nations received uniform acclaim for both its generosity and spontaneity. He earmarked the money for children, land mines, and refugees. The United Nations needed the money. Its UNICEF program for children alone was budgeted at $900 million in 1997. And the organization was not upset that Turner left the dinner to rush to Manhattan's CNN studios and break the news to his friend Larry King and the world at large. "He went with his heart," said wife Jane Fonda after the fact.[7]

Perhaps. Yet, in giving his money to the United Nations in the hope that it would be spread throughout the world for Turner's noble causes, the media crusader elevated himself to the position of charity elite while pursuing his own political agenda. It was a grand gesture and an even grander example of the trickle-down theory that had failed to work in the past, essentially because the money fed the bureaucracy of the institution rather than the needy waiting for its help.

The drama surrounding the gift became its reason for life, rather than for the good Turner proclaimed he wanted to achieve. Newspapers and magazines were tripping over each other to crown Turner the king of munificence. Four months after the gesture received neon headlines, it made news all over again when Turner appointed Timothy Wirth to head his new United Nations Foundation, with the assigned duty of distributing the wealth as it became available. Wirth, undersecretary of state for global affairs under President Clinton and previously a senator from Colorado, was described by Turner as someone who "shares my vision for the future." Presumably one billion dollars' worth.

That exact figure was rumored to be the likely cost to Rupert Murdoch for an indiscretion in Hong Kong with a young executive named Wendi Deng, a vice president of Sky TV who was born the same year Murdoch married his current wife, Anna, 31 years ago. Anna found out about the affair one week before their wedding anniversary in April, and soon moved out of the house.

Theirs had been a marriage so stable, so completely invincible from outside threats that few among their friends believed Anna's departure to be anything more than an effort to get her husband to back away from his business and spend more time at home. Then Deng began accompanying Murdoch on trips apparently outside of her executive duties. Gossip guru Liz Smith was the first to break the news of the split in the *New York Post.* It was a mention, nothing more. But it was all that was needed for the world to take notice.

He would have continued to make headlines for his dalliances had it not been for a far bigger story that pushed his private life down on the list of fascination. The newest boondoggle being played out in the media was the Murdoch-mandated cancellation of *East and West,* the memoirs of Christopher Patten, the last governor of Hong Kong. Patten's less than flattering depiction of the Chinese was initially said to have nothing to do with Murdoch's failure to publish the book, which had been bought at auction by Murdoch's HarperCollins U.K. for $200,000.

Stuart Proffitt, publisher of HarperCollins' trade division, went so far as to label *East and West* "the best and most lucidly written book I've read by a politician in fifteen years of publishing" at a dinner for distributors and senior staff.[8] That was before Murdoch found out about the deal, which previously had gone unnoticed by the globetrotting mogul and sometime Wendi Deng escort. Unfortunately, the word from HarperCollins to Proffitt was that the book had been deemed "disappointing and uncommercial." The difficulty, of course, was not in Patten's writing, but rather in his political posture, which conflicted with Murdoch's own. Rather than risk offending the Chinese, Murdoch opted to offend Patten (who quickly found another publisher and sued HarperCollins for breach of contract), Proffitt (who quit the firm over the dispute), and much of the literary community (who judged the official HarperCollins stance as indefensible).

When the book was finally published by Macmillan in England and Times Books in America, it carried the tag line, "The Book Rupert Murdoch Refused to Publish." The *New York Times* said of *East and West*: "that rarest of literary products: a book that is as delightful to read as it is enlightening to ponder." HarperCollins later issued an apology to Patten and paid an out-of-court settlement reportedly in the tens of thousands of pounds.

Murdoch unconsciously moved to smooth his hair and felt his scalp. Where there once was a thatch of black mane, now stretched a barren forest of skin populated by an ever-decreasing number of determined holdouts, gray and wispy. Each hair as independent as Murdoch himself, dogged to grow in a direction at odds with the others. His hair—or was it his entire face?—was his only clue that he was now old. He felt the same as he did 40 years earlier. Hell, he felt better. His body was still thin, kept fit through exercise, and his heart was still strong. There was, of course, a small worry weighing on his mind ever since he arrived at his sixty-seventh birthday. *Father's heart gave out at 67, for crying out loud,* he thought.

Determined to outrun fate, Murdoch felt young and happy for the first time in years, for he had found love. His nervousness, his excitement every time he saw Wendi Deng convinced him that he was not just some foolish old man in a midlife crisis, but rather a vibrant mogul in charge of every shred of his person.

The news of the affair had hit his family hard, each member learning from the other first in pass-the-hat fashion, then through telephone conversations with a man who typically remained available for his children. His older daughter Prudence, always the most vocal, broke the silence with the press in a tele-vised interview aired years later. "I couldn't believe it, actually. I thought, *You dirty old man.*" His other daughter, Elisabeth, now general manager of BSkyB, dodged the press completely, but she was having marital discord of her own. Her husband, Elkin Pianim, had lost a small fortune in his efforts to launch the black-community newspaper *New Nation,* and the couple sepa-rated soon after the birth of their second child. After Pianim left England to return to Ghana, Elisabeth pursued a relationship begun prior to her divorce with Matthew Freud, a young press agent and great-grandson to Sigmund. Her father's own marital difficulties thus were better left not commented upon.

While friends held out hope for some sort of divine interven-tion to reunite Murdoch and Anna, any hope of reconciliation was dashed by the announcement in July 1998 that Anna had filed for divorce. Initial reports suggested that she would remain on the board of News Corporation and that the family was moving forward, united in its efforts to remain private and above the focus of the Murdoch press.

That Murdoch juggled his personal crisis and business jugger-nauts as well as he did speaks legends of a man whose discipline manifested itself in days that were structured down to the minute. It was a period when the unexpected became routine, and the routine found Murdoch racing to remain virtually in a static position.

The Justice Department filed a suit to keep Murdoch from his long hoped-for DBS dream by questioning the motive behind his sale of assets to PrimeStar in exchange for stock. According to the filing, "In the months following the ASkyB announcement, Murdoch discovered that he was being blackballed because of his DBS plans [with EchoStar]. Most of the large cable operators were giving [Murdoch] a slow 'no' on carrying his channels."[9] In contrast, the Justice Department continued, after Murdoch agreed to the PrimeStar trade, "Certain of PrimeStar partners' cable systems began to widely carry Murdoch's program networks."[10] The Justice Department wondered aloud about a deal with John Malone and any pressure brought to bear.

The department's reservations about the Malone–Murdoch PrimeStar connection were only the beginning, however. Lawyers from the same government agency were working to unravel any unexplained motives behind Murdoch's sudden sale of his favored *TV Guide* to Malone's Tele-Communications Inc. Under the terms of the surprise $2 billion deal, the TCI-controlled United Video Satellite Group would get ownership of *TV Guide* in exchange for $800 million in cash and $1.2 billion in United Video stock, representing a 40 percent share of the company.

Murdoch, who had been slowly selling off various components of his Triangle Publications purchase years earlier, wanted to greatly reduce his magazine business in the United States, according to insiders. With the sale of *TV Guide*, he was well on the way, leaving the relatively new *Weekly Standard* as one of the few Murdoch-controlled magazines in America.

United Video, whose Prevue Channel was the dominant on-air cable programming guide, was being rechristened the TV Guide Channel as part of the deal. Included as an adjunct, United Video also was absorbing its rivals, Cable Guide and Total TV, in a sale worth $75 million, leaving TV Guide the only on-air programming guide as well as the dominant program magazine. Despite the complexity of the transaction, the sale was concluded in record time with almost no publicity. The major change was reflected in the on-air promos from the Prevue Channel itself, hawking its new image and name with the gusto of a car dealer bannering next year's models.

Meanwhile, Murdoch found himself in the increasingly uncomfortable position of sinner, placed there by his wife, the Roman Catholic, who continued to play the betrayed spouse, spurned in middle age for a much younger woman. The thought of Anna filing for divorce in California, an equal-opportunity state where matrimonial splits were concerned, scared Murdoch enough to keep a team of divorce attorneys occupied on and off for 11 months.

If there was a positive side to the divorce drama, it made other aspects of Murdoch's life look simple by comparison. Unexpected trouble in India, for one. When he learned from his attorneys that a warrant had been issued for his arrest in India, he met the news with a languished grin and a shake of the head. He was a wanted man from the Arabian Sea to the Bay of Bengal for failing to appear in court to answer charges that his Star TV network had broadcast material labeled "vulgar and obscene." It was the kind of charge that surely begged for a comment from Ted Turner, but then Turner was hardly in a position to be casting stones.

The Murdoch arrest warrant occurred at a rather low point in the history of CNN, to which Turner now remained related only by marriage. For the first time in its history, the news channel had to retract an entire story. The piece, which aired as the featured presentation on the first installment of *NewsStand,* a new CNN series, purported to reveal the use of lethal sarin nerve gas in a 1970 Pentagon operation in Laos. A subsequent investigation by *Newsweek* suggested that there were substantial errors in the conclusions drawn during the program and voiced by CNN reporter Peter Arnett.

The ensuing fallout from the program, which ironically was designed to showcase the new synergy between *Time* magazine and its on-air stepbrother CNN, resulted in the resignation of the series' executive producer, the firing of two line producers, and Arnett receiving a humiliating reprimand. Turner, to his credit, faced television critics in Pasadena, California, without the benefit of a team of public relations interceptors, apologizing for the story not so much because it was inaccurate, but because "we didn't have evidence beyond a reasonable doubt." He also labeled CNN's retraction "probably the greatest catastrophe in my life." Turner then resorted to his vintage act, offering to "take my shirt off and beat myself bloody on the back" to beg forgiveness from the nation's veterans. It was classic Turner disarming the attack dogs. Or, as *Electronic Media* saw the moment: "There was little left to ask, nothing more to dig and pick and gnaw. When the bear stands up and surrenders, the hunter finds little joy in a kill."[11]

It was time to surrender for Murdoch as well. After finding himself unable to jockey around the Justice Department's determination to scuttle his PrimeStar deal, he announced that ASkyB was withdrawing from the project. Again Murdoch was left without a satellite, without a DBS partner, and with fewer and fewer options to cushion his loss.

Those who say that persistence is the mother of success could take a page from Murdoch, who in October 1998 proved the point by reapproaching EchoStar's Charles Ergen waving a white flag the size of Colorado. That Ergen agreed to meet with Murdoch in spite of the $5 million lawsuit he had pending against News Corporation suggests something of the limited number of opportunities that existed at the time in DBS. Now, of course, Ergen was in control, and he intended to take his time enjoying the sight of Murdoch, vulnerable and suppliant. It was a dangerous game. To play with Murdoch was to play the pipe in front of the cobra. There was no room for error. And regardless of appearances, Murdoch was not a desperate man.

At the close of 1998, Fox Films was reaping the benefits from the gigantic hit *Titanic,* which had earned more than $600 million in American grosses alone and went on to add another $1.6 billion in international receipts. Fox also released the films *The Full Monty, Dr. Dolittle,* and *There's Something About Mary* that year to box-office gold. Over Turner's objections, Murdoch had successfully purchased the Los Angeles Dodgers despite having never attended a baseball game. He had sold *TV Guide,* bought the Family Channel, and moved into Soho's Mercer Hotel with his 31-year-old girlfriend, occupying a suite with leather curtains and a bathtub built for two. Clearly, this was not a man to be toyed with. Yet, in the year ahead there were those who would try, and in the process alter the way the world received its news and, even more alarming, what news the world received.

# NINETEEN

# A Family Affair

*I try to speak to Dad every day*
*to see what he's doing*
*or to say, you know, 'I love you.'*

Lachlan Murdoch
*Entertainment Weekly*
July 30, 1999

The home was more like Anna than Rupert, its manicured lawn and garden a serene oasis high atop the anxiety of Los Angeles' traffic and commerce. Hidden behind thick iron gates at the end of a long driveway, Misty Mountain was a Tuscan palace on six grand acres. Designed in 1926 by noted California architect Wallace Neff for silent film star–turned–director Fred Niblo, the estate was dubbed "one of the most important houses in Los Angeles" by real estate broker David Mossler.[1]

Anna Murdoch's taste was everywhere—in the antiques, the art, the polished brass, the flawless crystal. She reigned at Misty Mountain until April 1998, when she turned her back on the house, husband, and life she loved, exchanging the placid surroundings for the melodrama of divorce.

Disney Studios chief Michael Eisner came to look at the mansion when it was placed on the market for $19.5 million. So did actor Will Smith and agent Michael Ovitz. Dreamworks' Jeffrey Katzenberg was another lookyloo, but when no one made a serious offer, Murdoch removed the house from the market in April 1999.[2] Two months later, Anna Murdoch's divorce from her

371

husband of 32 years became final, with her settlement reported at a conservative $200 million. A bargain price, but it was more than enough for Anna. She had negotiated well, and saw to it that her children and stepdaughter Prudence were protected as the legal heirs to their father's share of News Corporation.

While it was Anna who had formally filed for divorce, there was little doubt that her husband had pushed for it, a fact confirmed by Anna in an interview in *Australian Women's Weekly*. "I think that Rupert's affair with Wendi Deng—it's not an original plot—was the end of the marriage," she said. "He was extremely hard, ruthless, and determined that he was going to go through with [the divorce] no matter what I wanted or what I was trying to do to save the marriage. He had no interest in that whatsoever."

What Murdoch did have an interest in was Wendi Deng. Friends admitted that he looked like a "teenager in love," not an easy illusion to carry off at age 68. Seventeen days after his divorce was final, Murdoch invited 80 guests to New York's Chelsea Piers for a special evening aboard the *Morning Glory*, Murdoch's 155-foot yacht. Among them were his four children. The host that greeted his guests looked less like a teenager than a banker who had lost his shoes. Murdoch was dressed in a dark blue suit and was barefoot, as was Deng, who left the crowd dining on lobster napoleon to change from a short-sleeved dress into a floor-length gown designed by Australian Richard Tyler. At 8 P.M., under a sky filtering the haze from Manhattan, Murdoch took his third wife and proclaimed himself "the luckiest man in the world."[3]

It was a decidedly different approach to a wedding than his elder son, Lachlan, had chosen just four months earlier. Security guards roamed Murdoch's Australian estate Cavan, which sat on thousands of acres along the Murrumbidgee River with its rainbow trout and Murray cod. There was a pool and tennis and horses too, but this day, amid cold weather and showers, there would be none of that. Instead, under a tent bedecked with flowers and a makeshift chapel constructed of lattice next to the riverbank, Lachlan Murdoch married Sarah O'Hare, an elegantly thin model who had achieved fame for her Wonderbra advertisements.

Wendi Deng accompanied Murdoch to Australia but did not attend the wedding, remaining instead in the hotel suite she shared with her then fiancé. Guests to the event were shuttled in buses with windows blocked by Murdoch newspapers to keep unauthorized photos to a minimum. In an effort to reduce the intrusion of the press, the family had arranged to supply photographs of the ceremony "free of charge."

Other than the weather, which not even Murdoch could control, the wedding was a true celebration, with the entire Murdoch family in attendance. Anna, looking particularly elegant, seized the spotlight from the wedding couple, if only briefly, when she rose to make a toast. "Now I have the microphone," she said, "and one man in the room must be rather nervous."[4]

Lachlan had been deemed the heir apparent to his father's $33 billion media empire when, weeks before the wedding, Murdoch had appointed him senior executive vice president of News Corporation, dubbing him "first among equals" where his children were concerned. Lachlan's two tattoos—one of a snake, the other of a gecko—and his penchant for riding his Ducati motorcycle to work had not reduced his potential in Papa's eyes, which remained firmly focused on the bottom line.

Back in New York after a monthlong honeymoon in Italy, Murdoch plunged immediately into his nonstop schedule, seemingly invigorated by his newlywed status and the prospect of coming home to a wife eight years younger than his oldest child. His detractors, while never completely out of ammunition, had found even Murdoch's *New York Post* recently lacking in controversy and the man himself abnormally quiet. The arrival, however, of a piece in *Vanity Fair* eclipsed that lull and stirred the pot of contention.

Author William Shawcross, whose biography *Murdoch* was a best-seller, discovered a new Murdoch—a man who wore all black to look younger and "in." Underneath the clothes, though, lurked the same manipulator, willing to mold the truth to fit the moment, particularly where his business in China was concerned—a presence he said was nonexistent, even though Star TV's channels blanketed the country. "How many people watch those channels? I can't tell you," he said. "It's meant to be illegal to have dishes, but if you go anywhere you'll see a lot of dishes pointed at the satellite we are on."[*5]

Murdoch crossed the line of legitimacy when he declared that he didn't think "there are many Communists left in China. There's a one-party state and there's a Communist economy, which they are desperately trying to get out of and change."[6] Murdoch's most malicious comments were directed at the Dalai Lama, who Murdoch seemed to suggest was a "very political old monk shuffling around in Gucci shoes."[7] He laid credit for the quote on cynics without denying that he was among them. Further, Murdoch claimed that "half the people of Tibet still think that the Dalai Lama is the son of God."[8]

Time to rewrite the religious texts, or perhaps tell Murdoch that the people of Tibet believe the Dalai Lama to be the fourteenth incarnation of Buddha, who was a teacher, not a god. Oblivious to the fact that he was spouting propaganda or, worse, uttering it deliberately, Murdoch went on to picture Tibet as an "authoritarian, medieval society without any basic services."[9] This from the mouth of a man who had been married less than a month to a woman born in China.

The commotion created by the comments inspired columns, commentary, and letters. Not only did Murdoch find no need to apologize, but he also repeated his opinions. Meanwhile, Wendi

---

[*] Murdoch failed to mention that China's prime minister, Zhu Rongji, confessed that his favorite television celebrity appears on Star.

Deng wisely refused to comment. She chose to shelter herself from the public, accompanying Murdoch on trips but, unlike Anna, remaining silent on his business and his politics.

Murdoch managed to mix both when he hired departing Speaker of the House Newt Gingrich as a commentator on Fox News. After barely surviving the brouhaha over his book contract with Murdoch's HarperCollins back in 1995, the House Leader of Family Values found himself caught up in a messy divorce from his second wife, Marianne. Though the *New York Post* reported allegations of adultery with the headline NEWT'S FOOLING AROUND WITH HIS GIRL ON THE HILL, this did not prevent Murdoch from offering Gingrich a seven-figure contract to analyze politics on Fox News. There, Gingrich joined fellow adulterer Dick Morris, the prostitute toe-sucking adviser to Bill Clinton, whom Murdoch had previously hired and kept from the unemployment lines after he was tarred and feathered in true Washington fashion.

In expanding into nonpublishing areas of Australia, Murdoch had taken a page from Southern California's Universal Studios with Fox Studios Australia, a complex of six soundstages for production, a public entertainment area divided into a studio tour called Backlot and a shopping and eating area named Bent Street. Production designer Jeremy Railton, the genius behind the innovative Saturday morning TV show *Pee-Wee's Playhouse* as well as productions around the world, created the look.

In November, traveling to Sydney for the opening of Fox Studios Australia and News Corporation's annual stockholders meeting, Murdoch stepped back onto the soapbox to criticize the policies of the current conservative government, which had refused to bend the country's restrictive media regulations in Murdoch's favor. "I think the individuals involved in making decisions are overawed by some of the existing players," Murdoch suggested, in a veiled reference to his competitor Kerry Packer, owner of Australia's Nine Network and the country's major publisher of magazines. "For a free-enterprise, market-friendly country to give existing businesses absolute monopolies for decades is unthinkable, but it's happened here," he continued. "It sounds like Indonesia under Suharto." To which Australian prime minister John Howard responded, "Australia will decide our own constitutional reforms [without] the leave or permission of any foreigner."[10]

Closer to home on his own Fox News, Murdoch looked directly into the camera and spoke with the wisdom of a sage in discussing the competition on NBC. "I understand the business has been offered to Time Warner for $25 billion, and one or two well-known people on the board are very much in favor of buying it, and the rest are very much opposed."[11] His words immediately trickled down to the front page of the *New York Post*. GE OFFERS UP NBC read the headline. That it wasn't true didn't matter to the Murdoch press. This was news—sort of.

Ted Turner, being the aforementioned well-known person on the board, could not decide if he was disappointed that it was not accurate, or happy that Murdoch had made a fool of himself. Now restricted in his own outbursts by contractual obligations at Time Warner, Turner said nothing in response, although he did speak out a month later to Larry King, saying he still was in favor of buying NBC, even though Time Warner had already launched the Warner Bros. Network.

"I'm like Noah," Turner said. "I want two of everything. It's double your pleasure, double your fun, have two broadcast networks instead of just one."[12]

"We have no intention of selling it," countered GE chairman Jack Welch. "I've tried to say that as many ways as I can, even when Rupert went off the reservation."[13]

As it happened, all the talk of NBC and networks and Ted Turner's desires amounted to little more than smoke screens for what was actually happening in the Time Warner boardroom. The real news that was about to rock the corporate world was far bigger than Murdoch's suggestion that the Peacock Network was for sale for $25 billion. It was Time Warner itself that was for sale, and for a whopping $165 billion plus change.

When the merger of America Online and Time Warner was announced on January 10, 2000, Ted Turner appeared to be happy. True, there was a scowl on his face, but that might have been expected. Just the week before, Turner revealed he and Jane Fonda had separated after almost nine years of marriage. Much was happening in Turner's world, and regardless of what the media were reporting, the AOL Time Warner merger was not at the top of his list.

Fonda's walkout had left Turner stunned. There had been earlier reports of marital discord and visits by the couple to a marriage counselor. "Jane wants me to become a saint," Turner had said. "And I'm not."[14] What Turner was was disappointed. After selling his companies to Time Warner, he had lost himself in the process. No longer in charge, no longer making decisions, no longer changing the world and standing center stage had taken Turner down another path, one full of too much time and too few challenges.

As the deal to merge Time Warner into AOL was announced, Turner sat on stage with AOL chairman Steve Case and AOL president Bob Pittman, as well as Time Warner's Jerry Levin, but it was Case and Levin who were in the spotlight. It was no longer Ted's show, and despite his claim that he was thrilled and approached the merger "with as much excitement as I did when I first made love some forty-two years ago,"[15] it placed him one more corridor removed from the center of the action.

In the months that followed the creation of the largest media conglomerate in the world, there were endless analyses of the impact of the merger. Jim Ledbetter, from the New York bureau of the *Industry Standard,* saw a much larger Time Warner benefiting by gaining instant access to the Internet through AOL, and AOL acquiring the reach of a major global conglomerate in Time

Warner. David Bennahum, author of *Extra Life: Coming of Age in Cyberspace*, saw it as natural synergy, "the beginning of a profound transformation," one in which the world would receive "all our entertainment and our news through this global Internet network."

While Turner suddenly felt like the once-powerful racehorse now watching from the pasture, Murdoch looked upon the merger as a wake-up call to the future of communication, one in which he was not playing a large part. Murdoch knew better than anyone about a missed opportunity, and with AOL he had definitely missed the mark.

Back in 1996, Murdoch had briefly flirted with scooping up AOL for $5 billion and probably would have if he hadn't known so little about the Internet. Hoping for some sound advice, he went to Microsoft chairman Bill Gates, who turned him off to the concept by saying that AOL didn't even have a business plan. Later, commenting about AOL to host Willow Bay on *CNN Moneyline*, Murdoch said, "We had an opportunity to come in when it was four or five billion, and it went up to being worth $150 billion. It was a pretty serious opportunity that we missed there."[16]

Almost immediately, as if shocked into action, Murdoch reacted with a flurry of announcements to counter what he saw as a loss of momentum. He proclaimed record profits for News Corporation in the first half of 1999/2000, pegging the number at $818.09 million, and adding that "television, newspapers, cable programming and book publishing all posted sharp operating income increases." Fox's chief operating officer, Peter Chernin, said there was a "tremendous sense of urgency throughout News Corp. to transform our platforms and our content to exploit the lucrative opportunities of this new digital age."[17]

It was a time for fast reorganization. Nearly overnight, Murdoch had been reduced to what appeared to be an also-ran at his own game when compared with the aggressive stances of AOL

Time Warner and Microsoft with its push into both cable and the Internet. "A lot of us used to be big fish in a big pond. Now we are all minnows with two huge sharks," he said.[18]

As if rushing toward some goal line, Murdoch laced together a number of alliances. First, he won a license to beam his content over Bulgaria via its government-owned Channel 2, becoming that country's first commercial broadcaster and leading his entry into southern Europe.[19] Then in March, Murdoch joined with Singapore Telecom to provide Internet and wireless service to Asia after losing a short but intense takeover battle for Hong Kong's Cable & Wireless HKT. Richard Li, son of Hong Kong business tycoon Li Ka-shing (with whom Murdoch had also done business), stole the prize of Cable & Wireless from under Murdoch, and used Murdoch's own money to do it. Li's 10-month-old Pacific Century CyberWorks had been grubstaked with money from his initial sale of Star TV to Murdoch back in 1992. Gareth Chang, head of Star TV, resigned hours after his company's bid for C&W was foiled, reportedly after an argument with Murdoch.

By June, Murdoch had filled the opening by transferring his son James to Hong Kong as the chief of Star TV. Like his brother, James had a tattoo on his forearm—this one in the shape of a lightbulb—as well as great admiration for his father and no time to talk about lines of succession to the throne. "Pop's going to be around a long time and we're all very young," the bespectacled and sarcastic heir said.[20]

As James was ascending within the corporate structure, his sister Elisabeth opted to exit, leaving behind her legacy at BSkyB in favor of forming a TV production company. "Elisabeth is an extremely talented film and television executive," her father said, "as her work at Sky has demonstrated. Starting her own production company is purely a personal decision, one that has my full blessing. Elisabeth has made a great contribution to News Corp."[21]

Rumors floated immediately that Elisabeth had fallen into disfavor with her father since her divorce from Elkin Pianim, and had been asked to leave BSkyB when she became pregnant by her current boyfriend, Matthew Freud. Everyone in the Murdoch family insisted, however, that Elisabeth's decision was based solely on her desire to demonstrate her abilities away from the Murdoch spotlight.

Elisabeth did attend James' June wedding to longtime fiancée Kathryn Hufschmid, a former model and later a publicist for *Gear* magazine. Beautiful and chummy, Hufschmid matched James' acerbic wit and colorful tongue and was a particular favorite of Dame Elisabeth, who once again traveled from Australia for yet another Murdoch clan wedding. This one was held in Old Saybrook on the Connecticut River. Amid the lush greenery that is Connecticut in spring, Kathryn read from James Joyce during the ceremony. James read from a work by Chilean poet Pablo Neruda. As Rupert watched, his eyes filled with tears at the very real prospect of his own mortality.

The previous April in Los Angeles, during a routine physical examination, doctors discovered cancer in Murdoch's prostate. It was a devastating blow to the man who considered himself invincible. Nine weeks of radiation therapy were prescribed, and Murdoch had finished the exhausting regimen shortly before the wedding. He had refused to cut down on his schedule during the treatment and beamed with joy that at this moment, he was alive and fine and watching his youngest child get married.

That's when the tears began to flow. Unconsciously, yet in full view, the man who commanded terror in the hearts of businessmen around the world felt his young wife's hand in his and cried. For what he had accomplished and what he had left to do, for the glory of the river and the flowers and the air that still smelled damp from the rain, Rupert Murdoch cried.

It's a safe bet that Ted Turner was tearful that day as well, for he was crying with regularity these days. AOL's Robert Pittman had been to Atlanta, roaming the halls of CNN and snooping, as Turner loved to call it. Snooping for ways to save money and make over the news network to better fit within the framework of a reworked Time Warner. Pittman was not a Turner kind of guy. He was a smooth operator, a jet-setter who started his show-biz life in Mississippi as a teenage disc jockey. Pittman helped create MTV, and at AOL he had earned his stripes as the company's marketing wiz. At the new AOL Time Warner, Pittman had been given the title of co-chief operating officer (with Time Warner's Richard Parsons). He had been awarded the combined companies' cable networks, cable systems, magazines, advertising, and subscription business. No, he was not likely destined to be a Turner favorite.

The way Turner actually learned that he was being stripped of his authority over the companies that he had birthed, suckled, and raised came via a telephone call from Jerry Levin. Despite appearances to the contrary, when the merger was announced Turner had not played a role in any of the decisions relating to the operation of the company. He did not take part in any meetings and was advised only on a need-to-know basis or as a courtesy as Time Warner's largest stockholder.

According to Levin's memory, when he told Turner that Pittman was now in control of Turner Broadcasting, Turner reacted by attempting to go over his head to AOL Time Warner chairman Steve Case. Case listened, Case understood, and Case apparently did nothing, for when the official announcement was released several weeks later regarding the breakdown of responsibility at the combined AOL Time Warner, Turner was out and Pittman was in. As Turner told it, he was fired. The way Levin saw it, Turner was a senior adviser and vice chairman, even though he had no direct responsibility.

Turner received *that* news by fax at his ranch in New Mexico, where he was hosting Liberty Media chairman John Malone, who had sold his ownership of TCI to AT&T and was now an "adviser." Malone knew all too well what Turner was going through. He had absorbed some of the same shockwaves himself. Malone handled the situation by investing in Rupert Murdoch, a familiar name to both.

Murdoch had decided to spin off his satellite interests into a new division called Sky Global Networks and announce an initial public offering (IPO), according to paperwork filed with the Securities and Exchange Commission. Sky Global would include Murdoch's BSkyB network in the United Kingdom, in which Murdoch owned 37 percent; his German investment in 24 percent of Premiere World, a pay-TV service; Stream TV in Italy (42 percent); his 100 percent ownership in Star TV; plus portions of Japan's Sky PerfecTV, Brazil's Sky Brazil, Mexico's Sky Mexico, Latin America's Sky Multi-Partners, NDS (formerly News Datacom), and *TV Guide*. By spinning off those companies and raising additional capital through an IPO, Murdoch had visions of purchasing DirecTV from General Motors' Hughes Electronics division, thus completing his quest for world satellite domination.

Malone wanted to be a partner in Murdoch's expansion. In one of the most complicated exchanges of company stocks, he agreed with Murdoch to do the following: receive 18 percent of nonvoting stock in News Corporation in exchange for 21 percent of Malone's Gemstar International** stock, adding to the 22 percent of Gemstar Murdoch already owned to peak his ownership at 43 percent. Sky Global would then absorb Gemstar, including its most valuable asset, *TV Guide,* and bid to buy DirecTV from General Motors.

While the mechanics of such an involved stock exchange gave headaches to the governments' various regulatory bodies that had to approve the transfers, the real test came in explaining the elaborate swap-and-shop to the public, who was expected to race

---

** Gemstar is a global media company specializing in on-air programming guides and
  services.

to buy shares when and if Sky Global became a reality. At the moment, however, it was all so much paper, with the majority of it in press releases and filings with the SEC. Unorthodox mergers and acquisitions had a way of becoming reality, however, as Ted Turner learned with AOL Time Warner.

Turner was admittedly in a free fall, spiraling out of control, and the world as he had known it became a stranger. There were moments when despair crowded out reason, and thoughts of suicide made unwelcome sounds. The man who wanted to save America and bring peace to the world found he was the neediest person of all.

On April 16, 2001, Jane Fonda filed for divorce from Turner, calling their marriage "irretrievably broken." Turner later said it was the saddest, loneliest day of his life. He was unwanted by his company and his wife, who it seems had replaced him with Jesus.

"I had absolutely no warning about it. She didn't tell me she was thinking about doing it. She just came home and said, 'I've become a Christian,'" he explained.[22]

For the agnostic Turner, it was a mystery how the entire thing happened. It was less a mystery to his soon-to-be ex-wife. "I chose not to discuss it with him because he would have talked me out of it," Fonda said. "He's a debating champion. . . . He needs someone to be there one hundred percent of the time. He thinks that's love. It is not love. It's babysitting." Then she added, "We went in different directions. I grew up."[23]

# The Emperor Has No Clothes

*I never felt we were different in any way.*
*Even when one cover of* Time *magazine*
*featured Dad as King Kong.*
*That's the first memory I have of Dad at school,*
*on the cover of* Time *magazine*
*portrayed as this monster.*

Lachlan Murdoch
*Inside the Murdoch Dynasty*
June 20, 2002
BBC2, London

September 11, 2001. At 8:45 A.M., Eastern time, an American Airlines passenger jet crashed into the North Tower of the World Trade Center in New York City, and life in the United States would never be the same. For a news organization, there is no greater test than performance during a national disaster, and for both the Cable News Network and Fox News, September 11 was a study in both contrasts and efficiencies. Each network was on the scene immediately, with live coverage televised to the world 15 minutes before the president of the United States, reading to children in a classroom in Florida, learned America was under attack.

Americans turned to television for information and comfort that day, drawn to video replays like rubberneckers at the scene of a horrible accident. But this was no accident. This was murder,

and an outraged country began a mourning process than continues still. On that day, CNN was at its expected best. It was the
official news station relied upon for the latest on the tragedy
across the nation and indeed the world. From the White House
to, presumably, the al-Qaeda terrorist network, CNN, while cen-
tering its focus on breaking news at Ground Zero in Manhattan,
also pulled comments and commentary from its bureaus in the
Middle East and Europe. It was timely, efficient, and seemingly
objective.

Fox News was saturated with viewers that day as well. The
demographics of its audience skewed younger, more conservative, a direct result of the efforts of Fox News chairman and CEO
Roger Ailes, an extremely savvy and well-connected Republican.
Ratings had been climbing, albeit slowly, ever since its debut as a
full-flung network (complete with an outlet in New York).
Though still running a distant second to CNN, Fox News took
on added legitimacy that day. New viewers who discovered Fox
News on September 11 found a network that made little secret of
its opinions, pushing them out front, attacking, evaluating, challenging, accusing. Many, it seemed, liked what they judged to be
an aggressive brand of honest reporting and dogmatic analysis.

Much of the initial popularity of Fox was linked to the
appeal of commentator Bill O'Reilly, who had emerged as its
star. O'Reilly's argumentative style and no-holds-barred opinions acted like a whirlpool, attracting virtually everything that
dared near his eddy. Whereas many were ultimately repulsed by
his overbearing, combative approach, others gravitated toward it,
often finding validation of their own opinions through his ultra-
conservative views.

*The O'Reilly Factor* was more than just the title of his hourlong
nightly show. It spawned two best-selling books by its host and
helped Fox find its identity. Though the news network was still
using the slogan "Fair and balanced," it had added another that
helped cover the fact that it was obviously reflecting Murdoch's

conservative posture. The new slogan, "We report, you decide," left it open to viewers to evaluate Fox's stance, which Murdoch characterized as neutral and unbiased, challenging anyone to point out an example of the network's right-wing leanings.

Murdoch conveniently overlooked that Fox's managing editor, Brit Hume, charged with shaping the scope of daily coverage, was a contributor to the conservative journals *American Spectator* and Murdoch's own *Weekly Standard*. The network's daytime anchor, David Asman, hailed from the Manhattan Institute, which the *Boston Globe* characterized as "a conservative think tank that was founded by Margaret Thatcher's mentor and Ronald Reagan's spymaster" and called it "the most influential source of political ideas."[1] Tony Snow, a former speechwriter with the senior Bush administration and noted conservative columnist, was the host of *Fox News Sunday*. All with Roger Ailes, onetime producer for conservative poster-boy Rush Limbaugh, running the show.

Murdoch went to such extraordinary lengths to insist that his news network was neutral that his protests themselves drew attention to the conservative nature of Fox News and that of its owner. What made the effort even more suspect is that Murdoch had never made a point of hiding his personal involvement in imprinting his political views on his newspapers. He did just the opposite, routinely using endorsements and editorials to gain influence by helping to elect candidates likely to favor his businesses.

With the arrival of the George W. Bush White House in January 2001, Murdoch was in a position to reap the benefits of a renewed acceptance of big business in Washington. The change of administration was particularly timely given his two latest attempts to increase his hammerlock on the media. The first, a $5.3 billion takeover grab of Chris-Craft Industry television stations, had a far-reaching impact on broadcast regulations. Chris-Craft owned a group of 10 stations, including outlets in New York, Los Angeles, Salt Lake City, and Phoenix—cities where Murdoch currently owned stations. The acquisition was technically legal due to changes in the FCC ownership rules in 1999 that allowed broadcasters to buy a second station in certain markets to help promote the success of fledgling networks like those started by Paramount (UPN) and Warner Bros. (WB). In Murdoch's case, of course, his only purpose for the purchase was to increase the number of Fox-owned stations and, ultimately, his profits.

Making the purchase more intriguing was the fact that 8 of the 10 stations were affiliated with the UPN Network, a direct competitor to Fox. Should Murdoch be permitted to buy the stations and subsequently keep the outlets' UPN affiliation, he would essentially be competing against himself in those four markets in which he had two stations. Yet while Murdoch's efforts to break old taboos and establish new beachheads in American broadcast ownership were generating the most publicity, they were not occupying the majority of his time. That distinction fell to his increasingly aggressive efforts to acquire DirecTV from General Motors.

Since March 2000, when GM announced it would divest itself of its Hughes Electronics DirecTV satellite division, Murdoch had been bidding for the unit, said to be worth $40 billion. The man who had repeatedly tried and failed to launch a satellite service in the United States now intended to acquire one as the largest part of a bold plan for global satellite dominance. Murdoch placed so much emphasis on the purchase that he was willing to merge his Sky Global into Hughes Electronics to get it.

DirecTV, with its 10 million subscribers, not only was the largest satellite broadcaster in America, but it also represented the last piece in a patchwork of companies that spiderwebbed Murdoch's control of the media across the world. While acquiring DirecTV—and through it, control of Hughes Electronics—had long been Murdoch's dream, it was hardly an easy acquisition. Finances aside, the legalities of the transaction required approval by multiple government agencies. First, however, Murdoch had to convince Hughes that Sky Global was an appropriate suitor.

On the surface, the fit between DirecTV and Sky Global was perfect: large American satellite firm merges with international satellite firm to make a media giant that would be virtually untouchable by the competition. Yet, news stories of the day, regaling in praise over the potential of the merged companies, failed to take note of Michael Smith, chairman of Hughes and brother to General Motors chairman Jack Smith.

If Murdoch succeeded in coaxing Hughes into his fold, he, not Michael Smith, would be chairman of the combined companies. Having been charged by brother Jack to strike the best for Hughes and generate needed cash for parent GM, Mike Smith planned to start shopping the product around, hoping not only to find a sweet deal financially, but also to keep his job in the process.

Certain that he had the front position in any negotiation for DirecTV, Murdoch began laying the extensive groundwork required for such a major merger. The ever-present John Malone agreed to take a $1 billion dollar position in the venture, having bought into the Sky Global restructuring. Bill Gates of Microsoft pledged to take a $4 billion stake in anticipation of providing Internet links via the DirecTV set-top descrambler. GM was to spin off Hughes Electronics as a separate, publicly traded company. Sky Global would merge into Hughes Electronics in exchange for Hughes stock. And Rupert Murdoch would end up owning 35 percent of the resulting company, DirecTV–Sky Global—then worth in excess of $70 billion. It all looked so easy—on paper.

Murdoch knew how to play out this merger in the news and in trade papers around the world, maintaining his image, building his stock value, increasing his worth as the emperor of communications, the king of media. He approached his offer from a position of strength. Few companies in the world either were in the market for a digital satellite service or could afford the premium price General Motors was demanding.

Underneath its veneer of success and profitability, GM needed this sale even more than Rupert Murdoch did. With $38 billion in underfunded pension programs,[2] GM needed an immediate influx of capital to avoid having its credit rating downgraded, and a Hughes merger with Sky Global was a speedy way to achieve that goal.

On February 6, 2001, Rupert Murdoch had what he felt was an agreement with GM for Hughes Electronics and Sky Global to merge. In what had been several months of intense business planning, negotiations, and crunched numbers, Murdoch had his satellite service across America and the linchpin in a global network that would transform communications on a scale never seen since the invention of the printing press.

The last time Murdoch had depended on a handshake, however, was with Jerry Levin and Time Warner Cable. The memory of that debacle and the press frenzy that followed it lay close to the surface, the raw skin colored by emotional irritation that time had not yet soothed. As news reports continued to flood from GM's Detroit headquarters, choreographed to obtain extended coverage of the done deal, Murdoch found himself strangely uneasy, a nonbeliever in his own achievement.

It was easy enough to understand. DirecTV, for all its current value, was, after all, the last visage of Howard Hughes, a billionaire not exactly notorious for his stability. When he created the company in the twenties, it was to develop aerospace and defense products. And, indeed, it became the largest defense contractor of its era. With those divisions long since spun off to Boeing and Raytheon, Hughes Electronics had been reduced to DirecTV, one last fabulous example of the visionary that Howard Hughes was.

USA Networks CEO Barry Diller called it "a transforming transaction," this merger of giants in communication.[3] Seemingly all the pieces of Murdoch's puzzle had meshed seamlessly with GM's needs at the moment. All, of course, except those of Michael Smith, the Hughes chairman who wanted to keep his job. Smith called Murdoch during the second week of February and requested one last meeting at Fox Studios. It was to be a review of the various elements of the deal, the synergy of the multiple divisions of Sky Global and how DirecTV would play a part in the massive communication empire of Emperor Murdoch. A "due diligence" meeting, Smith called it; for the bankers, he said.

Faced with the potential for delay, Murdoch once again summoned his top executives from the various divisions of the Sky Global nebula. News Corporation chief Peter Chernin; Chase Carey, newly appointed head of Sky Global; Abe Peled of NDS; Gemstar head Henry Yuen; BSkyB's Tony Ball; Lachlan Murdoch, now deputy COO of News Corporation; and his brother, James, head of Star TV—they all gathered on February 20, 2001, in the News Corporation boardroom and began what was to be the final presentation before the victory celebration.

Although the presentations proceeded flawlessly, Murdoch described the meeting itself as weird. The bankers asked no questions, and Mike Smith, sitting in the rear of the room, appeared bored and argumentative.[4] There was only the shuffling of chairs as Smith rose from his seat a little after 2 P.M. and announced he was leaving. Something about another appointment. And with that, the chairman of DirecTV left the room a little more than halfway through James Murdoch's presentation on Star TV.

Rupert Murdoch was not one to tolerate disrespect, and Smith's behavior was blatant disrespect—of Murdoch, of his offer, and of the seriousness of GM to complete the deal. As his disbelief turned to indignation, he started a telephone campaign that began with Smith's brother Jack and raged through the executive suite of DirecTV's parent company. To his dismay, Murdoch learned that Mike Smith had continued to shop DirecTV around, and had found a willing accomplice in Charlie Ergen of EchoStar.

While maintaining a positive public posture, Murdoch lobbied tirelessly to regenerate interest in his DirecTV–Sky Global proposal. It was a negotiation being driven by a dream: Murdoch's vision of his global satellite service. Ironically, for all its stalling, Hughes Electronics was desperate for cash to pay for overdue improvements and expansion of its system, not to mention GM's own need for a cash infusion. News Corporation, by comparison, had no such urgency. "Is Sky Global viable without a U.S. presence?" Murdoch said. "Of course it is. That's a bit like asking whether the Louvre could exist without the Mona Lisa. We, like the Louvre, have plenty of other treasures."[5]

Ah, but the dream. There was the rub. This was not just about good business. This was about the culmination of a life's work. Rupert Murdoch, controller of information. A man who, to hear him talk, was running out of time. In an interview in March with PBS' Charlie Rose just before Murdoch's seventieth birthday, Murdoch removed a piece of paper from an inside pocket and reflected on his remaining time. By his calculations, he had lived 613,000 hours, 201,000 in childhood. Of the remaining 412,000, Murdoch had decided to set some of them aside, reducing his "productive time" down to 275,000 hours. "I take out a month for holidays, at least half a weekend, family time, evenings, etc., and you're down to at the very minimum a couple hundred thousand hours I've been at work," he told Rose. "And then I go, 'What have I done?' How much time have I wasted in endless meetings with no decisions? I guess I've wasted half my life. So if I'm pretty healthy and have a normal life expectancy, I've got about another 175,000 hours to go, of which maybe I can spend 75,000 productively at work . . . and hopefully it won't all be spent talking to General Motors."[6]

There was, of course, other business transpiring at News Corporation. It just wasn't being noticed amid the klieg lights focused on DirecTV. Murdoch invested in a 12 percent share of China Netcom, the Internet provider across mainland China. Penetrating into China's closed market was another of Murdoch's dreams, a dream now shared by son James, who had taken well to his position as head of Star TV and had even adopted his father's conciliatory attitude toward the ruling government's lack of tolerance for alternate opinion. James labeled the Falun Gong, a decade-old organization that mixed religious philosophy and meditation, as a cult "that clearly does not have the success of China at heart." The youngest Murdoch additionally cautioned that the Western press was presenting a distorted picture of human-rights abuses in the country and that "these destabilizing forces today are very, very dangerous."[7]

In early May, Rupert Murdoch visited British prime minister Tony Blair to talk about Blair's reelection campaign and share the news that Murdoch's wife, Wendi, was going to have a baby, further cementing the media giant's Chinese-American relations. Blair's reaction was shared by many: amazement at the news and curious how it would affect the line of succession as carefully dictated in Anna Murdoch's divorce settlement. Dame Elisabeth, when questioned about the pregnancy, reacted with typical low-key deflection. "Oh, it's just family news, that's all," she said. "I think honestly and truthfully it's very early on to be talking about these things. People talk about these things so early these days, don't they?"

While Murdoch's own family might have been off limits, Murdoch's Fox family was very much in play. Back in January, Murdoch's partner in the enterprise, Haim Saban, had taken advantage of a clause in his contract and opted to sell out his 49 percent. The move prompted Murdoch to seek a buyer for the network, which Saban had valued at $6 billion. What Murdoch eventually settled for in July was a $5.3 billion payout from Disney Studios, who eagerly absorbed the network started by televangelist Pat Robertson, renaming it the ABC Family Channel.

That irony brought out a plethora of columns salting wounds and casting stones, pointing out the fact that Robertson had taken part in an advertising campaign that lambasted Disney's *Ellen* TV series. According to those advertisements, the award-winning show, starring comedian Ellen DeGeneres as Ellen Morgan, a lesbian bookstore owner, was "insulting to millions of Americans who once looked at Disney as a beacon of family entertainment."[8]

Though the sale of the Fox Family Channel amounted to nearly $2 billion in profit for Murdoch, the man was unhappy. Clearly, his bid for DirecTV, the final cog in his quest for world dominance, was not moving forward, not even after Michael Smith was fired from his position for bollixing what otherwise might have been an easy sale. In the months since Murdoch made his initial offer, the stock market had plunged, right along with DirecTV sales to home users and GM car sales to consumers. As May pushed into June and met the heat of summer in July and August, News Corporation maintained its vigilance on Hughes Electronics, as did feisty Charlie Ergen. Despite the relatively small size of his company, EchoStar, Ergen was not retreating in the face of pressure from Murdoch, and in fact was increasing his efforts to convince GM that he was a serious bidder for its DirecTV jewel.

Ergen, like Murdoch, was a gambler. In this case, he was gambling on Hughes Electronics' ability to see that his official offer, a $32.3 billion mostly paper bid, was preferable to Murdoch's complicated though cash-heavy proposal. Of Ergen, Murdoch would only say, "There's been a lot of speculation that he is playing a clever hand of poker here, holding things up as long as he can while he's increasing his share of the market, [and] we will just have to see how he plays his hand. He certainly won't show us his cards in advance."[9]

Ultimately, Ergen did not need to show his hand, for in the tradition of fine poker, Murdoch folded and walked away. On October 27, 2001, after a meeting of the board of directors of General Motors failed to produce a winner in the bidding for DirecTV, Murdoch withdrew his offer, essentially leaving Ergen the winner. Twenty months after the game began, it was over, or so the investment community thought.

Immediately Murdoch's stock dropped $2 billion, as it appeared that the media giant had given up in distress, frustration, or both. The GM board quickly approved the offer from EchoStar and prepared to clear the regulatory hurdles of the FCC and the Justice Department. With stock reevaluation, the deal that was now being bantered· for approval was said to be worth $25.8 billion. As part of its deal, GM found itself lending Ergen $2.75 billion, secured by EchoStar stock, while he shopped around for additional financing. Already GM should have been concerned. Instead, pictures of a grinning Ergen with GM's CEO Rick Wagoner were spotted across the front pages of newspapers around the world, including many owned by Rupert Murdoch, who publicly expressed "no regrets" over his loss.

In November, few media analysts even noticed when Murdoch's shares in News Corporation dropped to 16.25 percent as John Malone's Liberty Media concluded its agreed-upon stock swap. The deal increased Murdoch's share of Gemstar to 43 percent, for which Malone received 115 million preferred shares of News Corporation. As a result, Malone held 18 percent of Murdoch's company, though it was mainly in nonvoting shares. At the time, all eyes were still on Charlie Ergen, pushing his way through FCC hearings. Murdoch actually had taken a break from business to welcome his fifth child, a nine-pound baby girl named Grace Helen, who was born on November 19. He took a breath and reflected on his life and the brand-new one he held in his arms.

It was a time for reflection for Ted Turner as well. No longer married, no longer working, Turner watched as bits and pieces of his empire were being sold or dissolved. Sand through an hourglass. *Showbiz Today,* for 17 years Turner's favorite show on CNN, was dropped, replaced by entertainment segments that would air throughout the day. Cut as well was *People Count,* an ecological program hosted by Jane Fonda.

There were glimpses of the old Turner, but they were flashes so small that the light they created was nearly transparent.

Turner launched the Nuclear Threat Initiative with Senator Sam Nunn of Georgia, pledging $250 million to disarm and destroy nuclear stockpiles around the world.

And there was the occasional slip of the tongue. "I was looking at this woman, and I was trying to figure out what was on her forehead. At first I thought, you were in the Seattle earthquake. Now I realize you're just Jesus freaks. Shouldn't you guys be working for Fox?" He later apologized for his insensitivity on Ash Wednesday.

For the most part, Turner remained silent, introspective, wondering how he had suddenly become anachronistic. The visionary without a vision to speak of. A man lost in his own wilderness. There were moments of hope, even laughter, as he traveled the globe in a restless search to recapture his dream. And there were women still, of course, including longtime ex-girlfriend Frederique D'Arragon, now 50 and still ravishingly beautiful.

In August, his daughter Jennie's young child, Maddox Garlington, died suddenly at the age of two of complications from Hurler's syndrome, a rare genetic disorder that causes defects in a variety of organs and tissues. Turner immediately canceled his travel and business plans and was inconsolable over the loss. "He literally disappeared," said an AOL Time Warner aide. "There were no calls in and no calls out."[10] Even the *Wall Street Journal* seemed to be burying Turner before his time, reporting that the vice chairman was not expected to renew his contract. The small item appeared in the second section on page 6.

On December 5, 2001, a beleaguered Jerry Levin announced his sudden decision to resign as chief executive officer of AOL Time Warner in the face of dropping stock prices. His replacement, former co-chief operating officer Richard Parsons, extended an olive branch and encouraged Turner to reconsider returning to the company as an active vice chairman. It was not a job Turner necessarily coveted, and he was slow to deliver his answer.

There were evenings when Turner would stare for hours across the man-made pond he designed to reflect the Spanish Peaks. Crimson skies washed with gold. Or was it bronze? He couldn't decide. Yet, for all the calmness, he was far from a man at peace. His wealth now cut by 70 percent due to falling stock prices, he had been on antidepressants since the tragedy of September 11.

Turner did not reemerge until the end of the year for an appearance at a cable convention in Anaheim, California. Smiling, alert, he seemed revived in spirit and eager to attack AOL Time Warner for its problems, its waste, but mostly its outgoing CEO, Jerry Levin.

Calling the merger "the biggest mistake I ever made," he lamented the unfolding of events. "I never thought in my wildest dreams I would lose my job." He said that if he had waited a few years, he should have purchased Time Warner. "I could have fired Jerry Levin before he fired me. I was his friend. I would have had a hard time firing him—at that time."[11] A month later, Turner signed a new two-year contract as vice chairman of AOL Time Warner.

Ted Turner and Rupert Murdoch are two storm fronts colliding. And like weather patterns, no amount of scientific analysis can accurately predict the outcome when these two astonishing individuals interact, cross paths, play God. For these are not ordinary men. They are manipulators of world opinion—nothing less. So it was in the year 2002, and continues still today.

Turner is back at his post at AOL Time Warner, reenergized by his position as vice chairman and sous chef in charge of stirring the pot. His latest efforts were directed to improving the stock price of his company and repairing the dilution of his wealth, which he had laid at the feet of chairman Steve Case.

There have been more verbal gaffes. In February 2002, during a lecture at Brown University, Turner compared President Bush to Julius Caesar and called the September 11 hijackers "brave but probably a little nuts." Turner later said his comments were taken out of context.

In June, he suggested that Israel was engaged in terrorism. "Right now, aren't the Israelis and the Palestinians both terrorizing each other?" he said in London's *Guardian*. "The rich and the powerful, they don't need to resort to terrorism. The Palestinians are fighting with human suicide bombers—that's all they have. The Israelis, they've got one of the most powerful military machines in the world. The Palestinians have nothing. So who are the terrorists? I would make the case that both sides are involved in terrorism." Israel reacted by adding the Fox News Channel to its cable system after parliamentary deputy Avraham Hirschson called for a national boycott of CNN.

The Fox News Channel was making inroads in America as well, beating CNN for the first time in its history and increasing its viewership 75 percent on 34 percent more stations. According to MSNBC chief Erik Sorenson, "Fox is doing the tango while CNN and MSNBC are waltzing. We're doing a beautiful waltz, but the tango is the dance of the day."[12]

Murdoch's *Post* continued to run its garishly clever headlines, including one that read THAT'S AOL FOLKS, accompanied by a cartoon of Porky Pig, while the breaking news was that the Securities and Exchange Commission was investigating AOL Time Warner for accounting improprieties.[13] Reporter Nikki Finke sued the paper for $10 million when she was fired after writing about the Walt Disney Company's alleged irregular accounting practices under the headline DEEP POOH POOH.

After airing a collection of al-Qaeda videos that allegedly demonstrated chemical testing on dogs, CNN ran aground with initial claims that it did not pay for the tapes, only to later admit it had indeed purchased them for $30,000. Fox News took out a full-page advertisement in *USA Today* to point out the discrepancy and its newest trademarked slogan: "The Network America Trusts for Fair and Balanced News.™"

The Fox Network had the top-rated show the first Wednesday in September with the two-hour finale of *American Idol: The Search for a Superstar*. The success of the series prompted a spin-off, planned for Fox's FX cable channel. Titled *American Candidate*, the reality show promised to showcase ordinary Americans vying for a chance to run as the People's Candidate during the presidential elections of 2004.

On October 10, the FCC rejected EchoStar's bid to merge with Hughes Electronics DirecTV, citing its effect on competition. This opened the door for Murdoch to pick up the satellite service at a rummage-sale price, estimated to be at least $10 billion less than his previous offer. He said he intended to look into the potential merger "very carefully."

Odds appear to be excellent that he will succeed. If so, Rupert Murdoch would have control of the skies with his Sky Global division and the pipeline through which world news will travel. Likewise, Ted Turner, now firmly in control of the ultimate destiny of AOL Time Warner, would dominate the Internet and cable arenas.

Two men, operating with competing political agendas. Two men, never shy about using the media to further their causes. And all the while making extraordinary profits under the guise of educating and entertaining the masses. They will clash and they will win, with the power to determine what is seen, how it is received, and what message the world takes away from the experience. Until there is one.

*The game is over because, like it or not,*
*when you own all of the real estate on the board*
*and there's nobody left to pay rent, you win.*

Ted Turner
Anaheim, California
November 29, 2001

# A C K N O W L E D G M E N T S

**F**inishing a book is a cause for celebration. Arriving, as it does, at the end of an often grueling exercise in research, composition and editing, it is also a time for giving thanks, especially to those who helped shape the final product.

My publisher, Michael Viner, deserves special mention for conceiving *Clash of the Titans*. His encouragement and advice are priceless to me—then, now and always. Mary Aarons, of New Millennium Entertainment, assembled a team to protect me from my concept of spelling and grammar, including editor Dianne Woo and typesetter Carolyn Wendt. They joined researcher Cathy Dawson, proofreaders Aimee Dow and Robert Kent, indexer Pam Rider, jacket designers Steve Edelman and Sonia Fiore, and cover illustrator Rob Fiore. This book is theirs as much as mine.

Thanks as well to Jane Weimer and her staff at the Port Orange branch of the Volusia County (Florida) Library—Pia Andersen, Kim Dolce, Liz Huffman, Beth Masterson, Charlotte Nettles, Mary Ann Sumner, and Agnes Rivera; Shelly McCoy and her staff in the Microforms Unit of the Morris Library at the University of Delaware—Georgia Basso, Nadine Burroughs, Richard Campbell, Joe Daley, Regina Fitzpatrick, Carrie Happoldt, Feroz Klyani, Kholiswa Laird, Jillian Morra, Allyson Short, and Tim Wojtek; the reference librarians at the Public Library of Cincinnati and Hamilton County (Ohio); the periodical librarians at the Savannah branch of the Live Oak Public Libraries (Georgia); the manuscript librarians at the British Library (London), the State Library of NSW (Sydney, Australia), and the National Library of Australia in Canberra; Brad Gernand in the Manuscript Division of the Library of Congress, Washington, D.C.; and especially Debbie DeJonker-Berry and Laine Quinn at the Provincetown Public Library, Provincetown, Massachusetts.

Carole White bid me welcome in Beverly Hills, California, where her home was my home for weeks at a time, and my secrets became her secrets. Carole, I've still got the key and will be back. Patrick Briggs allowed me to use his home in Washington, D.C. as a research base, and pretended not to notice the piles of documents from the FCC that invaded his living space. Thanks again Patrick. And Joyce Outlaw, who allowed me free roam of her compound in Orlando, Florida. Bandit, you are one-of-a-kind.

My sister, Joan Henn, once again donated her guest room in Newark, Delaware, while I conducted interviews in New York, Philadelphia, Boston, and Maryland. Plus Patti and Harry, Traci and Michael, and Melissa and Richard—because.

The burden of entertainment fell to Troy Stratos, Tony Melluzzo, Ronald Saleh, Evan Harlow, Sterling Richardson, Daniel Eastman, Valerie Reynolds, Anne Jordan, Shelley Herman, Marilyn Richards, Jill Vaughan and Deb Breedlove, plus a special thanks to Alberto Proia.

Charlie Leporacci, who knows the reason why.

And, as always, to my mother Anne for her kindness and joy in daily life and her wisdom told through gentle words. You inspire us all.

*—Richard Hack*
*Provincetown, Mass.*

# E N D N O T E S

## Prologue

1 Masters, Burrough, *Vanity Fair,* January 1997.
2 Mermigas, *Electronic Media,* September 23, 1996.
3 Yelland, *New York Post,* September 27, 1996.
4 Masters, Burrough, *Vanity Fair,* January 1997.
5 Ibid.
6 Harper, *Washington Times,* November 3, 1996.
7 Gay, *Newsday,* October 7, 1996.
8 Author's interview of confidential source.
9 Yelland, *New York Post,* September 28, 1996.
10 Peers, *Variety,* September 30, 1996.
11 Sherman, *New York Post,* October 4, 1996.
12 Topousis, *New York Post,* October 8, 1996.
13 King, Lewis, *New York Daily News,* October 8, 1996.
14 King, Lewis, *New York Daily News,* October 11, 1996.
15 *New York Post,* October 15, 1996.
16 Lewis, *New York Daily News,* October 19, 1996.
17 Deposition transcript, U.S. District Court.
18 Ibid.
19 Ibid.
20 Janison, *New York Post,* October 19, 1996.
21 Janison, *New York Post,* October 21, 1996.
22 Sandomir, *New York Times,* October 22, 1996.
23 Nicholson, Lewis, Jamieson, *New York Daily News,* October 22, 1996.
24 Lewis, *New York Post,* October 23, 1996.
25 Usborne, *Independent on Sunday,* November 24, 1996.
26 Masters, Burrough, *Vanity Fair,* January 1997.

## Chapter One

1 Zwar, *In Search of Keith Murdoch,* p. 13.
2 Ibid., p. 16.
3 Ibid.
4 Monks, *Elisabeth Murdoch: Two Lives,* p. 48.
5 Ibid., p. 67.
6 Ibid., p. 68.
7 Ibid., p. 72.
8 Ibid., p. 101.
9 Ibid., p. 130.
10 Ibid., p. 311.
11 Murdoch, *Six Australians: Profiles of Power, Australian Broadcasting Corporation,* January 1, 1966.
12 Ibid., p. 157.
13 "The Areopagus," *Corian,* July 1947.
14 "The Areopagus," *Corian,* August 1948.
15 Shawcross, *Murdoch,* p. 50.
16 Ibid., p. 157.
17 Monks, *Elisabeth Murdoch: Two Lives,* p. 166.
18 Ibid., p. 174.

19   Shawcross, *Murdoch,* p. 58.
20   Ibid.
21   *Cherwell,* June 11, 1952.
22   Monks, *Elisabeth Murdoch: Two Lives,* p. 178.
23   *New York Times,* October 6, 1952.

### Chapter Two
1   Truex, "Surprising Son," *Atlanta Constitution,* May 9, 1977, p. 4D.
2   "Profile: Ted Turner," *Atlanta Constitution,* May 12, 1973, p. 23.
3   Author's interview of confidential source.
4   Vaughan, *The Grand Gesture,* p. 99.
5   Smith, *Sports Illustrated,* p. 78.
6   Vaughan, *Ted Turner,* p. 152.
7   "Florence Turner," *Atlanta Constitution,* p. 38.
8   Vaughan, *Ted Turner,* p. 154.
9   "Profile: Ted Turner," *Atlanta Constitution,* June 12, 1977, p. 23.
10   "Florence Turner," p. 38.
11   Kirkpatrick, "Going Real Strawwng," *Sports Illustrated,* August 21, 1978, p. 78.
12   Williams, *Lead, Follow or Get Out of the Way,* p. 26.
13   Vaughan, *Ted Turner,* p. 153.
14   "Profile: Ted Turner," *Atlanta Constitution,* June 13, 1977, p. 28.
15   Author's interview of confidential source.
16   Goldberg, Goldberg, *Citizen Turner,* p. 56.
17   Ibid., p. 62.
18   Kirkpatrick, "Going Real Strawwng," p. 79.
19   Bibb, *It Ain't as Easy as It Looks,* p. 33.
20   Williams, *Lead, Follow or Get Out of the Way,* p. 34.
21   Marriage certificate on file, Chicago, Illinois.
22   Goldberg, Goldberg, *Citizen Turner,* p. 92.
23   Bibb, *It Ain't as Easy as It Looks,* p. 40.
24   Goldberg, Goldberg, *Citizen Turner,* p. 95.

### Chapter Three
1   *Savannah News,* March 6, 1963, p. 1.
2   Kiernan, *Citizen Murdoch,* p. 18.
3   Goldenson, Wolf, *Beating the Odds,* p. 214.
4   Leapman, *Arrogant Aussie,* p. 26.
5   Ibid., p. 32.
6   Shawcross, *Murdoch,* p. 85.
7   Leapman, *Arrogant Aussie,* p. 34.
8   Monk, *Elisabeth: Two Lives,* p. 199.
9   Goldberg, Goldberg, *Citizen Turner,* p. 108.
10   Turner, Advertising Age, Nov. 1982.
11   Goldberg, Goldberg, *Citizen Turner,* p. 113.
12   Vaughan, *Ted Turner,* p. 186.
13   *Atlanta Constitution,* January 13, 1976.
14   *New York Times,* March 30, 1966, p. 46.
15   Howard, *Good Housekeeping,* June 1988, p. 47.
16   Cotts, *Illustrated London News,* August 1988, p. 14.

## Chapter Four

1 Goldberg, Goldberg, *Citizen Turner,* p. 125.
2 Williams, *Lead, Follow or Get Out of the Way,* p. 65.
3 Author's interview of confidential source.
4 Goldberg, Goldberg, *Citizen Turner,* p. 124.
5 Williams, *Lead, Follow or Get Out of the Way,* p. 65.
6 Bradshaw, *Television/Radio Age,* June 24, 1974, p. 26.
7 Ibid.
8 Williams, *Lead, Follow or Get Out of the Way,* p. 67.
9 Wintour, *The Rise and Fall of Fleet Street,* p. 225.
10 Lewis, *New York Times,* October 1, 1969, p. 46.
11 Leapman, *Arrogant Aussie,* p. 56.
12 Transcript, *Frost on Friday,* London Weekend Television.
13 "Australian Agrees," *New York Times,* September 27, 1969, p. 51.
14 Murdoch, *Sun,* November 15, 1969, p. 1.
15 Shawcross, *Murdoch,* p. 123.
16 "'New Boy' on Fleet Street," *Newsweek,* May 10, 1971, p. 97.
17 Ibid.
18 Bibb, *It Ain't as Easy as It Looks,* p. 88.
19 Kirkpatrick, *Sports Illustrated,* August 21, 1978, p. 80.
20 Waters, *Newsweek,* July 14, 1975, p. 53.
21 Gardner, *Cosmopolitan,* July 1986, p. 104.
22 Waters, *Newsweek.*
23 *Providence Journal-Bulletin,* May 13, 1986, p. 14.

## Chapter Five

1 Breasted, *New York Times,* November 21, 1976, p. 39.
2 Gelman, *Newsweek,* November 29, 1976, p. 84.
3 Gupte, *New York Times,* November 21, 1976, p. 42.
4 *New York Times,* January 7, 1976, p. 24.
5 *New York Times,* April 4, 1976, p. E1.
6 Fimrite, *Sports Illustrated,* July 19, 1976, p. 25.
7 Ibid.
8 Bonventre, *Newsweek,* June 7, 1976, p. 60.
9 Chass, *New York Times,* January 3, 1977, p. 29.
10 Ibid.
11 McFadden, *New York Times,* January 3, 1977, p. 28.
12 Ibid.
13 Ibid.
14 Carmody, *New York Times,* January 4, 1977, p. 36.
15 "Turner Buys the Hawks," *New York Times,* January 4, 1977, p. 33.
16 Ibid.
17 Kirkpatrick, *Sports Illustrated,* August 21, 1978, p. 70.
18 New York Times, January 25, 1977, p. 34.
19 Meeting transcript; Williams, *Lead, Follow or Get Out of the Way,* p. 145.
20 *Atlanta Journal,* April 23, 1977, p. 24.
21 "MacPhail Backs Kuhn's Power," *New York Times,* April 29, 1977, p.21.
22 Bibb, *It Ain't As Easy As It Looks,* p. 117.
23 Hannon, *Sports Illustrated,* May 23, 1977, p. 67.
24 *New York Times,* May 14, 1977, p. 9.
25 Hannon, p. 68.

### Chapter Six

1 Lehr, *King Lehr and the Gilded Age with Extracts from the Locked Diary of Harry Lehr,* p. 38.
2 Vaughan, *Ted Turner,* p. 22.
3 Ibid., p. 26.
4 Bonventre, *Newsweek,* September 12, 1977, p. 12.
5 "'Mouth of the South' at the Helm, *Time,* August 8, 1977, p. 44.
6 Hersey, *Yachting,* September 1977, p. 189.
7 Kirkpatrick, "Going Real Strawwng," *Sports Illustrated,* August 21, 1978, p. 80.
8 "Deputy Mayor Criticizes," *New York Times,* July 19, 1977, p. 26.
9 "Beame Calls The Post," *New York Times,* August 28, 1977, p. A42.
10 "Robert Lipsyte Quits at The Post," *New York Times,* September 28, 1977, p. B10.
11 Winfrey, *New York Times,* October 5, 1977, p. B2.
12 Kihss, *New York Times,* April 14, 1978, p. B5.
13 "Some Unions Assailed," *New York Times,* April 21, 1978, p. 78.
14 Kiernan, *Citizen Murdoch,* p. 213.
15 Reeves, *Esquire,* October 10, 1978, p. 12
16 Raskin, *New Yorker,* January 29, 1979, p. 69.
17 Ibid., p. 70.
18 Welles, *Esquire,* May 22, 1979, p. 51.
19 Brogan, *New Republic,* June 24, 1985, p. 12.
20 "A Separate Peace," *Time,* October 16, 1978, p. 104.
21 Clark, *New York Times,* July 27, 1979, p. D2.
22 Collins, *New York Times,* August 16, 1979, p. 1.

### Chapter Seven

1 Whittemore, *CNN: The Inside Story,* p. 27.
2 Schorr, *Staying Tuned,* p. 303.
3 Ibid., p. 304.
4 Williams, *Lead, Follow or Get Out of the Way,* p. 258.
5 Whittemore, *CNN: The Inside Story,* p. 78.
6 Cronkite, *CBS Evening News,* December 7, 1979.
7 Ibid., p. 91.
8 Author's interview of confidential source.
9 Williams, *Lead, Follow or Get Out of the Way,* p. 257.
10 Whittemore, *CNN: The Inside Story,* p. 128.
11 Bibb, *It Ain't as Easy as It Looks,* p. 192.
12 Zoglin, *Atlanta Constitution,* June 2, 1980, p. D1.
13 Ibid.
14 *Variety,* June 4, 1980, p. 43.
15 Waters, *Newsweek,* June 16, 1980, p. 63.
16 Ibid., p. 61.
17 *Home Video Magazine,* June 1980, p. 16.
18 *National Review,* June 27, 1980, p. 768.
19 *Donahue,* April 1, 1981.
20 Waters, p. 66.

### Chapter Eight

1 Schardt, "A Fate Worse Than Death?" *Newsweek,* p. 74.
2 Shawcross, *Murdoch,* p. 170.
3 Leapman, *Arrogant Aussie,* p. 195.

4   Schardt, "A Fate Worse Than Death?" p. 74.
5   Ibid., p. 193.
6   Evans, *Good Times, Bad Times,* p. 199.
7   Author's interview with confidential source.
8   Range, "Ted Turner," *Playboy,* p. 90.
9   Kilpatrick, "Captain of Cable," *Interview,* September 1980, p. 36.
10  "Can Ted Turner's Cable News Hang In?" *Business Week,* November 3, 1980, p. 92.
11  Halliday, "Cable Makes 'Cowards,'" *Backstage,* May 15, 1981, p. 1.
12  Fingleton, "Know Your Market," *Forbes,* August 7, 1981, p. 36.
13  Ibid., p. 37.
14  "Cable News Team Wants Equal Rights," *Business Week,* p. 45.
15  Gelman, "How Dare They!" *Variety,* p. 66.
16  Goldberg, *Citizen Turner,* p. 283.
17  *Atlanta Constitution,* February 20, 1982, p. 15.
18  Smith, "What Makes Ted Run?" *Sports Illustrated,* June 23, 1986, p. 76.
19  Goldberg, *Citizen Turner,* p. 285.
20  Range, "The Demons of Ted Turner," *Playboy,* p. 63.
21  Henry, "Shaking up the Networks," *Time,* August 9, 1982, p. 50.

### Chapter Nine

1   Evans, *Good Times, Bad Times,* p. 296.
2   Munster, *Paper Prince,* p. 235.
3   Kiernan, *Citizen Murdoch,* p. 244.
4   Whittemore, *CNN: The Inside Story,* p. 241.
5   Author's interview of confidential source.
6   Rudnitsky, *Forbes,* November 7, 1983, p. 82.
7   Ibid.
8   Shawcross, *Murdoch,* p. 193.
9   Evans, *Good Times, Bad Times,* p. 404.
10  Goldberg, *Citizen Turner,* p. 309.

### Chapter Ten

1   Author's interview of confidential source.
2   Fabrikant, Bianco, Laderman et al., *Business Week,* March 18, 1985, p. 28.
3   *Folio,* February 1985, p. 13.
4   *Broadcasting,* April 22, 1985, p. 31.
5   Stewart, *Wall Street Journal,* April 23, 1985, p. 3.
6   *TV Digest,* May 6, 1985, p. 2.
7   Block, *Outfoxed,* p. 103.
8   Martin, *Advertising Age,* May 9, 1985, p. 55.
9   Christopher, *Advertising Age,* July 8, 1985, p. 62.
10  Loftus, *Variety,* August 7, 1985, p. 41.
11  Beerman, *Variety,* August 7, 1985, p. 41.
12  Castro, *Time,* August 19, 1985, p. 33.
13  Ibid.
14  Monks, *Elisabeth Murdoch,* p. 279.
15  Shawcross, *Murdoch,* p. 250.
16  Ibid., p. 253.
17  Light, *Advertising Age,* September 16, 1985, p. 72.

### Chapter Eleven

1 Melvern, *The End of the Street,* p. 62.
2 Ibid.
3 Kelly, *Time,* March 3, 1986, p. 52.
4 Laver, *Maclean's,* February 10, 1986, p. 64.
5 Ibid.
6 Shawcross, *Murdoch,* p. 275.
7 Kelly, *Time,* March 3, 1986, p. 52.
8 Goldberg, *Citizen Turner,* p. 375.
9 Green, *People,* July 14, 1986. p. 64.
10 Weisman, *New Republic,* December 29, 1986, p. 16.
11 Henry, *Time,* July 21, 1986, p. 76.
12 *People,* August 4, 1986, p. 7.
13 Taaffe, *Sports Illustrated,* July 21, 1986, p. 55.
14 Henry, p. 77.
15 Gay, *Advertising Age,* October 6, 1986, p. 1.
16 Goldberg, *Citizen Turner,* p. 378.
17 Ibid., p. 373.

### Chapter Twelve

1 Author's interview of Gene Jankowski.
2 Gold, *Variety,* April 1, 1987, p. 3.
3 Grover, *Business Week,* June 1, 1987, p. 50.
4 *New York Times,* March 2, 1989, p. 1.
5 Chenoweth, *Virtual Murdoch,* p. 81.
6 *Television Digest,* February 1, 1988, p. 6.
7 Zuckerman, *Time,* January 18, 1988, p. 19.
8 Ibid.
9 *Broadcasting,* January 11, 1988, p. 42.
10 Griffin, *Time,* February 8, 1988, p. 57.
11 Cockburn, *The Nation,* March 12, 1988, p. 331.
12 Guider, *Variety,* June 15, 1988, p. 33.
13 *Atlanta,* November, 1988, p. .
14 Mason, *People Weekly,* March 29, 1991, p. 62.
15 Ibid.
16 Mitchell, *Marketing,* August 18, 1988, p. 7.
17 *Broadcasting,* August 15, 1988, p. 96.

### Chapter Thirteen

1 Shawcross, *Murdoch,* p. 357.
2 *Business Week,* March 20, 1989, p. 32.
3 Shawcross, *Murdoch,* p. 384.
4 Stephen J. Simurda, *Worldbusiness,* unpublished cover story, 1995.
5 Chenoweth, *Virtual Murdoch,* p. 71.
6 Geraldine Brooks, *New York Times,* July 19, 1998, sec. 6, p. 20.
7 Shawcross, *Murdoch,* p. 23.
8 Ibid, p. 26.
9 Glenn, *Broadcasting,* December 24, 1990, p. 16.
10 Bart, *Variety,* January 21, 1991, p. 1.
11 Townsend, *Punch,* July 4, 1998, p. 18.

12 Author's interview of confidential source.
13 Harris, *Forbes,* September 2, 1991, p. 40.

### Chapter Fourteen

1 Stutz, *Audubon,* October 1991 p. 112.
2 Ibid.
3 *Advertising Age,* October 28, 1991, p. 6.
4 Burkhart, *Atlanta Constitution,* November 12, 1991, p. D1.
5 Ibid., p. D10.
6 Shawcross, *Murdoch,* p. 414.
7 Mermigas, Mandese, *Advertising Age,* March 2, 1992, p. 1.
8 Coe, *Broadcasting,* March 2, 1992, p. 4.
9 Coe, *Broadcasting,* June 29, 1992, p. 17.
10 Michaels, *Forbes,* September 28, 1992, p. 47.
11 Chakravarty, *Forbes,* January 4, 1993, p. 84.
12 Ibid., p. 85.
13 Ibid.
14 Gross, New *York,* February 8, 1993, p. 32.
15 Mirabella, *Crain's New York Business,* April 5, 1993, p. 4.
16 Diamond, *New York,* April 12, 1993, p. 16.
17 Lindorff, *Business Week,* September 20, 1993, p. 50.

### Chapter Fifteen

1 Monks, *Elisabeth Murdoch: Two Lives,* p. 298.
2 Hird, *New Statesman & Society,* September 16, 1994, p. 19.
3 Michaels, Rotenier, *Forbes,* March 14, 1994, p. 84.
4 Ibid.
5 Zoglin, *Time,* June 6, 1994, p. 54.
6 Robins, *Variety,* May 30, 1994, p. 1.
7 Reibstein, Hass, *Newsweek,* June 6, 1994, p. 46.
8 *Television Digest,* June 27, 1994, p. 6.
9 Roush, *USA Today,* July 12, 1994, p. 3.
10 *InterActive Week,* October 10, 1994, p. 72.

### Chapter Sixteen

1 Larson, *Time,* April 17, 1995, p. 46.
2 Ibid., p. 45.
3 *New Yorker,* February 6, 1995, p. 27.
4 Lewyn, *Business Week,* May 15, 1995, p. 43.
5 *Business Week,* May 29, 1995, p. 29.
6 *Folio,* June 1, 1995, p. 16.
7 Author's interview with Larry King.
8 Bates, Dutka, *Los Angeles Times,* August 31, 1995, p. A49.
9 Ascher-Walsh, *Entertainment Weekly,* September 15, 1995, p. 22.
10 Sanger, *Newsday,* September 23, 1995, p. 28.

### Chapter Seventeen

1 Mundy, *Mediaweek,* March 4, 1996, p. 22.
2 Ibid., p. 24.
3 Williams, *Variety,* July 15, 1996, p. 1.

4   Time Warner, Turner Broadcasting System merger prospectus.

5   *New York Post,* October 25, 1996, p. 6.

6   *News International & Others v. Michael Clinger & Others,* CH 1996 N4257 & 5450, number 104, High Court, London, November 17, 1998.

7   Neil, *Full Disclosure,* 1996, p. 3.

8   Author's interview of confidential source.

9   Chenoweth, *Virtual Murdoch,* p. 180.

10   Ibid., p. 182.

11   Roberts, *Newsweek,* March 10, 1998, p. 46.

12   Author's interview of confidential source.

13   Transcript of Larry King's interview with Ted Turner at the NCTA's Vanguard Awards in New Orleans, March 1997.

## Chapter Eighteen

1   Zoglin, *Time,* May 12, 1997, p. 65.

2   *Television Digest,* May 19, 1997, p. 5.

3   *Across the Board,* July/August 1997, p. 13.

4   Mermigas, *Electronic Media,* September 29, 1997, p. 3.

5   Peers, *Variety,* September 22, 1997, p. 4.

6   Lenzner, *Forbes,* October 14, 1996, p. 40.

7   Cohen, *Time,* September 29, 1997, p. 32.

8   Richardson, *Publishers Weekly,* March 9, 1998, p. 11.

9   Stern, *Variety,* May 18, 1998, p. 35.

10   Ibid.

11   Alridge, *Electronic Media,* July 20, 1998, p. 30.

## Chapter Nineteen

1   Griffin, *New Yorker,* April 19, 1999, p. 25.

2   Ibid.

3   *People,* July 12, 1999, p. 80.

4   Chenoweth, *Virtual Murdoch,* p. 315.

5   Shawcross, *Vanity Fair,* October 1999, p. 320.

6   Ibid.

7   Ibid.

8   Ibid.

9   Ibid.

10   Woods, *Variety,* November 8, 1999, p. 6.

11   Mermigas, *Electronic Media,* November 29, 1999, p. 1.

12   Jessell, *Broadcasting & Cable,* December 20, 1999, p. 10

13   Ibid.

14   Hewitt, *People,* January 17, 2000, p. 116.

15   *Newsweek,* January 24, 2000, p. 35.

16   *CNN Moneyline,* September 20, 1999.

17   *AsiaPulse News,* February 10, 2000, p. 924.

18   Beale, *Campaign,* February 18, 2000, p. 20.

19   Nadler, *Variety,* February 21, 2000, p. 34.

20   Brooks, *Gentlemen's Quarterly,* October 1999, p. 140.

21   Dawtrey, *Variety,* May 8, 2000, p. 110.

22   Auletta, *New Yorker,* April 23, 2001, p. 156.

23   Ibid.

### Epilogue

1  Kaplan, "Conservatives Plant a Seed in NYC," *Boston Globe,* February 22, 1998, p. 1.
2  Chenoweth, *Virtual Murdoch,* p. x.
3  Hogan, *Multichannel News,* March 5, 2001, p. 50.
4  Rohm, *The Murdoch Mission,* p. 14.
5  Higgins, *Broadcasting & Cable,* April 9, 2001, p. 14.
6  *Harper's Magazine,* May 2001, p. 25.
7  *New Republic,* April 9, 2001, p. 12.
8  Lease, *Sarasota Herald Tribune,* July 30, 2001, p. A11.
9  Forrester, *Interspace,* August 29, 2001, p. 14.
10  Author's interview of confidential source.
11  Donohue, *Multichannel News,* December 3, 2001, p. 8.
12  Johnson, "Fox News Enjoys New View—From the Top," *USA Today,* April 4, 2002, p. D1.
13  Cox, "That's AOL Folks," *New York Post,* July 25, 2002, p. 1.

# B I B L I O G R A P H Y

**A Note from the Publisher**

Over 5,000 periodicals were consulted by the author as he researched this book. In an attempt to keep the page count down, to make the book more affordable and accessible to readers, we have decided not to print these in the book. This list is available on our website, *www.newmillenniumpress.com.*

Anderson, Christopher. *Citizen Jane: The Turbulent Life of Jane Fonda.* New York: Henry Holt and Company, 1990.

Ashmead-Barlett, E. *The Uncensored Dardanelles.* London: Hutchinson, 1928.

Auletta, Ken. *Three Blind Mice.* New York: Random House, 1991.

Auletta, Ken. *The Highwaymen: Warriors of the Information Superhighway.* New York: Random House, 1997.

Baistow, Tom. *Fourth-Rate Estate.* London: Comedia, 1985.

Barber, Lionel, and John Lawrenson. *The Price of Truth: The Story of the Reuters Millions.* London: Sphere Book, 1986.

Barry, Paul. *The Rise and Rise of Kerry Packer.* Sydney: Bantam, 1993.

Bean, C.E.W. *The Story of Anzac.* Sydney: Angus and Robertson, 1941.

Belfield, Richard, Christopher Hird and Sharon Kelly. *Murdoch: The Decline of an Empire.* London: Macdonald, 1991.

Bertrand, John, and Patrick Robinson. *Born to Win.* New York: William Morrow, 1985.

Bibb, Porter. *Ted Turner: It Ain't As Easy As It Looks.* Boulder, Co.: Johnson Books, 1993.

Block, Alex Ben. *Outfoxed.* New York: St. Martin's Press, 1990.

Bonner, Elena. *Alone Together.* New York: Alfred A. Knopf, 1986.

Botkin, B.A. *A Treasury of Southern Folklore.* New York: Crown Publishers, 1962.

Bower, Tom. *Maxwell the Outsider.* London: Mandarin, 1991.

Bowman, David. *The Captive Press.* Ringwood, Victoria, Australia: Penguin, 1988.

Brand, Stewart. *The Media Lab.* New York: Viking, 1988.

Brendon, Piers. *The Life and Death of the Press Barons.* London: Secker and Warburg, 1982.

Bruck, Connie. *Master of the Game: Steve Ross and the Creation of Time Warner.* New York: Penguin, 1994.

Calwell, A.A. *Be Just and Fear Not.* Melbourne: Lloyd O'Neil, 1972.

Cannon, Michael. *The Land Boomers.* Melbourne: Melbourne University Press, 1966.

Carey, John. *The Intellectuals and the Masses.* London: Faber and Faber, 1992.

Carroll, V.J. *The Man Who Couldn't Wait.* Melbourne: Heinemann, 1990.

Chadwick, Paul. *Media Mates.* Melbourne: Macmillan, 1989.

Chenoweth, Neil. *Virtual Murdoch: Reality Wars on the Information Highway.* London: Secker & Warburg, 2001.

Chippindale, Peter, and Chris Horrie. *Stick It Up Your Punter.* London: Heinemann, 1990.

Chippindale, Peter, and Suzanne Franks. *Dished! The Rise and Fall of British Satellite Broadcasting.* London: Simon & Schuster, 1991.

Clurman, Richard M. *To the End of Time.* New York: Simon & Schuster, 1992.

Cockerell, Michael, Peter Hennessy and David Walker. *Sources Close to the Prime Minister.* London: Macmillan, 1984.

Coleman, Fred. *The Decline and Fall of the Soviet Empire, Forty Years that Shook the World, from Stalin to Yeltsin.* New York: St. Martin's Press, 1996.

Conquest, Robert. *Tyrants and Typewriters.* London: Hutchinson, 1989.

Cooper, William. *Shall We Ever Know? The Trial of the Hosein Brothers for the Murder of Mrs. McKay.* London: Hutchinson, 1971.

Coote, Colin R. *Editorial.* London: Eyre & Spottiswoode, 1965.

Cudlipp, Hugh. *Walking on the Water.* London: Bodley Head, 1976.

Curran, James, and Jean Seaton. *Power Without Responsibility: The Press and Broadcasting in Britain.* London: Routledge, 1988.

Dear, Ian. *Ocean Racing, an Illustrated history.* New York: Hearst, Main Books, 1985.

Dizard, Wilson P., Jr., and S. Blake Swensrud. *Gorbachev's Information Revolution: Controlling Glasnost in a New Electronic Era.* Boulder, Co.: The Center for Strategic and International Studies, Westview Press, 1987.

Dizard, Wilson P., Jr. *The Coming Information Age.* London: Longman, 1989.

Dizard, Wilson P. *Old Media/New Media: Mass Communications in the Information Age.* New York: Longman, 1993.

Duke, Patty, and Gloria Hochman. *A Brilliant Madness.* New York: Bantam Books, 1992.

Dunkley, Christopher. *Television Today and Tomorrow: Wall to Wall Dallas?* Harmondsworth, U.K.: Penguin Books, 1985.

Dunne, John Gregory. *The Studio.* New York: Farrar, Straus & Giroux, 1969.

Edgar, Patricia. *The Politics of the Press.* Melbourne: Sun Books, 1979.

Edwards, Robert. *Goodbye Fleet Street.* London: Jonathan Cape, 1988.

Eisler, Riane. *The Chalice & the Blade.* New York: Harper & Row, 1987.

Evans, Harold. *Good Times, Bad Times.* London: Coronet Books, 1984.

Felshman, Neil. *Gorbachev, Yeltsin and the Last Days of the Soviet Empire.* New York: St. Martin's Press, 1992.

Fields, Robert Ashley. *Take Me Out to the Crowd: Ted Turner and the Atlanta Braves.* Huntsville, AL: Strode Publishers, 1977.

Gans, Herbert J. *Deciding What's News?* New York: Pantheon Books, 1979.

Gelb, Norman. *The Berlin Wall.* New York: Random House, 1986.

Gilder, George. *Microcosm.* New York: Simon & Schuster, 1989.

Giles, Frank. *Sundry Times.* London: John Murray, 1986.

Godenson, Leonard H., with Marvin J. Wolf. *Beating the Odds.* New York: Charles Scribner's Sons, 1991.

Goldberg, Robert, and Gerald Jay Goldberg. *Citizen Turner: The Wild Rise of an American Tycoon.* New York: Harcourt, Brace & Co., 1995.

Goodhart, David, and Patrick Wintour. *Eddie Shah and the Newspaper Revolution.* London: Coronet, 1986.

Grose, Roslyn. *The Sun-Sation.* London: Angus and Robertson, 1989.

Hall, Richard. *The Secret State: Australia's Spy Industry.* Sydney: Cassell, 1978.

Hamilton, Denis. *Editor-in-Chief.* London: Hamish Hamilton, 1989.

Hammond, Eric. *Maverick.* London: Weidenfeld and Nicolson, 1992.

Harris, Robert. *Gotcha! The Media, the Government and the Falklands Crisis.* London: Faber and Faber, 1983.

Harris, Robert. *Selling Hitler.* London: Faber and Faber, 1986.

Henderson, Gerard. *Australian Answers.* Milsons Point, New South Wales, Australia: Random House, 1990.

Heren, Louis. *Memories of Times Past.* London: Hamish Hamilton, 1988.

Hetherington, John. *Australians: Nine Profiles.* Melbourne: F.W. Cheshire, 1960.

Howard, Philip. *We Thundered Out: A Bicentenary History of the Times.* London: Times Books, 1985.

Inglis, K.S. *The Stuart Case.* Melbourne: Melbourne University Press, 1961.

Jacobs, Eric. *Stop Press: The Inside Story of the Times Dispute.* London: André Deutsch, 1980.

Jenkins, Simon. *Newspapers: The Power and the Money.* London: Faber and Faber, 1979.

Jenkins, Simon. *The Market for Glory.* London: Faber and Faber, 1986.

Jobson, Gary, with Ted Turner. *The Racing Edge.* New York: Simon & Schuster, 1979.

Josephson, Jessica J. *European Media Hard Data.* London: International Media Publishing, 1991.

Kennedy, Trevor. *Top Guns.* Melbourne: Sun Books, 1988.

Kiernan, Thomas. *Citizen Murdoch.* New York: Dodd, Mead, 1986.

King, Cecil. *The Financial Times: A Centenary History.* London: Viking, 1988.

Kornbluth, Jesse. *Highly Confident: The Crime and Punishment of Michael Milken.* New York: William Morrow, 1992.

Lamb, Larry. *Sunrise.* London: Papermac, 1989.

Lawrenson, John, and Lionel Barber. *The Price of Truth.* Edinburgh: Mainstream Publishing, 1985.

Leapman, Michael. *Arrogant Aussie: The Rupert Murdoch Story.* Secaucus, N.J.: Lyle Stuart, 1985.

Leapman, Michael. *The Last Days of the Beeb.* London: Allen and Unwin, 1986.

Lehr, Elizabeth Drexel. *King Lehr and the Gilded Age with Extracts from the Locked Diary of Harry Lehr.* Philadelphia: J.B. Lippincott Company, 1935.

Lowe, Janet. *Ted Turner Speaks: Insights from the World's Greatest Maverick.* New York: John Wiley & Sons, 1999.

Lundy, James L. *Lead, Follow, or Get Out of the Way: Leadership Strategies for the Thoroughly Modern Manager.* San Diego: Avant Books, 1986.

MacArthur, Brian. *Eddie Shah,* Today *and the Newspaper Revolution.* Newton Abbot, U.K.: David and Charles, 1988.

MacArthur, John R. *Second Front: Censorship and Propaganda in the Gulf War.* New York: Hill & Wang, 1992.

McLuhan, Marshall. *Understanding Media: The Extensions of Man.* New York: New American Library, 1964.

McQueen, Humphrey. *Social Sketches of Australia 1888-1975.* Ringwood, Victoria, Australia: Penguin, 1978.

Martin, J. Stanley. *A Tale of Two Churches: From West Melbourne to Box Hill.* Melbourne: Box Hill, St. Andrew's Presbyterian Church, 1967.

Mayer, Martin. *Making News.* New York: Doubleday, 1987.

Melvern, Linda. *The End of the Street.* London: Methuen, 1986.

Moorehead, John. *Gallipoli.* London: Hamish Hamilton, 1956.

Munster, George. *Rupert Murdoch: A Paper Prince.* Ringwood, Victoria, Australia: Viking, 1987.

Munster, George. *Family Business.* London: Collins, 1988.

Murdoch, Reverend Patrick. *Laughter and Tears of God and Other War Sermons.* Melbourne: Arbuckle, Waddell and Fawckner, 1915.

Nolan, Sydney. *Nolan's Gallipoli.* Canberra: Australian War Memorial, 1978.

Pacini, J. *A Century Galloped By: The First Hundred Years of the Victoria Racing Club.* Melbourne: Victoria Racing Club, 1952.

Packer, Clyde. *No Return Ticket.* Sydney: Angus and Robertson, 1984.

Pearl, Cyril. *Wild Men of Sydney.* London: W.H. Allen, 1958.

Penniman, Howard R. *Australia at the Polls: The National Elections of 1975.* Washington, D.C.: American Enterprise Institute for Public Policy Research, 1977.

Pool, Ithiel de Sola. *Technologies of Freedom*. Cambridge, MA: Harvard University Press, 1983.

Porter, Henry. *Lies, Damned Lies and Some Exclusives*. London: Chatto and Windus, 1984.

Porter, Jeffrey. *Men, Money and Magic: The Story of Dorothy Schiff*. New York: Coward, McCann and Geoghegan, 1976.

Postman, Neil, and Steve Powers. *How to Watch TV News*. New York: Penguin, 1992.

Povich, Maury. *Current Affairs: A Life on the Edge*. New York: Putnam, 1991.

Randall, Mike. *The Funny Side of the Street*. London: Bloomsbury, 1988.

Richey, Michael W. *The Sailing Encyclopedia*. New York: Lippencott & Crowell, 1980.

Righter, Rosemary. *Whose News Anyway?* London: Burnett Books, 1978.

Robertson, John. *Anzac and Empire: The Tragedy and Glory of Gallipoli*. Melbourne: Hamlyn, 1990.

Rousmanierre, John. *Fastnet: Force 10*. New York: W.W. Norton & Co., 1980.

Rusher, William A. *The Coming Battle for the Media*. New York: William Morrow, 1988.

Sampson, Anthony. *The Midas Touch*. London: Hodder and Stoughton, 1989.

Shawcross, William. *Murdoch*. New York: Simon & Schuster, 1992.

Silverman, Stephen M. *The Fox That Got Away*. Secaucus, N.J.: Lyle Stuart, 1988.

Smith, Anthony. *Shadows in the Cave*. Champaign, Illinois: University of Illinois Press, 1973.

Smith, Anthony. *The British Press Since the War: Sources for Contemporary Issues*. Newton Abbot, U.K.: David and Charles, 1974.

Smith, Anthony. *The Newspaper*. London: Thames and Hudson, 1979.

Smith, Anthony. *The Geopolitics of Information*. New York: Oxford University Press, 1980.

Smith, Anthony. *Goodbye Gutenburg*. New York: Oxford University Press, 1980.

Smith, Anthony. *The Age of Behemoths: The Globalisation of Mass Media Firms*. New York: Twentieth Century Fund, 1991.

Smith, Major General Perry M. *How CNN Fought the War*. New York: Birch Lane Press, 1991.

Somerfield, S.W. *Banner Headlines*. Shoreham-by-Sea, U.K.: Scan Books, 1979.

Souter, Gavin. *Company of Heralds*. Melbourne: Melbourne University Press, 1981.

Souter, Gavin. *Heralds and Angels*. Melbourne: Melbourne University Press, 1991.

Stefoff, Rebecca. Ted Turner: *Television's Triumphant Tiger*. Ada, OK: Garrett Educational, 1992.

Stephens, Mitchell. *A History of News*. New York: Viking, 1988.

Stewart, James B. *Den of Thieves*. New York: Simon & Schuster, 1992.

Stonier, Tom. *The Wealth of Information*. London: Methuen, 1983.

Swanberg, W.A. *Pulitzer*. New York: Charles Scribner's Sons, 1967.

Taylor, Philip M. *War & the Media*. Manchester, U.K.: Manchester University Press, 1992.

Thompson, Peter, and Anthony Delano. *Maxwell*. London: Bantam Press, 1988.

Thomson, Lord. *After I Was Sixty*. London: Hamish Hamilton, 1975.

Tuccille, Jerome. *Rupert Murdoch*. New York: Donald I. Fine, 1989.

Twitchell, James B. *Carnival Culture*. New York: Columbia University Press, 1992.

Vaughan, Roger. *The Grand Gesture*. Boston: Little, Brown & Co., 1975.

Vaughan, Roger. *Ted Turner: The Man Behind the Mouth*. Boston: Sail Books, 1978.

Walker, Mike. *Australia: A History*. London: Macdonald Optima, 1987.

Whitlam, Gough. *The Truth of the Matter*. Harmondsworth, U.K.: Penguin, 1981.

Whittemore, Hank. *CNN: The Inside Story*. Boston: Little, Brown & Co., 1990.

Wiener, Robert. *Live from Baghdad*. New York: Doubleday, 1992.

Williams, Christian. *Lead, Follow, or Get Out of the Way*. New York: Times Books, 1981.

Williams, Huntington. *Beyond Control: ABC and the Fate of the Networks*. New York: Antheneum, 1989.

Williams, Valentine. *The World of Action*. London: Hamish Hamilton, 1938.

Wintour, Charles. *The Rise and Fall of Fleet Street*. London: Hutchinson, 1989.

Wriston, Walter B. *Risk and Other Four-Letter Words*. New York: Harper & Row, 1986.

Zwar, Desmond. *In Search of Keith Murdoch*. Melbourne: Macmillan, 1980.

# INDEX